THE STEPHEN BECHTEL FUND

IMPRINT IN ECOLOGY AND THE ENVIRONMENT

The Stephen Bechtel Fund has

established this imprint to promote

understanding and conservation of

our natural environment.

*The publisher gratefully acknowledges the
generous contribution to this book provided by
the Stephen Bechtel Fund.*

OUR DYING PLANET

OUR DYING PLANET

An Ecologist's View of the Crisis We Face

Peter F. Sale

UNIVERSITY OF CALIFORNIA PRESS

Berkeley   Los Angeles   London

University of California Press, one of the most distinguished university presses in the United States,
enriches lives around the world by advancing scholar-
ship in the humanities, social sciences, and natural
sciences. Its activities are supported by the UC Press
Foundation and by philanthropic contributions from
individuals and institutions. For more information,
visit www.ucpress.edu.

University of California Press
Berkeley and Los Angeles, California

University of California Press, Ltd.
London, England

Library of Congress Cataloging-in-Publication Data

Sale, Peter F.
    Our dying planet : an ecologist's view of the crisis
we face / Peter F. Sale.
        p.   cm.
    Includes bibliographical references and index.
    ISBN 978-0-520-26756-5 (cloth : alk. paper)
        1. Nature—Effect of human beings on.
2. Environmental responsibility.   3. Ecology.
I. Title.
    GF75.S25   2011
    304.2'8-dc22   2010051606

Manufactured in the United States of America

20   19   18   17   16   15   14   13   12   11
10   9   8   7   6   5   4   3   2   1

The paper used in this publication meets the
minimum requirements of ANSI/NISO Z39.48-1992
(R 1997) (*Permanence of Paper*).

CONTENTS

PREFACE

My neighbor and I were mowing our lawns one morning in the spring of 2005. We paused to talk. It was an early spring; the grass was growing furiously. I commented that unusual weather is what we should come to expect with climate change. His response floored me—climate change was nothing to worry about, and humans weren't responsible anyway. When I pressed, he replied that from what he could deduce from the newspapers, the overwhelming majority of climate scientists were convinced there was nothing serious going on. I tried to suggest he had it backward, that the great majority thought the problem was serious. I realized then that intelligent members of the public were not well informed on the matter. That same spring, while teaching a new community ecology course to senior undergraduates, I saw that even life science majors were frequently ill informed. Most were either naively committed conservationists or sublimely comfortable in a worldview that admitted no concerns about environmental matters. That spring, I decided to write this book.

Since that time, there has been enormous growth in information and interest about climate change, although many people remain unconvinced. Books on climate change tend to deal with it in isolation from all the other things we are doing to the environment, and this tendency to avoid confronting the full spectrum of problems makes our situation seem less critical than it really is. As I wrote recently[1] with reference to the global decline of coral reefs, they "are not becoming degraded because of over-fishing, or pollution, or inappropriate coastal development, or global warming, or ocean acidification, or even because of an increase in intensity of storms. It is the synergy of all these impacts which is causing the progressive collapse of coral reef ecosystems." It's possible that as a marine scientist I am particularly attuned to the importance of multiple impacts, because ocean processes do merge and blend. In any event, I do not think the issue of the multiplicity of impacts—our ecological footprint—is getting nearly enough attention.

Although I began my studies at the University of Toronto, I have spent most of a rewarding academic career doing marine ecological research in the tropics. I spent nearly twenty years at the University of Sydney, doing research on the Great Barrier Reef, before I moved in 1988 to the University of New Hampshire and subsequently the University of Windsor, Canada, continuing tropical research in the Caribbean. I am now based at the United Nations University's Institute for Water, Environment, and Health, located in Hamilton, Canada. UNU–INWEH is a small U.N. agency where I seek to use the best available science to advance environmental management of tropical coastal environments.

Coral reefs, the ecosystem I know best, have been clichéd as the canaries in the environmental coal mine, and they seem very likely to disappear this century—the first ecosystem we will have eliminated from the earth. That staggers me: we are likely to eliminate a whole ecosystem from the planet. What science is learning about coral reefs and our impacts on them is truly alarming, and this book is in part an attempt to let the public know about that. However, as an ecologist, I reach beyond my own special system to look at our impacts in other areas, and I see lots of other bad news—bad news that still has not caught the attention it should. By focusing on several of our different negative impacts on the global environment rather than on just one, this book is my attempt to educate without preaching. I want people who read the book to understand, better than they did before, the seriousness of our situation and to subjectively appreciate it. I use coral reefs as a motif, a link that quietly ties the various chapters together,

1. P. F. Sale, *Marine Pollution Bulletin* 56 (2008): 805–809.

but the book is really about us, about what we are doing to our world, and about what we must do to repair our damage and create a better future. I hope that my research background and particular perspective will permit some new examples, alternative metaphors, and novel linkages that will make the messages fresh, distinctive, and compelling.

While the book deals with what may seem like an overwhelming amount of bad news, the overall message is positive. There still is time for us to salvage most of what we are destroying, and there are ways to transition toward a future that combines a high quality of life and a sustainable environment that is biologically diverse. The choice is not between economic progress and environmental conservation, or even between civilization and the natural world—it is between an intelligently managed, low-impact but advanced civilization and the widespread disaster that will come if we continue business as usual. The final chapter sets out the changes that have to occur very soon if we are to avoid the abyss we have been digging for ourselves.

I owe a number of people thanks for their help in making this book possible. My colleagues Jon Lovett Doust and Jake Kritzer read early versions of some chapters and provided needed encouragement when progress was slow. Donna, my wife, and Michelle, my daughter-in-law, read most chapters, helping me to see where I was in danger of losing the reader. Donna also provided numerous examples of our environmental impacts from her own active reading of the media. Randy Olson, Bob Steneck, and Jake Kritzer commented "anonymously" on later drafts, and while I did not make it more detailed, as Bob wanted, or less like "science-talk," as Randy wanted, I did take their advice very seriously as I rewrote, while also incorporating the comments that Jake provided. I know it became better with their input. Yvonne Sadovy, Terry Donaldson, Meg Lowman, Bob Steneck, Ove Hoegh-Guldberg, and Andy Hooten were all generous with photographs. At University of California Press, Chuck Crumly, science publisher, was immediately positive when I approached him about the book. He was involved in the publishing of my first book through Academic Press in 1991 and has been a supporter since. The UC Press team, including Chuck, Lynn Meinhardt (who never lost a file I sent), Jacqueline Volin (who took the book through production), and copy editor Jimmée Greco (who worked diligently to make my text clear), made the tasks of putting the book together almost fun. Along the way, Eric Engles of

Editcraft Editorial Services used his expertise as a developmental editor to turn what I thought was a good book into something a whole lot better and taught me a lot in the process. My son, Darian, and my wider family have been uniformly supportive, but Donna, in particular, has consistently provided that love and steady understanding that she has always provided throughout our lives together. Living with a scientist must have its lonely moments, and I am always grateful (and even a bit surprised) that she chose to be with me. Needless to say, all the errors in this book are mine alone.

INTRODUCTION

April 1984, Heron Island, southern Great Barrier Reef. The helicopter landed in a swirl of sand on the circular pad near the resort. I grabbed my gear, walked across the island to the research station for a hasty hello, then headed down the beach to the waiting skiff. Fifteen minutes after landing, I boarded the *MV Hero,* joining my research team. They had just spent a week under trying circumstances of high winds, rough seas, and cold rain doing scuba surveys of the Capricorn Group on the southern Great Barrier Reef. Naturally, on my arrival, the seas had flattened and the sun had come out. I was regarded with some suspicion mixed with irritation: once again Sale had avoided the bad weather. We steamed north through the night to the Swains Reefs, a vast labyrinth of mostly unnamed reefs that lies 200 to 300 km off the Queensland coast.

Over the next nine days, under sunny skies and glorious starlit nights, with continuing calm seas, we surveyed some fifteen reefs, searching for ones with a northwestern face of relatively uniform slope and high coral cover, chiefly of platelike and branching corals. This was the first year of a new project, and we wanted to choose five reasonably similar reefs that we could visit late each summer for the next three years. We saw many amazing places—steep drop-offs, isolated coral pinnacles ris-

Facing page: Agaricia tenuifolia, Glovers Reef, Belize, 2003. Photo courtesy of R. S. Steneck.

ing nearly to the surface, narrow passes between reefs with tidal waters surging through, dense forests of soft corals, and the gently sloping reefs covered with platelike corals that we wanted to find. One reef held the densest population of sea snakes I had ever encountered—snakes up to five feet long, on the bottom, in mid-water, and at the surface—and I learned which members of the team carried that deep-seated fear of serpents that is, unfortunately, so common. On each reef that proved suitable, we conducted counts of fish using standard transect methods. We set out tape measures 30 meters long, then swam along them, counting fish of each species and tallying them on underwater slates. We focused on juveniles, fish that had been hatched and recruited to that reef during the past summer season. We also described the habitat along each transect, recording coral forms and other structural elements. During the week in the Swains, we encountered only one other vessel. It appeared on the horizon and then disappeared fifteen minutes later. Otherwise it was us, a brilliant bowl of a sky, a circular ocean world, and the reefs.

At the end of the trip, I flew home to Sydney, and less than a week later I was in the Florida Keys, where I met Jim Bohnsack, a reef fisheries scientist based at NOAA's Southeast Fisheries Science Center on Key Biscayne. Bohnsack knows the Keys intimately and took me to Looe Key, which at that time was one of only two protected portions of the Keys and one of the best examples of reef development in Florida. It was my first visit to Florida, and he wanted to show me the best.

We headed south by car to Key Largo, and then by boat south along the curving chain of islands. When we arrived at Looe Key, we tied up to a convenient mooring, suited up, and got in the water. I saw several other small boats in the vicinity, and during my dive I almost bumped into two other divers as we came around a massive coral head from opposite sides. I do not know who they were, but that was the first time in years that I had nearly run into a stranger underwater. Things got worse. At the end of my dive, I was on the surface, about to throw my mask and snorkel over the gunwale and haul myself aboard, when I realized I had surfaced at the wrong boat. I discreetly retreated and swam over to the right boat. Moorings to tie up to, lots of boats, and diver traffic jams: although Looe Key was a fascinating example of a Caribbean reef and a pleasure to visit, it was definitely not the picture of isolation I had experienced at the Swains Reefs.

The close juxtaposing in time of these two field trips jolted me into recognition of something I had thrust to the very back of my mind since my graduate student days in the late 1960s: people and the things they do are a significant factor in most natural environments, and thinking about ecology without also thinking about people is unrealistic. Until then, my research had centered on reefs in a "natural" condition, meaning "without people," or more accurately, "with so few people that human impacts could be ignored." In taking that approach, I was like most other ecologists at the time, but fewer and fewer reefs were like that. A quarter century later, ecologists like me think frequently about people and the impacts they have on natural ecosystems. The problem is that most of our impacts are far less benign than what's caused by divers swimming past, watching and enjoying a coral reef.

.   .   .

It is now widely accepted that humans affect the natural environment deleteriously through overfishing, deforestation, release of greenhouse gases, and in many other ways, including anchoring small boats near reefs and bumping into reefs while diving. What is not broadly appreciated is that these many impacts are linked in multiple ways, both in the causal factors leading to them and in their consequences. They are not suited to a solve-one-at-a-time strategy, nor can they be ignored, because they each are becoming more serious every day. Also not fully appreciated is the seriousness of the changes these impacts are causing in the functioning of the natural world—seriousness for the ecosystems concerned and seriousness for us. In the West, our wealthy civilization's ability to import resources from far afield and protect us from bad outcomes has become an enormous, warm, and fluffy duvet that we have pulled over ourselves—a duvet that keeps us from seeing what is really happening outside. Our wealth protects us from reality, and that reality is one of serious jeopardy.

We remove too many fish from the sea and too many trees from the forest. We replace grasslands with agricultural fields and fields with towns. We divide land into patches separated by concrete barriers we call highways. And we poison natural systems (and sometimes ourselves) when we send the by-products of our technology (not to mention our used and unwanted items), into landfills, waterways, and the air around us. Now our impacts are so large that we are altering the chemistry of our atmosphere and oceans in ways that change the climate on a global scale. One consequence is a mounting loss of biodiversity around the world. We are causing what might become the greatest of all the mass extinctions that have occurred since organisms first roamed the earth, certainly the most rapid of the mass extinctions on record. Yet while we recognize these varied impacts, we still do not really see what is happening to our world, nor do we comprehend what the consequences might be for us.

People may know a lot about each different impact but less about their full significance. We all know of extinctions that have occurred in the recent past and of species that might be on the edge. We take steps to conserve threatened species, even to the point of flying ultralights to guide threatened birds on their annual migrations. But few people understand the consequences of biodiversity loss. We know of instances of overfishing (usually after the fish are all gone), but we are less familiar with the reasons why fisheries keep on failing one after another, and we do not see the long-term consequences for our food supply or for ocean ecology. We appreciate the fact of deforestation but not its scale or its significance to the global water cycle or the climate. Desertification, the process by which productive lands turn into arid wastelands, is seen—if it is thought of at all—as something that happens to other people and not as the natural endpoint of years of mismanagement of forests, grasslands, and water resources. We know that pollution can have consequences for human health as well as environmental health. We even sense that recycling can make economic as well as environmental sense, but we do not appreciate the growing scale and complexity of pollution or its subtle ramifications. We generally understand the greenhouse effect and the fact that our carbon-intensive economy is changing the atmosphere and thereby altering the climate, but we mostly think of climate change as merely a slight increase in average temperature rather than a radical reordering of the ocean–atmosphere climate engine. Having lots of facts does not build a visceral appreciation of our various impacts on this planet.

We also tend to examine each of our deleterious impacts separately and out of context when we should be seeing them as interconnected, mutually reinforcing parts of a larger problem. And living under our duvets, we in the West like to keep the separate parts of that larger problem at arm's length. Sometimes we treat them as problems of specific regions, as if the dead zone in the Gulf of Mexico were a unique phenomenon unrelated to the four hundred other dead zones we have created around our shores. Or as if the desertification in West Africa shares nothing with the 1930s dust bowl of the American Midwest. But the separate problems are really one problem, a global problem, our problem.

Some parts of the natural world are more sensitive to our impacts than others. As a coral reef ecologist, I study one of the most sensitive systems on Earth. Worldwide, reefs have deteriorated measurably in my lifetime, and it is not an unrealistic prediction to say that we risk having no reefs that resemble those of today in as little as thirty or forty more years. None. Although many of us have never seen a coral reef and do not live anywhere near one, our activities have still degraded this marvelous ecosystem almost everywhere it occurs. An understanding of how our impacts interact to affect this particularly sensitive system could go a long way toward helping us anticipate the kinds of problems we are likely to face as our impacts begin to have major consequences for less-sensitive ecosystems. In this way, the coral reef can serve as an important sentinel, an early warning of the problems to come, a canary in the environmental coal mine. As a scientist, I am certain that a deeper understanding of the ecology of all natural systems, and of the details of how our activities modify that ecology, is an important and fundamental element in preparing ourselves for the tasks we now face. More sensitive ecological systems—the canaries—can help us gain that knowledge sooner.

.   .   .

In his 1994 autobiography, the Harvard University biologist E. O. Wilson advised us to "keep in mind that ecology is a far more complex subject than physics." Unfortunately, this counsel does not seem to have permeated very far into our communal psyche. Instead, we tend to think of ecology as something like advanced nature study—all notebooks, binoculars, and funny sun hats. Most of us know little about this science, having gleaned what we could from half-remembered high school or college courses, supplemented by information in the media. While there are sophisticated treatments of this discipline in the better universities and in some excellent textbooks on the subject, there also exist quite weak texts and university courses taught with little excitement and no imagination. Ecology in high school courses tends to be kept very simple, and the media usually do a poorer job of reporting on this field than they do on many other areas of science. I often find that otherwise informative "educational" videos dealing with ecological subjects are best viewed with the mute button depressed, because of the misinformation in the narration. The result is that the great majority of people, if they know much at all about the science of ecology, have a very superficial sense of what this science is about, and a rather simple picture of its central concepts—the population, the community, and the ecosystem. Just at the time our growing impacts require that we really understand the nature of ecological communities, our educational systems become even less effective in providing the necessary knowledge than they had been, bogged down by the widespread misconception that the only growing points in the biological sciences are at the molecular level.

To fully understand human impacts on ecological systems, we need to understand the systems' normal functioning. What world leaders, policymakers, and average citizens need today is a crash course on the nature of ecological communities—how they function, how they change over time, and why they change in the ways they do. Unfortunately, the conventional wisdom on these subjects can be pretty far from the truth. Conventional wisdom relies heavily on an out-of-date, early-twentieth-century understanding of ecology that is at odds with what we now know to be the case. A profound revolution in ecological thinking took place in the latter years of the twentieth century, which revealed a world that is very different from— and far less capable of self-regulation and repair than—the world we believed in until then. I'll take up this topic in a later chapter, but for now remember that we live in a world we need to understand correctly if we are going to be able to anticipate the likely consequences of our impacts on it. And believe me when I say that our world is far more fragile ecologically than our conventional wisdom would suggest. We cannot assume it will always be able to repair itself when we carelessly damage it.

.   .   .

The human footprint on the natural world is unsustainable already, but it is becoming larger every day because of the growth of human population and per capita[1] consumption. We do not have the option of ignoring this problem for much longer. The ecological underpinnings of our way of life are rapidly deteriorating, so the sooner we peek out from under our duvet and recognize that there is a problem we have to attend to, the greater our opportunity to make wise choices and create a good future.

Our apparently separate impacts all trace back to the growing number of people and each person's growing use of natural resources and environmental services.[2] The most obvious difference between now and past times is that there are many more of us than there used to be, and given that each of us requires a certain amount of food, water, shelter, and other perquisites of life, we are requiring more from the earth than we used to. As well as becoming much more numerous, we have, in many countries, become more profligate in our use of things the earth provides, consuming far more food, water, energy, and other resources per capita than our ancestors did.

Consider our use of energy. Humans used to be like other animals, deriving all our energy from the food we ate. Sometime during the Pleistocene, we first harnessed fire, using wood as the source of fuel, thus increasing our per capita use of energy about 2.5 times. With the invention of agriculture, we had more work to be done, and we harnessed additional sources of energy to do it. Horses, oxen, and camels were domesticated as additional muscle power, increasing per capita use of energy another 2.5-fold. Adding use of wind and water power doubled energy use, and the harnessing of coal at the start of the Industrial Revolution brought the total increase in per capita use to 37.5 times that of pre-fire hominids. Our per capita rate of consumption has increased more or less exponentially since that time, and our increase in numbers makes the increase in total energy used enormous. While per cap-

1. Since I will use this term frequently, remember that *per capita* means "the rate per individual." If population size is growing, use of resources will also grow, even if the per capita rate of use remains constant.

2. The environment provides us with both goods, such as foods and building materials, and services, such as degradation and recycling of wastes, protection from storms, and cycling of nutrients and energy. We tend to treat the goods as ours for the taking and to take the services for granted. It is relatively easy to see our growing use of goods (resources), but our use of services is also important. Frequently, our overexploitation of resources leads to changes in the environment that impact its capacity to provide these critical services.

ita use of energy has grown most rapidly, our use of other resources has also tended to grow substantially as our civilization has become more sophisticated.

Some people point to the differences among nations in resource consumption, as if this is the problem that needs to be solved. In fact, the differences among nations in per capita use of resources are substantial and important, but the overall growth in average per capita consumption is also real—it's not only Americans who like to own cars. This increasing average individual rate of consumption means that the growth of our population has a far greater impact on the earth than it would otherwise have. In many cases, we are using resources at rates that are unsustainable, either because these are nonrenewable resources that exist in finite amounts or because these are renewable resources that cannot be renewed at rates any faster than they are at present. In still other cases, there are ample supplies of these resources, but they cannot be transported to the places where people need them with sufficient rapidity to meet the growing demand. As a consequence, there are many instances in which we are running out of important natural resources either locally or globally. It is also the case that our use of resources impinges upon the use made by other organisms, with the result that our growing demand for resources leads to other radical changes within the ecosystems of the earth. Our growing demand is capturing more and more of what the earth produces, to the detriment of other species and of the ecosystems on which our lives depend.

As we consume more resources than we did in the past, we also produce more waste products, and their impacts on the ecosystems of which we are a part are correspondingly greater. To complicate matters, our advanced civilizations have created many new materials, so that our waste products include items that were not part of the natural world before the development of civilized societies. Some of these items can be toxic to people or to other organisms that may be important to us.

Some of our effects upon the earth may seem quite subtle at first, but they can have a way of turning out to be much more serious than initially suspected. On land, because of our recently developed capacity and apparent enthusiasm for broad-scale terraforming, literally reshaping the physical environment in which we live, we have tended to chop up ecological systems such as forests and grasslands into ever smaller pieces more widely separated from one another by our monoculture agriculture and cityscapes. In the coastal oceans, by contrast, we have tended to simplify and homogenize the environment through trawling, beach "reclamation," and coastal "improvement." Both trends lead to loss of species and simplification of ecosystems. Both on land and in the ocean, as our own international shipping and travel have grown, we have unintentionally increased the opportunities for other organisms to gain transport from one place to the next. One result is that ecological differences among locations are being reduced, because those species best suited to disperse and most capable of establishing new populations become ever more cosmopolitan, while other species are lost forever. The wave of extinctions that we have let loose upon Earth is likely to become as substantial as any of the five so-called mass extinction events of the geological past, and we risk far more than the aesthetics of rich biodiversity by this gross simplification of the natural world. We risk losing the capacity for ecological resilience—the ability of ecosystems to cope with stresses without being permanently damaged by them. That we are risking loss of resilience on a global scale rather than in a few local places should be a cause for real concern, because we only have this planet to live on. Some of our activities, particularly the spread of cities and highways, have measurably altered what happens to rain after it falls and how the energy in sunlight is absorbed. And some of our waste products have turned out to have significant impacts on aspects of climate, locally and globally. To put it bluntly, we are numerous enough and sufficiently powerful to be making a mess of the world.

.   .   .

One argument used to minimize the importance of human impacts contends that conditions on the earth have always fluctuated, sometimes radically, and that life has shown sufficient resilience to contend with these "natural" changes. A corollary argument contends that the changes seen today are themselves "natural" and not caused by human activity. I've always been surprised that this argument holds so much sway among nonscientists, because most of us are not used to thinking in terms of such long time frames. But that might be precisely why this idea has gained some traction in the popular mind: because the chain of argument begins with a proposition (that change is an unavoidable fact of Earth history) that is attributable to scientists, who *do* think in the long term, the wider argument (that present changes are natural and life is resilient enough to adjust to them) can be painted with a patina of authority that effectively masks the lack of logic in the proposition.

So let's begin at the beginning and acknowledge that throughout geological history the world *has* undergone environmental changes, sometimes even profound ones. Its early atmosphere was largely devoid of oxygen until the first microbial stromatolites and other cyanobacteria (also called blue-green algae) introduced photosynthesis about two and a half billion years ago and increased oxygen content a thousand-fold in just four hundred million years.[3] In the more recent past of the last five hundred seventy million years (from the start of the Cambrian period), the world has been both warmer and colder than it is now; the continents have been redistributed into substantially different patterns; mountain ranges have been formed and eroded away; absolute sea level has fluctuated at least 120 meters, alternately covering and exposing the continental shelves. As earth and climate scientists have improved the precision of their records of past change, it has become apparent that many changes have not been smooth and gradual. Instead, ecological systems appear to live within a modest level of "background" change but have been periodically stressed by relatively abrupt shifts that have pushed them beyond their limits of resilience. Then tipping points of various kinds have been reached, resulting in sudden, catastrophic change into a new ecology, usually with the loss of most of the species previously present. It's a more dynamic world than we are used to thinking of, and a more dangerous one too.

It would be naive to pretend that all present-day changes in the world are due to human activities, but the fact that some changes would have occurred whether or not we were here scarcely matters if the overall changes that are occurring are potentially risky for our future well-being. If there are actions we can take that will mitigate these changes, it would be prudent to take them. The complication, of course, is that when talking about environmental change, we are not talking about

3. This was the most profound environmental change ever caused by living organisms; it allowed the development of organisms that breathe oxygen and of ecological systems as we know them today. You can see living stromatolites today in the shallow waters of the Exuma Cays, Bahamas, and at Hamelin Pool at the inner, southern end of Shark Bay, Western Australia. They look a lot like their Archean relatives of 2.5 billion years ago. They are also easily mistaken for slimy rocks.

simple single-cause, single-effect processes. We are talking about a complex system with multiple causal agents and multiple consequences. This complication helps create the differing opinions concerning our role in environmental change and the differing views on its overall seriousness.

Given that the world has changed, sometimes drastically, in the geological past and is changing today, we must recognize that it may change drastically in the future. When I look at the available data, I see three factors suggesting that the changes happening now or the ones likely to happen in the future are somewhat special—which is science talk for "alarming." First is that the changes, climatic and otherwise, that are presently occurring are more rapid than any in the past, except for rare cases when events such as the arrival of a large meteorite caused change very quickly. Second is that some of the changes occurring now are different from any that have happened before, and many different kinds of change are occurring at once. Third is that the more severe changes in past periods have led to mass extinctions, including the removal of the dominant organisms. We are the dominant organisms of today's world, and I'd personally like us to remain present for a few more years. Putting it simply, I aim to convince you that we live in challenging times, and that our challenge is not to manage the world so that it does not change, but to manage our impacts so that patterns of change do not become so severe that devastating tipping points are exceeded.

.   .   .

This book is divided into three sections. The first and longest looks at four specific examples of how our activities impact the natural world. Overfishing is dealt with first. As a relatively simple issue of overexploitation with just a few subtleties, it is perhaps the most straightforward example. It's also an issue we have struggled with ever since we began to manage fishing activities. Our impacts on forest ecosystems—the next topic—are also largely a problem of overexploitation, but with the complication that we deliberately clear away forests to create agricultural land and then turn the agricultural land into cities. Talking about forests is also a good way to introduce the important concept of environmental services. Our direct impacts on the oceans and atmosphere are dealt with next, because without understanding climate change, it is difficult to comprehend the perfect storm that is currently smashing into the world's coral reefs and other ecosystems, too. The unfolding tragedy of the reefs themselves finishes this first section.

The second section deals with a question that has been nagging at me for twenty-five years: In view of all the human-caused devastation described in the first section, why do we not get it? Why do we not understand that we have a big and growing environmental problem? Why do we not live up to our name as *Homo sapiens* and approach the problem and the possible solutions rationally? Why do we not deal politically with the need to prioritize, reach consensus, and act?

I think there are several reasons why we have difficulty coming to grips with our environmental problems. Some of them have to do with politics and the marketplace—but as root causes of our lack of understanding and action these are well outside my expertise, and other authors have explored them at length. The reasons I focus on in this section have more to do with how people perceive and think. We tend first of all to constantly readjust the reference points that would otherwise allow us to perceive and appreciate troubling changes, a phenomenon that's been called "the problem of shifting baselines." Second, we share a pervasive (and, as I will explain, ill-founded) faith that the natural world is a well-regulated system that can absorb all the insults we throw at it without being permanently damaged. This helps us rationalize all our impacts on the environment.

So if we really are fundamentally altering the world's ecosystems and drastically reducing biodiversity, why does it matter? And if it does matter, how should we respond? These two questions form the basis of the third section. It begins with the human-caused mass extinction now under way and explains biodiversity's role as the foundation of all the ecological processes on which we depend. The importance one ascribes to biodiversity depends to a considerable degree on one's particular view of the extent of human responsibility for our planet, but it also depends on one's understanding of basic biology and ecology. How we view the relationship of humans to the rest of nature will probably also determine our attitudes to other aspects of our current dilemma and our preferences among possible solutions. The section continues with a look at our use of energy, because if there is one aspect of our global environmental problem that requires the most urgent attention, it is the need to reduce our releases of greenhouse gases into the atmosphere. Central to this task is changing our patterns of energy use.

The chapter on energy is followed by a short exposition of the current patterns of growth of the human population. Population growth has been a taboo subject for discussion over the past thirty years or so, but we can no longer delay talking about it. The simple fact is that the growth in the size of our population that will take place over the next forty years if we do not change our ways is fundamentally incompatible with a future in which people enjoy quality of life in an environment that is sustainably managed. In short, we cannot get a good outcome to our environmental problems without seriously tackling population growth.

The final chapter tries to look forward and anticipate the possible futures ahead of us. In it, I point to the few pieces of good news around us as evidence that we are capable of making appropriate decisions. Indeed, we are remarkably capable of rapidly changing our attitudes once we are convinced a change of perspective is needed. Our challenge now is to make these needed changes globally. My personal challenge is to help us make our decisions quickly enough to minimize the pain and maximize the positive outcome, both for us and for the bountiful natural world upon which our lives ultimately depend.

PART ONE

INFORMATION

What We Are Doing to Our World

I

OVERFISHING

We have always been fishermen.[1] Fishing extends far back into our human past, and as our last remaining hunter-gatherer activity it ties us to that past in a tangible way. We capture wild aquatic organisms for personal use and to trade with other people. Most, but not all, of these fishery products are used for food. A trout fisherman on a Scottish stream who ties his own flies and approaches his sport with a quasi-religious fervor may have very little in common with the Malaysian peasant who fossicks at low tide for edible shellfish and crabs to feed her family, but both are part of fishing. So too are the giant multinational corporations, with their fleets of factory trawlers, their thousands of miles of longlines and nets, and their flash-frozen tuna air-lifted from deck to jet to Japan. Fishing is a vast global enterprise with a sophisticated array of technology and millions of people all engaged in extracting aquatic organisms from rivers, lakes, and oceans, trading them around the world, and consuming them in many different ways.

While we have always fished, we seem also to have usually overfished, leading to the reduction and sometimes the loss of formerly

---

Facing page: Tuna auction, Tokyo Fishmarket. Photo courtesy of Terry J. Donaldson.

1. The word *fisherman* is considered politically incorrect, even though many women in the industry proudly consider themselves fishermen. The gender-neutral term, *fisher,* is actually the name of a rather beautiful North American weasel.

valuable fishery resources. Until recently, the consequences of such overfishing were generally local and temporary. Now, for the first time in human history, we face the possibility of widespread, essentially permanent collapse of the most important fisheries around the globe. Our continuing tendency to overfish is surprising given the investment in fisheries management around the world; on the surface, it does not seem to be that difficult to manage catch so that it does not exceed the capacity of the fished populations to supply.

Coastlines throughout the world provide scattered evidence of ancient fishing successes in the form of aboriginal middens—large piles of shells, bones, or other debris resulting from the capture, butchering, and presumably eating of the catch over many days and years by members of past cultures. In many middens, the size of the shells and bones varies with depth, with the largest buried deep in the oldest layers and the smallest occurring in the younger layers near the surface. This is evidence of ancient overfishing.[2] The sizes of organisms being caught declined over time because, in all probability, the fishing was sufficiently intense to lower the life expectancy of the fished species. They lived less long, on average, before being caught and no longer reached the sizes they had in past years. And while we cannot tell this from examining a midden, it is very likely that as they became smaller over time, the animals being caught also became less common and harder to catch. Ancient fishermen often overfished and at some point had to search for new fishing grounds.

Most fish are remarkably fecund animals, producing thousands, sometimes millions, of eggs in a lifetime. Most also reproduce through external fertilization so that the female matures a clutch of eggs within her body before mating with a male. Most fish also grow in size throughout life, and because eggs take up space in the body cavity before they are laid, older, larger females are markedly more fecund than youngsters. Many fish also live for decades if not caught first. These life-history characteristics mean that fish populations can be remarkably productive, able to replenish their numbers rapidly following a decline in population size. The relative lack of parental care and

2. An alternative possibility, that the people came to prefer smaller specimens, is a comforting thought, but that is hardly likely given the modern success of all-you-can-eat restaurants.

the small size of newly hatched fish ensure that fish breeding success is strongly dependent on environmental conditions and a certain amount of luck—a fish population of a given size can produce an enormous cohort of young fish one year and far fewer the next.[3]

Fishing is currently big business and vital to our food supply. The United Nations Food and Agriculture Organization (FAO) reports that, according to 2008 data, fishing provides 15.3 percent of the animal protein needs of the human population worldwide, or about 16.7 kg of fish per person per year. Commercial fishing directly employs about 44 million people and brings about 92 million metric tons of product to market every year, while aquaculture provides an additional 51.7 million metric tons. These fishery products are worth about US$91.2 billion and $78.8 billion per year, respectively, and the international trade in fishery products exceeds $92 billion per year. Adding in so-called illegal, unreported, and unregulated catches and the fish caught by recreational fishermen and by artisanal fishermen to feed their families around the world further increases the total tonnage of fishery species captured to 130 million metric tons per year.

The FAO also reports that the total world catch has been declining at the rate of about 0.7 million metric tons per year since about 1988, despite increases in fishing efforts. Globally, fishing is still very big business, but fisheries are failing to provide as they used to.

The decline in total commercial catch is one of several signs that our tendency to overfish is pushing us up against firm limits and that future catches may become far less bountiful than they have been. In this chapter we will look at fishing, sustainable fishing, and overfishing. We'll get into the science behind fisheries management and the reasons why management so often fails. I hope you'll become more aware

---

3. These statements about the reproductive biology of fishes are all qualified because fishes are a remarkably diverse group of vertebrates, displaying a bewildering variety of reproductive physiology and behaviors. While most fish spawn a large clutch of eggs and offer no parental care, some species give birth to free-swimming fry after internal fertilization, some lay eggs in nests that are vigorously defended, some carry the eggs around in their mouths until hatching, and one quaint Australian fish carries its eggs hanging from a hook on its forehead. Most fish have a distinct breeding season and may spawn only once a year. Others may spawn daily. And while most fish appear not to care too much about romantic ties, there are some that mate for life. And then there are a handful of species that are hermaphroditic, all female, but dependent on nondiscriminating males of other closely related "normal" species to give them a quick stimulus to ovulate.

of what takes place to make those fish available in grocery stores, and that you will appreciate the need to fish much more sustainably than we currently do. Along the way I will also touch on the more general problem of overuse of natural resources.

THE COD FISHERY OF THE NORTHWEST ATLANTIC

When John Cabot returned to England in 1497, he brought with him tales of plentiful Atlantic cod *(Gadus morhua)* of such size and abundance that catching these fish was simple. There were even claims that the fish were so abundant as to impede the progress of ships. Southern Europeans came to refer to the lands Cabot had found as Baccalaos, from the Spanish *bacalao,* the cod. The Portuguese had commenced fishing for cod off Newfoundland by 1501, followed shortly by the French and Basques. This commercial cod fishery was to last for almost five hundred years.

Initially, fishing off Newfoundland was an entirely ship-based operation. Ships sailed from Europe in the spring, fished intensively, salting down the catch in barrels, and returned home to the markets. But early on, the British, French, and Basques established shore camps where they could land the catch, salt it, and air-dry it. It was then packed dry for transport to the European markets; as a lighter product it was more economical to ship and, as a less heavily salted product, it was preferred by the public. To this day, many Europeans along the Mediterranean coast prefer dried, salted cod to the fresh product.

The colonization of Newfoundland was a direct consequence of the growing commercial fishery. Initially it involved the construction of seasonal dwellings for the people who worked the fishery, processing the catch for shipment home. Gradually, seasonal dwellings became year-round homes as investments in real property began to require guarding it through the winter, but it was always the cod industry sustaining the development. Wars in Europe altered the overall fishing effort and the countries involved in the trade, and periodically the cod stocks failed, but on average the overall harvest grew year by year. As early as 1683, the problem of "overcapacity" was recognized by the Colonial Office in London—an excess demand for fish had fueled development of excess capacity (too many ships and nets) to catch them, and fishery stocks were failing.

Farther south, the Gulf of Maine cod fishery was "discovered," and Cape Cod named, by the crew of the *Concord,* a British ship sent to the New World to hunt for supplies of sassafras in 1602. Fishing vessels followed soon after, using the shores and the offshore islands of the gulf as suitable fish-drying sites. Fishing, and a Europe-based industry using seasonal dwellings on suitable shorelines, was well established by the time the first colonial settlements were being established in New England in 1620. However, the industry quickly became an American-based one, as local populations took up fishing, first in their immediate vicinity, and later in larger vessels venturing as far afield as the Grand Banks and northern Newfoundland. This was in contrast to the situation farther north, where the local Newfoundland and Nova Scotia populations operated inshore fisheries from smaller vessels and left the offshore fishery on the Grand Banks and the Labrador coast to be operated by larger vessels whose home ports were mostly in Europe. By the start of the eighteenth century, the Grand Banks fishery included vessels from England, France, Spain, and Portugal along with vessels from New England.

The cod trade grew so important that it became a vital source of foreign exchange for the developing American and Canadian colonies. It was incorporated into a profitable transatlantic trade in which the vessels that shipped dried cod to Europe returned with African slaves for the West Indies and southern American colonies, stocking up with sugar and salt in the West Indies before moving again to the fishing grounds of New England and the Grand Banks. Simultaneously, some vessels shipped the lower-quality fish south to feed the slaves in the West Indies and transported sugar back to Europe.

In these early days, fishing was done by hand-line from the decks of the vessel. Beginning in the nineteenth century, however, new methods were developed. Cod seines, gill nets, and cod traps were used to a limited extent in coastal waters, and small dories began to be carried by the offshore vessels so that hand-liners could spread out over a wider area to fish. By the 1850s, longlines with hundreds of hooks began to replace hand-lining in the offshore fishery, but it was at the start of the twentieth century, with the arrival of trawling, that fishing methods made a major advance in effectiveness.

The otter trawl was introduced to the U.S. Atlantic seacoast in 1908 but was not used in Newfoundland waters until 1935. An otter trawl consists of a large baglike net that can be dragged across the seafloor, with two large otter boards, or doors, mounted on the towing lines at the ends of the trawl's wings—the outer corners of its mouth. The doors can be as big as garage or barn doors and may each weigh 1,000 kg in commercial trawls that have mouths 100 meters wide. The doors are rigged so that hydrodynamic forces tend to move them outward, spreading the wings and pulling the mouth of the net open. Floats or kites lift the headline of the net to keep the mouth open vertically, and the footline is weighted and protected in various ways to keep the net in close contact with the substratum. The otter trawl proved to be very efficient at catching cod and other groundfish, and trawling became the principal method of capture in this fishery.

In addition to the introduction of trawling technology, the twentieth century saw increased use of steam and diesel power, of refrigeration and flash-freezing, and of long-distance rapid transport to market by truck, train, and plane. The result was that the Northwest Atlantic fishery was presented with an ever-expanding market and the temptation to continue to expand the fishing effort to supply the demand.

So what do we see when we look at the catch of cod? Detailed examination of the early fishery, region by region, reveals many examples of stock declines and resulting poor catches, but the solution was simply to expand to new fishing grounds. For example, a failure of the southern and southeastern inshore Newfoundland fishery in 1715 provided the impetus for expansion to the northeastern Newfoundland shore and for a progressive expansion of fishing on the Grand Banks. And with each shift to more distant fishing grounds there was a shift toward larger vessels and more fishing effort to cover the additional costs. The growth in the catch proceeded as the area being fished expanded, as technology advanced, and as markets opened up. By 1765, the total catch for Newfoundland, the Grand Banks, Georges Bank, and coastal waters was about 180,000 metric tons, supporting a brisk trade with Europe and the West Indies. Catches declined during the American War of Independence but then recovered. By the mid-1800s, the total catch of cod from the Northwest Atlantic was about 200,000 metric tons, but it increased further, reaching 260,000 by the early 1870s. By 1895, the Northwest Atlantic cod fishery was landing 420,000 metric tons, and it continued at about this level, fluctuating between 400,000 and 700,000 metric tons, through to the Second World War. By 1955, the catch had reached about 1,000,000 metric tons, and it peaked at about 1,900,000 metric tons in 1968. Thereafter, catches declined progressively, to about 500,000 metric tons in 1975 and 80,000 metric tons in 1990. The Canadian government closed the northern cod fishery in 1992 and all groundfishing in Canadian Atlantic waters in 1993. Since then, cod stocks have shown minimal recovery. A commercial fishery that had provided enormous economic and nutritive benefits over five hundred years was finished.

From the commencement of commercial fishing, there were local declines or outright failures in the cod fishery. With hindsight, it's possible to see that in a situation in which anyone with the funds to secure a vessel could join the fishery, there was always a tendency to overfish local cod stocks. In the 1600s and 1700s, fishing was restricted to those locations that were near to land or home ports. When fishing yield declined in those locations, it was possible to travel to new locations. The result was that diminished stocks often had a chance to recover, while the fishery was sustained commercially by turning to previously unfished stocks. However, once the fishery grew so large that all fishable locations in the region were being fished, the tendency to overfish still reduced stocks, but there was nowhere else for the fishing effort to go.

If fishermen were not inventive and had continued using hand-lines from relatively small boats, it is possible that the catch of cod would never have grown to the size it did, and the collapse of the 1990s would not have occurred. But that is not the nature of fishing. Fishermen are wily predators, always looking to innovate to capture their prey faster and more economically.

The collapse of the cod fishery provides three clear lessons. First, there is a profound difference between the local failures that occurred from time to time during the early years of the fishery and the final overall collapse. Second, the combination of growing demand and improving technology led to ever-expanding effort and ever-growing yield up until the eventual collapse. Third—but not evident from the information I've provided so far—the fishing effort acted in concert with other factors to bring about the decline in cod populations. To fully understand what happened, it is necessary to move beyond a focus on effort and catches to examine the myriad factors that determine how abundant a population of fish will be and how fishing changes that. To do this we have to dip into theory. It's not particularly complicated theory, so bear with me.

EFFECTS OF FISHING ON FISH POPULATIONS

Logic dictates that populations of fish (or other species) grow when more fish are born than are dying, and they decline when more fish die than are being born. Ideally, a population will remain at constant size if each female produces, on average, the number of offspring needed to ensure that exactly two of them will reach adulthood and breed in their turn. (Two are required because in most species of fish, as in other animals, 50 percent of offspring are males.) That a female cod spawns millions of eggs each year and can live up to twenty more years after reaching maturity at five or six years tells us that very few hatched cod eggs grow up to become adult spawning cod. There are lots of things that happen to kill cod, nearly always well before they reach sexual maturity. Only one of these is fishing, which principally kills older fish.

From the perspective of the fish, fishing is just one more form of predation—one more challenge in its struggle to survive and reproduce. When fishing commences on a previously unfished population, it increases the chance of mortality, with the result that fish live, on average, less long before they die. In addition, fishing is a size-selective form of predation that tends to have the greatest impacts on the larger and older members of the population. While Atlantic cod can live for twenty-five years or more, by the early 1990s fishing was so intense that most cod were being caught before they were seven years old.

Because of these basic facts, there are several consequences of starting to fish a population. First, because animals tend to die younger, the population tends to become smaller than it was before, because each individual is present for a shorter period of time. Second, because the animals tend to die younger, they have fewer seasons after reaching sexual maturity in which to spawn—two or three seasons versus as many as twenty seasons in the case of cod. The result is that each successful fish (one that reproduces at least once) produces fewer offspring over its (shortened) lifespan. Furthermore, because fish are more fecund when they are older, the actual reduction in the production of offspring is substantially greater than the reduction in the number of spawning seasons might suggest.

Given these simple facts, how do we manage a fishery so that it can be maximally profitable without leading to the decline and extinction of the fished population? Managers have relied traditionally on three factors that may make it possible for fishing to increase predation on a population without wiping it out. These are density dependence, the storage effect, and the relationships among cost, catch, and effort in a fishery. The first two are aspects of how populations grow; the third is an economic relationship in the fishing activity.

Density dependence is central to ideas concerning the regulation of numbers in a population and for that reason has featured importantly in the history of ecology. It is also central to the simplest ecological model of population growth—the *logistic* model. As already noted, the pattern of growth of any population is determined by the pattern of births and deaths within it. Both birth and death rates depend upon the average age and condition of the individuals that make up the population, and by convention we speak of a *per capita rate of increase,* meaning "the rate per individual at which the population grows."[4] Each member of the population requires food, shelter, and other resources in order to survive, grow, and potentially reproduce. When a population is small relative to its available resources, its individuals are likely in good condition—well fed, growing at maximal rates, healthy. They should possess a relatively high life expectancy and should produce offspring at a higher rate than individuals of a larger and denser population. The high per capita rate of increase causes that population to grow, but, following the logistic model, as the population grows the individuals will begin to experience shortages of resources such as food or shelter space. These shortages will cause the individuals to grow more slowly, be less fit overall, produce fewer offspring, and die at a younger age on average. As a result, per capita rate of increase falls, leading to a decline in the rate of growth of the population. Thus we can see that per capita rate of increase is dependent on the density of the population relative to its resources; because the dependence is negative, there is a tendency for any episode of population growth to cease and for the size of the population to stabilize. The population size at which this occurs is termed the *carrying capacity* of its environment—that size at which the availability of resources relative to the numbers of individuals competing for them sets birth and death rates to be exactly equal (see Figure 1).

4. The concept of a per capita rate of increase of a population may seem peculiarly complex, but it simplifies the math. It also conforms to the idea, to be explored in detail in chapter 6, that it is individuals, not populations, that give birth and survive or die. The per capita rate of increase is the average individual's share of the overall rate of growth of the population. It becomes progressively smaller as the population grows larger, and it reaches zero when overall birth rates and death rates are exactly balanced.

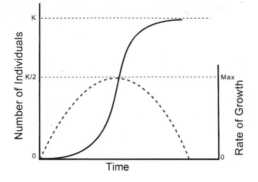

FIGURE 1. A population obeying a logistic pattern of growth exhibits an S-shaped change in population size over time (solid line, left axis) as the rate of growth (dotted line, right axis) increases to a maximum and then declines to zero when the carrying capacity of the environment (K) is reached.

Animals are still busily growing, reproducing, and dying, but the rates at which these happen balance one another and keep the size of the population constant. The logistic model can be redrawn to show the rate of growth of the population at any given population size. The growth rate is at a maximum when the population is half the size it will ultimately reach at carrying capacity.

Looked at from the perspective of the fishing industry, this logistic curve indicates that if fishing reduces the size of the population from where it was before fishing started (its virgin state when it was presumably at carrying capacity), the capacity of the population to grow will become progressively greater until the point that the population has been reduced to half its virgin size. By fishing at a rate that removes individuals quickly enough to keep the population at this size, the fishery will gain the maximum sustainable catch that the fish population is capable of providing. (This statement is correct, but doing this in a real fishery is more difficult than it might seem.)

Very similar approaches are used to maximize yields in other harvested populations. We mow pastures for hay at a frequency designed to capture the burst of rapid plant growth before the plants become large and crowded. We harvest forests on a longer cycle but follow the same principle. And we take cattle and pigs to market at an age that optimizes growth prior to sale. In all these examples, we maximize yield because of density dependence, relying on the idea that younger and less-crowded organisms grow more rapidly.

Theoretically, by doing sufficient fishing to keep a fish population at this one-half of maximum size, a well-managed fishery will be able to fish indefinitely, taking the maximum sustainable yield (MSY) of fish per year, and the population will continue to produce into the distant future. Clearly this rosy future did not befall the cod or any of a number of other species.

There are two important things to notice about this simple model of density-dependent logistic growth. First, while the capacity of individuals to grow and reproduce is highest when the population is smallest (because there are ample resources available for each individual), the overall capacity of the population to grow more abundant will decline once the population is pushed below one-half of its virgin size (because a few individuals cannot produce large numbers of offspring quickly). The desirable one-half of virgin size for the population is not a stable equilibrium—the population will tend to move away from this point unless fishing is very closely regulated, and the further it is pushed below this point, the less capacity it will have for growth and recovery. If one is interested in the long-term yield of the fishery, seeking to fish at a rate that will achieve MSY is a very risky goal that demands exquisite control of the rate of fishing.

Second, this model assumes that the production of resources and the status of all other things in the environment that impinge on the condition of the fish are unvarying. If the availability of resources varies independently of the size of the fish population, if environmental temperature changes (so that metabolic rates, and therefore rates of growth for given caloric intake, change), or if any other environmental feature changes in a way that modifies the growth, fecundity, or survivorship of the fish, then carrying capacity, rate of population growth at a given population size, and the size of the population at which maximum yield is obtained all change. Under these circumstances, maintaining the population at the magic equilibrium size can become a very difficult task indeed. Needless to say, environments are rarely unvarying.

Variability of environmental characteristics is so pervasive that we should never forget it, even if the simple logistic model of population growth assumes variability is unimportant. In fact, fish populations have been telling us for a long time just how variable their environments are. They do this by demonstrating tremendous variability in recruitment.

Recruitment is the addition of a cohort to a population. It happens to armies when raw recruits go to boot camp, and it happens to biological populations when new groups of juveniles are added to the population each breeding season or when new groups of juveniles reach adulthood. Recruitment is a measure of progress through the ranks of the population, and it can be measured at any life stage. Fishery biologists frequently measure recruitment at the time that young individuals become large enough to be caught by the particular fishing gear being used. Ecologists tend to measure recruitment to specific life stages, such as to the juvenile stage following a larval period or to the adult stage at the time of maturation.

In a fish population, recruitment—whether you measure it at the end of larval life, at sexual maturation, or at the time the fish get big enough to be caught by a gill net of a particular mesh size—is profoundly variable from year to year. Science has known about this since 1914, when the Norwegian fishery biologist Johan Hjort documented the very great variation from year to year in recruitment to populations of a number of commercial fishery species in the North Sea. In the years since, it has become abundantly clear that the production of a new cohort of fish is a very risky business that is sometimes crowned with massive success and is at other times an absolute failure. Looked at another way, while only two of a female cod's millions of offspring are likely, on average, to reach maturity, the actual breeding success of individuals varies very widely around this average, and thus the breeding success of populations varies very widely from year to year.

In species that have relatively lengthy lives, such as most fishes, the population at any particular time is composed of a number of cohorts of individuals, each the product of recruitment in a particular year. Recruitment variability means that these successive cohorts start out at very different sizes and will probably preserve these differences throughout life. Indeed, the main conclusion of Hjort's classic study was that variation in recruitment results in the formation of occasional particularly abundant cohorts, so-called strong year-classes, that tend to dominate the catch and sustain the fishery over several years.[5]

The main reason in fishes for variation in production from year to year is that there are years when greater proportions of newly hatched

5. Strong year-classes occur in humans as well as in fish, although our recruitment variability is far less pronounced. At present there is a great deal of media interest in the baby boom generation reaching retirement age. The baby boom generation is a strong cohort of humans (most pronounced in Western countries) that was produced immediately after World War II, when all those soldiers came home and everyone was optimistic

eggs survive and years when smaller proportions do. Why this happens is less easy to explain but has to do with environmental variability that modifies the likelihood of survival in these early stages. Given that a cod lays several million eggs in a season, it's clear that the probability of survival is normally very low indeed (or we'd be up to our necks in cod), so very modest changes in the chance of survival will lead to very large changes in the number of fish recruiting.[6] Among the environmental changes that may be important are weather patterns that delay the plankton blooms the newly hatched fish depend on for food, ocean current patterns that carry the larvae to places that are quite unsuitable (or, alternatively, very suitable) for their survival and development, and temperature patterns that cause them to grow more quickly or more slowly than usual and thus alter the risk of predation on or the demands for food by these tiny larvae. (A slowly growing larva is small for a longer time and runs a greater risk of getting eaten because of this.)

In a population made up of relatively long-lived individuals, the effects of good recruitment can be "stored," meaning that the reproductive capacity of strong year-classes remains for many years, buffering recruitment variability. While a population with many year-classes of animals present will receive only a modest boost in overall numbers in years when recruitment is highly successful (because each year-class is only a small component of the total population), it can survive many years with very poor recruitment (because there will still be animals maturing and reproducing). By contrast, a population of short-lived individuals containing only a handful of year-classes will exhibit far greater fluctuations in overall size as good and bad recruitments occur and will be able to tolerate only short runs of poor recruitment without going extinct.

One consequence of fishing is that, because it increases mortality and lowers average age, it tends to reduce the storage capacity of the fish pop-

---

about the future. The abundance of baby boomers generated a slightly less conspicuous strong cohort, the echo boomers, produced when the baby boomers reached reproductive age. The baby boom and the echo boom resulted from increases in reproductive activity due to greater numbers of individuals entering their reproductive years during a period of peace and prosperity.

6. If the average female produces 1,000,000 eggs, about 999,998 of every 1,000,000 offspring die before reaching adulthood. That is a mortality rate of 0.999998. Reducing that rate by only 1 percent, to 0.989998, means that 10,002 fish of every 1,000,000 reach adulthood—an increase in recruitment of about five thousand times.

ulation. This makes a fish population more vulnerable to a series of years of poor recruitment than it would otherwise be. When fishing pressure is relatively light, however, storage in the population makes it possible to continue having good catches despite variation in rates of replenishment of the population through reproduction and recruitment. The good year-classes sustain the fishery through years of poor recruitment.

Fishing is predation, and fishermen are efficient predators—they do not waste effort, and they are skilled or they do not survive. Fishing was a very important activity to the Melanesians and Polynesians who migrated out from Southeast Asia to populate all the scattered islands of the South Pacific, nearly one-fifth of the surface of the planet, by 1000 A.D. During this expansion into the Pacific, they developed a very broad range of fishhook styles and materials. Differences in design and manufacture of fishhooks have been used extensively by archeologists to track cultural connections, and bone or shell fishhooks of various designs are now sold as tourist curios throughout the region wherever tourists with pocket change congregate. But these fishhooks—the finely crafted tools of their trade—are really a testament to the sophisticated fishing skills of these island-dwelling people. Each hook was specifically designed to catch a particular species of fish with particular jaw structures or behaviors, in particular ways, and at a particular time and place. The level of sophistication easily rivals that of the flies tied by that Scottish trout fancier I mentioned earlier, but the Polynesians used their tools to provide food rather than for sport. Worldwide, coastal peoples still use hooks, hand spears, nets, and traps of various types, and they use their hands to pick up slower-moving species such as mollusks. They fish effectively, and fishery products form an important part of their diets and provide trade goods, including jewelry, medicines, and other materials.

Yes, fishing is predation, but it is also an economic activity: commercial fishermen fish to make money. Being an economic activity, fishing should be subject to market forces, and in many ways it is. Fishing has costs. These include the cost of the boat and the equipment and wages for the crew. Costs are linearly related to the amount of effort expended by the fishery in catching fish. Effort is a measure of the overall investment—in dollars and time—by the fishery. A fishery involving ten ships of a particular size and type costs about half per year what a fishery involving twenty ships of this type would cost. And the ten-ship fleet exerts about half the predatory pressure on the fish population that the twenty-ship fleet does. A fishery using faster, more wide-ranging vessels or vessels carrying more sophisticated gear for tracking fish costs more per year than a fishery using smaller, less elaborate vessels and exerts correspondingly greater predatory pressure on the fish population. If the value of the yield in marketable fish exceeds the cost of catching the fish, profits are made and fishing continues. If the yield does not match the cost of catching, losses are incurred, and we may anticipate some fishermen getting out of this business into something more lucrative.

Ideally, the economics of the marketplace should provide a very reliable regulator of fishing effort, because the value of the catch does not increase linearly with effort. Because fishing reduces the average age and therefore size of individuals as well as the overall abundance of the fished population, it becomes more difficult to obtain fish of high market value (larger sizes usually) as the fishing effort increases. Given that there is a certain rate of production of fish available to be caught, it follows that the value of the catch obtained will increase with effort only to a certain point. Beyond that point, increasing effort will result in a yield of lower value because few fish remain to be caught. Increasing effort still further should lead to a yield of less value than the cost of catching the fish, and fishing harder still could lead to the removal of all available fish (extinction). As Figure 2 shows, the interaction of cost, yield, and effort should lead to a stable if rather unhappy equilibrium in which effort rises to that point at which costs equal yield (and the fishery does not make a profit), but effort should not rise higher than this. This should be so even when all fishermen are thoroughly selfish and fish to obtain the maximum catch possible, so long as they do not go broke doing so.[7]

Drawing these three factors together—storage capacity, density dependence, and the links among cost, catch, and fishing effort—theory suggests that it should be rather easy to ensure that fishing be a long-term, sustainable pattern of exploitation. The storage effect ensures that the fish population will be buffered from the natural variation in production as well as from any modest fluctuations in fishing pressure. Density dependence in demographic properties provides confidence that the fish population can compensate by increasing rates of

7. The MSY shown in Figure 2 as the point at which net profit is greatest occurs at the point where fishing pressure has reduced the population to about 50 percent of virgin (unfished) abundance.

FIGURE 2. Fishery economics—
the relationship between the cost
of fishing and the yield or income
derived from the catch. Costs rise
linearly with the effort expended
to catch fish. Yield rises steeply at
first but falls off at high levels of
effort because few fish remain to
be caught. The intersection between the cost and yield curves,
a, is a stable equilibrium at which

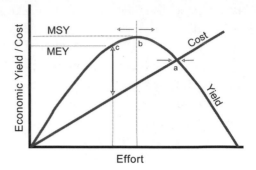

the fishermen make no profit. The maximum sustainable yield (MSY, point *b*), when
catch is greatest, and the maximum economic yield (MEY, point *c*), when profit (difference between cost and yield) is greatest, are both desirable goals, but neither is a stable equilibrium point.

production of new fish when fishing pressure reduces fish density. And
the economic links between the cost of catching fish and the value of
the yield at market should mean that fishermen, being rational beings,
will never increase effort to levels that would be truly detrimental to
the fish population. Would that it were all this simple.

This ideal situation is not reality. The economic extinction of the cod
fishery is only the latest example in a long series of apparently well-managed fisheries that have been overexploited and have collapsed. But why
is this so? Part of the problem lies in the simplicity of our model—fishing has strong ecosystem effects beyond those of simply removing some
fish, and fish populations are impacted by things other than fishing. The
graph in Figure 2 does not account for fishing's reduction of the storage
effect, which makes the fish population less capable of weathering a series
of poor years. Nor does it provide for the environmental variability (the
poor years) that results in the demographic variation that makes the effort
required to obtain the maximum sustainable yield (or indeed any specific
yield) change from year to year. In fact, it assumes environmental variability does not exist. A more realistic Figure 2 would show two blurry
clouds of points in place of the cost and yield curves that intersect so precisely at a single point. Above all, Figure 2 provides no way of showing
the several other ecosystem effects of fishing that may radically alter the
challenges facing fishes as they seek to survive and reproduce.

The other part of the problem lies in our tendency to think of fishery management as the management of a simple interaction between a predator and its prey. Fishermen are indeed predators—rational, intelligent predators—but they are also members of real human societies participating in an economy. Figure 2 does not include the effects of political decisions made to sustain human communities and the fishing industries they depend on for livelihood when they experience hard times—the debt relief, the unemployment benefits, and the other governmental actions intended to help families in need but that also allow people to remain fishermen when cold economic reality should be causing them to turn to other employment. Government policies intended to mitigate economic misery in the short term can have unintended negative consequences for the long-term sustainability of the fishery.

In the remaining sections of the chapter, I describe what is currently happening to fisheries worldwide. I then review the important ways in which real fishing differs from our simple theory and discuss some of the ways in which fisheries managers have been able to deal successfully with these departures from theory to make fisheries sustainable.

CURRENT GLOBAL TRENDS IN FISHERIES

Overall global fishery production has declined slightly in recent years, despite continued growth in effort. Unless we can reverse this pattern, it probably signals the beginning of the end of our ability to extract fishery products from wild stocks in a commercially viable way. Just as long ago we learned to farm animals and plants instead of harvesting wild game and wild plant products, we will come to rely on aquaculture for our fishery products, and the eating of wild fish will become as exotic as the eating of wild game (really wild, not farmed bison or elk). The scale of modern commercial fisheries is such that this transition will represent a major shift in the ways in which we feed the world's human population, and the nature of aquaculture suggests it will not be a transition to a rosier future.

Daniel Pauly of the University of British Columbia has spent his career in efforts to improve our management of fisheries, particularly in developing countries where there was rarely an adequate management infrastructure or reservoir of expertise. Pauly and colleagues raised the alarm in a series of papers in *Nature* and *Science* at the close of the twentieth century. We had reached the point where we were no longer able to increase the tonnage of fish removed from the world's oceans, and in the process we were making substantial changes to the structure of fish populations and the ecosystems to which they belonged. Scientists from other universities who have looked at the data independently have largely supported these claims.

In fairness, Lewis (Loo) Botsford of the University of California at Davis had reported the perilous state of global fisheries in 1997, documenting the high proportion of fisheries classified by the FAO as fully or overexploited and the extent of indirect ecosystem impacts due to fishing activities; and the FAO itself has always reported dispassionately on the difficulties facing world fisheries and the relatively limited improvements in management that have occurred. The FAO predicted a limit in global marketable catch of about 80 million metric tons as early as 1971 and showed that limit as having been reached in the early 1990s. Pauly's alarm call, therefore, was based on information that had been around and publicly available for several years. Figure 3 shows the world fishery yield from 1950 to 2006.

Unfortunately, dispassionate reports by the FAO to the United Nations and its member states do not always attract media attention, and the eyes and ears of the public, in the same way that a prominent article in *Science* or *Nature* may. Fisheries management is ultimately a national responsibility, and political decisions by many nations are strongly influenced by public opinion. It's good that there are scientists such as Pauly who work in universities and nongovernmental organizations and are able to get the message out to the wider public.

Figure 3 is based on the worldwide commercial fishery data compiled by the FAO since 1950. These data are based on national statistics provided to the FAO by individual countries. The FAO cross-checks the national submissions, works with member countries to improve their fishery data, and, where necessary, makes adjustments based on other available sources of information on fisheries in each region. The FAO statistics are not perfect, but they represent the best data available on commercial fisheries per country. They include a variety of types of information beyond annual catch and include information on aquaculture yields. They provide the basis for the biennial technical reports produced by the FAO and for much of the international policy developments that have enabled fisheries management to improve to the extent it has, and they are publicly available via the FAO website for others to use. What Pauly did was to draw attention to the over-reporting

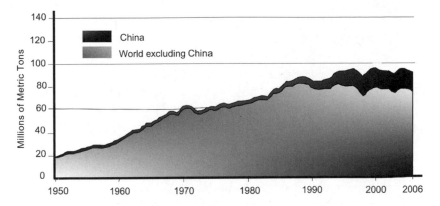

FIGURE 3. Total world capture fishery yield from 1950 to 2006 as reported by FAO, with the catch by China shown separately. A slight negative trend in yield is evident beginning in the mid-1980s. Figure redrawn from figure 1, page 4, *State of World Fisheries and Aquaculture 2008*, published by the Fisheries and Aquaculture Department of the Fisheries and Agriculture Organization of the United Nations.

of catches in the Chinese fishery, make reasonable corrections for this bias, and remove from the global total catch the widely fluctuating catch of Peruvian anchoveta in order to see the underlying global trend in total catch.[8] The underlying trend is downward.

Over-reporting of catches is an unusual bias. (Commercial fishermen usually prefer to under-report; only recreational fishermen tend to over-report, at least when it comes to the sizes of the ones that got away.) It happens when there is political pressure on the industry to meet high catch targets. The centrally planned economy of China was routinely setting targets for all industry managers, including targets for fish to be landed, and by the early 1990s targets had grown well beyond what the fishery was able to catch. For Chinese fisheries managers, keeping one's job was dependent on meeting the set goals, whether or not the fish actually got caught. The FAO had become aware of this problem with the Chinese data at about the same time Pauly drew public attention to it and worked with the Chinese authorities to remedy the situation. Part of the remedy was a characteristically diplomatic move by the Chinese government—a public declaration of a "zero-growth" policy in 1998

8. Pauly removed the catch of anchoveta simply because this catch varies so extensively in response to el Niño, and he wanted to make the overall trend in global catch clear.

that fixed catch targets (which will presumably remain in place until real catches no longer require an "upward nudge" as the data are compiled). Another part was the FAO's decision, commencing with its 2006 report, to report Chinese catches separately from those of the rest of the world.

Pauly corrected for the Chinese over-reporting, revealing a downward trend of 0.66 million metric tons per year that began in 1986. This downward trend has occurred despite the fact that the global fishing fleet is about 30 percent larger than it needs to be—the global decline in catch occurs in spite of a more-than-sufficient effort to catch fish because sufficient fish are simply no longer there.

The sizes of fish being caught have also been falling because fish are being caught at younger and younger ages. This phenomenon appears universal, and in many instances the reduction in size and age attained is profound. In 2003 Ransom Myers and Boris Worm of Dalhousie University in Halifax, Canada, documented the global extent of this phenomenon, reporting that industrialized fisheries typically reduced the community biomass (the total weight of living organisms present) by 80 percent within fifteen years of starting to fish and that the larger species are most severely impacted. They estimated that the biomass of large predatory species was on average now about 10 percent of what it had been prior to the onset of commercial fishing. This removal of 90 percent of the biomass of the larger species brings with it a marked reduction in size (and age) attained. For example, whereas Atlantic swordfish once regularly lived 20-plus years and grew to weigh more than 450 kg, the average one landed in 1995 weighed about 41 kg and was only three to four years old.

While the reductions in size are impressive, it is the reduction in average age at capture that is of most importance ecologically because of the obvious effects on the storage capacities of the populations. With fish living less long, there are fewer annual cohorts present in a species' population, and its capacity to withstand years of poor recruitment is reduced. In addition, the total lifetime production of offspring per individual is reduced because females reproduce over fewer years. Indeed, for species such as the Atlantic swordfish, the average age at capture is less than the age at maturation, meaning that the average fish is being caught before it reproduces.

The overall effect on fecundity is, of course, greater than the reduction in number of episodes of reproduction might imply. As fish grow older and larger, fecundity of the females increases exponentially because their larger body cavities can contain much greater numbers of eggs. For example, in the red snapper, *Lutjanus campechanus,* which commonly lives nine to eleven years and may live to twenty years, a single 61 cm (12 kg) female eight to ten years old will spawn the same number of eggs as two hundred twelve smaller females 42 cm in length (1.1 kg) and three to four years old. And that is just in the one year. While the overwhelming majority of these eggs are going to die very young, the reduction in average maximum size of the fish must greatly reduce the number of larvae being produced, making it less likely that the population will be able to produce outstandingly large cohorts of offspring in the occasional good years. This further erodes the ability of the species to capitalize on good years and thereby survive the poor ones.

Finally, in a number of fishes, including the groupers *(Serranidae)* and snappers *(Lutjanidae)* that are some of the most important fishery species in tropical coastal waters, animals normally mature as females, only to transform into males later in life. In such sequentially hermaphroditic species there is an additional potential impact of overfishing: By selectively removing the larger, older fish, the fishery selectively preys upon males, and the risk exists that the number of males may become so small as to limit the availability of sperm to fertilize the eggs. In some such species, the regulation of sex change may be strongly age based—an automatic developmental event that occurs at a specific age—but in the majority of cases it is mediated socially through behavioral interactions or pheromonal communication within the social group. With social mediation, the problem of male depletion is probably reduced—animals will simply become male at smaller sizes—but it is not eliminated.

Scarcely studied at all, but almost certainly as important as disruption of sex ratios, is the simple fact that when overfishing is sufficient to change population density and age structure, it must also disrupt social structures in those species that have social organizations more complex than a simple school. Disrupted social structures can be expected to result in reduced reproduction, regardless of whether the fish are hermaphroditic. Behavioral and ecological studies of fish on coral and rocky reefs using snorkel and scuba to permit direct observation and experimentation show us that the great majority of demersal fishes in these structurally complex habitats have complex social organizations. The idea of fish as anonymous individuals drifting haphazardly through a uniform environment and waiting to be caught makes it easy to think of fishing as a two-agent interaction involving the fisherman and his prey with nothing else being important. The reality of fish as individuals interacting differentially with other members of their population in a spatially variable environment means that fishing does have effects that depend on which of the various individual fish are caught. Catching all the older members of a population can have different consequences than catching some of the younger members; however, as yet we have paid far too little attention to this impact of overfishing.

It is not only the total marketable catch that has deteriorated. In 1998 Daniel Pauly and his coworkers used *Science* to alert the world to another sign of problems for world fisheries stocks. Again using the FAO database, they reported that the mean trophic level of species taken by the world's fisheries had declined between 1950 and 1994. They described the phenomenon as "fishing down the world's marine food webs."

To understand this concept, we must first appreciate the modern quantitative method for measuring an organism's trophic level. When he first introduced the concept in 1927, the Oxford ecologist Charles Elton described the trophic level of an organism quite simply: organisms exist at differing levels in a food chain, with primary producers at level 1, herbivores at level 2, carnivores that eat herbivores at level 3, and so on up as high as level 4 or 5. Omnivores that eat a mixture of plant and animal species or that eat a diet of several different types of animal from several different trophic levels were conveniently overlooked in Elton's scheme. The more quantitative approach used by Pauly requires detailed diet data for each species in the ecosystem being fished. The trophic level of a given species is determined as the average trophic level of the foods it eats plus 1. Thus a species that eats 40 percent plants (trophic level 1) and 60 percent strict herbivores (trophic level 2) sits at trophic level 2.6 ($0.4 \times 1 + 0.6 \times 2 + 1 = 2.6$).

Pauly and his coworkers computed the trophic level of each species being caught commercially; then, for each year from 1950 to 1994, they calculated the species composition of the catch for each of the major marine fishery regions of the world and for the global catch. They were then able to determine the average trophic level of the catch each year. Their results demonstrate a gradual downward trend in average trophic level of the global fishery catch, for both salt water and freshwater fishes. The global trends are each comprised of sets of trends for each major fisheries region of the world, and these are not identical. In marine regions, the majority of trends are downward, but a few regions show no significant change (e.g., Indo-west Pacific) or even a trend toward higher trophic levels (e.g., southwest-central-southeast Atlantic). These atypical trends can usually be explained by commencement of fishing in new locations or depths or on previously untapped resources—a process that is unlikely to continue much longer since all regions are now being fished.

What causes this downward trend, and what is its significance? Fisheries target species that are economically valuable. Indeed, the enormous quantities of bycatch that characterized most fisheries until recently were simply those fish that were of so little economic value that they were not worth bringing to shore. Traditionally, economically valuable species have tended to be large-bodied, usually older, and almost always piscivorous (fish eating). A decline in the average trophic level of the catch is a clear signal that fisheries have changed their targets through time. The catch has come to be comprised increasingly of fish that feed at lower trophic levels, and these tend to be smaller, younger animals.

If you have been buying fish to feed your family over the past several years, you have seen evidence of fishing down the food web, even though you may not have realized it. All those new kinds of fishery products on the supermarket shelf are there because those are the species that are now being caught. They used to be avoided or thrown back as bycatch. In the Northwest Atlantic region, the traditional target species were initially cod and, shortly thereafter, haddock. Both of these are relatively large, high-trophic-level piscivores that are of high economic value because of the relative ease of capture and the quality of the meat. By the time the trawl fishery largely collapsed in the Northwest Atlantic in the 1990s, the catch from that region was made up in about equal parts of demersal fishes, pelagic fishes, crustaceans, and mollusks.[9] As well as cod and haddock, the catch now included hake, Atlantic redfish and American plaice (all demersal), the pelagic herring, crustaceans (shrimp, crabs, and lobster), and mollusks such as scallops. All of these additional species exist at lower trophic levels than cod and haddock. Similar changes have occurred in other regions. Large piscivores that formerly dominated catches have been replaced

9. Demersal fishes are those that forage near the substratum while pelagic fishes forage in mid-water, often far from any solid surfaces.

by smaller-bodied piscivores, planktivores, and fishery species that are not fish—the squid, clams, lobster, and shrimp that are now major parts of world fisheries. (The situation is even more obvious in the markets in developing countries, where tiny fish prevail; we in the West, snuggling in our duvets, still see lots of the high-value species because we can afford to pay for the few of them being caught.)

What is the significance of fishing down the food web? If it were just a case of changing our food preferences, this would actually be a positive development. All biological production depends ultimately on photosynthesis (except for a tiny fraction of primary production by chemotrophic bacteria that occur in such places as deep ocean vents), and, obeying the Second Law of Thermodynamics, there is loss of energy at every level of the food web. A given amount of sunlight can be used to produce many grams of plant material, which will support production of fewer grams of cow, and still fewer of farmer eating steak. By cropping a lower trophic level of organism (eating grain rather than cow, or smaller rather than larger fish species), we harvest a more plentiful supply of food resources. Unfortunately, however, the shift of fisheries to lower trophic levels has not been voluntary. It appears to have been forced due to the elimination of the higher-trophic-level species. Those large piscivores are not yet extinct (in most cases), but they have been made too rare to sustain fisheries, and in the majority of cases they are not recovering their former numbers.

That we are fishing down the food web is a clear indication of the pervasiveness of overfishing in the world's oceans. The danger is that we now are reaching the limit of fishable species, because we are already fishing organisms at an average trophic level of 3.1. Trophic level 3 in marine systems is organisms that feed on zooplankton. Our next step, if we continue this downward journey, will be to harvest krill and other tiny crustaceans. While krill do feed the giant baleen whales, grilled krill on toast will be a sad replacement for a tuna steak, quick broiled so it remains blue in the center, or many of the other quality fish products that have graced our tables.

OTHER ECOSYSTEM EFFECTS OF OVERFISHING

So far, I have considered only direct effects of overfishing on the species being targeted. But given that fishing has routinely reduced the standing biomass of most fishery species by 80 to 90 percent, it should be no surprise that we have altered the structure of marine ecological communities. They are becoming simplified, as fewer species are present and fewer trophic connections exist. Jeremy Jackson of Scripps Institution of Oceanography in San Diego and the Smithsonian Tropical Research Institute in Panama together with several coworkers made this point cogently in 2001 in an article in *Science,* drawing attention to chronic long-term overfishing of marine systems and the resultant loss of larger, older, higher-trophic-level species. Jackson's focus was not on how this trend reduced our options for fishery products, but on how the losses were causing dramatic changes to the structure of the ecosystems being fished. In this article, Jackson broadened the meaning of *fishing* to include hunting for maritime mammals such as seals, the sea otter, and Steller's sea cow (extinct since 1768) that feed in marine environments. Using paleontological, anthropological, historical, and current ecological and fisheries management data, he documented a distressingly common and very long-term tendency to overfish larger, usually higher-trophic-level species and to cause pronounced changes to ecosystem structure as a consequence. His examples include the West Coast of North America, where the loss of Steller's sea cow and the sea otter led to a great increase in sea urchins, which reduced the capacity of kelp beds to recover from storm damage because grazing by urchins prevented the establishment of new juvenile kelp plants. As a result, the complex ecosystem of species of fish and invertebrates that depend upon the kelp to provide habitat structure and sometimes food is replaced by a simpler, less productive community occupying a largely bare, rocky habitat termed an *urchin barren.* He makes a similar argument for the Gulf of Maine, where overfishing of cod and other groundfish allowed urchin populations to explode. The large urchin populations led to the replacement of kelp forests by extensive urchin barrens. Paradoxically, in both of these cases, new fisheries for sea urchins (part of the fishing-down process) have allowed some recovery of kelp; however, the forests now lack the higher-trophic-level consumers that were formerly present.

Regarding coral reefs, Jackson suggests that overfishing has gone so far that in many locations major populations of herbivorous fishes have largely disappeared along with the larger piscivores. While the story is complex (see chapter 4), it appears that, at least in the Caribbean, overfishing, together with an outbreak of disease that virtually eliminated another major herbivore, the *Diadema* sea urchin, has been responsible for a shift from coral-dominated to algae-dominated benthic communities. The latter are notably less valuable for tourism, less diverse, and less productive of valued fishery species. Overfishing of turtles, manatees, and dugong may have made sea grass beds around the world much more susceptible to the diseases and pollution that are now prevalent causes of reduced abundance and ecological complexity, and overfishing of oysters appears to have been a primary cause of the eutrophication and consequent ecological simplification of the Chesapeake Bay. Jackson argues that overfishing has been widespread for a long time, that it predictably (thought not always) removes the larger, higher-trophic-level species, and that it causes substantial changes to the ecosystems being fished. In particular, it appears likely that in some if not all cases, overfishing changes ecosystems in ways that make them more vulnerable to other human or natural disturbances such as pollution, outbreaks of diseases or invading species, storms, and climate change. This synergism between overfishing and other forms of disturbance should be an issue of great concern because, as we shall see, our other kinds of impact on natural systems are also becoming more severe year by year. We need to recognize that by avoiding overfishing we also may be able to mitigate the effects of these other disturbances.

Overfishing also impacts species other than the ones being targeted. These impacts can be separated into bycatch issues and habitat effects, and they vary in importance depending on the fishing techniques a particular fishery uses.[10] In 1994 the FAO reported on rates of bycatch in global fisheries during the 1980s and early 1990s. Quantities were enormous. The global bycatch was estimated to be 27 million metric tons, more than one-third of the marketed catch of 77 million metric tons. This "wasted catch" was widely recognized as undesirable, and there was widespread support to improve the situation. U.N. resolutions and the FAO's Code of Conduct for Responsible Fisheries all called for steps to reduce bycatch. An update by the FAO in 1998 reported global bycatch as 20 million metric tons, and its 2004 assessment reported

10. The term *bycatch* makes it sound as if this is a pretty minor issue, as in "by the way." The industry is fishing for cod, halibut, or tuna; other species are caught incidentally, accidentally. The fishermen seek ways to avoid bycatch because it gets in the way. Yet for many kinds of commercial gear, the bycatch can be very substantial, sometimes a greater biomass than the catch of economically desired species.

bycatch at 7.3 million metric tons, or 8 percent of the global marketable catch. That's quite an improvement in ten years, and by 2006 the FAO did not bother to mention bycatch at all. As we will see, that does not mean the problem has disappeared, only that it has changed.

Bycatch is a mixture of uneconomic specimens caught unintentionally and not worth bringing to market. These consist of undersized members of the target species and individuals of undesired species. Because these organisms are not valued, they are discarded at sea, and rarely are any data collected concerning the amount or the species composition of the bycatch. Now, consider first the bycatch comprised of small specimens of the desired species, and consider a fishery being managed very close to or exceeding its MSY. The bycatch is unreported, and therefore is an excess catch of unknown extent that may not be fed into the equations used to monitor the fishery and the state of the population being harvested. Further, because these are small (therefore young) individuals, the bycatch is reducing the number of new juveniles entering the fishery in subsequent years. The result of a substantial bycatch of this type is that the population performs less well than expected under a given level of fishing, because the fishing (including bycatch) is substantially more intense than the level intended.

The bycatch that is comprised of unvalued species poses a different and more serious problem. This bycatch is an unmonitored fishery on a group of species that together provide the ecosystem that sustains the species of fishery interest. Assuming the different species making up this ecosystem are variably susceptible to being caught and variably able to sustain the level of fishing that is being imposed on them, some populations will barely be modified by the slight levels of bycatch, while other species may be severely overfished. As a consequence, over a period of time there will be definite changes in the relative abundances of the various species that make up the community. Now remember that the capacity of a fish population to grow in size depends upon a full suite of environmental factors that affect the individual's capacity to survive and reproduce—a supply of food is one of these factors. If some of the bycatch species are more important than others as prey for the commercially targeted species, and if these happen to be the ones that are overfished as bycatch, the ecosystem becomes less able to sustain populations of the economically valued fishes.

There is a lot of variation among fisheries in the extent of bycatch, based on differences in gear and in uses of the fish. Bycatch in artisanal fisheries is very low (less than 1 percent of catch) or nonexistent; people who fish to feed their families eat the bulk of what they catch or sell it to raise funds for other needs. Among commercial fisheries, trawling has a particularly bad record—both bottom trawling for a range of groundfish such as cod and mid-water trawling for shrimp. A trawl catches everything that enters its mouth and is larger than the mesh-size of the cod end. On a good day, as the net fills, even organisms that might have passed through the mesh can become trapped because the mesh becomes plugged by the mass of fish, invertebrates, and algae that have already been caught. Shrimp trawlers typically discard about 62 percent of the catch as bycatch, while bottom trawlers discard 10 percent as bycatch. The reported bycatch in the long-line fishery for tuna and other open-ocean, migratory species is surprisingly high at 29 percent, but this number includes the carcasses of "finned" sharks. (Finning is an exceptionally wasteful practice in which the fins are cut off sharks for the Asian shark fin trade and the carcasses dumped back into the ocean, often still alive but unable to swim.) Bycatch also varies geographically, depending on the nature of fishery practice in different locations, from a high of 22 percent of catch, or 1.7 million metric tons, in the central Atlantic fishery (where long-lining predominates) to less than 7 percent in the Pacific and Indian Oceans. (All percentages are 2004 values.)

Reductions in bycatch have been achieved in two ways. The first has been through the refinement of gear and fishing practices to reduce the capture of unwanted fish. Most notably, the Gulf of Mexico shrimp trawl fishery has improved its (still disappointing) record by developing nets with exclusion devices of various types to prevent unwanted organisms, from small fish to large turtles or dolphins, being trapped even if they enter the mouth of the net. (It takes some skill to build a net that will sift out and retain the small creatures while rejecting the large creatures, so there are limits to what can be expected in modifying this gear.)

The second way in which bycatch has been reduced is the more important one and is paradoxically part of our fishing down the food web. Bycatch has been reduced by finding ways to make these species and small sizes marketable. Changes in regulations have eliminated minimum size limits in some fisheries so that younger fish, when caught, can still be marketed. Reduced availability of the former target species means that vessels have excess hold capacity and can afford to bring less valuable species ashore. And new ways of processing have been developed that make use of smaller specimens or different species.

For example, many fish that would formerly have been discarded as bycatch are now used in the manufacture of surimi—that amazing Japanese product that looks and tastes almost like crabmeat but does not put people with allergies to crustacea into anaphylactic shock. Madison Avenue has stepped forward and convinced the public that some other fish that would previously have been avoided are in fact highly desirable foods. One case in point is the monkfish—the name is applied to several species of the genus *Lophius*—a large, ugly, bottom-dwelling anglerfish that was routinely discarded as bycatch until the early 1980s. It was not considered attractive enough to be marketable. This fish has an enormous head and a much smaller body, but the flesh in the trunk and tail is delicious. Consumers rarely ever see a monkfish with its head on or learn that it is an anglerfish—marketers decreed that it should be brought to market already reduced to the tail section or a fillet, probably to disguise its appearance and avoid turning consumers away. It became a viable fishery in many regions including the United States, Europe, and Australia without most consumers in these locations knowing what it looked like. Of course, as in so many fishing tales, this one has mixed endings. Since the early 1980s, increased pressure on this slow-growing, deep-water fish has led to chronic overfishing of many populations, some fishery closures, and a few apparent recoveries under better management. So, the monkfish went from bycatch to mostly overfished in two short decades, but its use has indeed reduced bycatch.

Changes to marketing practice do not mitigate the damage caused to ecological communities by bycatch. Fisheries are still removing large numbers of young fish from populations and are removing individuals of many different species, frequently at unsustainable rates, because these are an incidental catch not being targeted (and management pays less attention to incidental species). Still, if we consume more of what we catch, perhaps our need to catch ever more fish will grow more slowly.

Some kinds of fishing also have profound effects on habitat. Again, bottom trawling is a particularly egregious example. If you think about it, trawling involves dragging a rather heavy net and a couple of heavy barn doors across the substratum in an attempt to catch those organisms that swim about just above it. To be effective, the trawl must hug the bottom so that fish can't escape underneath. As a consequence, trawling has substantial effects on the structure of the substratum, particularly when that structure is relatively delicate, made up of various sponges, bryozoans, oyster reefs, algae, and corals. Trawling rips these up while generally leveling any topography of the ocean floor. This is a little like clear cutting a forest but using a bulldozer to do the clearing. (Actually, it may be quite a lot like clear cutting because many of the structure-forming benthic organisms such as sponges can be quite slow-growing, long-lived creatures—five hundred years is possible for many sponges. These are removed by trawling, much as old-growth trees are removed from forests.)

Now if trawling occurs at a rate such that a trawl crosses a particular area only once every decade or so, the system is probably capable of recovering, and in any event there will be ample undisturbed area in the vicinity. But with overfishing, trawling can become so intense that the disturbance occurs repeatedly, and there is seldom time for the system to recover its former structure before it is trawled again. In 1998 Les Watling from the University of Maine and Elliott Norse of the Marine Conservation Biology Institute in Redland, Washington, examined catch and effort data from shrimp fisheries to reach an estimate for the total amount of trawling (of all types) taking place around the world. They found that trawls sweep over an area equal in size to all the world's continental shelves once every two years! Trawling is not uniformly distributed, however, and they noted that while there were shelf locations that had never been trawled, other locations may be trawled as many as four hundred times per year.

Some other forms of fishing also have undesirable effects on habitat. Chief among these are the use of dynamite and other explosives and the use of various chemicals, from household bleach to cyanide, to catch fish on coral reefs for the aquarium trade or food. The explosives or chemicals make collection in this structurally complex habitat much more effective. They also severely damage other components of the community, particularly the corals that provide the habitat on which the rest of a reef biota depends. Using dynamite and chemicals is universally condemned, and these methods are illegal in virtually every jurisdiction that has laws to manage use of coral reefs. That does not mean these methods are seldom used. Of the two, "blast fishing" with dynamite has the more serious environmental effects. A 1-kg beer bottle bomb produces a rubble crater 1–2 meters in radius and kills most of the coral in that area. While occasional damage on this scale is easily repaired by natural processes, it is the extensiveness of the practice that causes the problems. In Indonesia, blast fishing has been estimated to destroy 3.75 square meters of live coral cover per 100 square meters of reef per year—a rate substantially above the rate at which reef growth can regenerate the habitat. By contrast, cyanide fishing (and fishing using other chemicals) has more modest impacts on nontarget species. The damage is primarily the physical destruction of delicate coral growth, which occurs while extracting the catch and so is really incidental to the use of chemicals. Still, the habitat destruction can be substantial when the fishing effort is high. Since both forms of fishing are peculiar to coral reefs, I discuss them in more detail in chapter 4.

COLLAPSE OF FISHERY STOCKS: DO THEY EVER RECOVER?

Conventional thinking suggests that if we reduce the abundance of a fish species by overfishing it, reducing or suspending fishing will permit the population to recover. The history of overexploited fisheries does not support this expectation, however. There are now innumerable instances of fish species, such as the Atlantic cod, whose numbers have been greatly reduced and have not recovered, even though fishing has been abandoned, banned, suspended, or in other ways halted. That they tend not to recover should be a very clear message to us: Our simple notion of the natural world as one in which sizes of populations are carefully regulated by mechanisms that will tend to protect them from extinction is a flawed one. That attractive, dependable world is apparently not the world in which we and fishes live.

Why fish populations that have been severely overfished do not recover can be understood by reviewing the various aspects of overfishing enumerated in this chapter. Overfishing reduces the size of the fished population and can disrupt social structures vital to population integrity in the process. Overfishing severely depletes a population of its older individuals, dramatically reducing its capacity to weather periods of poor recruitment and its capacity to rapidly increase its numbers when conditions are favorable for recruitment. Overfishing usually also depletes many other species from the community of which the target species is a member. Some of these other species may play particularly important roles, as prey or in other ways, in facilitating the success of the target species. Frequently, overfishing leads to increases in abundance of those species that are less susceptible to being caught by the fishing gear in use, and these now more abundant species use many of the resources formerly available to the species that have now been depleted. Finally, overfishing can have substantial habitat impacts that may make the environment one that is no longer favorable for populations of the target species.

In addition to all of these factors, it is also extremely difficult for societies to reduce their fishing efforts until overfishing has become extreme. And it is equally difficult to refrain from starting to fish again before the fish population has had sufficient time to recover (assuming that the fishery is one in which some recovery of abundance does take place). Before turning to why we overfish and whether we can do anything about the sorry state of the world's fisheries, let me briefly squelch the idea that aquaculture will come to our rescue and the rescue of the world's coastal ecosystems.

THE LIMITED PROMISE OF AQUACULTURE

Aquaculture is an enormous and growing industry around the world. In practice and effect, it is very different from fishing, although many of the fish, crustaceans, and shellfish we consume today are aquaculture products, and it is often difficult to tell the difference. Extensive areas of freshwater ponds and lakes and coastal wetlands are employed to raise aquaculture species, and pen culture (also termed *sea ranching*) is extending aquaculture out across the continental shelves. A logical and commonly held view is that just as agriculture replaced hunting and gathering as a much more efficient way of acquiring terrestrial food products, aquaculture will eventually replace fishing of wild stocks. It is quite true that aquaculture has become important and will continue to grow in importance, and it is probably also true that our seafood diet will become predominantly based on aquaculture species over the next few years. Indeed, the only way of further increasing our global consumption of seafood is through increased aquaculture. But it would be unwise to anticipate that a shift to aquaculture will permit us to market ever-greater quantities of seafood while permitting natural marine systems to recover from the present state of overfishing.

Marine systems and terrestrial systems are very different in structure, and we enter them at very different ecological places when we seek to consume their species for food. Humans consume a broad range of plant products and a number of animal species, particularly herbivores, from the land. By contrast, plants from the ocean play a tiny role in human food products, even in Japan, where the use of algae as food has been taken furthest. Most oceanic plants, after all, are single-celled phytoplankton. Nor do we make much use of marine herbivores as food—most of these are minute zooplankton. Instead, we prefer to fish for top carnivores, the tuna, swordfish, grouper, cod, and so on that feed on smaller fish and are at levels 3.5 to 4.5 on the trophic web. There are of course some interesting exceptions to this rule. Among the marine herbivores we consume are abalone, conch, sea urchins, and parrot fishes. We also eat a number of suspension feeders (consuming phyto- and zooplankton and suspended organic matter), such as oysters, mussels, and certain sea cucumbers, and various detrital feeders, including many burrowing clams. Perhaps the most unusual herbivore we eat is the giant clam, which both suspension feeds and obtains nutrients from the symbiotic zooxanthellae (single-celled algae) that occupy the surface layers of its mantle.

Now, if you find you have not eaten very many of the animals on this list of exceptions, you need to eat more sushi and to try some of the more unusual dishes in other types of Asian restaurants. The nature of the list justifies my claim that feeding on fishes other than top carnivores is an unusual event—although it becomes ever more common as we fish down the food web.

If one plans to farm on land, it's possible to focus attention on specific species of plants, providing them with sunlight, water, and nutrients, or to focus on herbivores, supplying them with plant food. Farming the ocean is a different matter. There are no marine plants with the potential to become human staples in the way that grain crops have become, although certain suspension feeders such as oysters can be farmed in a manner analogous to that of terrestrial plants by providing them sites with a steady supply of plankton-filled water. The animals that are of sufficient economic value to be worth raising under aquaculture nearly all require foods derived largely from animal tissues. These animal-derived foods are obtained primarily by fishing wild stocks of small fish. So, far from ameliorating the need to fish, the rise of aquaculture is generating a new market for fishery products—products that used to be bycatch. Aquaculture is both energetically and economically expensive because of the food requirements of the species being raised, and it has proved difficult to develop aquaculture species that can be raised for a cost that is less than the cost of catching them in the wild. Obviously, this difficulty will be eased as all seafood becomes more expensive due to its reduced availability in the wild, and we can anticipate ever more aquaculture products on the supermarket shelves.

This increase in aquaculture, however, is going to come at a real cost. While some progress is being made in developing plant-derived foods, we will continue to need to fish wild populations to obtain much of the animal protein for the aquaculture enterprise. In addition, the enormous densities of animals living in aquaculture pens or ponds create local aquatic pollution due to their own production of waste and to the usual practice of providing surplus feed to maximize rates of growth. Then there is the problem of the introduction to the coastal marine environment of antibiotics, used to maintain the health of the crowded fish. And through inevitable escapes or releases, individuals with novel genetic makeup have been introduced to native populations—strains that have been selected for fast growth under crowded conditions, not necessarily for traits that will be adaptive in the wild. Each of these problems is real and growing as the use of aquaculture grows, but the biggest may be the continued need for animal food.

In its 2008 report on world fisheries and aquaculture, the FAO reported that global aquaculture production reached 51.7 million metric tons in 2006, having grown 8.7 percent per year since the early 1970s. The FAO stated that there was going to be a need for increased fish production, that it was unlikely that capture fisheries could provide much increase, and that it was going to be necessary for aquaculture to make up the difference. By evaluating national plans for increases in aquaculture production through the next thirty years, the FAO suggested that there was reason for cautious optimism that the world's need for fishery products in 2030 could be met by growth in aquaculture. It noted, however, that among other things the availability of fishmeal (for feed) was a "much-debated issue." This cautious report is about as close as the FAO has ever gotten to suggesting we will not be able to achieve stated goals for fishery production, and nothing was said concerning the mix of species that we may be eating in 2030. In 2006 world aquaculture was using 3.06 million metric tons of fishmeal and 0.78 million metric tons of fish oil as feed—56 percent and 87 percent of total production, respectively. While there have been impressive developments in aquaculture feeds (so that salmon diets, for example, now are only 30 percent fishmeal), I suspect we will be fishing the oceans for krill after all—to feed to aquaculture species. And after the krill, what then?

WHY DO WE OVERFISH? HOW CAN WE STOP?

We are officially *Homo sapiens,* the wise humans. If overfishing has been going on so long, if we have multiple stories of species that have been fished nearly to extinction and failed to recover, and if we have extensive efforts to manage fisheries, to monitor them, and to investigate what is going wrong, why are we still trying to catch more fish than are available to be caught? Surely it is in our collective best interest to do a much better job of managing these incredibly valuable resources. Are we less wise than we believe?

On a positive note, we are doing a much better job than we used to do. When the cod fishery began in the sixteenth century, it was an open access, unregulated fishery. Anyone who wanted to enter it and had a vessel and crew was free to do so. This has been the typical state of fisheries when they first start and has been the usual state of fishing enterprises since our Pleistocene ancestors speared fish and collected shellfish on their shores. Such a fishery is far from being a logical interaction between fish and fisherman acting together to achieve a long-term stable output of product. It is a scramble by a group of competing individual fishermen, each seeking to maximize his or her catch and to take fish as rapidly as possible, reasoning, "If I do not catch the fish, someone else will take them."

Garrett Hardin coined the phrase *tragedy of the commons* to describe the problem inherent in this type of interaction. Before they are caught, fish are a commons in that they belong to nobody and are available for all to make use of, much as the commons of the English village was a pastoral area on which any farmer was free to graze his cattle. The tragedy is that in such circumstances, it is in nobody's best interest to moderate his or her behavior to ensure that the commons will be fit for grazing next week or next year. If I don't catch those fish, somebody else will. Marine fishery resources were treated as a commons for many years, partly because most of the world's oceans were outside the territorial waters of any nation and laws governing the use of the oceans did not exist. Now that the Law of the Sea has established the right to an exclusive economic zone extending 200 nautical miles out from shore, most countries are claiming national ownership of fishery resources within this zone, and many fisheries are managed on a limited entry basis. This means that the yet-to-be-caught fish are collectively owned by the fishery and that the fishery is of a fixed size. A new fisherman can enter the fishery only by purchasing a license from someone seeking to leave it.[11] Indeed, it is now widely recognized that limited entry is an essential part of the management of any fishery, if that fishery has any real chance of being sustainable.

In other words, we now have established law governing the use of marine resources, and there are mechanisms that can be put in place to avoid the tragedy of the commons. However, the great majority of fisheries are still not being managed effectively. Some are unmanaged, some are not managed effectively, and some are managed in ways that permit unlimited entry and the resulting growth in effort that results. Inadequate management is widespread in developing countries that either lack the resources to provide effective management and enforcement or could muster the needed resources but lack the political will to do so. Developed countries also have poorly managed fisheries. They occur under three types of circumstances: the fishery is a new one, tapping a previously unfished resource; it could be managed more effectively but there is a lack of political will to do so; or it is in international waters or on populations that straddle boundaries of different nations' territorial waters.

It takes time for a management agency to recognize the need to develop management policies for a newly targeted species. Personnel must be deployed to work on this new species, and data must be collected to determine its basic demographic characteristics. Laws governing the fishery must be introduced and implemented. Sometimes management agencies are simply less nimble than they should be. Unfortunately, in recent years, new fishable stocks have frequently been discovered in deeper, colder waters. Such fish tend to be very slow growing and long-lived. The initially bountiful catches are comprised mainly of old

11. It is still a commons, but with some control on the number of people competing to use it. Catch share programs, now gaining in popularity, are still more effective (chapter 10).

individuals, and these animals are removed in a short time, because the population lacks the capacity to rapidly replace itself. The result is that an initially promising fishery quickly shows declining catches of much smaller, younger animals and can become unprofitable almost before the management agency has begun to gather the information needed for sustainable management. Fisheries for monkfish and for orange roughy provide many examples, although some of these are now managed sustainably. (A roughly parallel problem can develop even in an established fishery when new technology leads to rapid changes in effective effort. Unless the management agency is alert to the innovations, the fishery can overfish even while obeying the regulations to the letter.)

Lack of political will arises because fishery management is a governmental activity that exists partly to sustain a fishery resource but primarily to ensure the continuation of an economically valuable industry that creates jobs and wealth. When fishermen have extensive investments in the vessels and fishing gear and when fishing is a primary source of employment and income in a region, governments have a way of pressuring management agencies to permit fishing effort to remain as it was or to grow, even if the data say that the population is being overfished and that effort must be reduced. Sometimes the pressure is quite indirect. Canada's particularly favorable regulations governing unemployment insurance for "seasonal workers" such as fishermen seem, on the surface, socially responsible, but they have had the effect of keeping people in the fishing industry long after economics would suggest they seek other employment. A large population that wants to earn a living by fishing and that is able to hang in through lean years because the unemployment benefits are pretty good remains a constant spur to the management agencies to provide good news in the form of renewed opportunities to fish.

In many developing countries with large coastal populations dependent on artisanal fishing for their own food as well as their livelihood, overfishing gets ignored because there are no obvious alternative sources of employment or food. How do you tell an artisanal fisherman to stop fishing when he has no other way of feeding his family? As often as not, these countries have so little invested in fisheries management that the data to confirm that the resources are being overfished are simply not available, and if they were available, lack of will and of viable alternatives to fishing would ensure that little attention would be paid to them.

Finally, there is the issue of straddling stocks (species whose distributions and fishery cross two or more different jurisdictions) and of stocks that are fished primarily in international waters. In the case of straddling stocks, differing management regulations may not be complementary or may not be equivalently enforced, and damage to the stock caused by overfishing within one jurisdiction is transferred to all regions of the fishery. In the case of open-ocean fisheries, management policies depend far more on consensus among fishermen from different nations than on enforceable regulations, and all the problems of open access and limited management effectiveness remain. That it is still possible to buy whale meat legally in Japan and that the finning of sharks continues as the primary way of harvest for the shark fin trade are testaments to the lack of effective management of high seas fisheries in the twenty-first century. Both cases are clear examples of unsustainable fishing practices, widely condemned except by the people who make money engaging in them.

So, what does the future hold for fishing? There is reason for limited optimism because of a number of improvements in both the science and the sociology of how we manage fisheries. Scientists understand that the oceans cannot provide ever-increasing quantities of fish, and we know that much of the demographic theory that led to the concept of managing for MSY was overly simple and was, in any event, asking for a much finer control of effort than would ever be possible in the real world. There is widespread acceptance among fishermen, managers, governments, and the general public that fisheries management requires adoption of the precautionary principle—that we should fish cautiously, erring on the side of taking less than the resource can sustain—to maximize the chance that fishery resources will remain available to future generations. The creation of various types of marine protected areas, particularly so-called fishery reserves, as a way of both conserving species and sustaining fisheries has been widely adopted as a useful additional tool for managing fisheries in coastal waters (discussed in chapter 4). There is also widespread appreciation that fishery species are embedded in marine ecosystems and cannot be extracted without attention to the impacts on the sustaining ecosystems. With this deeper understanding, we are in a much better position to devise effective ways of managing fisheries sustainably.

There is also much better appreciation of the linkages among government, society, management agency, and fishermen and of the complexities (contradictions, perhaps?) involved in trying to manage in a way that both sustains resources and ensures economic viability for the industry. (Coincidentally, our better understanding of fisheries management also serves to inform our management of other types of resources, such as forest products.) Considerable success has been achieved in some jurisdictions in efforts to make fishery management a cooperative, shared responsibility between the industry and the management agency, and the FAO Code of Conduct for Responsible Fisheries is being adopted widely. Best of all, perhaps, fisheries that are being managed sustainably are being marketed as "green," and the public that ultimately buys fish is beginning to differentiate and buy from the responsible fisheries instead of from those that are being managed less well.

Despite these reasons for optimism, however, I remain concerned. The human population is still growing, and coastal populations are growing more quickly than those inland. Fisheries provide 15.3 percent of the animal protein we consume, and the need for that protein is not going to disappear if fishery yield continues to decline. Too many fisheries are overfished, and there are few available stocks that have not yet been targeted. And while aquaculture might manage to fill our increasing needs, it's more likely that it will not. My fear is that, in the final analysis, it is going to become more important to put food into people's mouths today than to ensure that fishery resources remain available for use in the next decade or next century. With the loss of fishery resources will come a need for more food production from agriculture, more use of limited water supplies for farming or pond aquaculture, and the resulting stresses on terrestrial ecology that these changes could bring. In other words, the possible loss of fisheries is not a local problem or a marine problem. It has ramifications that will ripple across other parts of the world as we struggle to grow the food that fisheries formerly provided for us. I hope I am wrong, but I fear that the bountiful and nutritious food we have obtained from the oceans throughout our history is no longer going to be available to us, and that in the process of exploiting it to the very end we are going to irrevocably change the structure of marine ecosystems. Wild fish are going to become as rare as wild game or wild forests (never mind the fish that will become extinct). Ultimately, even if we can get that 15.3 percent of protein from some other source, we become poorer because we occupy an impoverished planet.

2

REMOVING FORESTS

I first met Meg Lowman when she came to Australia as a graduate student in the mid-1980s to study herbivorous insects in eucalyptus forests.[1] We both traveled north to Queensland—my graduate students and I to dive on the Barrier Reef, she to climb into forest canopies. For a time she provided an important window onto a kind of ecosystem with which I had little direct experience. I vividly remember one conversation in which she lamented the difficulty of getting up to the canopy where she suspected all the action took place. I understood exactly what she meant, because I had long desired to get down below the dense "canopy" created by thickets of the branching coral *Acropora*. These thickets are physically very close to being forests in miniature. With the right conditions and the right species, the thickets can extend 100 meters or more along

---

Facing page: Hemlock grove, Algonquin Provincial Park, Canada. Photo by P. Sale.

1. Trees of the genus *Eucalyptus,* native to Australia, are particularly copious producers of toxic gums and oils that they pack into their leaves, making them distinctly less easy to eat. Eucalyptus, brought to North America without their native insect pests, grew tall and unblemished throughout California—to the extent that some American ecologists had reported that their chemical defenses made them immune to insects. Back in Australia, they were immune to many but had their share of insects that chewed their way carefully through the leaves alongside the koalas, which also seem not to mind the flavor. Meg Lowman wanted to know what role insect herbivores played in eucalyptus forests. She is currently director of the Nature Research Center, North Carolina Museum of Natural Science.

a reef face and stretch upward as much as 2 meters above the substratum on which the corals grow. The *Acropora* thickets are occupied by a myriad of small fishes, crustaceans, mollusks, echinoderms, and other taxa, and during dives I'd often paused to peer deep into the twilight gloom among the branches, trying to see what was going on down there. But I despaired of ever getting a better look into this world, because I could not conceive of a nondestructive way of getting inside.

Unlike me, Meg Lowman solved her problem, becoming an important member of a stalwart group of forest ecologists who conquered the technical challenges of exploring the sunlit tops of tropical forests. In her Australian work, Meg used standard utility linesman's climbing gear and rock-climbing ropes and tackle. Subsequently, she went on to use rope ladders and catwalks, which enabled her to move away from the trunk, but she was still stuck within the canopy, not on top of it. Later still, in various places around the world and with various colleagues who shared her passion for the treetops, she has used canopy webs (a sort of spider web of wires and platforms for scientists to move about on), cranes that lower the scientists into the canopy from above, and a dirigible balloon that tows a 27-meter-diameter raft just above the canopy surface. In rainforests, the canopy is where the ecological action takes place and where a large portion of the biodiversity spends its life.

Coral reefs and forests are analogous in several ways. In each, certain sessile (fixed in place) species provide a complex three-dimensional structure within which numerous other species make their lives. In each, these sessile species, the trees and corals, are relatively slow growing and long-lived. In each, they play a major role in the nutrient and energy cycling that drives the dynamics of an ecological community.

While my experience of forests has been quite limited, as an ecologist I know that they are, indeed, the coral reefs of the terrestrial world—structurally complex, enormous storehouses of biodiversity, biogenic environments built through the activities of one set of their species, the trees. In all cases, forests provide a wide array of ecological services: they moderate winds, ameliorate weather, regulate the water cycle, cycle nutrients, control run-off and erosion, and absorb and store carbon. While I have seen coral reefs become degraded over the years, Meg Lowman has seen the forests shrink as we overharvest their trees or clear them away to use the land for other purposes.

Commercial logging is now an industry that uses mechanized equipment to harvest whole forests quickly and efficiently, but humans have been consuming forests at a slower pace for at least the last ten thousand years. Consequently, there is less forest now across the world than at any time in the past several thousand years. With the progressive loss of forested land, we are losing not only forests' store of valuable timber products, but also their suite of even more valuable environmental services and the often substantial biodiversity of other forest organisms. I believe there is now little doubt that the loss of forests worldwide is having important effects on global climate and biodiversity.

OUR USE OF FORESTS

In 2005 commercial harvest of forests worldwide was valued at US$64 billion in wood products and a further $4.7 billion in nonwood forest products. These numbers do not include the firewood harvested by rural communities for their own use or the trees cleared for slash-and-burn agriculture and not taken to market. While we harvest the oceans for food products and relatively little else, we obtain a much broader range of products from forests—building materials, energy sources, food, and many more. Simply put, forests, like oceans, are of enormous economic value for the resources they provide us.

Overall, our use of forests has not been sustainable, and while the situation has improved, there continues to be a net loss of forest cover. Worldwide, we are deforesting about 13 million hectares of land per year, although natural regeneration, reforestation, and afforestation[2] reduce the net loss to about 7.3 million hectares a year.[3] The total forested land remaining in 2005, including secondary forest but not tree plantations, was just shy of 4 billion hectares. Four billion sounds like a lot of hectares of forest: about 0.6 hectares, or nearly 1.5 acres, per per-

2. *Reforestation* is the reestablishment of forest on formerly forested land, while *afforestation* is the establishment of forest on land that has not been forested for a very long time, if ever.

3. There is some uncertainty regarding extent of forested land and rate of deforestation because of differences in numbers reported by different countries and different definitions of what constitutes a forest. FAO statistics (used here) are conservative (optimistic) and have been criticized by some environmental organizations because they too readily accept "land with planted trees" as equivalent to "forest." In this view, a planted monoculture of single-age trees is unable to provide many of the environmental services that a diverse, multi-age natural forest provides and therefore should not be called a forest.

son now alive on Earth. And the 7.3 million hectares lost per year seems rather small by comparison—it's less than 0.2 percent of the total.

As is the case with many of the trends discussed in this book, it is the unceasing nature of forest loss, 0.2 percent, more or less, *every* year, rather than the absolute magnitude of loss in a single year that is the problem. There are good reasons to believe that humanity will enjoy a better quality of life and will solve a variety of environmental problems more economically if we work to save the forests we now have and even increase their extent. Most of these reasons are tied to the environmental services that forested land provides—services of far greater economic value than can be derived by harvesting timber.

Forests are being lost because of deliberate policies to remove them and use the land for grazing or other agricultural purposes, but they are also disappearing and being degraded because of the ways in which we extract their products. At low intensities, removing trees, firewood, animals, and other products from forests can be sustainable, but across the globe increased need and demand for these products has pushed the rates and modes of extraction far beyond what is sustainable, with grave consequences for forest ecosystem integrity.

Because the specifics of forest resource extraction matter, we need to begin with a brief look at the different ways in which humans are currently using forests. The most consequential type of use, of course, is timber harvest or logging, which can be divided into two main types: selective logging and clear cutting. Forests are also used noncommercially (and increasingly commercially) by rural communities, mostly in developing countries, for the gleaning of a wide variety of products, including construction materials, food, and firewood. This latter type of use, called artisanal, was once largely sustainable, but in recent decades it has become a leading cause of deforestation, habitat degradation, and biodiversity loss.

Commercial selective logging involves choosing individual trees for harvest while leaving the forest community more or less undisturbed. A mixed-age, mixed-species tree community remains following logging, although preferred species may become progressively rarer over time. Selective logging was the prevailing commercial practice until the development of modern machinery. In many parts of North America, such as in central Ontario where I live, the opening up of the region to European settlement was driven largely by logging. Individual trees were selected, felled, dragged to water, and floated to saw mills. Many of the towns of central Ontario began as sawmill locations or as particular points on the downstream journey of logs to the mills. The logging industry has virtually ceased in this region now—the land is more valuable for recreation and tourism. Around these towns, the largely recovered present-day forests still include a number of overstory trees, trees that were inaccessible, imperfectly formed, or for other reasons not logged. These now tower above the second-growth forest like beacons or watchtowers, silent reminders of what once was here.

Selective logging is costly because of the one-tree-at-a-time approach, the need (usually) to use smaller-scale machinery, and the difficulty of getting felled trees out of a forest. Despite this, selective logging is still practiced in regions where the market is primarily for high-quality wood for cabinet making and fine construction or in high-diversity tropical forests when a market for a few highly valued species can mean that the desirable trees will be widely scattered. However, in the majority of logging situations—regions where the market can use the great majority of the trees, such as in low-diversity forests and in single-species tracts resulting from deliberate planting programs or in richer forests where the market is for wood chips or pulp—selective logging has largely been replaced by clear cutting.

Clear cutting is now the dominant method of commercial forest harvest. Theoretically, clear cutting is a harvest of the forest when the trees reach an optimum size, similar to the harvest of field crops such as corn. To fit forests more neatly into the logic of clear cutting, natural forests are increasingly being removed and replaced by planted, single-age monocultures that will in turn be harvested several decades later. Clear cutting is frequently described by proponents as "the farming of trees." Ideally, it is efficient, makes use of larger-scale machinery favoring larger-scale operations, and yields a more uniform product.

Clear cutting is also a drastic alteration to the forest community. In many cases the regrowth that follows the harvest of trees is less successful than proponents maintain. Without significant post-cut mitigation and remediation,[4] significant regrowth of forest can take many

---

4. Typical actions include efficient removal of slash wastes, protection of soil structure, prevention of erosion, and planting and sometimes extended care of seedlings of desired species.

decades to occur naturally. During this time large areas of former forest remain denuded and are subject to erosion, flooding, and deterioration of water quality, with a concomitant loss of many forest-dependent species of plants and animals. It is not a coincidence that logging companies, nearly universally, leave buffer strips of uncut forest along highways and waterways. The latter are necessary and usually mandated for erosion control, but the former are likely there simply to prevent the public from seeing what a clear-cut forest really looks like.

While tree farming may seem an economically logical form of forest management, even with best practices it can have significant negative impacts on natural forest ecosystems. Environmentally responsible logging companies put significant investment into post-cut management and usually include extensive replanting of favored species as a part of the process. Even with active replanting, however, clear cutting still involves the complete removal of forest from an area, a lengthy period of regrowth, and the production of a second-growth forest that is single- or nearly single-age and usually much less diverse in tree species than the forest it replaced. These effects of clear cutting can be further ameliorated if the logging company sets up a "crop rotation" strategy by cutting several smaller patches within a forested site on each cutting cycle. Over time, this builds a mosaic of differently aged stands within the site. However, even logging companies that make a serious effort to operate in an environmentally sustainable way inexorably shift primary forest to secondary forest and ultimately to forest plantations, and at each step along this path there are losses of biodiversity, of environmental services, and of ecological resilience because of the progressive simplification—fewer species, narrow age range—of the tree community being managed. And multinational logging companies operating in remote parts of developing countries often do not make even minimal efforts toward sustainability.

Artisanal forest use, the other major type of use, can be both extensive and varied in developing countries. It is also the only way in which we interacted with forests prior to the last five hundred years or so. There are three main classes of artisanal use: the use of fire to maintain or expand forest clearings and adjacent grasslands, the application of slash-and-burn agriculture, and the collection of forest products, including firewood and bushmeat. Our use of fire to maintain preferred vegetation has a history extending back to the Pleistocene, and the extent to which we used it, on every continent, keeps getting revised upward as paleoecologists and anthropologists investigate further. A belief that the world was a lush primary forest, within and around which primitive peoples lived, is unrealistic as far back as our information can project. Once we got fire we began changing landscapes. Although pre-agricultural humans changed landscapes with fire more extensively than we previously believed, modern humans have done a more thorough job with axes, chainsaws, feller bunchers, and mechanical harvesters. The extent to which we have changed landscapes has grown immensely as our numbers—and our demand for forest products and cleared land—have increased.

Slash-and-burn agriculture makes use of the pulse of nutrients released when trees are cleared and much of the wood burned to create small plots of briefly fertile soil in which one or two crops can be raised. The nutrients are rapidly used up by the crop plants, and because so many forests sit upon relatively unproductive soils, the slash-and-burn cycle has to be repeated every few years, progressively converting forested land into rather poor agricultural land.

At low intensity, slash-and-burn agriculture has trivial impacts on the forest. It may even open the forest up to regeneration in much the same way that natural tree falls create light-filled gaps used by the next generation of trees during its period of rapid growth to reach the canopy. As human populations grow, however, the increasing frequency of slash-and-burn activity has the same effect on the forest as overfishing does on fish stocks. The forest retreats, and exhausted soils remain behind.

Collecting forest products also has a trivial impact if extraction rates remain low. For thousands of years, human communities have supported themselves by using what they could glean from adjacent forests or grassland habitats. Fuel, construction materials, fruits, nuts, tubers, other edible plant products, various small animals, and medicinal supplies are all gleaned to provide for the community's needs. Traditionally, this was women's work, while the men pretended to help out by fishing and hunting for larger prey. But with growing human populations, this gleaning of forest products can become overharvesting too, and its impacts can be severe.

For example, hunting of game and gleaning of smaller species comprise the most common form of animal resource extraction in the forests of South America and Africa, but because little of this meat finds its way into official trade routes, it is difficult to accurately gauge the extent of the harvest. Studies assessing the present-day sustainability of these activities invariably find that rates of extraction far exceed rates of production. Rates of extraction increase as human populations grow, as improved capturing technology becomes available, and as improved transport and refrigeration and a growing market economy encourage commercialization even on a modest scale. In 1998 David Wilkie and Julia Carpenter of the Wildlife Conservation Society investigated the consumption of bushmeat for equatorial Africa (Cameroon, Central African Republic, Republic of the Congo, Democratic Republic of Congo, Republic of Equatorial Guinea, and Gabon). They found that, on average, 1.2 million metric tons were consumed per year, or 35 kg per person and 645 kg per square kilometer of forest each year. More recent calculations by the Durrell Wildlife Conservation Trust's John Fa and his colleagues put the consumption for equatorial Africa at 4.9 million metric tons of dressed bushmeat per year (or over 2,600 kg per square km per year), a substantially greater rate and one that is definitely unsustainable. It is widely recognized that consumption of bushmeat has been increasing in all forested regions; however, the rate of extraction of bushmeat in the Amazon basin (0.15 million tons per year, or 39.5 kg per square km per year) is substantially less than in Africa and occurs at a rate of exploitation that Fa suggests is sustainable. It is reasonable to anticipate that the extraction of bushmeat will become progressively more efficient and less sustainable as forest cover is reduced and patches of forested land become smaller and more widely separated. While there is little information on the extent to which forest tree communities are dependent on their animal occupants, the bushmeat story means that the long-term viability of forest ecosystems is not dependent solely on sustainable extraction of trees. We must also find ways to manage our use of the nonwood resources sustainably.

In many parts of the developing world, wood provides the chief or only form of fuel for cooking and heating, and the collection of firewood is the other major part of women's gleaning activity. Wood accounts for about 5 percent of the world's total primary energy supply (2002 data), but wood is about 22 percent of all fuel used in Africa, 12 percent of fuel used in South America, and less than 1 percent of fuel used in the developed countries that comprise the G8. While people prefer dry, dead wood as firewood, in situations where demand exceeds the rate of supply of dead wood, the collection of firewood also consumes live timber. In addition to the artisanal gleaning by rural communities, there exists a growing commercial harvest that is sold in cities as firewood or charcoal. Together, these can constitute a substantial harvest, but again, the extent of harvest varies geographically.

Firewood (including wood harvested for charcoal production) accounts for 87 percent of all wood harvested in Africa and about 62 percent of wood harvested in Asia but less than 15 percent of wood harvested in Europe and North America. The FAO anticipates a modest increase in the production of firewood and charcoal in Africa and South America in the next several decades. To put some numbers on these percentages, in 2002, African nations were harvesting 546 million cubic meters of wood for fuel per year, out of a total harvest of 629 million cubic meters of wood products. Africa's supply of firewood for that year, if stacked neatly into one-meter-high, one-meter-wide piles, would have stretched almost fourteen times around the earth. This is nearly three and a half times the amount of wood fuel harvested in all North and Central American countries, yet the total wood harvest in Africa is only two-thirds of that in North and Central American countries.

To make sense of statistics on rates of forest loss, it's necessary to distinguish between primary forest (also called old growth), secondary forest, natural forest (which may be old growth or secondary growth), other wooded land (which the FAO defines as treed land with canopy cover of 5 to 10 percent, not including tree plantations), and forest plantations (which are never natural or old-growth or other forested land).[5] The most dire descriptions of forest loss focus on the loss of primary forest, forest that has not previously been significantly exploited by humans. The most rosy descriptions, which the FAO seems to prefer, are based on areas of tree-covered landscapes, including plantations of spruce, pines, eucalyptus, and even date palms (the FAO reports 4.8 percent of the world's forests are plantations). And there is enough

5. This rich but confusing nomenclature helps obscure the facts of deforestation. Primary forest (and, to a substantially lesser extent, secondary forest) provides the full range of goods and services from forested land. The other types of forest, as categorized by the FAO, provide a much-reduced set, and, as discussed later, most of the deforestation that occurs is ultimately loss of primary forest.

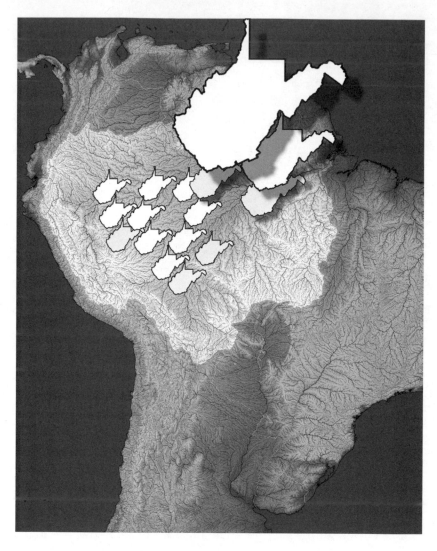

FIGURE 4. How many West Virginia–size patches of land can be fitted into the Amazon rainforest? We lose the equivalent of the area of West Virginia from the world's forested land every year, due to unsustainable logging and land clearing. Image of Amazon basin is from the National Aeronautics and Space Administration's Earth Observatory website, http://earthobservatory.nasa.gov. NASA image by Jesse Allen, using SRTM data courtesy of the University of Maryland's Global Land Cover Facility, and river data courtesy of the World Wildlife Fund HydroSHEDS Project.

variability in the data available to allow different authors to present different numbers and rates. Even the rosy descriptions show that forestry practice is not generally sustainable at present: In its 2007 report on the state of the world's forests, the FAO shows a global rate of net loss of 0.18 percent of forest area annually, with losses for individual countries as high as 5.2 percent annually (in Burundi). The FAO reports the global total is 7.317 million hectares lost per year.[6] This is equivalent to the loss every year of a forest a bit bigger than Ireland or West Virginia. (The FAO also reports a 3.8 percent annual gain in forest area in that notably forested country, Bahrain—date palms in tidy rows perhaps?)

Because reforestation and afforestation never create new primary forest, and because much logging in developing countries centers on primary forest, almost all (about six million hectares) of that West Virginia–size forest lost globally each year is primary forest. Primary forests currently account for just over 36 percent of all forests, but we are disproportionately harvesting our primary forests and replacing them with secondary forests, plantations, or cleared land. So the question of forest decline has to be recast: Are there disadvantages to losing primary forests in particular? Or, to put it more bluntly (see Figure 4), how many times can you remove a West Virginia–size forest from the Amazon and still have an Amazon rainforest?

HOW VALUABLE IS A FOREST?

Forests are not just timber. I've already mentioned the considerable annual harvest of bushmeat and other nonwood products that we obtain from forests. To what extent can such products be derived from secondary forests or plantations? And what about the environmental services that forests provide?

The biggest difference between primary forest and secondary forests or plantations is the diversity. Primary forests are biologically rich, and not just in the tropics. It's a no-brainer to conclude that a secondary forest or plantation, with fewer species and a narrower age distri-

6. The annual rate of net loss is the annual rate of loss due to deforestation minus the gains due to regeneration, replanting, and afforestation. In a preliminary announcement for the 2010 report, the FAO has slightly reduced these rates, but the numbers are disputed by many conservation organizations.

bution of trees, will support a less rich biota. But how much less rich? And other than for the harvest of bushmeat, does the difference really matter? How good a job do these "lesser" forests do of ameliorating climate, mitigating effects of severe weather, preventing run-off and erosion, sequestering carbon, and putting oxygen into the air? There is room for considerable new research because the task of measuring, let alone the task of assigning value to, many of these services can be quite challenging.

Another way to come to grips with what we are losing is to consider the value of a forest equivalent in size to Ireland or West Virginia, because that is how much forest we lose each year. In taking this approach, I am going to cheat and pretend that the forest being lost is "average"—some strange amalgam of primary forest, secondary forest, and plantation with a capacity to produce valued products that is also globally "average." I do this because that makes it possible to use the FAO's global average data, but it is cheating because most of this lost forest is primary forest and thus definitely of more than "average" value. So, the values derived will all be underestimates. The FAO data reveal that the world's 3.9 billion hectares of forest generate roughly US$68.7 billion per year in forest primary products. Therefore, we can anticipate our West Virginia–size forest should yield about $127 million per year at current "average" rates of extraction. To this direct economic value of its timber and other raw products, we can add the money made through pulp and paper manufacture, wood processing, and other downstream activities usually included as part of the forest sector of an economy. This adjustment brings the total economic output per year of our forest to about $585 million. (Remember, it's an underestimate.)

Now, if we can stop counting beans and think more broadly, it's clear that this direct economic value is only the start. All those wood products generate employment in the industry, and there could be other ancillary economic benefits, such as the revenue and employment from a vibrant tourist industry nestled in one corner of the forest. The more tricky part is to determine the value of the environmental services this forest is providing, a value that can frequently exceed the value of the resources harvested. The challenge to determine the total economic value (TEV) of a forest has been grappled with by ecologists and economists working together over the past thirty years, and more intensively during the last decade. It is a difficult challenge because most environ-mental services do not enter the economy directly and are therefore not easily valued quantitatively. Furthermore, the results are usually surprising to people accustomed to looking only at conventional bal-ance sheets. Chapter 7 will explore this issue more generally, but we can look now at a couple of examples that show the surprising value of forests.

One approach, taken by Andrew Balmford of Cambridge University, Robert Costanza, then of the University of Maryland, and their col-leagues was to seek out examples where it was possible to compare the TEV of an area of relatively undisturbed natural habitat with that of a nearby comparable area that had been exploited and modified. The economic value of the latter included the direct value to consum-ers of exploited resources as well as the more general societal values and environmental services. In an article published in *Science* in 2002, they reported the results of a review of more than three hundred stud-ies. Only five met their criterion of a comparison of nearby relatively undisturbed and transformed habitats, but these included two forest systems: tropical forests in Malaysia and Cameroon. The Malaysian and Cameroon studies showed an average 18 percent benefit to keeping the land forested instead of clearing it and converting it to small-scale farming (TEV of $2,570 compared to $2,110, per hectare). (All amounts in this section are in U.S. dollars.) That 18 percent benefit ($460 per hectare) is a marginal value that accrues every year as a net profit for not replacing the forest with farmland. It is an amount in addition to the value of the forest products harvested each year. Under economic conditions that apply today, most conversion of unexploited ecosys-tems into exploited (and usually degraded) ones is economically costly. However, private economic benefit frequently attaches to the conver-sion as the logger harvests all the trees or the farmer plants new fields, in much the same way that fishermen gain economic value from the catch even as they overfish the resource.

Other studies have approached the question of forest TEV in a dif-ferent way. In 2002 Brooks Kaiser of Gettysburg College and James Roumasset of the University of Hawaii did a valuation for the single benefit of conservation of water provided by protected forests of the Ko'olau Mountains of Oahu, Hawaii. These 40,000 hectares of pro-tected forest are critical to replenishing the Pearl Harbor aquifer, the primary source of drinking water for Honolulu. By estimating the cost of using desalination to replace the water that would be lost if the forest was degraded, they found a value for the forest of between $1.42 and $2.63 billion. Their lower estimate works out to about $35,500 per hectare, substantially more than the values for the Malaysian and Cameroon forests. And this is the value for a *single* environmental service.

In 2004 Taylor Ricketts of the World Wildlife Fund and colleagues ran experiments on pollination effectiveness in Costa Rican coffee plantations that were different distances from remnant patches of forest more than 20 hectares in size. They showed a measurable positive effect on the coffee crop for sites within 1 km of a patch of forest due to more effective pollination. They used these experimental results to compute the value of the pollination services provided by two small patches of forest (111 and 46 hectares). A total of 480 hectares of coffee plantation were within 1 km of one or other of these patches, and the coffee yield was 20.8 percent greater for these plantations than for plantations farther away from forest. This represented a total additional yield worth $62,000 per year, putting the value of the two patches at $395 per hectare per year for their pollination services alone. Again, this is not TEV but the value of forest for a single environmental service. These valuations for forested land are not out of line with what has been determined in other studies.

With these values for forest services, it is possible to estimate the cost of the loss of services from that West Virginia–size forest that is being removed every year by deforestation. Using the Malaysian and Cameroon marginal value of $460 per hectare, the cost is $3.4 billion per year, every year into the future. The Costa Rican pollination value yields slightly less ($2.9 billion per year), while the Ko'olau Mountains water conservation value yields a whopping $259 billion dollars per year. Each of these amounts is *in addition to* the value of wood and non-wood products sustainably harvested from a forest of this size ($585 million per year). None of these are trivial amounts,[7] and since another forest of the same size is lost each subsequent year, this economic cost of deforestation grows rather large rather quickly—about US$185 billion

7. All amounts are also substantially larger than the value of the goods harvested in removing that patch of forest. This may be a general trend: environmental services are much more valuable than the goods we harvest.

in lost services plus $32 billion in lost opportunity for sustainable harvest after ten years of continuing loss using the Malaysian-Cameroon valuation. Do we need to value our forests more than we do? You be the judge.

WHAT DOES THE FUTURE HOLD?

Deforestation has led to the collapse of civilizations in past eras. Jared Diamond has recently documented the sad history of deforestation on Easter Island in making the more general case that human civilizations have a penchant for overtaxing their environments. In his view, it is the subsequent failure of resource supplies or related factors rather than war or other societal adjustments that is the usual cause of the demise of civilizations. In our very interconnected world, the demise may be delayed and global, but it will still occur unless we learn how to harvest sustainably.

One thing we can count on, unfortunately, is that, unless forestry practices change substantially, there will continue to be deforestation in many parts of the world and, along with this, the expansion of deserts. The loss, year by year, of that West Virginia–size forest leads ultimately to the expansion of unproductive drylands and deserts. Drylands are places in which shortage of water limits crop, forage, or timber production or other ecosystem services dependent on plant growth. To be sure, deforestation is not the only cause of expansion of drylands and deserts. Growing human populations overexploit available supplies of water or damage the capacity of their environment to retain water in the first place. Climatic changes result in droughts that reduce the capacity of the environment to support plant communities. But in too many instances, the elimination of forests is the first step on a path that leads eventually to badly eroded land that does not retain water effectively. This path from lush forest to arid dryland or desert can be difficult or impossible to reverse.

Drylands currently occupy 41 percent of the earth's land surface, and desertification currently affects 10 to 20 percent of drylands. As such, desertification directly impacts the lives of 100 to 200 million people at present and threatens to impact many more in the future (the FAO speaks of 1 billion). It is particularly severe in sub-Saharan Africa, where productivity of arable land is falling 1 percent per year and has dropped 20 percent in the past forty years. With less efficient retention of water, soils dry out. Movement of soils, liberated when plant cover fails, smothers surrounding vegetated regions while simultaneously creating an environment where seeds are unlikely to germinate and are incapable of surviving if they do. While there have always been deserts and factors that create deserts, these causal processes are synergistic and particularly likely to cause serious problems at the present time.

Global climate change exacerbates the problem of desertification, because global patterns of rainfall and evaporation are changing in ways that substantially modify the moisture regimes in soils. In many places, soils are becoming drier than they have been in the historical past (see chapter 3). The global impact of the problem is perhaps best illustrated by the fact that reasonably good evidence now exists showing that dusts lifted off the new deserts in western Africa have brought novel pathogens to the coral reefs of the Caribbean (see chapter 4).

While desertification can be a final step on the path beginning with deforestation, there are two more immediate impacts of overharvesting of forests that have gained particular attention recently. By degrading forests, we reduce their capacity for slowing the water cycle, retaining humidity within the forest, and generally ameliorating local climate. In places such as West Africa, deforestation exacerbates the reductions in rainfall that are occurring as part of global climate change, with the result that locations are becoming even drier than they would otherwise be, making land less fertile even while hastening the progression toward desertification. The second impact is even more important. The release of the sequestered carbon in forest trees as their wood is burned or allowed to decay and the loss of sequestration capacity that the forest formerly provided are twin mechanisms by which deforestation speeds up climate change directly by permitting more of the carbon dioxide that we release to remain in the atmosphere.

There is a brighter side to the future when it comes to forests. Our growing ability to properly value the environmental services provided by forests and to correctly identify which members of society benefit from those services has made it obvious that values of forest services are immense and do not accrue solely to the landowners. (If they did, landowners would take much better care of their forested land.) It's also clear that many environmental services are distributed quite widely beyond the local population. In the most obvious cases, the weather-ameliorating and water-regulating services of forests extend well beyond their immediate boundaries, and their climate-regulating services—through their capacity to sequester carbon that would otherwise be released to the atmosphere—are truly globally distributed. With an economics of forests that includes the value and distribution of beneficial services comes the possibility of a market for those services. A number of local, regional, and global mechanisms are now in existence, but probably the most important is the developing carbon market, encouraged by the Kyoto Accord and other global mechanisms to stem climate change. By providing money to local populations to care for their existing forests or to undertake reforestation or afforestation programs, it is possible to increase the local sequestration of carbon, thereby ameliorating climate change. In the process, the new or revitalized forests provide all the other environmental services as well. It is too early to tell how effective such markets are going to be, but it seems likely that they will help to slow, if not reverse, the deforestation of recent years.[8]

In addition, the growing interest in managing forests sustainably has led to a number of explorations of intercropping and other forms of agroforestry—the management of forests for a variety of agricultural products. In creating agroforestry systems, we may be rediscovering an ancient way of capturing the resources of forests in a sustainable way while preserving their ability to provide environmental services.

The forest that intrepid explorers of the Amazon found in the nineteenth century was not the "forest primeval" they thought it to be. Archeological research over the past thirty years or so has established that, while not yet widely recognized by the public, pre-Columbian populations throughout the Americas were both much larger and much more advanced culturally than had been thought previously. William Denevan of the University of Wisconsin reported in 1996 that within the Amazon Basin, advanced agricultural communities supported large populations on the river bluffs and upland savanna, a total of perhaps 5.5 million people in all of Amazonia (including the Amazon and

8. One of the few encouraging outcomes of the Copenhagen conference on climate change in December 2009 was the pledge made by Australia, France, Japan, Norway, Britain, and the United States to provide $3.5 billion toward the cost of slowing and eventually reversing deforestation in poor countries. Particularly interesting was their stated appreciation of the environmental services provided by forests beyond the sequestering of CO_2. Details were sparse, and the pledge needs to be fulfilled.

Orinoco watersheds and the Guianese highlands between them). Their intensive agriculture both expanded savanna at the expense of forest on upland savannas and created a rich black soil, *terra preta,* that is clearly anthropogenic, widely distributed throughout the region wherever there were settlements, and up to two meters thick. These fertile soils confirm the long history of settlement at each site and the effectiveness and sustainability of the inhabitants' agricultural practices. As well as cultivating crops on fields that were mounded, irrigated, or both, they appear to have maintained orchards of fruit- and nut-bearing trees and to have managed nearby forest by the selective cultivation of species that yielded valued food or other products in a sophisticated type of agroforestry that was effective in capturing useful resources while maintaining biodiversity and forest cover.

With the arrival of Europeans and the diseases they brought, this advanced forest management collapsed as native populations were decimated in a few brief decades. Surviving small groups of natives reverted to a much simpler and less sustainable slash-and-burn agriculture, and areas previously cleared and farmed became reforested to produce the "virgin rainforests" that later Europeans saw. The irony is that Amazon natives could have taught Europeans ways of sustainably managing forest ecosystems if only exotic diseases and aggressive oppression had not killed them off before they had a chance to instruct us. If we have come to better understand the value of forested land in recent years, as I think we have, there is hope that we can learn new ways of farming the forests that will be as effective as the ways of pre-Columbian natives of Amazonia.

The awareness of the true value of forests is growing in many parts of the world as we learn how to value their environmental services and as many of those services grow in importance under current patterns of climate change. Yet the pace of deforestation has been remarkably fixed over the past twenty years, and the time may be fast approaching when we simply can no longer afford to further reduce the area of the earth's land surface vegetated with forest. The challenge will be to devise effective ways of living with forests and using them sustainably rather than clearing them away to create open land. Population growth, consumer culture, the differential distribution of the costs and benefits of overexploitation, and our failure to recognize that the replenishment of natural ecosystems after they have been degraded is problematic at best can be extraordinarily difficult issues to deal with, yet all contribute to the challenges we will face as we try to move toward real sustainability. In this, our use of forests and fisheries is distressingly similar, and I anticipate similar difficulties in making real improvements.

The FAO's *State of the World's Forests 2007* begins with the following declaration concerning global progress toward sustainability: "The overall conclusion is that progress is being made, but is very uneven. Some regions, notably those including developed countries and having temperate climates, have made significant progress; institutions are strong, and forest area is stable or increasing. Other regions, especially those with developing economies and tropical ecosystems, continue to lose forest area, while lacking adequate institutions to reverse this trend. However, even in regions that are losing forest cover, there are a number of positive trends on which to build." In this fragile sense, and with considerable caution because of the FAO's known tendency to be optimistic, we may conclude that our management of forests has been somewhat more skillful than our management of fisheries. Indeed, it should be, because as terrestrial organisms we are much better informed about the ecology of forests than we are that of coastal waters and have a much longer history of interacting with them. On the other hand, the pressures that lead to deforestation are many and are quite difficult to alter, and impacts of deforestation will continue to rest squarely on our remaining primary forests, with their rich and immensely valuable environmental services.

3

DISRUPTING THE OCEAN-ATMOSPHERE ENGINE

Sudbury, Ontario, was a surreal place when I drove through it in 1962. Heavily industrialized, a mining town, it was not a pretty place to begin with. But the coal-fired power plants and smelters delivered a constant stream of sulfur compounds to the atmosphere, and the resulting acid rain had produced an ugly result. For miles around Sudbury, particularly downwind of it to the east and north, the landscape looked like something very bad had happened—some places resembled a lunar landscape, with rocky hillsides devoid of trees, while other places had only stunted and twisted trees. The boreal forest that used to be present had disappeared.

I was on my way to my field site in the Temagami region northeast of Sudbury, where I was to begin my research career by investigating the ecology of the Aurora trout, a relict species known from White Pine Lake and just one other nearby lake. I drove north from Sudbury to Kirkland Lake, an old gold-mining town, then flew southwest to White Pine Lake, where my assistant and I made good use of an old trapper's log cabin. (The cabin was old; I never knew the trapper.)

White Pine Lake was beautiful and totally undeveloped (although the area had been logged early in the century). It was at least a two-day canoe trip from civilization and was 100 km northeast of Sudbury. I saw three

Facing page: Chamberlain Point, Maine, February 2006. Photo courtesy of R. S. Steneck.

people that summer, other than my assistant and the ones who came on the plane with my groceries. It was one of those lakes that makes Central Ontario such a special place, with crystal-clear waters, lots of smooth rock sculpted by the Pleistocene glaciation, and a forest of cedar, spruce, and stately white and red pine. It looked like heaven to me.

I fished in vain, however, using many meters of gill netting rather than a rod and reel. My records show over fifty twenty-four-hour sets of a gill net 100 meters in length in White Pine Lake that year. But the lake held no Aurora Trout or indeed any other fish and probably had not since the late 1950s. Its pH was 5.4. Although I did not recognize the problem, it had become too acid for them to reproduce successfully. Acid rain was "discovered" as a phenomenon a few years after I completed my work.

Fortunately for the Aurora Trout, there was a captive breeding population in one hatchery operated by the Ontario Ministry of Natural Resources, and this population was carefully maintained. The species was listed as threatened by the Committee on the Status of Endangered Wildlife in Canada in 1987. Whole-lake liming (addition of lime) in the early 1990s restored the pH of the lake, and fish were successfully reintroduced from the hatchery stock to both White Pine and neighboring Whirligig Lake as well as to ten other suitable lakes in the region. The species has now bred successfully in its native lakes, which remain closed to fishing. Very limited angling for Aurora trout is permitted on some of the non-native lakes, and this beautiful species remains listed as threatened.

With the threat of global climate change, many people have forgotten acid rain, a problem that first came to notice in the industrial cities of Europe in the late 1800s and became recognized as a more widespread problem in the latter part of the twentieth century. Acid rain is a consequence of burning coal under conditions that permit the sulfur dioxide and nitrogen oxides it releases to escape into the atmosphere. These compounds react with oxygen and water in the atmosphere to form acidic compounds that fall to the earth with rain. Subsequently, this acidified rain impacts both terrestrial and aquatic ecosystems, particularly in places—such as eastern Canada, the northeastern United States, and Scandinavia—where soils and water are poorly buffered and unable to tolerate the additional acid without showing measurable shifts in pH. Acid rain kills forests and lakes, although with appropriate scrubber technology on smokestacks, it can become a problem of the past.

The scientific understanding of acid rain developed initially in Scandinavia, and Svante Odén, a Swedish soil scientist, is generally credited with recognizing the insidious and transnational nature of this type of pollution. On 24 October 1967, Odén published a report detailing the way in which industrial pollution from the countries of Western Europe was impacting the forests and lakes of Sweden. Unusual for a scientist, he chose to publish not in a technical journal but in Sweden's largest daily newspaper. This very public step initiated global action: to reduce acid rain, international treaties were developed that demanded strict controls on what chemicals left the smokestacks of power plants and smelters in Europe and subsequently North America.

Sudbury, north of Lake Huron, sits on top of the richest nickel deposit in the world as well as rich deposits of copper. Mining began in 1886, and by 1916 the coal-fired smelters and power plants were pumping an estimated 600,000 metric tons of sulfur dioxide (SO_2) into the atmosphere each year. Sudbury was the greatest point source of SO_2 emissions in North America and provided a laboratory for the study of acid rain.[1]

Still, it was not until the late 1960s that aquatic ecologists such as Richard Beamish and Harold Harvey of the University of Toronto put together the evidence for impacts on lake ecosystems and their fish, and not until the late 1970s did North American scientists recognize the widespread nature of acid rain pollution on that continent. Sudbury's giant INCO mining operation (now Vale INCO) began to tackle its SO_2 problem in 1972 by building the "superstack," which at 380 meters tall was then the tallest smokestack in the world and lifted the polluting gases high into the sky, almost out of sight and, it was hoped, out of mind. Indeed, improvements to air quality in the immediate vicinity did occur, but the pollution simply traveled farther. Beginning in the early 1980s, under regulatory pressure from the government, INCO began a major investment in research and new technology to clean up its Sudbury operation. By 1994 about 90 percent of the SO_2 was being captured before it escaped into the air. Trees are now growing in Sudbury again.

I use the example of acid rain to begin this chapter because the inter-

---

1. Globally, the burning of coal is responsible for over 50 percent of SO_2 emissions, with oil responsible for a further 25 to 30 percent, but in Sudbury's case, about 80 percent of emissions come from the ores themselves and less than 20 percent from the coal used in smelting.

national scientific and regulatory effort that allowed us essentially to solve this problem was perhaps the first demonstration that the nations of the world can come together to solve a major environmental problem that crosses national borders. A response of equal resolve and cooperative spirit is required for the problem of climate change, which is truly global in scope and far more serious. It affects not just temperatures but also rainfall patterns, atmospheric circulation, ocean currents, ocean temperatures, and ocean chemistry. Since a large part of the cause of climate change lies in our patterns of use of energy, that's the topic I turn to first.

NO SHORTAGE OF ENERGY

For the last couple of centuries, industrial societies have been burning fossil fuels at ever-increasing rates to release and harness the energy stored in their chemical bonds. This has released into the atmosphere large amounts of carbon dioxide, which works to trap heat from the sun's radiation near the earth's surface, instead of having it radiate outward into space. This release of the waste product of fossil fuel combustion is why energy use is central to understanding human impacts on the atmosphere and, because of atmospheric change, on the oceans.

Humans use a lot of energy, and people in developed countries use a lot more energy than people in developing countries. The good news is that there is nothing fundamentally wrong with using energy. Using energy does not, by itself, cause undesirable environmental effects, and the sun delivers a lot more energy to the earth every day than we currently use. Virtually all of this energy is dissipated as heat.

To be specific, the average amount of electromagnetic energy continuously arriving from the sun at the position of the earth (mostly as visible light) is 1.366 kilowatts per square meter, which translates to 174,000 terawatts (174×10^{12} kilowatts) for the entire earth, a target 127 million square kilometers in area. This solar constant of 1.366 kilowatts per square meter varies seasonally (± 3.5 percent) as the earth moves closer to and farther from the sun.

Much of this continuous rain of energy does not reach the earth's surface because it is reflected into space or absorbed by the atmosphere. In addition, particular sites on Earth are variously experiencing night or day, cloud cover or clear skies, and variable inclinations toward the sun. As a consequence, the average rate of receipt of solar energy at a specific site on the earth's surface is about 0.250 kilowatts per square meter continuously throughout the year, or about 32,000 terawatts for the entire earth. To put these numbers into perspective, of the 174,000 terawatts of energy arriving from the sun, only 18.3 percent (32,000 terawatts) gets through the atmosphere and reaches the earth's surface. Of this 18.3 percent, all photosynthesis uses just 0.06 percent (100 terawatts). The rest (18.2 percent) moves water around the hydrologic cycle, generates winds and therefore weather, and dissipates as heat. At present, humans are consuming about 13 terawatts of energy at any particular moment; if all this came directly from sunlight, we would be using just 0.007 percent of what reaches the earth's surface. I'll repeat my point: there is way more than enough energy arriving on the surface of the earth every day to provide for all our current energy needs, so the *amount* of energy we use is not the problem.

The problem arises because we do not sit quietly gathering sunlight. Mostly we derive our energy from organic materials such as coal, oil, and gas that were created initially through photosynthesis over many years in the distant past, and then sequestered (and chemically changed) deep in the earth. As I noted earlier, our burning of these fuels to release their energy also releases CO_2 and some other compounds into the atmosphere and leads to a major disruption of the giant ocean–atmosphere engine that powers our climate.

Our per capita use of energy grew slowly as early humans learned to make fire and then to domesticate plants and animals. It grew more rapidly as we began to harness wind and water and to develop industries. By the beginning of the Industrial Revolution, with the harnessing of coal-fired steam power, we were using about 37.5 times as much energy per capita as in pre-fire days (and there were many more of us using energy, so the overall increase was substantially larger). From the start of the Industrial Revolution, we in the West commenced an exponential increase in demand for energy that has scarcely slowed. A similar exponential rise has now commenced in a number of developing countries such as China and India. The amount of energy consumed by humanity, although small relative to the amount arriving from the sun, is now many orders of magnitude larger than when we first began using fire, and a major portion of it comes from burning of fossil fuels.

The Energy Information Administration of the U.S. government provides abundant data on energy production and use across the world since the mid-twentieth century. It reports that total world energy use during 1980 was 83 trillion kWh, of which U.S. use totaled 23 trillion kWh.[2] (One trillion kWh is enough energy to power a million typical North American homes for 109 years.) These numbers had increased to 136 trillion and 30 trillion kWh, respectively, in 2005 and are projected to reach 204 trillion kWh and 35 trillion kWh by 2030. These are all very big numbers compared to the 2,000 to 2,500 kilocalories (2.3 to 2.9 kWh) we each use per day in food energy.

The burning of fuels to provide the energy we use generates yet another big number. Oxygen from the air combines with the organic fuel to produce heat, CO_2, water, and a few organic compounds usually left in the ash after the fire has spent itself. CO_2 is a harmless, colorless, odorless gas that is essential for plant photosynthesis and is also produced in respiration by all living things. As such, it is not a compound one would think of as a pollutant. And yet the quantities of CO_2 now being produced and discharged into the atmosphere through our use of fossil fuels are having major effects on the world's climate.[3]

Because the carbon released from fossil fuel burning was last in the atmosphere many millions of years ago and has been sequestered underground since then, its return in the form of CO_2 represents a current net gain in atmospheric concentrations of this gas. Globally, our use of fossil fuels currently releases 30 billion metric tons of CO_2 into the atmosphere annually, and the amount increases year by year. Even though about half of that released CO_2 moves quickly out of the atmosphere and into the ocean (40 percent) and forested lands (10 percent), the amount added each year is sufficient to measurably increase CO_2 concentration in the atmosphere and raise global temperatures as a consequence. While we also release greenhouse gases through our farming and forestry activities, the CO_2 produced by our use of coal, oil, and gas is the main cause of warming and atmospheric change. It's our release of this greenhouse gas that is the real problem, not our use of energy.

2. The Energy Information Administration website insists on using the quad BTU (quadrillion British thermal units) as the measurement of energy use—I have converted this to the more usual kWh (kilowatt hours). One quad BTU = 0.293×10^{12} kWh.

3. The burning of wood also releases CO_2, but the CO_2 released was removed from the atmosphere via photosynthesis only years to decades ago, so its return does not really alter the total amount of CO_2 in the system.

GREENHOUSES, GASES, AND OUR WARMING WORLD

Wander into a sunroom on a warm, sunny day and it can be oppressively hot, especially if the air circulation system is not operating. On a cold winter day, it can be warm and inviting. The reason for this is that glass is variably transparent. It allows visible light (wavelengths from about 400 to 700 nanometers) to pass through it, but it is relatively opaque to ultraviolet (UV, less than 400 nm) and infrared (IR, greater than 700 nm) wavelengths. You can sit in the sunroom all day, getting very hot, but you won't get a suntan because the windows block the UV wavelengths. You get hot in that room because much of the light entering through the windows is absorbed by the surfaces of the room to be re-emitted as heat (IR), which cannot escape easily through the windows. The tendency of glass to transmit visible light but not heat makes sunrooms and greenhouses possible.

Our atmosphere behaves a lot like glass. The broad range of frequencies of energy coming from the sun is filtered because the atmosphere is more transparent to light but somewhat less transparent to both UV and IR wavelengths. Its reduced transparency to UV wavelengths has made it possible for people to bask in the sun without suffering the DNA breakdown that unfiltered UV light will cause. (We just get sunburn and tan lines, and, after years of such behavior, dry, leathery skin, retinal damage, and occasional skin cancers and melanomas.) The atmosphere's reduced transparency to IR radiation or heat has made it possible for the average surface temperature on Earth to hover around +10°C while temperatures on the moon, where there is far less atmosphere, remain about 50° to 150°C colder. Sunlight hitting the earth is partly re-emitted as heat, but much of that heat is trapped here by the atmosphere.

Among the various gases that make up our atmosphere, certain ones make it less transparent to heat. These have been labeled *greenhouse gases* and include carbon dioxide (CO_2), methane (CH_4), nitrous oxide (N_2O), and a number of others. Ozone (O_3) is one of the main gases that make the atmosphere less transparent to UV wavelengths. The hole in the ozone layer was of great concern a few years ago because it was growing, and it risked exposing large portions of the planet to increased UV irradiation and the attendant biological damage that this would produce.[4]

---

4. I mention ozone and UV wavelength transmission, even though this is only tangentially related to climate change, because it was our releases of chlorofluorocarbons

Now, if you change the concentrations of greenhouse gases in the atmosphere, you alter the degree to which the atmosphere is transparent to heat. An increase in concentrations of greenhouse gases makes the atmosphere a better insulator (it allows less heat to escape into space), and our climate warms. Broadly speaking, the average temperature at the surface of the earth is a balance between the amount of light energy that arrives from the sun, is absorbed by objects, and is then radiated as heat, and the rate at which that heat is able to escape from the earth to space by passing back through the atmosphere.

Of course, the global pattern of temperature is not determined quite so simply. For one thing, the world does not exist at a single average temperature—there are diurnal, seasonal, and geographic differences in temperature. These differences occur partly because more sunlight per unit area arrives in equatorial regions than in regions closer to the poles, and more sunlight per unit area arrives at any particular location during the summer months—all because the earth happens to be a globe tilted on its axis. This differential arrival of sunlight means that the earth is warmer at the equator than at the poles and that there are warmer and cooler seasons.

Heat does not stay where it is generated, however, and the geographic differences in temperature are also strongly influenced by the transport of heat from warmer to cooler portions of the globe in currents of air and water. About 60 percent of the heat transferred from the tropics to the poles is moved within the atmosphere, both through movement of warm air masses and through the evaporation of water in the tropics and its subsequent condensation as rain farther north or south (evaporation consumes heat, which is subsequently released when water vapor condenses as rain). The remaining 40 percent of heat is transferred from the tropics toward the poles via ocean currents that move masses of warmer tropical water toward temperate regions. Today, the giant "heat engine" comprised of the atmosphere and the oceans ensures that our tropical regions are cooler and our polar regions substantially warmer than they would be if heat simply stayed where it

---

(as escaped refrigerants) that caused the hole. Once the problem was identified, nations rallied, regulations were passed, and certain refrigerants were phased out. The hole now seems to have stabilized and may be becoming smaller. In other words, human actions can affect climate, and, as with acid rain, humanity is capable of recognizing a serious problem and working collectively to repair it. There is hope.

was generated by absorbed sunlight. This heat engine drives the atmospheric phenomena that we think of as weather—cold and warm fronts, storms, rainfall, and so on—and comparable phenomena in the ocean—fronts, eddies, gyres, and ocean currents. Weather, averaged out over years, produces what we call *climate.*

Our climate can change for many different reasons. The amount of solar radiation that reaches the earth can increase or decrease. The atmosphere can change to cause more or less of that solar radiation to be reflected into space before it reaches the surface, or to allow more or less of the heat radiating from the surface to escape back through the atmosphere to space. And the earth's surface can change to alter the relative balance between the amount of light reflected and the amount absorbed and then re-emitted as heat.

The amount of solar energy reaching the earth changes in response to several extraterrestrial cycles. The approximately eleven-year sunspot cycle causes an alteration in the amount of energy released from the sun and has a small effect on climate. The various Milankovitch cycles, with periodicities ranging from approximately nineteen thousand to four hundred thousand years, cause changes in the shape of the earth's orbit and the distance from the sun at the closest and most distant points of the orbit. They introduce a larger variation in the amount of energy arriving at the earth and create measurable, though still modest, effects on our climate.

Events on the earth that change the transparency of its atmosphere or alter the albedo (reflectivity) of its surface also affect climate by modifying the proportion of arriving energy that is absorbed, converted to heat, and retained. Volcanic eruptions, snowfall, and changes in greenhouse gas concentrations all create these effects. When Mount Pinatubo erupted in 1991, it put large quantities of sulfates into the high atmosphere as aerosols. These increased the reflectivity of the upper atmosphere, thus reducing the amount of arriving sunlight that was able to reach the earth's surface. The result was measurably cooler climate over several years. Snow and ice cover substantially increase the albedo of the earth's surface, thus reducing the proportion of arriving sunlight that is absorbed and converted to heat. Snow-covered land reflects up to 90 percent of incident light compared to typical green vegetation, which reflects about 10 percent. Thus an increase in snow cover results in a cooler climate. Finally, increases in the concentration of greenhouse gases in the atmosphere increase the extent to which heat is trapped and lead to a warming of climate.

PAST CLIMATES

L'Anse aux Meadows, bleak and windswept, is at the very tip of the long peninsula that marks the northern limit of Newfoundland and is a place from which you can watch the icebergs floating south out of the Arctic Ocean. It also boasts a sparse collection of ruins, remnants of the only well-verified Norse settlement in North America. That settlement provides historical verification of the ancient Norse saga that tells of Leif Erikson's journey west from Greenland around A.D. 1000 to a new country he called Vinland in honor of its abundant grapes.

Erikson's journey was the final thrust in a westward expansion of the Norse civilization from Norway to Iceland, to the outer Scottish islands, to Greenland, and on to North America in the eighth and ninth centuries. In Greenland, the Norse established several successful settlements that built an economy on farming livestock and hunting seals; from Vinland they traded timber, grapes, and raisins or wine as far east as Iceland. Although L'Anse aux Meadows is too small to have been other than a way station on the route to Vinland, the still undiscovered Vinland may not have been much farther south or west. Grapes have never grown in northern Newfoundland, but Jacques Cartier reported abundant grapes farther west on the northern shore of the St. Lawrence River in 1535. The Vinland outposts were occupied only twenty to thirty years; however, the Greenland settlements endured until the fifteenth century before finally collapsing because of a changing climate. The last recorded event in Norse Greenland was a wedding in September 1408.

This tale of Norse expansion and collapse, of farming and wine growing in northern lands, coincided with the Medieval Warm Period (lasting from about 800 to 1300), when temperatures in the northern hemisphere were very slightly (0.1°C) *cooler* than today but about 0.5 to 1.0°C warmer than in the so-called Little Ice Age spanning the sixteenth to nineteenth centuries. During that onset of cooler weather, farming in Greenland failed, and there are numerous historical references to particularly cold winters, crop failures, and famine throughout Europe. One degree can make a big difference.

Just outside the tiny Italian village of Bolca, in the foothills of the Alps, two small sites a few hundred meters apart have yielded an abundance of beautifully preserved fossils of early Eocene age (50 million years ago). The Museo Civico di Storia Naturale in nearby Verona houses a comprehensive collection of these fossils, many including details of soft parts and even traces of surface coloration. They are fishes and other organisms typical of a coral reef and represent the earliest comprehensive record of a "modern" coral reef community.[5] In the early Eocene, Bolca was part of the Tethyan seaway that extended from the Atlantic, through the Mediterranean, across the Middle East, to Southeast Asia. Given that the Panama Isthmus was not yet formed, there existed a circumtropical oceanic seaway at that time, and the climate was notably different from today's. The uplift of Italy to form the Alps later in the Eocene was part of a general closing off that also eliminated the central portion of the seaway from Israel through to Bangladesh and Burma and built the Himalayas. But 50 million years ago, Bolca was a tropical lagoon filled with fishes that are typical of coral reefs today.

Where I live in central Ontario, east of Lake Huron and north of Lake Ontario, the topsoil is thin and poor, and the frequent exposures of bedrock have been polished smooth by the several-kilometers-thick slab of ice that ground over them as recently as ten thousand years ago. Outside my house, I have several large, rounded boulders the size of Volkswagen bugs, just sitting there where the ice left them behind. And the land is rising slowly year by year, only a millimeter or so per year where I live, bouncing back after being depressed by the great weight of that ice. I still shovel snow every winter, and the lakes freeze over for several months, but one has to travel 2,000 km north to find permanent snow cover now.

Yes, climate has changed in the past for various reasons, and it will do

---

5. The Scleractinian corals had evolved in the mid-Triassic and gradually moved into the important reef-building niche that was vacated by the extinction of the rugose and tabulate corals in the End Permian mass extinction 245 million years ago. Coral-dominated reefs were again prevalent toward the end of the Jurassic but declined in abundance during the Cretaceous and were essentially absent for 10 million years following the End Cretaceous mass extinction 65 million years ago, although a few coral species survived. Modern Scleractinian genera evolved during the early Eocene and Miocene, and modern reef fish genera also appeared at this time. Bolca was not the first modern reef, but it is the best early example of a well-preserved reef fish fauna and is early in the history of modern coral reefs.

so again. Even apparently slight changes can have profound effects—the change from the Medieval Warm Period to the Little Ice Age involved no more than a 1°C shift in average temperature, yet it canceled Norse expansionism and led to frequent crop failures and famine in Europe. The seventeen-million-year-long Eocene was notably warmer and more equitable across the world than the climates before or after this period. This has been attributed to a collection of interacting factors, including the circumtropical circulation of the oceans permitted by the spatial arrangement of continents at that time, massive releases of methane from subsea clathrates[6] at the start of the period, and a progressive reduction in concentration of CO_2, driven perhaps by the evolution of new types of plants at the Eocene's close.[7] The cyclic Pleistocene glaciation that left boulders in my yard during its last retreat has been variously attributed to long-term Milankovitch cycles in the earth's orbit that modify the extent of the difference between summer and winter insolation, to changes in greenhouse gases such as CO_2, and to peculiarities (notably the nearly closed-off Arctic Ocean) of the modern arrangement of the continents and the resulting constraints on patterns of global ocean circulation. The Milankovitch explanation might be preferred except that our climate has not always cycled in this way. Why should always-present cyclic changes in the planet's orbit have begun to modify climate only in the last two million years?

Our ability to determine past climates becomes less precise the further back we go. Over the last one hundred fifty years our measurements have been quite accurate because we have been measuring weather systematically using reliable instruments in many parts of the world over

6. Methane clathrates are complexes in which methane is trapped within the lattice of water ice. They are denser than water and stable at temperatures close to 0°C but can melt to release methane if warmed or brought to the surface. Volcanic activity could have generated the initial warming at the start of the Eocene, and human-induced climate change could do the same thing in the future. Once clathrates start to melt, the released methane, which is a potent greenhouse gas, will ensure that warming continues.

7. Plants differ in the way in which they manipulate carbon during photosynthesis. If a new type of plant appears with methods of handling carbon that make it more efficient, it will tend to become more abundant than other plants and will gradually pull down CO_2 concentrations in the process. Something pulled CO_2 concentrations down from about 1,000 parts per million (ppm) during the Eocene to 280 ppm at the end of the Pleistocene, and more efficient photosynthesizers could have done this. Remember that plants put all the oxygen into the atmosphere much earlier.

that time period. Further back we must rely on less direct methods. Annual growth rings in trees can get us back two hundred years or so,[8] telling us in which years the tree grew well (warmer, wetter years). By matching patterns in the width of rings in living trees with ones that died some time ago, it's possible to extend this record back a couple more hundred years. Growth rings in massive corals also tell which years were good for growth (warmer), and here there are some individual corals that are several hundred years old. The ice of glaciers shows fine layers representing the snow that fell during a single year. More important than the thickness of these layers are the minute bubbles of air that are encapsulated there. These are samples of the atmosphere at particular times in the past, and ice cores in Greenland and Antarctica have retrieved records extending back thousands of years. Ratios of oxygen isotopes ^{18}O and ^{16}O and concentrations of CO_2 in these bubbles both correlate very closely with temperature records over the past one hundred fifty years and with temperatures inferred from tree rings prior to that. Therefore, oxygen isotope ratios and CO_2 concentration can both be used as proxies for temperature at even earlier times. The Vostok ice core from a site near the Russian base in Antarctica provides these correlates of temperature for the past four hundred fifty thousand years. Oxygen isotope ratios in some oceanic sediments can take us back even further.

Further back still, we have to rely on interpretations of sedimentary rocks and the fossils they may contain. There are abundant reasons to interpret the presence of reef-forming coral fossils as evidence that the site was a shallow tropical sea at the time they were alive. In the same way, the presence of pollen or other fossil evidence of pine forests indicates a cool, temperate environment, and shallow inland seas can be expected to have moderated local climates millions of years ago just as they do today. Similarly, those polished but scratched rock surfaces and the occasional large rounded boulders lying about near my house report the presence of a glacier some time in the past as clearly as if the glacier had only recently retreated. Past climates have been both warmer and cooler and wetter and drier than the one we presently enjoy.

8. Unless that tree happens to be a bristlecone pine! This very long-lived tree, found in the Sierra Nevada, includes the oldest living individuals of any organism on this planet, with some individuals now over forty-five hundred years old.

ANTHROPOGENIC CLIMATE CHANGE

The notion that humans might alter the climate by modifying the composition of the world's atmosphere is not a recent one. Continuous monitoring of the atmosphere commenced in the late 1950s at Mauna Loa, and this revealed that the concentration of CO_2 was increasing, primarily due to combustion of fossil fuels and deforestation.[9] The physics of the greenhouse effect was well understood by climate scientists, and so the possibility of climate change was quickly recognized. Calculations done as early as 1967 showed that a doubling of atmospheric CO_2 concentration would raise the world's average temperature by about 2.4°C, and Wallace Broecker of the Lamont-Doherty Geological Observatory outside New York published an article in *Science* in 1975 that reported, "The exponential rise in the atmospheric carbon dioxide content . . . by early in the next century will have driven the mean planetary temperature beyond the limits experienced during the last 1000 years." He added, "We may be in for a climatic surprise." That surprise is happening right now.

In 1981 James Hansen, who had recently become the director of the Goddard Institute for Space Studies in New York, published a landmark article in *Science* with several colleagues. They reported that average global temperature rose 0.4°C in the century since 1880, that this increase was consistent with that expected based on measured increases in atmospheric CO_2 concentration, and that the increase in CO_2 was due primarily to burning of fossil fuels. They predicted significant further warming during the 1980s and that there would be substantial climatic consequences in the coming century. Their article was unusual for the specificity and generality of its predictions, and the predictions have come true one after another (see Figure 5). In many ways, this article marked the beginning of serious attention to a developing major global problem. By the close of 1988, the United Nations General Assembly had resolved that the threats posed by climate change required significant international cooperation to develop strategies for prevention and adaptation, and the United Nations Environment Programme and the World Meteorological Organization had jointly established the

---

9. It is still being measured, and CO_2 concentration is still increasing. The Mauna Loa data are graphed at www.esrl.noaa.gov/gmd/ccgg/trends/. The raw data show a monthly mean CO_2 concentration of 384 ppm in October 2009, compared to 316 ppm in March 1958. The annual curve has been continually upward—there is more CO_2 in our atmosphere every month, year after year, and our world grows warmer as a result.

Intergovernmental Panel on Climate Change (IPCC) with the goal of providing a scientifically rigorous assessment of all aspects of climate change, including the role of humans in causing these changes and their likely impacts on human populations.

The IPCC is now over thirty years old and has proved to be an exceptionally effective mechanism for achieving consensus across the international science community. It presents that consensus view clearly and in terms that can be understood by both policymakers and the general public. The IPCC produced its preliminary assessment report in 1990. Its second assessment report in 1995 was a substantive set of documents identifying what was known and what was still uncertain at that time. This was followed by a third assessment report in 2001 and a fourth in 2007. The IPCC is currently preparing a fifth assessment report, which will appear in 2014. The third and fourth reports are currently available for download on the IPCC website (www.ipcc.ch).

One feature of this series of reports is that the predictions of one have an uncanny tendency to be proven correct in the next. A more distressing feature is that it's usually the worst-case predictions that prove to be correct. The climate continues to surprise us in small ways, usually providing worse outcomes than we had anticipated. Another important but nonobvious feature is that these reports are what economists call "lagging indicators"—they tend to report today what was the case a few years ago. This is a normal feature of science: the investigations take time to do, then the results must be prepared for publication, then the manuscript must be rigorously reviewed by other scientists in the field, and then the article (probably revised following review) is finally published. Scientists are used to seeing their work of one to three years ago finally getting published, and they all know that to keep up to date with what is happening in their fields, it is necessary to go to conferences and have discussions with other scientists; they cannot simply rely on published materials. In the case of the IPCC, the importance of the reports is such that the process of writing and reviewing them is even slower than it is in conventional science. To begin with, the teams of scientists working on any report are large and scattered across the globe. The report prepared by Working Group 1 (physical science) for the fourth assessment lists seven editors and more than five hundred "authors," some of whom had major roles in the research and writing while others simply commented on text provided by others. Coordinating the efforts

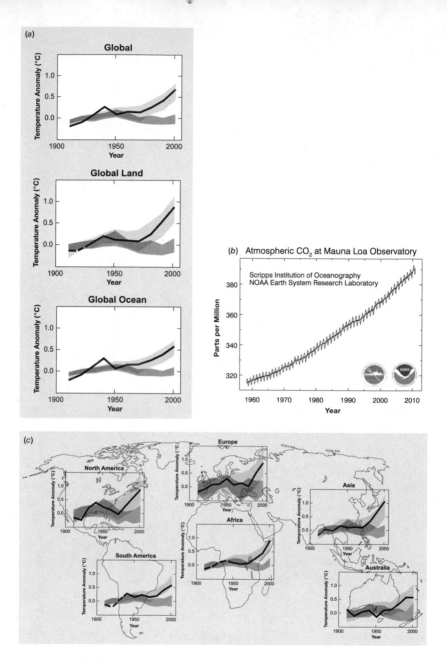

FIGURE 5. World temperature has been warming and will continue to warm, due primarily to our release of CO_2 and other greenhouse gases into the atmosphere. Shown are (a) the overall global, land, and sea surface temperatures from 1906 to 2005; (b) the increasing concentration of atmospheric CO_2 as measured at Mauna Loa, from 1958 to the present; and (c) the individual trends of temperature for six world regions from 1906 to 2005. Each climate plot shows observed temperature

of all these people is a prodigious task, and every section had to gain approval because these reports are public documents that are meant to express the consensus view of the global science community.

That *only* four assessment reports have been produced over thirty years does not mean people have not been working hard, but the time required for the writing and publishing process means that what we were told by the IPCC in the fourth assessment was old news by the time it was released in 2007. This lag time should make the information in these reports of even more concern to readers, because the situation is changing quickly.

In the IPCC's third assessment report (2001), the question, "Is the Earth's climate changing?" was followed by "The answer is unequivocally 'Yes.'" Scientists do not write this way unless they are really certain of the result, and stating such an emphatic consensus from such a large number of scientists is definitely unusual. Intransigent political leaders, a tiny number of climate skeptics, and the media's belief in the need to always present both sides of every story have delayed our becoming aware of what climate scientists have known for a decade or more.

The synthesis report of the fourth IPCC assessment (2007) begins with the following statement: "Warming of the climate system is unequivocal, as is now evident from observations of increases in global average air and ocean temperatures, widespread melting of snow and ice and rising global average sea level." A figure beside this text shows strong upward trends in average global surface temperature and sea level since 1850 and a slight decrease in northern hemisphere snow cover. In

---

(ten-year mean, black line) plotted as the deviation from the mean temperature during 1900 to 1950. Also shown are results simulated by climate models using only natural (darker band) or both natural and anthropogenic forcings (lighter band). In every case, the observations fit more closely the simulations that include anthropogenic factors. Temperature graphs in parts (*a*) and (*c*) are redrawn from figure SPM.4 in *Climate Change 2007: Synthesis Report. Contribution of Working Groups I, II, and III to the Fourth Assessment Report of the Intergovernmental Panel on Climate Change,* published by IPCC, Geneva, Switzerland. CO_2 record in part (*b*) is redrawn from the Mauna Loa atmospheric CO_2 record on the website of the National Oceanographic and Atmospheric Administration's Earth System Research Laboratory, Boulder, Colorado: www.esrl.noaa.gov/gmd/ccgg/trends/#mlo_full.

fact, if we consider average annual global temperature[10] as the measure, the ten warmest years on record until 2009 include all nine years from 2001 to 2009, while 2000 ranks fourteenth (data from NOAA National Climate Data Center State of the Climate reports). Put another way, of the one hundred thirty years with adequate records up to and including 2009, the ten warmest all occurred within the last fourteen years (1998 plus 2001 to 2009). If I was a betting man, I'd wager my life on the fact that the earth is getting warmer. As I proof this manuscript, 2010, which started out warm in my part of the world but then cooled in late summer, looks like it will be tied with 1998 as the second-warmest year on record. It looks like the trend is continuing.

Not only have recent years all been warm. The upward trend in temperature appears to be increasing, and the IPCC fourth assessment reports that the trend during the fifty years between 1956 and 2006, 0.13°C per decade, was nearly twice that of the trend over the one hundred years from 1906 to 2006 (0.07°C per decade). This increase in the rate of warming is what we might expect given the increase in the rate at which CO_2 concentrations are increasing. In other words, the situation is getting worse more quickly.

If we turn to regional temperature, the complexity increases. Polar regions are warming substantially more rapidly than more tropical regions, and land areas are warming more rapidly than oceans (see Figure 5). Yet the oceans have taken up about 80 percent of the extra heat being added to the earth system (it takes more heat to warm water than air), and if the world were a drier place, we'd be a lot warmer than we are. There is also variation from year to year both globally and locally. The temperatures from 1998 averaged across the globe were warmer than from any year before or since, and 2009—relatively cool in eastern North America—was still one of the hottest on record globally. People experiencing a cool summer, or politicians talking to those people, frequently see a warming climate as not exactly the most pressing problem they confront.

10. NOAA data are quoted here, but global average temperatures, whether calculated by NOAA or the IPCC, are a rigorous extrapolation from numerous weather stations across the world (currently about two thousand), including terrestrial and marine stations. The IPCC has carefully evaluated the procedures used and has expressed high confidence in the use of this statistic as a simple way of stating the average condition on Earth for a given year.

Late in 2009, a group of twenty-six leading climate scientists, including many lead authors of chapters in the fourth IPCC report, published a scary document, *The Copenhagen Diagnosis, 2009: Updating the World on the Latest Climate Science*. Sixty pages long, it began as follows:

> Global carbon dioxide emissions from fossil fuels in 2008 were nearly 40% higher than those in 1990. Over the past 25 years temperatures have increased at a rate of 0.19°C per decade, in very good agreement with predictions based on greenhouse gas increases. A wide array of satellite and ice measurements now demonstrate beyond doubt that both the Greenland and Antarctic ice-sheets are losing mass at an increasing rate. Summer-time melting of Arctic sea-ice has accelerated far beyond the expectations of climate models. (It has recently been melting about 40% faster than models had predicted back in 2007.) Satellites show recent global average sea-level rise (3.4 mm/yr over the past 15 years) to be ~80% above past IPCC predictions. By 2100, global sea-level is likely to rise at least twice as much as projected by Working Group 1 of the IPCC, in the 4th report.

Look at the adjectives used, the lack of qualifiers to give wiggle room *(approximately, more or less, other things being equal)*, and the extent of overshoot reported. Scientists do not write this way unless the data are exceptionally clear. We have a very serious problem on our hands.

FUTURE CLIMATES: THE NEXT FEW DECADES

The modest changes in temperature and other climate factors that have been reported to date make it difficult to convey the urgency of the situation. Most people do not yet appreciate how an average change of a degree or so will have profound effects on climate, on agriculture, and on our way of life. The changes also impact natural systems in diverse ways, and these changes are not stopping—remember that accelerating rate of increase in CO_2 concentration: 0.07 parts per million (ppm) per decade, then 0.13, and now 0.19. The projections for future warming and consequent climate modification are one of the most important products of the IPCC and worth serious reflection, especially given that what was projected in the fourth IPCC report is almost certainly less severe than what now appears likely.

When it comes to predicting the future, the IPCC approach has been to develop a series of scenarios that deal with likely changes in the pattern of greenhouse gas emissions and therefore in the concentrations of these gases in the atmosphere. Our release of greenhouse gases depends upon the extent of energy use, the type of energy we use, and on other activities we engage in, such as deforestation and land clearing. These in turn depend upon such things as human population growth, growth in GDP, the level of economic development, and the extent of discrepancy in average wealth of people in developed and developing countries. A series of forty coherent, quantitative scenarios was developed by the IPCC, falling into four families that have generally similar assumptions about these socioeconomic issues. The A1 family is the largest, including seventeen scenarios that describe a future world of rapid economic growth and a global population that rises until midcentury and then declines again. While they all describe a rapid introduction of newer, more energy-efficient technologies, they are divided into three groups that differ on the details of this transition. The B1 family of nine scenarios describes a world with the same global population trajectory as in the A1 family but with rapid shifts toward a service and information economy, with reduced resource-intensive activities and the introduction of clean and resource-efficient technologies. The A2 (six scenarios) and B2 (eight scenarios) families are intermediate to these. Six of the forty scenarios have been chosen (one for each group within A1, one each for the other families) as illustrative scenarios in most IPCC modeling. These span the range of likely trajectories with the A1FI scenario, which features continued reliance on fossil fuels, showing the highest output of greenhouse gases, while the B1 scenario, with its rapid shift to carbon-free energy sources, shows the lowest output. By adopting this approach, the IPCC is able to display a series of possible futures depending on specific socioeconomic assumptions, rather than pretending to predict the future—almost certainly an impossibility.

By running a climate model and inputting one of these scenarios to specify changes in greenhouse gases, it is possible to generate climate projections globally or locally at various times into the future. Obviously results become less precise the further into the future they are projected, and the IPCC has seldom projected beyond 2100. By using multiple climate models and multiple scenarios (the usual IPCC practice), it is possible to generate a range of likely future outcomes and to compare the effects on outcomes of particular scenarios. When this is done for average world temperature from 2090 to 2099, results range from 1.8°C (B1 scenario) to 4.0°C (A1F1 scenario) warming relative to temperatures from 1980 to 1999.

These temperature increases, like the high temperatures already measured in recent years, do not seem very great to most people, but remember the transition from the Medieval Warm Period to the Little Ice Age involved a change of less than 1°C in average annual temperature. The *most optimistic* IPCC prediction for the end of this century is twice as big. These changes in temperature have profound impacts on many aspects of climate and can lead to significant alterations in world ecology and in our quality of life and economic prosperity.

The IPCC's fourth assessment does a good job of exploring likely climate changes during the present century. To begin with, there is the climate change to which we are already committed. Even if we halted the release of all greenhouse gases this afternoon, the increase in atmospheric concentrations that has already occurred would produce a temperature increase of about 0.1°C per decade through this century—it takes that long for the planet's increased retention of heat due to the changed atmosphere to equilibrate across ocean, land, and atmosphere. We need to be anticipating close to half a degree more warmth by 2050 even if we stop releases of greenhouse gases right now, and we know we are not doing that.

On top of this inevitable warming, there is the warming that will occur because of our further additions of greenhouse gases to the atmosphere. This is somewhere in the range of 2 to 4°C. And increased temperature affects other aspects of climate as well. The warming will vary among regions; it will lead to a more energetic atmosphere with more wind and more intense windstorms; there will be changed patterns of rainfall and increased melting of ice and snow, with concomitant rises in sea level. All of these changes have begun—the evidence is all around us. Then there are the other influences on the water cycle such as reduced snow melt, increased evaporation from the land and ocean surface, increased transpiration by plants, increased aridity and desertification, and changes in river flows, lake levels, and extent of wetlands.

Warming is expected to be most severe over continents and in far northern latitudes and least severe over the southern oceans and Antarctica. Snow cover area will diminish, and Arctic sea ice will disappear seasonally within a few decades. With these reductions in ice and snow, the earth's surface will absorb more of the light hitting it, so that the production of heat will increase more rapidly—a classic positive feedback mechanism that has been resulting in temperature changes in Canada's far north that regularly exceed the earlier projections from the IPCC and require frequent adjustments of climate models. The warming of northern Canada and Siberia is resulting in melting of the permafrost, the extensive, permanently frozen ground of these regions. With that thaw comes the release of an as yet unknown quantity of methane, a potent greenhouse gas, and the start of another positive feedback loop. The world's temperature is going to continue to rise at an increasing rate as this century progresses. Bad things are going to happen faster than we expect because of this.

There are other interesting (that is, alarming) possibilities. Sea level is rising because of both thermal expansion of the warming ocean waters and the melting of glaciers, although the fourth assessment is uncertain about the precise rate and extent of sea level rise under various scenarios. Sea ice, such as that found in the Arctic, does not change sea level as it melts because it is already floating. Thermal expansion will continue for several centuries because of the very slow mixing processes that will distribute heat throughout ocean waters. The melting of glaciers across the world appears likely to be the biggest immediate problem. It will lead to global sea level increase, and the rate of melting appears to be significantly faster than scientists had predicted based on information gained in the less-warm years of the twentieth century. Greenland is currently losing an estimated 300 cubic km of ice per year—which creates a lot of water. If all of Greenland's glaciers were to melt—an increasingly likely situation given expected temperatures later this century—sea level would increase 7 meters. This was the situation that prevailed during the last interglacial, 125,000 years ago. Add in some melting in Antarctica, and the situation gets a lot worse. Even a 1-meter rise in mean sea level will flood major cities, devastate many coastal communities, and submerge a number of island nations. Don't buy land in Florida.[11]

11. Melting of glaciers creates yet another problem. Many important rivers, such as the Indus, the Ganges, and the Yangtze in Asia, the Rhône in Europe, and the Columbia and Yukon in North America, are fed by glaciers. They are going to decline in flow or even dry up without this water, and agricultural regions that depend on meltwater from glaciers and snow in the uplands are going to become more arid.

Scientists had not seen glaciers that were melting rapidly until recently, and it turns out that ice does not melt only on the glacier's surface. Instead, surface meltwater tends to tunnel through the glacier mass and collect as rivers underneath, melting the inside and bottom of the glacier as well as its surface. James Hansen has recently argued that there is a real risk of portions of a large glacier in Greenland or Antarctica breaking off, sliding rapidly downhill on its lubricating cushion of meltwater, and plunging into the ocean. If an event of this type occurred, there would be a catastrophically sudden rise in sea level, a small but global flood. While we have mostly experienced gradual change in climatic conditions (at least as it appears to us; the current pace is exceptionally rapid in a geologic time frame), there may be some sudden, unpleasant surprises in store for us.[12]

The changing temperatures are going to have significant impacts on patterns of rainfall, but IPCC data still are relatively imprecise about changes to rainfall patterns because the complexity of processes driving the changes is greater than that for temperature. Three things will happen to rainfall. Warmer temperatures over tropical oceans are going to result in increased evaporation from the ocean surface, putting more water into the atmosphere that is then available to fall as rain. The more dynamic (windier) atmosphere means that global patterns of monsoonal rainfall are going to shift so that the rain arrives in different places and times than it does now. Warmer temperatures over continents are going to increase rates of evaporation (and transpiration), meaning that the rain that falls is going to be put back into the atmosphere faster, resulting in a drier environment than at present, when much water remains on the surface or in groundwater. Put together, these three factors

12. Those who scoff at the possibility of a large piece of glacier breaking off and slip-sliding downhill into the ocean should ponder the following: An asteroid hit the Yucatán peninsula at the end of the Cretaceous with devastating effects worldwide. Vesuvius erupted explosively over two days in A.D. 79, showering Pompeii with hot ash that suffocated and entombed the inhabitants almost before they had time to stop doing whatever they were doing. Mount Saint Helens erupted so forcefully on the morning of 18 May 1980 that the blast pressure flattened forests as far as 30 km away in minutes, and people such as USGS volcanologist David Johnson, who was taking measurements 10 km away, were killed instantly by the heat and blast. The 9.2-magnitude earthquake off Sumatra, Indonesia, on 26 December 2004 generated a tsunami that raced across the Indian Ocean to the shores of Africa, bringing death and destruction to coastal communities across a quarter of the earth's circumference. Bad things happen suddenly, on a large scale, without much warning.

ensure that water will cycle more rapidly from atmosphere to surface and back, that rain may fall in different places and in different seasons, and that rainfall patterns will change. There will still be a monsoon, but its new location hundreds of kilometers away will not help the rice farmer dependent on it.

THE EFFECTS ON OCEAN CLIMATE

The world's oceans are the other half of the climate engine because of their capacity to store heat and absorb gases. While surface waters are warm, the bulk of ocean water is cold, and the very slow oceanic mixing processes mean that the oceans will continue to take heat (and CO_2) out of the atmosphere over the next thousand years. Unfortunately, we cannot wait a thousand years for the oceans to correct our mistakes. Surface waters have also absorbed about half the CO_2 we have released into the atmosphere, but the absorption of CO_2 has special consequences for ocean water.

As CO_2 concentration in the ocean increases, the CO_2 reacts chemically with the water to produce hydrogen (H^+) and bicarbonate (HCO_3^-) ions, and the pH of the ocean falls. This "ocean acidification" is quite trivial at first glance—about 0.1 pH unit (from 8.2 to 8.1) since the start of the Industrial Revolution. It's likely to get down to pH 7.9 or 7.8 by 2050, still on the alkaline side of neutral.[13] The ocean is not turning into lemon juice.

However, just as the slight changes in average world temperature are proving to have substantial impacts on climate and agriculture and therefore on human lives, these minute changes in pH will have profound effects on calcification processes in the ocean. As pH is reduced, the saturation state of calcium carbonate ($CaCO_3$) is reduced, meaning that $CaCO_3$ becomes more soluble. As a result, calcification—effectively the taking of $CaCO_3$ out of solution—requires more energy to be accomplished. Calcification is the process by which corals build reefs. It also is involved in the building of skeletons by a broad range of other sea creatures: mollusks, echinoderms, bryozoans, coralline algae,

13. The pH scale is a logarithmic one, so the drop from a pH of 8.2 in pre-industrial times to 8.1 today actually represents about a 30 percent increase in the "acidity" of the ocean, although seawater remains well on the basic side of neutral (pH = 7.0).

and many other taxa, including a number of common phytoplankton and zooplankton. In short, the great majority of marine creatures with shells or skeletons will become compromised in their ability to build these essential body parts. What happens then?

Coral reefs give us some insight, because the chemical and physiological processes involved in calcification and skeleton building by corals are well studied. As will be discussed in chapter 4, there is now evidence that some corals are growing more slowly than they did as little as twenty years ago, with profound results for reef ecosystems. The impacts of acidification, however, are likely to be even more profound for open-ocean and coastal ecosystems that depend upon phytoplankton production to power their economies. As yet, scientists know too little about the calcification process in such species or how it may respond to acidification. Major planktonic groups such as the forams and coccolithophores are going to become uncommon or rare if their ability to grow their carbonate skeletons is compromised.[14] At present, the data on effects of acidification are sparse. Most marine organisms that have been tested are less able to produce their skeletons (or they produce thinner skeletons) in water with lower pH levels; however, the extent of this effect varies among species. Some are scarcely affected while others show a very strong response. When organisms such as coccolithophores, at the very base of oceanic food webs, or forams, close to this base, are compromised in their ability to grow, we can anticipate substantial changes in overall biological activity and productivity. Fishery yield is likely to be hit, but we are not yet in a position to assess the degree of this impact.

The effect of pH on calcification processes varies from place to place across the world's surface waters because temperature also plays a role.

14. Coccolithophores (phylum Haplophyta) are nearly spherical photosynthesizing cells less than 0.02 mm in diameter. They are so abundant that, despite their small size, they play a major role in oceanic primary production. Each cell is covered by a set of calcareous plates, the coccoliths. Foraminifera, or forams (phylum Sarcomastigophora), are much larger, mostly around 1 mm in diameter, although some species can be more than 1 cm across. These are amoeboid protists that feed on smaller plankton. Each is encased in a calcareous test, or shell, often of quite beautiful design. Both coccolithophores and forams have been abundant over long geological time and are prominent microfossils; their skeletons can be so abundant that they produce a fine-grained limestone, such as found on the white cliffs of Dover. On reefs, forams can be abundant in shallow water, and their skeletons contribute substantially to those idyllic white sand beaches that we associate with the tropics.

In general, it is more difficult to build calcareous skeletons in cooler temperate regions than in tropical regions because the $CaCO_3$ is less soluble (that is, easier to take out of solution and incorporate into a skeleton) at higher temperatures. However, calcification is becoming more difficult in all locations as pH declines. Modeling studies have shown how tropical surface waters, where coral reefs occur, were quite conducive to calcification in pre-industrial times. The zone of excellent calcification has progressively diminished so that at present many coral reefs are bathed by waters that are only marginally conducive to calcification. By 2050, assuming the concentration of CO_2 in the atmosphere reaches 450 to 500 ppm, most reefs will lie in waters in which calcification is a slow and energetically demanding process.

Another consequence of climate change on the world's oceans concerns the deep ocean and anoxia. Our present oceans are well stratified: warm water is at the surface, and cold but well-oxygenated water is below. Surface waters cooled in the Antarctic, north Atlantic, and north Pacific sink and carry oxygen down to deep layers, eventually dispersing this oxygen to all parts of the deep ocean. Oceans have not always been like this. On many occasions in past epochs, the deep ocean has been anoxic and occasionally also high in concentration of sulfur dioxide (SO_2) and even hydrogen sulfide (H_2S). Such periods of low oxygen and high sulfur content tend to occur during or immediately following periods of warm temperatures or high atmospheric CO_2. These periods are believed to play a substantial role in mass extinction events, most notably the End Permian event, in which nearly all oceanic species became extinct.

One plausible mechanism for shifting the ocean toward anoxia begins with an increase in greenhouse gases (through major volcanism or human activities, as is occurring today). This leads to higher temperatures and greater rates of biological productivity in surface waters. At the same time, the warmer temperatures mean that near-polar surface waters are less cold and therefore less capable of carrying dissolved oxygen than they are today. These warmer surface waters may also be less prone to sinking, as I will discuss in a moment. They likely continue to sink but do so more slowly, carrying less oxygen into the depths. Meanwhile, the heightened productivity in surface waters yields a greater drift into deep water of dead organic matter that uses oxygen as it decomposes. The result is local, then regional, and ultimately widespread anoxia. There are three signs that we may be now on the first steps of this pathway: (1) the size and number of "dead zones" in continental shelf waters such as off the mouth of the Mississippi River and in the Black Sea are growing;[15] (2) there is a pronounced warming of surface waters in the north Atlantic; and (3) the oxygen minimum layer, typically at 200 to 1,000 meter depth, is expanding. Because the global ocean is so immense, processes are usually slow and happen over what are by human standards long periods of time. If we are moving toward deep anoxia, it will likely take several thousand years, which makes this not an immediate concern compared to the other aspects of global climate change that we seem to have initiated. But it is still important for creatures that live in the deep ocean!

A related problem concerns the potential slowing or stopping of major ocean currents. The Gulf Stream is such a major current. It is a surface component of what is called the global ocean conveyor, a system of major surface and bottom currents in the oceans of the world that transports water and its associated heat, dissolved oxygen, and other components. The Gulf Stream transports warm, salty water from the Caribbean up to the north Atlantic, where it cools and releases its heat to the atmosphere. In this way, it transports heat and substantially ameliorates the climate of the north Atlantic and Western Europe. As this salty water becomes cooler, it also becomes denser, dense enough to sink below the less salty water from the Arctic Ocean. This "thermohaline" sinking transports oxygen to the deep waters of the Atlantic and very slowly to other parts of the world and acts as a major driver, almost a pump, for the global ocean conveyor. Critical to the operation of this pump is the relative temperature differential among Gulf Stream water, Arctic water, and the atmosphere. Some oceanographers fear that global warming due to greenhouse gases may be sufficient to make the less-salty Arctic water warm enough to float on top of the salty but still warmer Gulf Stream water, thereby restricting the opportunity for heat to be lost to the atmosphere but also slowing or halting the sinking of the no-longer-cooled

15. Dead zones result from excess nutrification of surface waters due to agriculture and pollution, which stimulates excessive primary production in surface waters. The resulting rain of dead and dying organisms into deeper water stimulates microbial decomposition processes that initially use up all dissolved oxygen. This creates an anoxic environment with microbially driven anaerobic decomposition processes predominating, usually releasing sulfur as SO_2 or H_2S.

Gulf Stream waters. If there is no sinking, there is no possibility for more Gulf Stream water to move north and no chance to deliver all that heat. The North Atlantic and Europe would cool down, even though the global climate continued to warm. Is the global ocean conveyor now stalling? Some data during the first years of this century suggested it was, but more recent data suggest it may not be . . . yet. It has happened in the geological past, and it could happen again, but at present this issue is just one more ticking time bomb waiting to go off.

The ocean–atmosphere climate engine is a complicated one with many parts, all linked by multiple processes. It does not run like clockwork. Good clocks keep impeccable time. In contrast, this engine shows a pattern of performance that wanders about. The wandering is undoubtedly due to perfectly understandable processes, but they are complicated ones, and we do not yet fully understand them. This engine is exquisitely sensitive to slight differences in temperature or salinity of water masses and to differences in temperature between the sea surface and the atmosphere. It is also definitely sensitive to the chemical composition of the atmosphere. When atmospheric chemistry changes, there are usually commensurate changes in patterns of heating. These in turn set off a suite of other changes that alter rainfall, change patterns of wind and storms, shift dynamics of glaciers and sea ice, change sea level, and even alter the strength of major oceanic currents, including those that distribute heat away from the tropics.

Such intricate systems, with their positive and negative feedback loops and their sensitive responses to changing conditions, are precisely the types that yield unexpected and sometimes suddenly changed outcomes. Just as we have been overtaxing the capacity of oceanic ecosystems to provide us with fishery resources and the capacity of forest ecosystems to provide our timber and other products, we have been overtaxing the capacity of our atmosphere to absorb the CO_2 and other greenhouse gases that our economies are generating and that we wanted to simply throw away. In all three instances, we can see evidence (less clearly so far for the atmosphere) that our overtaxing has shifted each system toward sets of conditions that may lead to rapid and potentially irrecoverable change. And the new ecological conditions that will result may not be as suitable for us as the ones we have become used to.

·   ·   ·

The available data on climate change are growing rapidly, increasing our knowledge of what is happening, strengthening our models of what may happen, and clarifying both the severity of the likely changes in climate and the urgency with which we must deal with them. As I was finishing the first draft of this chapter in December 2009, the Copenhagen climate change conference was under way. Science and politics do not find life easy when they get into bed together, and recognition of the climate change problem and its likely consequences for people around the world gets pushed aside by the usual political jockeying for advantage (economic and otherwise) among nation-states. Prior to the conference, both the United States and China announced plans to curb emissions of greenhouse gases, and while these announcements were generally welcomed, they both fell well short of what the science tells us is needed.[16] Canada, meanwhile, was a distinctly reluctant participant, even though a majority of its citizens recognize the need for action and express frustration with their government and the opposition parties for not treating climate as an important issue. By the time of Copenhagen, Canada had committed to reducing emissions by 3 percent below 1990 levels by 2050—very far behind the reductions the science says are needed. And Canada is proving to be a master of backpedaling.

Along the way to Copenhagen, the precautionary principle seems to have been forgotten. Time and again, whether in fisheries management, forest conservation management, pollution control, or other instances when environmental sustainability or human health is at stake, we have learned that it is best to adopt a precautionary stance. Take all the actions that appear to be needed even if, subsequently, further scientific study shows it would have been safe to do less. The alternative approach—to not act until the science shows beyond question that action is needed—is a recipe for disaster, and a path we have taken far too often. This is the path we have trod through 2010. I hope we find a better path soon.

16. Just prior to Copenhagen, the United States pledged to cut emissions by 17 percent from 2005 levels by 2020—equivalent to 4 percent from 1990 levels and well below the EU pledge of 20 percent from 1990. China pledged a cut in *carbon intensity* of 45 percent from 2005 levels by 2020. Carbon intensity is a measure of the rate per unit of production at which an economy releases carbon to the environment rather than a measure of the absolute rate of emissions. Given China's rapidly growing economy, this is a pledge only to have emissions *increase* at a slower rate.

4

THE PERILOUS FUTURE
FOR CORAL REEFS

It was a clear, sunny day in the summer of 1973. Summer days are usually sunny on the southern Great Barrier Reef, but in truth, the winds had been up for the past couple of days, and diving conditions were marred by reduced visibility. I was at 15 feet, motionless, watching my fish and writing on my Plexiglas slate. I'd spent a lot of time over the last couple of years at this spot on the edge of Heron Reef, directly south of the Heron Island Research Station. I was investigating real estate transactions, of a sort. I was alone, or thought I was.[1]

I call them "my fish" because I knew them as individuals: a group of around thirty fish of three species of damselfishes (Pomacentridae). They were herbivores, territorial, and pugnacious in defending their individual plots of ground where the algal turf they fed on flourished. The algae flourished because the damselfishes were so good at defending their feeding grounds from other fish: parrotfish, surgeonfish, and, yes, their damselfish neighbors. They had divided up all the space in a 50-square-meter patch of dead coral plates and rubble formed long ago

Facing page: Reef seascape in Palau, November 2007. Photo courtesy of R. S. Steneck.

1. Coral reef scientists used to dive alone routinely, before the diving safety nannies forced dive buddies upon us. Now we follow approved if overdone protocols, but in truth, the diving buddy is often out of sight, making his or her own observations. Same-boat, same-ocean buddy diving! The safety rules have doubled the data we collect!

when a storm cut down the branching corals that had been growing there. My interest was in how the three different species had divided up the space. What were the rules? What were the mechanisms? I was studying coral reefs precisely because they offered me complex ecological communities in which I could pose such questions and then try to find the answers. (And also because I felt at home in a reef environment in a way I should perhaps not even try to describe.) I was not studying human impacts on coral reefs. Like most other reef ecologists of that day, I thought human impacts were something to avoid—we studied "natural" systems because we wanted to know how these systems worked in their natural state, that is, without human interference.

In any event, there I was, motionless in mid-water, being a scientist, and I got a feeling that there was something behind me. I was out from the reef face, looking in toward it. Behind me was the open water of the Heron-Wistari channel, seventy to eighty feet deep, with strong tidal currents and large tiger sharks that fed on the kitchen garbage regularly discarded in mid-channel by the Heron Island resort. I'd seen the sharks from the garbage boat. They were much bigger than I.

I was certain there was something behind me and decided, even though I was intent on watching neighborly disputes, to turn around. About forty eyes, arranged in an arc from my right to my left, motionless, were staring at me. The poor visibility made the creature a bit obscure in the gloom, but the eyes gradually resolved into pairs behind face masks, with regulators and bubbles. The resort dive master, having found visibility poor that day, had led his group of tourists into the shallows and, desperate to find something for them to see, had brought them past the scientist. I gave what I hoped was a friendly but uninviting wave and turned back to my fish. I had work to do. And doing it with an audience of tourists behind me was almost as bad as if there had been sharks back there, but I was not an arresting subject, and they moved on after a minute or two.

Looking back, I realize I threw away a chance to communicate the real nature of science to the public. I should have risen to the surface for quick introductions and arranged a date to meet on dry land later to talk about the fish, the science, and why reefs were worth caring about. I'd like to think I learned a lesson that day, but I fear it took me several lost opportunities to learn it properly. This book is one of the results, and in this chapter I say quite a bit more about the coral reef ecosystem than I would have told those tourists. Now, nearly forty years later, I have not only come to know a good deal more about this important ecosystem, I have also grown very concerned that we are on the verge of eliminating it from the planet. Accordingly, I focus on how and why we are degrading coral reefs so severely and highlight the clear lessons I think we can learn from this particular canary in the environmental coal mine. But to fully appreciate what we are at risk of losing, I will first outline what coral reefs are ecologically, and why they are wondrous natural phenomena that enrich our world. It's not yet too late for coral reefs, but they belong on an IUCN ecosystem Red List.[2] Let's begin with those fish I was watching.

THE COMPLEX CORAL REEF ECOSYSTEM

My three species of property owner, all relatively nondescript drab brown fish without common names, are currently known by people as *Stegastes apicalis, Stegastes wardi,* and *Plectroglyphidodon lacrymatus.* They are three members of a guild of about thirty species of territorial damselfishes with representatives throughout the tropics and into the temperate zone, where they live on rocky reefs. They belie the name *damselfish,* which more properly belongs to the much larger guild, also circumtropical, of planktivorous damselfishes—smaller, daintier, and more brightly colored. These hover in large groups to feed on plankton streaming by, the damselflies of the reef. I'm certain that if my fish ever think of themselves, they do not use those names, but we are stuck with them. *Apicalis* grows to the largest size (about 15 cm), *lacrymatus* is slightly smaller, and little *wardi* barely ever makes it to 10 cm. *Apicalis* and *lacrymatus* can easily reach ten to fifteen years in age, although here again *wardi* does well to reach half that. Each individual spends most of its life within a small territory of up to 1 square meter in area, patrolling the borders and chasing away intruders. They even nip at the spines of sea urchins to encourage them to move along and not graze that particular algal patch.

2. The International Union for Conservation of Nature, IUCN, publishes a Red List of species worldwide that have been evaluated by experts and are considered to be threatened with serious population decline or extinction. No such list exists for ecosystems, but if it did, coral reefs would be on it.

I visited that group of thirty fish and two similar groups nearby multiple times over a two- to three-week period every two to four months for three years. On each visit, for an hour or two (a tank of air lasts a long time at 15 feet), I would watch what was going on. And I would note my observations on a map of the patch. In this way, by seeing where each individual would "stand and fight," I determined the boundaries of each territory as clearly as if each fish had built a little white picket fence. I was particularly interested in what happened as juvenile fish grew in size or after fish died, because that is when real estate changed hands. And, being a scientist, I supplemented these observations with experiments in still other patches in which I used small spears, powered by a rubber band held between the fingers, to kill and remove territory holders, to watch what happened next.

Over three years, these fish educated me about how different but similar species really share the resources of their environment. Resource sharing was not done in the way I had been taught at school. These three species had such similar requirements that spaces in that patch were suitable for occupancy by a member of any of the three species, and coexistence depended to a significant degree on luck.[3] It took me some time and more research on groups of fish that shared small coral patches to get my head around this idea, but I was in time to participate in an amazing revolution in how ecologists understand the functioning of ecological communities—a subject we will visit in detail in chapter 6 because it has important lessons for how we understand our impacts on the natural world.

The details of any particular study are less important than the general principles I learned along the way. While I had always suspected it, my time watching fish on reefs has amply confirmed that these systems are neighborhoods in which the individual organisms have places they occupy, often on quite specific daily schedules. They use these places for specific purposes and share them with other individuals of myriad species whom they know as individuals and recognize as belong-

---

3. In the 1970s, a central tenet of community ecology was that each species had sufficiently distinct requirements so that competition for resources, such as habitat space, was primarily among members of the same species rather than different species. This harks back to Gause's studies of protist populations and the axiom that each species has a unique niche (see chapter 6). My studies were among those that chipped away at this belief.

ing. (Don't misinterpret. I am not attributing consciousness and deep thought to fish and crabs only centimeters in length, but I am claiming that the individuals that belong in a place recognize and accept as also belonging other individuals of multiple species.) Over those three years I spent watching the damselfish, I am confident that my fish recognized and put up with me.

I know they accepted one particular green turtle, an old female with a missing rear flipper. She used to drift past slowly in the early afternoons, traveling on the tide along the front of the reef, doing nothing in particular (unless she was enjoying the sunshine). She had a dense growth of algae on her upper shell, due no doubt to her age and her tendency to stay in the shallows, and my fish would stop whatever they were doing as she passed, swim up the several meters necessary, and browse across her shell together, not fighting, just for a few minutes, then go back down to homes with borders that needed defending. If you know any of the herbivorous damselfishes that occur throughout the tropics, you will recognize that grazing peacefully side by side is not typical behavior for any of them.[4] Nor is swimming a couple of meters above the substratum, where they risk being picked off by some large piscivore and turned into dinner. So, not only are the occupants of these neighborhoods members of highly structured communities, they are also capable of adapting to unusual circumstances. If an ice cream truck happens to float by in the form of an old three-flippered turtle, the neighbors recognize it is party time.

One of my regular field companions during those years at Heron Island was Ross Robertson. Then a graduate student at the University of Queensland, he went on to a stellar career at the Smithsonian Tropical Research Institute in Panama, where he still spends hours watching fish do what they do. At Heron Island, Ross was studying the cleaner wrasse, *Labroides dimidiatus,* a much more photogenic fish than my three and one that makes its living by removing parasites from the surfaces of larger fishes. Ross, who spent so much time in the water that his beard

4. My late colleague Art Myrberg of the University of Miami, a man who knew the behavior of territorial damselfishes better than most, referred to the three-spot damselfish of Caribbean waters as "pound for pound the most dangerous fish in the sea." The three-spot aggressively nips at divers' face masks and regulators, chews on their hair, and generally gets in their faces, despite being only about 12 cm long.

developed a distinct green tinge one summer, followed cleaner wrasses about. He found that the male fishes occupied much larger home ranges than the females and that each male patrolled his home range, following definite paths between particular "cleaning stations" where he would spend some time with the female or females present before moving on to the next stop on his daily path. The males were sultans, and their wives were scattered among a set of harems (or maybe they were just polygamist truckers with wives in every town). And every truckstop, or harem, was also recognized by other species as a place to get cleaned. There is something uncanny about a perfectly tasty, bite-sized cleaner wrasse entering the mouth of a large grouper or snapper, cleaning around its teeth, swimming farther in to pick parasites off the gill arches, and emerging through its gills—all while the larger fish patiently assists, rolling on its side, opening its mouth or operculum, moving its pectoral fins to provide access to its fishy armpits. How is such cooperative behavior learned—or is it? In any event, Ross Robertson's work, like mine, revealed the rich detail of the relationships among individuals that characterize the coral reef. The web of behavioral relationships that Ross and I saw is just one part of the very dense network of interrelationships among organisms that is the coral reef.

My conversations with ecologists who study other ecosystems and an abundant published record confirm that the coral reef is not unique in this degree of organization of individual relationships, although it is unique in many other ways. Ecological communities are complex assemblages of organisms of many different species living together in a particular place and interacting in ways that make sense. The web of interactions facilitates the processes that keep an ecosystem being what it is while providing the positive and negative feedback loops that are one of the fundamental properties of all ecosystems—just as they are of the ocean–atmosphere climate engine. Much as the ocean–atmosphere engine is prone to wandering, ecosystems wander rather than maintain a stationary, constant structure, and, also like the ocean–atmosphere engine, they are capable of wandering far enough that they reach tipping points and suddenly become very different from what they were before. Unfortunately, humanity is now impacting the natural world in many ways that variously impede the capacity of ecosystems to continue doing what they do, threatening their ability to provide goods and services upon which we and other species depend.

THE LUCK OF CORAL REEFS

If you fly from Los Angeles to Sydney or Brisbane and are fortunate to look out the window at the right time on a cloudless day, you may see a sea-green necklace floating on the Pacific waves. It's a coral atoll, one of the many strewn across the Pacific, and it's one of the most amazing natural phenomena on this planet. You have to be lucky to see it, and luck, good or bad, is a fundamental characteristic of coral reefs, whether they form atolls or the more widespread barrier and fringing reefs near continents.

"Every one," wrote Charles Darwin in 1842, "must be struck with astonishment when he first beholds one of these vast rings of coral-rock, often many leagues in diameter, here and there surmounted by a low verdant island with dazzling white shores, bathed on the outside by the foaming breakers of the ocean, and on the inside surrounding a calm expanse of water, which from reflection, is of a bright but pale green colour." Reefs and their associated sand cays (or keys) are the stuff of Robinson Crusoe tales, New Yorker cartoons about shipwrecked mariners, and winter vacations in the sun. The reefs themselves are perhaps the most gloriously improbable ecosystem on Earth. Their requirements are such that they can develop only in special places where temperature, depth, water quality, and clarity are all just right. They occupy just 0.1 percent of the total area of the world's oceans yet support about one-quarter of all marine species. Astoundingly rich and incredibly rare, they are also geologically ephemeral, and we are fortunate to live at a time when they are present.

A coral reef is a consolidated mass of limestone built up over time by the activities of a range of organisms that calcify, taking calcium dissolved in the water and combining it chemically with carbon and oxygen to create calcium carbonate ($CaCO_3$), or limestone. Major players in this calcification project are the corals themselves, but numerous mollusks, echinoderms, polychaete worms, crustaceans, protists such as the foraminifera, and coralline algae play important roles as well. In every case the $CaCO_3$ is used by the organism for skeletal support. Many calcifiers, including most corals, are colonial organisms. Their skeletons tend to have fine-scale structure in the form of cups or cells for individuals that are joined together in species-specific ways to produce a complex macro-scale architecture. They are often strangely beautiful, whether viewed under a microscope or from a distance. Other calcifiers live as solitary individuals, each with its own $CaCO_3$ skeleton. The foraminifera, for example, are predominantly solitary single-celled planktonic organisms, with fragile internal $CaCO_3$ skeletons that fall to the lagoonal floor at death, contributing to the sand that creates those white beaches. The mollusks are also solitary, but larger and with external skeletons, their shells. When they die, their shells, once broken up by wave action, also contribute to those sandy beaches. All the "rock" on a coral reef is biogenic—produced by calcifying organisms—except in rare cases where underlying basalt or granitic rock is exposed, where pumice has floated in from some distant eruption, or where new lava has flowed over the reef. Even the sand and mud is biogenic, although some coastal reefs will have these mixed with terriginous (from the land) sediments as well.

Reef-building corals are particularly rapid calcifiers because they are all really collaborations between a coral and a single-celled dinoflagellate alga called a zooxanthella, which lives within the cells of the coral animal. In a classic symbiosis, the coral uses energy provided by its algae to carry out calcification while the algae receive nutrients from the coral host. The algae generate that energy through photosynthesis, which explains why reef-building corals live only in shallow, clear water. (There are distantly related deep-water corals that lack zooxanthellae, produce their $CaCO_3$ skeletons much more slowly, and consequently do not build reefs of any consequence.)

With the exception of the mushroom corals (Fungiidae), reef builders are all colonial. The individual coral organism, or polyp, reproduces asexually by budding (splitting in two), and the pattern of budding results in a colony of specific form and branching pattern. Each polyp secretes its own $CaCO_3$ skeleton, which is fused to those of its neighbors to form the solid structure we recognize as the coral. The soft tissues of the polyps extend over the surface of the skeleton, joining to one another to create a continuous organic layer between the $CaCO_3$ skeleton and the water. Different species of coral have different patterns of budding, resulting in the diversity of forms on a reef: branching colonies of various types, flat platelike colonies, and almost spherical boulder colonies. Like all colonial organisms, corals are potentially immortal—even if a colony is severely damaged, the parts of it that survive can continue to grow and become replacement colonies.

In addition to budding, corals reproduce sexually by producing eggs and sperm within individual polyps. In so-called spawner species, these are released into the water, fertilization takes place, and minute larva are produced; in brooder species, the sperm is released to fertilize eggs within other polyps. The fertilized eggs then undergo some embryonic development before release into the water. Whether a coral species is a spawner or a brooder, the end result is a minute larval form that drifts in the water, settles to a hard substratum in a matter of hours to weeks, attaches itself, and begins the process of growing and budding to form a new colony.

Until the 1980s, scientists believed that the majority of coral species were brooders, because they found brooded eggs in polyps of some species and very little evidence of the spawner mode of reproduction. However, late in 1981 at a research facility on Magnetic Island, near Townsville, Australia, five graduate students (Peter Harrison, Russ Babcock, Jamie Oliver, Gordon Bull, and Bette Willis) made a sensational discovery. Studying coral reproduction with their mentor, Carden Wallace, they were culturing several different species of corals in aquaria. This can be painstaking work, even if it sounds like "fun in the sun."

In October, they noticed spawning in some aquaria five to eight nights after the full moon. A lunar month later, they observed spawning five nights after the mid-November full moon. In 1982 their corals only spawned once, but this was four or five nights after the full moon in early November. Their work and subsequent studies confirmed that the majority of coral species are spawners and that, at least on the Great Barrier Reef, spawning was remarkably synchronized, with the great majority of individuals of all spawner species reproducing on only one or two nights, five or so days following the full moon in November and occasionally also in October or December. In fact the bulk of spawning occurs about five nights following the largest spring tide of the year—which corresponds to the full moon and is usually in November. Wondrously improbable indeed. So wondrous that dive-tour operators now schedule night dives to see the corals spawn on those one or two special nights each year. Similar mass spawning occurs in other Indo-Pacific locations and in the Caribbean, but not necessarily on the same date as on the Great Barrier Reef, and in some places, such as the Caribbean, it is not quite so narrowly limited to one or two days. But enough about corals; this chapter is about reefs.

The reef, of course, is the full collection of coral colonies of different species and other calcifying organisms, which together form a complex mass of limestone with an architecture defined by the architecture of the various species, with cavities and lower horizontal surfaces filled with sand and rubble. A thin veneer of living tissue, whether of coral or coralline algae, covers most surfaces. Over time, the growth of corals and other organisms builds the reef up toward the surface of the sea but no farther, because these organisms cannot survive exposure to the air for any length of time. Under the most favorable conditions, when the substratum is sinking slowly relative to sea level, this upward growth can continue for many years, and the result is a thick mass of limestone comprised of all those old skeletons, with the living organisms over its surface. One of Darwin's major contributions to reef science was his hypothesis, subsequently largely vindicated, that fringing reefs, barrier reefs, and atolls are different stages in the gradual submersion of a (usually volcanic) island fringed by living reef. Drilling expeditions to various reefs, including the one at Heron Island, have documented the often hundreds of meters of limestone, all former coral and other calcifiers, underlying the modern reef. Of course, when the substratum is not subsiding or sea level is not rising, the opportunity for vertical growth is more limited and the limestone reef that develops will be thinner.

On coral reefs, the building process is not quite so simple as calcifiers building skeletons year after year. There is a continuing struggle between forces that break down the reef structure and forces that build it up. Calcification is the reef builder, while wave action, storms, and bioeroders are the main forces that wear it down. The bioeroders are a diverse group of species that scrape away at the surface (many parrotfishes, some sea urchins), drill through it, burrow into it, secrete acids to dissolve it, or otherwise tunnel out the reef from the inside (many worms, some mollusks, sponges, and other creatures). The reef grows up toward the light zooxanthellae need while the various destructive forces convert the limestone into sand and rubble, which is washed into holes and crevices toward the leeward side of the reef and very slowly dissolved.

The limited temperature tolerances of the corals keep reefs within the tropics. The zooxanthellae's need for light and the need of the corals to be fastened to a solid surface limit them to places where there is a rocky surface (which could be existing reef or other rock) no more than 40 meters or so below the surface of the sea. The need for light keeps reefs in clear water, and other water-quality needs of the corals restrict them to places that have open access to the sea and that lack serious pollution. Reefs grow best if the rocky substratum is subsiding slowly relative to sea level; they have less opportunity for growth if sea level is stationary relative to the substratum; and they are quickly killed if sea level falls or the substratum rises. They can also be killed if the substratum subsides too quickly for coral growth to keep the reef surface near the sea surface and light. Such "drowned" reefs occur on a number of sea mounts throughout the Pacific—they flourished during the Pleistocene when sea level was much lower than it is now but were drowned when sea level rose to near its present level.

Because reefs develop as a dynamic balance between calcification processes that add limestone and erosional processes that convert it to sand and rubble and then dissolve it away, any changes in the rates of calcification or erosion or to any one of the specific environmental requirements can cause the reef to die or fail to grow in the first place. It's not surprising that reefs occupy scarcely 0.1 percent of the world's ocean area. It's wondrous that they exist at all.

Reefs of one form or another have been present on Earth since the Precambrian. The earliest, first seen about 2 billion years ago, were structurally relatively simple hemispherical limestone mounds formed by stromatolites, a type of calcifying cyanobacteria, or blue-green algae. Stromatolites still exist in Western Australia and in the Bahamas—pillowlike mossy rocks that only a biologist could truly love. The earliest coral reefs (meaning that the primary calcifiers were corals) appeared in the early Ordovician, about 490 million years ago, and reefs have been present, off and on, ever since. I say "off and on" because there are some lengthy periods in which reefs appear not to have been present anywhere on Earth. In each such hiatus, some remnant species of corals survived to begin reef building again when conditions permitted.

The five largest mass extinctions (discussed in chapter 7) all affected coral reefs profoundly. Typically, the reef-building corals were among the first species to disappear, so that reefs were usually absent worldwide 0.5 to 1.5 million years before most other taxa succumbed, and each mass extinction was followed by a reef-free period as much as 10 million years in length. Modern reef-building corals (order Scleractinia) first appeared in the mid-Triassic, but reefs were globally absent for 6 to 8 million years following the End Triassic mass extinction. They flourished again through much of the Jurassic but became less extensive through much of the Cretaceous, and they disappeared completely for another 10 million years following the End Cretaceous mass extinction.[5] These global interruptions to reef growth are interesting: a hiatus of several million years suggests the conditions that caused the disappearance took a long time to be alleviated, and many other taxa did not experience such long interludes of relative absence. I will return to this punctuated history later in the chapter.

The complex limestone structures assembled by the calcifiers provide myriad opportunities for an enormous diversity of other species to find places to live and opportunities to feed. Among the fishes alone, there are planktivores that use the reef for shelter but shoal just above the reef's surface to feed on the plankton streaming by. There are fish that feed on organisms in the sands of lagoonal floors or in crevices in the reef structure. Some winnow mouthfuls of sand to extract minute crustaceans, while others detect larger mollusks or crabs just below the sand surface and grab them, letting the sand fall away from between their lips or through their gills. Some fish are specialized to feed on the coral polyps themselves or simply on the mucus that corals secrete to protect their outer surfaces. And of course there are fish that feed on other fish. There are fish that are active by day, by night, and only at dawn and dusk. There are fish specialized to live on every surface and within nearly every cavity on a reef—including one group of small fishes (the family Carapidae) that lives within the anal cavities of starfishes and sea cucumbers, returning home by swimming in reverse through the narrow orifice whenever danger threatens. The same exuberant diversity of lifestyles can be seen in every other major group of organisms, with the result that coral reefs are easily the most biodiverse environments on the planet.[6] An experienced biologist can consistently locate more than one hundred species of fish on a single dive on a Caribbean reef and more

5. In thinking about these periods of time, remember that our own genus, *Homo,* has been around only 2 million years. The scleractinian corals have been with us for about 240 million years, and their ancestors, the tabulate and rugose corals, take the lineage back almost 500 million years.

6. Paul Ehrlich of Stanford University long ago drew attention to this feature. While rainforests win the count of species hands down, supporting uncounted millions of species of insect, coral reefs have unrivaled diversity at the family, order, class, and phylum levels.

than two hundred species on a rich Pacific reef (the Pacific Ocean is far richer in reef organisms than the Caribbean). She or he can also locate representatives of all but three or four of all the animal phyla (the thirty or so major groups such as Echinoderms, Crustaceans, and Mollusks) found on the planet. With very few exceptions, every group of marine organisms occurs there in richness that is unrivaled in other environments, and many of these species have yet to be described by science. We have nothing resembling this concentration of richness on land.

So incredibly rich in species, coral reefs are located, paradoxically, in one of the most nutrient-poor deserts on Earth. The planktonic organisms and fishes that live in the surface waters of the tropical ocean drift to deeper waters when they die, if they are not eaten first, taking with them many of the nutrients they have acquired during their lives. As a consequence, there is a continuous removal to deeper waters of any nutrients that exist (and the colder deep waters do not mix easily with the warmer, less dense surface waters, so there is no easy way for nutrients to get returned to the shallows). Exactly the same process takes place in freshwater lakes if they are deep enough, and the open surface waters of deep tropical lakes are also nutrient-poor. (Lest you are wondering, the rain of nutrients into deeper layers of the ocean does not result in these being highly productive. These waters are even less abundantly filled with life than the surface layers. Nutrients without light provide no opportunity for phytoplankton to survive and grow, and without phytoplankton, there is little for zooplankton or any larger species to feed upon. No, the deep sea is also a desert, just a nutrient-rich one.)

The depth of the ocean makes return of nutrients to surface waters difficult, but upwellings occur in many places where a continental slope meets a strong onshore current, and in these places cold, nutrient-rich waters are brought up to mix into the surface layers. Where there are upwellings, the ocean is notably productive, and fish can be abundant. The northwest Atlantic cod fishery discussed in chapter 1 was as profitable and long-lasting as it was because it was sustained by strong upwellings caused as the Gulf Stream forced water against the continental slope of northeastern North America.

Many coral reefs gain some benefit from upwellings occurring on their seaward sides. Intermittent, storm- or tidally driven upwellings have been shown to be of primary importance in supplying nutrients to the reefs of the outer portions of the Great Barrier Reef, while the mid-shelf and inshore portions derive most of their nutrients from coastal runoff. Similar intermittent upwellings occur on other reefs adjacent to deep oceanic water. However, the main reason for the high abundance of life characteristic of coral reefs is that the members of this ecosystem have developed extremely efficient ways of gathering, conserving, and recycling nutrients so that they are retained within the living organisms and only slowly released to the environment and ultimately to deep waters.

We have already met one of the important partnerships in efficiency. The symbiotic association of coral species and their zooxanthellae enables high rates of photosynthesis because the waste products of coral metabolism become the nutrients needed by the zooxanthellae. Zooxanthellae are also symbiotic with a range of other reef species, including many sponges and, most conspicuously, the giant clams, *Tridacna,* and their relatives. Giant clams sit securely in protected lagoons on coral reefs, with their two shells opened so the fleshy mantle of the animal is exposed to sunlight. This mantle is iridescent, in a range of blues, greens, violets, yellows, and sometimes even reds—colors due mostly to the busily photosynthesizing zooxanthellae packed into its cells. The organic nutrients built through photosynthesis provide a major portion of the energy and nutrients needed by the clam for its growth. It supplements this with the plankton it filters from the surrounding water. Sponges with zooxanthellae also derive most of their nutrients from this cozy relationship.

Elsewhere on the reef, there are numerous filter feeders and other planktivores that sit patiently removing plankton and other nutritious particles from the water column as it streams by. The plankton are sparse compared to what you would find in more temperate waters (that's why the water is so clear), but since water streams past all day, a lot of plankton comes within reach. Some of these plankton harvesters are fish, ranging in size from the vast schools of minute damselfishes, cardinalfishes, and silversides that hover above the reef, picking at plankton one at a time, to the fewer, much larger manta rays and whale sharks that drift slowly past with their mouths open wide, vacuuming up their planktonic prey. Others are the sponges, bryozoans, oysters, and giant clams that filter volumes of water to strain out plankton or the corals and their relatives that capture plankton using tentacles armed with stinging cells. And there are still others, all stationary on the reef and together comprising a wall of mouths extracting all they can from the passing water, in the process adding their nutrients to the reef system.

Then there are numerous other particle-feeders that live within the reef, on or under the sand of the lagoons, ingesting any particles of organic matter they can. These include sea cucumbers, which scoop up sand and swallow it and any organisms living among the interstices, many burrowing worms, and a surprising number of fish, crabs, mollusks, and other creatures that nibble at what we would dismiss as dirt. So thoroughly do reef organisms police their environment for items that might have nutritive value that Ross Robertson once calculated that the average fecal pellet expelled by a parrotfish on a Panamanian reef would be consumed seven times by other fishes before it finally reached the substratum a meter or so below the parrotfish that started that particular chain of waste recycling.

The final players to mention in this game of nutrient management are the cyanobacteria, or blue-green algae. On reefs, these are profusely abundant in the shallowest depths, residing on and just under the surfaces of the sands, limestone, and rubble that occupy all spaces between the living corals and other sessile organisms. Cyanobacteria are nitrogen fixers. Other organisms cannot use atmospheric nitrogen for the nitrogen they need because its atoms are too tightly bound to one another. Nitrogen fixers take nitrogen gas dissolved in the water and cleave it to form nitrates, in the process making the nitrogen available to other organisms. The cyanobacteria of coral reefs happen to be particularly good at this and provide a steady stream of nitrates to the other organisms living there.

Together, the fixing of new nitrates, the importing of oceanic nutrients or nutrients from nearby land masses, and the very efficient recycling of nutrients among members of the reef community make possible very high levels of productivity, despite the nutrient-poor ocean that surrounds them. With rates of net primary production of up to 1,500 g $C.m^{-2}Y^{-1}$ (that is, grams of carbon incorporated into living tissue per square meter per year) on seaward reef faces, or 2,000 g $C.m^{-2}Y^{-1}$ at the coral colony itself, coral reefs rival rainforests as the most productive systems on the planet. However, these high rates of productivity can be deceptive because they are achieved by rapid recycling of organic material. While many fish are present and there's much food for the fish being produced, the reef remains a nutrient-limited environment. This means that harvesting those fish removes crucial nutrients from the system. Reefs cannot sustain an intensive fishery without showing a fall in productivity because of the limited nutrients that are available there.

VERY VALUABLE REAL ESTATE

Reefs are very valuable for the people who live near them. Although the odds are stacked against sustainable fishing on coral reefs because of the nutrient-poor environment, sustainable fishery yields can typically be 5 metric tons per square km per year. Many coastal populations obtain the bulk of their protein food from their reefs while also selling a portion of the catch to gain funds for other needs. In addition to the fish, crabs, lobster, octopus, giant clam, bêche-de-mer (sea cucumber), and other food fishery products that reefs supply, there are valuable fisheries for aquarium specimens and health products (such as seahorses that are dried, ground to a powder, and used in Asian folk medicines).

In many locations, reefs also support major tourist industries built around hotels, beaches, sun, sand, surf, and reefs. In most instances, this reef-based tourism far surpasses reef fisheries as an earner of GDP. In Australia, the Great Barrier Reef has been calculated to generate some AU$5.4 billion in GDP per year (2007 value), with the bulk of this money ($5.1 billion) coming from tourism. In comparison, commercial fishing brings in only $139 million, recreational fishing, $96 million, and other recreational activities, $57 million. This number—AU$5.4 billion per year—does not include factors such as the reef's value in coastal protection (which grows more important as development increases along the Queensland coast) or in cultural or aesthetic terms. For many Caribbean countries, tourism, chiefly or exclusively coastal, is the largest earner of GDP, while fisheries come in second or third. A recent valuation of two small reef regions in the Caribbean reported that reef-associated tourism and fisheries accounted for 40 percent of Tobago's GDP and about 21 percent of Saint Lucia's. This study also put the annual value of coastal protection at $18 to 33 million in Tobago and $28 to 50 million in Saint Lucia. On top of these immediate economic values, coral reefs have an enormous biodiversity value simply because they support such a high proportion of all marine species.

Given their very considerable value, coral reefs should be treasured natural environments that are carefully nurtured by the populations that depend upon them for livelihood and food. This is what would happen in a world that is managed rationally. It's not what happens in our world. Instead, we mistreat coral reefs in many different ways, and as a result their condition has been in decline for many years.

OVERFISHING OF CORAL REEFS

Reef fisheries have most of the problems discussed in chapter 1. Most reefs are in developing countries, which have limited resources for management and suffer from economic problems such as underemployment that limit opportunities for jobs other than fishing. Reef fisheries are also particularly difficult to manage: They are always multi-species, and even the routine recording of catch and fishing effort is difficult when fish are caught by a variety of methods and by numerous predominantly artisanal fishermen, then taken to market from many different landing sites (or simply taken home to feed the family). Enforcing regulations is difficult where fishing is an activity of last resort, and there are few economic mechanisms to cause fishermen to turn to other employment—mostly, alternative types of employment simply do not exist. The reef environment is architecturally complex but also easily damaged, and many fishing methods gradually destroy the habitat structure on which the fish depend. And the fish themselves are relatively site-attached, living in a patchily available habitat that reduces their scope for moving even if they were behaviorally likely to. This means that fishing impacts can be quite localized and that fish populations can become markedly depressed very quickly if fishing pressure is sustained at sites close to villages.

In addition to these general fishery management problems, coral reef fish populations suffer particular harm from three practices that are prevalent in coral reef fisheries: the fishing of spawning aggregations, the use of inappropriate methods, and the live reef fish restaurant trade.

Many reef fishes reproduce pretty much where they live. Some, such as the many damselfishes, build nests in which the females place their eggs to be defended by the male until they hatch. Others spawn in mid-water, the male and female rising together into the water column and expelling eggs and sperm at the peak of their arcing climb. The cloud of eggs and sperm then drifts away, and the fertilized eggs go on to complete embryonic development and hatch in mid-water. But a minority of reef fish species time their reproduction to specific times of year. These fish travel considerable distances to traditional sites, usually on the edge of the reef, where they aggregate over a couple of weeks until spawning in mid-water. Often the spawning fish all rise from the bottom at once in a large group. It happens that many fishery species, particularly the groupers and snappers, aggregate to spawn, and they are particularly vulnerable to fishing during the time they are at the spawning ground.

Remember that fishermen are intelligent and wily predators. They observe things. And around the world, fishermen have discovered the traditional spawning locations and have learned to assemble there at the appointed time of year. In an unregulated fishery (and most reef fisheries have been ones without catch limits), this results in excellent fishing at first, but the spawning aggregation becomes smaller year by year and then disappears.

Notice I called the aggregation sites "traditional." Scientists do not know for certain that all aggregating reef species have traditional spawning sites, but there is one small reef fish in the Caribbean that definitely does. The bluehead wrasse (so-called because the oldest males have blue heads) is a 15-cm fish of commercial value only as an aquarium species, but it shows the same spawning aggregation behavior, on a smaller spatial scale, as shown by many bigger relatives. Males travel tens of meters to spawning sites; they compete with one another for the most preferred locations; and females join them to be courted and to spawn. They do this every day for a large part of the year, timing their visits to the slack tide immediately after the daytime full tide. You can watch them doing it off any Caribbean resort beach—leave the pool and the swim-up bar and go see for yourself.

Robert Warner of the University of California at Santa Barbara has spent a large part of his life studying the life, particularly the sex life, of the bluehead wrasse. He did one memorable experiment to see if the spawning aggregation sites were chosen because they were particular kinds of places. Earlier work had disclosed that the males preferred the same locations year after year (the bluehead rarely lives longer than three years, so these were not the same males each year) and that these spawning sites tended to be promontories near the edge of the reef. But measurements of water flow, temperature, topography, and so on had not revealed any consistent pattern that distinguished preferred sites from many other similar sites nearby. Bob and his students collected all the blueheads from a couple of areas of reef and took them a kilometer or so down the coast to get them out of the way. They then collected fish from other areas of reef and released them in the newly vacated space. Then they watched. The new fish, not knowing where the "correct" aggregation sites were, set up a new group of sites, competed for access to some of these—the new preferred sites—and ignored some sites that had previously been used. The following year, the new sites were still being used.[7] The only way to interpret these observations was to conclude that the sites, apart from being acceptable according to broad criteria, were chosen arbitrarily and then established as preferred through a social process involving the passing along of the information from generation to generation, much as human cultures have established behaviors that have become solidified as traditions and customs.

It's not unreasonable to suppose that aggregation sites for larger species are also traditional. This helps explain why an overfished aggregation does not recover after the fishing has been abandoned. Why should it? Even if the fish population slowly recovers (and it is rare to have an intensive fishery at one aggregation site and no fishing for that species elsewhere), there are no experienced fish to show the way. The sad outcome of unregulated fishing of spawning aggregations is that aggregations disappear one by one until there are none left and the species declines to very low numbers. Who would have imagined that reef fishes would have traditions? Perhaps the fact that they do will help us understand that when fishing removes the great majority of individuals, especially the older individuals, it may have unanticipated consequences. It's like killing off all the parents in a village or town.

Inappropriate fishing methods were touched on in chapter 1, and in reality the tale is rather simple. Nets that rip up coral while catching fish, dynamite that blows up coral to catch fish, and poisons such

7. Bob Warner's experiment and many others mentioned in this book typify ecological research—ecologists ask testable questions and devise simple experiments to test them, thereby advancing scientific understanding. I think what we do is important, but I'm also aware that, in many ways, we are like children in a sand box. We have lots of fun doing things that most adults stopped doing when they grew up. I cannot imagine a life in which I had to have a real job!

as household bleach or cyanide that kill lots of other organisms while catching fish all lead to the same result—the progressive deterioration of habitat and a resulting loss of opportunity to catch more fish. Such inappropriate methods have been used in shallow waters wherever there are reefs but are a particular problem in many parts of Southeast Asia and the Pacific. These methods are difficult to eliminate because they obviously work, especially when overfishing has already made fish small and rare, and because managers rarely have sufficient resources to police large areas of reef. Eliminating such methods when human population growth is increasing demand for fish and when there are few alternative employment opportunities can be very difficult. But where they have been eliminated, the improvement in environmental quality, and therefore in fishing, is obvious to see.

The live reef fish restaurant trade was initially centered in Hong Kong. It is built on the idea that eating a colorful fish that was alive until tossed into a pan of sizzling sesame oil makes a fitting climax to a restaurant meal and on the notion that one's status can be enhanced by paying for this special occasion. Getting live fish from reef to restaurant costs far more than getting frozen fish there. With growing Asian affluence, this fishery exploded during the late 1980s and 1990s. Fish were being collected on reefs far out in the Pacific or Indian oceans, airfreighted to Hong Kong or a few other ports, rushed to restaurants, and put into aquaria to await the important businessman out to impress his guests with a lavish meal—a pan-sized, colorful reef species, the rarer the better, caught and cooked minutes before eating.[8]

Now, on the surface, there is nothing wrong with this fishery. The prices paid to fishermen for individual live fish, while considerably less than those at the restaurant, are considerably more than if the fish were caught and killed in the usual way. This greatly increases the value of the catch without requiring that more tons of fish be caught. However, when the value of a fish has as much to do with its rarity as with its weight or nutritive value and when fishing is done by targeting and capturing one fish at a time, the usual economic checks on fishing disappear. The more rare a species becomes, the higher its value, until the last one has been caught. The fishery exploded out into the Pacific pre-

8. The live reef fish restaurant trade is still growing in Hong Kong and has spilled out to other Asian population centers, including ones in western North America.

cisely because reef fish of the preferred species were becoming very rare closer to Hong Kong.

This fishery has two additional problems. The first is that many of the preferred species are fish that grow large and mature late. The pan-sized specimens sought by the trade have not yet reached maturity, and in most locations this fishery, usually preceded by other forms of over-fishing, quickly removes nearly all individuals of this size or larger. Decimating a reef of all fish old enough to breed is a pretty good way of ensuring there will not be any future generations. The final prob-lem has been purely economic. The high prices paid to the fisherman are more than sufficient to encourage illegal fishing, poaching inside no-take marine protected areas, fishing outside a permitted season, and so on. Thus, even if a particular nation has good fishery regula-tions for reef species, the economics of this industry encourages wide-spread flaunting of regulations. And the demand for fish continues to grow as more and more affluent businessmen seek to impress their din-ner guests. Perhaps it's not a surprise that of the nine species of reef fish (other than sharks) listed as threatened or extremely threatened on the IUCN Red List, six are fish that are threatened because of this particu-lar fishery.

What about the consequences of overfishing on coral reefs? The loss of species, reductions in size and age range, and loss of fishing yield hap-pen here in exactly the same way as for other fisheries. Fish approach extinction, and human populations dependent on those fish for food or economic well-being suffer. But there is another major impact of over-fishing. It changes the composition of the reef community, with poten-tially serious consequences for its continuation.

We fish primarily for the larger species on reefs. Typical preferred fishery species are carnivorous snappers and groupers. Included in the catch (and often filleted to be sold as snapper or grouper) are the larger parrotfishes. As overfishing continues, there is a progressive loss of any fishes larger than a few centimeters in length. Indeed, a quick indica-tor of the poverty level of a coastal community is the size range of reef fishes sold to the local population—smaller equals poorer.

The removal of parrotfishes in particular has a cascading effect because it removes a major ecosystem engineer. Parrotfishes are her-bivorous, feeding on filamentous algae, but their mouths are efficient scrapers, and larger parrotfishes bite off the algae and the upper millimeters of the rock beneath, capturing the organic material in the surface layers as well as the softer filaments. This scraping activity is a major erosional process on reefs, but the clean surfaces that result from this removal of algae provide opportunities for new corals to settle and grow without being overwhelmed by algae that compete with them for space. Many scientists now advocate banning the harvest of parrotfishes on reefs that are severely overfished as a way of helping to control algal growth. Otherwise, the reef does what has happened in so many places in the Caribbean—it becomes less and less a coral reef and more and more a rocky, boulder-strewn slope covered with a lush mat of filamentous algae. These algae-covered surfaces are far less productive overall and far less able to support the thousands of species of reef creatures or provide the continued coastal protection or tourism value of a healthy reef.

POLLUTION AND HABITAT DESTRUCTION

Given their need for clear ocean water, coral reefs are obviously susceptible to pollution. In a normally nutrient-scarce environment, excess nutrients stimulate algal growth, which can smother corals and other organisms, particularly if overfishing has already reduced grazing. Around the world, development has polluted coral reefs by leading to discharge of sewage and increased runoff. Enhanced sediment loads in rivers, due to inappropriate development or agricultural practices in the watershed, can damage reefs off river mouths, even when the waters are otherwise not polluted.

The lush reef community that once existed within Kaneohe Bay, a large (10 by 5 km) embayment on the northern shore of Oahu, Hawaii, had deteriorated by the late 1960s when Albert Banner of the University of Hawaii first described the rapid proliferation of a bubblelike green alga, *Dictyosphaeria cavernosa,* that was covering surfaces formerly lush with corals. Over the years, agricultural and, increasingly, urban development of the shores surrounding the bay had taken place, increasing run-off and the number of sewage outfalls. It seemed likely that nutrification was the cause of the switch to algae.

In 1978 the two main sewage outfalls, which had been in place for twenty-five years, were diverted to the ocean outside the mouth of the bay. Over the next eight years, water quality improved, and abundance of algae declined until it was about 25 percent as abundant as it had been in 1970. Coral cover doubled. The process stalled by 1986, however, and it appeared unlikely that the bay would ever return to its former state. Too many nutrients remained in the waters and sediments, too few grazers remained on the reefs to help keep algal abundances down, and coral cover was too low to rapidly refill the space formerly held by algae—any of these factors might have been the major cause of the stall.

To complicate the story, highly unusual weather in 2006 resulted in near continuous rains over forty-two days in February and March. The rainfall was not sufficient to create a deep, coral-killing freshwater lens over the surface of the bay, as can occur during intense storms, but in combination with the increased turbidity, it was continuous enough to greatly lower irradiance in bay waters. John Stimson, also at the University of Hawaii, identified the diminished light levels during those forty-two days as the cause of a dramatic die-off of *Dictyosphaerium* across the bay. Reef patches that had held 25 percent algal coverage in January had little or none of the algae present in June 2006 (0 to 2 percent cover), and reefs that had held 40 to 70 percent cover six years earlier were also largely devoid of the species. The low abundance persisted until 2008, when Stimson reported his observations, but there was little sign of corals taking advantage of the absence of algae to proliferate across the open ground. When I contacted John while writing this chapter (mid-2009), he told me that there had still been no recovery of the algae on the sites he was monitoring, but there had been some further recovery of coral in protected, shallow locations. It's still too early to tell whether the rainstorm permanently removed *Dictyosphaerium* or whether the algae or the corals will slowly return. Whatever the final chapter, the Kaneohe Bay story has long been a warning to people elsewhere to avoid polluting their reefs. Yet the pervasiveness of this problem remains, probably because humans have always washed their wastes downhill toward the ocean. It's hard to learn new tricks.

Along the Caribbean coast of Mexico, from Cancun south to Tulum, sits one of the most intensive tourism developments anywhere near reefs. The thousands of hotel rooms (and toilets) are serviced by an army of friendly hotel staff who live in far less salubrious accommodation away from the beaches and out of tourists' sight. These thousands of staff (the usual ratio in Cancun is ten employees per room) and their families also have toilets.

Let's just say that the hotels are supposed to provide secondary treatment and pump the treated effluent down deep wells. And let's add that the provision of sanitary services to the communities occupied by the armies of hotel staff is not regulated quite so strenuously as are the hotels themselves. Let's finally add that the Yucatán peninsula is a limestone bench (a pre-Pleistocene reef) riddled with caverns and underground rivers, some of which have become tourist attractions for those into cenote diving. Now, given the geology, it should not be a surprise that there are places out on the reef that run along this shore (the Mesoamerican Barrier Reef, the largest reef complex in the Caribbean) at which freshwater bubbles up through the substratum below.

I cannot say that sewage is finding its way to the Mesoamerican reef, because I have not made any measurements, and I do not know of any made by others. But I find it hard to believe that all that sewage is being adequately contained, and I also know that the reefs of Mexico's Caribbean coast are more lush with algae than they used to be. Is the cause pollution, overfishing, or both? On Mexican reefs, as in most reef locations, the extent of the impacts of pollution is not known because pollution has been one of those problems that has received relatively little attention. Pollution is in the too-hard basket—it requires money, technical expertise, and political will to address it, so it gets ignored.

How can a country manage coastal pollution to protect its reefs? This is always a difficult issue. Reef managers seldom have jurisdiction beyond reef borders, yet the sources of pollution can be far away. The cost of the environmental damage (declining value of the reef or its products) rarely impacts those responsible for the pollution directly— the sugarcane or banana planters, the golf course operators inshore, or the hotel operators themselves.[9] In the great majority of instances, as in Cancun, pollution of coral reefs is simply not dealt with. It is too difficult to tackle, both technologically and politically. Australia's experience could be a helpful lesson for other nations.

Australia's Great Barrier Reef Marine Park (GBRMP) is the world's

9. Serious beach pollution causing public health issues would impact the hotel operators directly and the golf course operators indirectly, but impacts that affect ecosystems happen long before this.

best example of coral reef management. From its inception, it was designed as a zoned management area, meaning that different activities are permitted in different parts of this vast area (344,400 square km) of managed marine environment. When it was established thirty years ago, the consensus was that pollution was likely to be only a minor problem for the marine park. The reefs were simply too far from shore. Still, steps were taken to gather information on water quality as part of environmental monitoring for the park, and by 2001 the management agency produced a report on water quality issues and a water quality management plan.

The Great Barrier Reef catchment area includes about a quarter of the land area of the State of Queensland and drains via a number of rivers to the coast. It is a predominantly rural area with low population density (seven hundred thousand people). European settlement commenced two hundred years ago, and development has progressed until 80 percent of the catchment is now agricultural, producing sugarcane and similar crops. There are some coastal towns with tourism, shipping, or natural resources industries. Gladstone, at the southern limit of the GBRMP, is the largest export terminal for coal and alumina (the aluminum oxide refined from bauxite ore) in Australia. River outflow fluctuates markedly in volume, and during tropical cyclones (Pacific hurricanes), some river plumes may extend out across the 100 to 200 km width of the park.

Great Barrier Reef locations now receive about 40 percent of their nitrogen and 55 percent of their phosphorus from coastal runoff, with the remainder coming from deepwater upwelling, rainfall, and nitrogen fixation within reef habitat. Inputs from the catchment are estimated to have increased fourfold since 1850, so in reef waters there has been about a 30 percent increase in the concentration of these nutrients over that time. The outer reefs of the Great Barrier Reef divide the open Coral Sea from the Great Barrier Reef lagoon. Circulation is predominantly southward on the outer reef due to the East Australia Current. It is northward in the inner part of the lagoon due to impact of the southeast trade winds, with relatively little mixing across the shelf. One consequence is that the many coastal and inner mid-shelf reefs are substantially more exposed to coastal runoff, while the outer reefs are only very seldom exposed to its effects (and rely more on upwellings for new nutrients).

There is now growing evidence that inner shelf reefs are deteriorating due to greater nutrification and associated algal growth. As well as nutrients and sediment, the coastal runoff contains pesticide residues, some heavy metals, and other pollutants from agriculture or industry, all in very low but still potentially damaging concentrations. These contaminants may be more problematic than the nitrogen and phosphorus because we simply do not know the physiological responses of many reef organisms to such things as pesticides, herbicides, heavy metals, and pharmaceuticals. However, the very strong public support for the GBRMP has made it politically possible to take steps to modify farming practices in ways that reduce harmful runoff to coastal and mid-shelf reefs. The problem of pollution on the Great Barrier Reef is undoubtedly replicated reef by reef around the world except in places where reefs are far from any land—it's just that the monitoring data used to describe and evaluate the situation and the political will to act are rarely present in other places. Think about this the next time you are enjoying a round of golf on one of those very green, ocean-side courses that dot the Caribbean—do you really think the herbicides and pesticides stay out of the water?

BEING LOVED TO DEATH

Over the years there has been a tendency to identify tourism as a potential savior of coral reefs. The argument goes that tourists from wealthy nations lacking reefs will pay to travel to poorer nations with reefs, and if a portion of that money stream can be captured, it can pay for the cost of maintaining reefs in good condition. Although I do believe that money from tourism could make an enormous difference, we need to be clear about the current situation, which is not always rosy. To begin with, large portions of the tourism "money stream" never get near the country with the coral reefs. Package tours and prepaid all-inclusive vacation specials feature prominently in tropical tourism. The hotels in most developing countries are mostly owned by large offshore multinationals, and the tourism industry is built around letting as little as is possible of the tourists' dollars, euros, and yen get lodged inside the country where the hotel is built. Then there is the unfortunate fact that many developing countries—as a matter of policy or of corruption—treat departure taxes, tourist taxes, and bed taxes as sources of general revenue. I have talked with many marine park operators in the Caribbean about the lack of funding to support the management activities, patrolling, and enforcement of regulations that marine protected areas need. Time after time, when I have made the point that increasing a country's tourist head tax by $1 to 2 per day would never deter any international tourists, the park operators have replied with fatalistic certainty that even if the tax was increased, the revenue generated would never find its way to the parks. And marine protected area (MPA) budgets bear them out. Once again the world of international business and government has figured out a way of keeping most of the profit from tourism out of the developing countries that provide the environments tourists come to enjoy. Tourism brings low-level service jobs to developing countries while using, and frequently slowly degrading, their natural environments. These beautiful coastlines and the reefs that sustain and protect them are providing tourism services to the multinational operators that are far more valuable than all those service jobs, all at no cost. They should be generating far more revenue for the local community than they do.

In 1999 I participated in a workshop in Cancun. It was one of my first visits to that part of Mexico, and I joined a snorkeling field trip to a site on the reef at the southern end of the Cancun hotel strip. We made use of a tourist operation that collected passengers from the hotels up and down the strip, put them onto two-person Sea-Doos, assembled these into "wagon trains," and journeyed down the lagoon, through channels in the mangrove forest, and out onto the reef where a floating "island" was moored. The island, a rather tacky set of barges with plastic palm trees, showers, toilets, restaurants, and bars, served as the center from which tourists could snorkel over the reef or take glass-bottom boat rides, fishing trips, and scuba tours to the deeper reef. We were told that the effluent barge traveled every day from the island to a discharge site back in Cancun, although there had been occasional problems with "overflows" at the island when the barge was late showing up. I noticed that all the snorkelers were wearing floatation vests that kept them on the surface and that there were more snorkelers per square meter of reef than I had ever seen before. I was told that the floatation vests were to minimize the chance of novices drowning but that they also played a major role in preventing the snorkelers from touching and damaging the coral. Even so, the eroded, broken shallower parts of the reef gave silent witness to the impacts of numerous fins and the occasional backside.

A couple of years later, off Key Largo, Florida, on a day-tripper scuba dive vessel operated by a friend, I witnessed divers climbing back on board after their dives with their fins and wetsuits slippery with coral mucus. For many, this had been their very first dive on a coral reef. They were thrilled by the experience. Their fins told me the corals were probably less thrilled.

There are many highly competent scuba enthusiasts and even more skilled snorkelers at vacation spots on reefs, but there are also many novices. They do not intend to damage the reef they have come to see, but they bump into it, kick it, and hold onto creatures that were never designed to be held onto. They return to their hotels sunburned, scratched up, tired, and happy. None of them realizes that they have contributed to the progressive decline of an area of reef. Multiply the impact of each boatload of innocent beginners by the number of boatloads per day and the number of sites where such things take place, and the statement that tourists can love a reef to death is easy to understand. Among effective coral reef managers, there is widespread acknowledgment of the value of restricting recreational snorkeling and diving to specific locations. It allows the inevitable damage to happen in one place, leaving other places to prosper, and it can be done easily by placing moorings at certain sites and requiring that the boats must moor rather than drop anchor. In the Great Barrier Reef Marine Park and a number of other well-managed locations, individual tourist operators are granted exclusive long-term leases on specific locations out on the reef where they undertake their in-water activities. This helps ensure that the operators, if not the tourists, will be working hard to keep the reef as undamaged as possible.

Direct damage to a reef by snorkelers or divers is just one tiny part of the problem. The hotels and their toilets are a much bigger part. So are the artificial beaches that are regularly "replenished" by bringing in sand from offshore. The mangroves that used to line many shores have been methodically uprooted to "improve" hotel sites, and beaches have been built where they were wanted, rather than using beaches where they naturally occurred. As a consequence, continual maintenance is needed because sand in the ocean goes where currents and waves take it, not where landscape architects would like it to be. What is lost in the process? Viable biological communities in the shallow back-reef areas disappear when the sand is stolen to create the beaches. Mangrove removal eliminates vital nursery habitats for numerous coral reef species, including many snappers and groupers, as well as a highly effective water purification system, not to mention the coastal protection of a mature mangrove forest. Sometimes the process of "aqua-scaping" to eliminate mangroves and build beaches changes water flow patterns sufficiently to result in the die-off of reefs some distance away.

Another problem generated by tourists is all those restaurants that must have reef species prominent on the menu. Now, much of the grouper sold in such restaurants is not grouper, but it still tends to be reef fish such as parrotfish, which are overfished to feed the continuous stream of greedy tourists. The advent of a tourism industry puts an additional heavy load on the backs of fisheries managers who are already struggling to manage overharvesting of their reef resources, and once the local sources are exhausted, the hotels purchase fish from ever farther away. Maintaining closed seasons at critical times when the fish are spawning or the lobsters are carrying their young is almost impossible when fisheries managers have limited capacity to police the waters and hotels deal directly with fishermen early in the morning. The tourists themselves are a mixture of people naively unaware of such things as overfished reefs, others self-important enough to assume that exceptions can always be made, and a small minority who might want to eat responsibly. Too many of us leave our environmental consciences at home when going on a tropical vacation; I sympathize with any restaurant operator who tries to act responsibly under such circumstances.

Finally, there are the cruise ships. Cruise tourism has been the fastest growing sector of international tourism since 2000, a trend probably strengthened by the fears generated by the attack on the World Trade Center. In coral reef waters, cruise tourism does four things, none of them good for reef ecosystems. It disgorges large numbers of restaurant, bar, and curio seekers onto local cruise ports daily. They promptly overload the water and sewerage capacity at the ports. It delivers equally large numbers of sun, surf, and snorkel enthusiasts daily to "idyllic deserted islands" to overtax the water and sewerage facilities on the islands while trampling, standing on, bumping into, and otherwise damaging the reefs they came to see. It brings in huge ships that drop anchor in anchorages where port facilities are limited and the anchor chains eliminate bottom topography as the vessels swing on the tide. And it creates a continuing, if traveling, demand for seafood and a source of minimally treated sewage, not all of which gets discharged at port facilities.

Passengers on cruise ships do not see this pattern because they only see the port or the idyllic island when they are there. They rarely appreciate that there will be another cruise ship using the same port and the same idyllic, deserted island the very next day. All season. And cruise ship companies would like to keep it that way. Let the passengers enjoy the meals without ever wondering where all that lobster and grouper came from. Cruise ship passengers, because they travel from port to port, never have a chance to get to know the locals or catch a glimpse of what goes on behind the curtains—they are more isolated from the developing countries they are visiting than even the tourists in their gated, all-inclusive hotels. Building responsible environmental attitudes in this community is especially challenging.

THE GREAT BLEACHING

In 1998 corals on reefs across the Indian Ocean turned ghostly white. Under stress, the corals had expelled their zooxanthellae, and zooxanthellae provide the only color pigments that corals "possess." This widespread "bleaching" was preceded by smaller-scale bleaching events elsewhere, beginning late in 1997. First there were reports of some bleaching of corals on the Galápagos Islands. By late January reports were arriving from Indonesia and the southern Barrier Reef, and by mid-February from the central Great Barrier Reef. I say "arriving" because the coral list server operated by the National Oceanographic and Atmospheric Administration, NOAA (coral-list@coral.aoml.noaa.gov), became a node to which scientists and others e-mailed their observations from around the world. Scattered reports were received from other Pacific locations, and then through April came news of the rapid bleaching across the Indian Ocean: Kenya, Mauritius, Comoro Islands, Sri Lanka, Maldives, Sulawesi, Lombok, Seychelles, Sabah . . . bad news from everywhere. These were not reports of occasional bleached corals. Estimates of extent were typically 75 percent, 85 percent, 100 percent of corals bleached. And the estimates of coral death were similarly high: 50 percent to 90 percent in Kenya, 100 percent of *Acropora* species at Maldives sites, 50 percent to 90 percent in the Seychelles, 70 percent in Sri Lanka. On through September, with Caribbean locations joining in as their summer progressed, the sorry reports kept piling up. What was happening, and why?

The expelling of zooxanthellae can occur in response to several different environmental stresses: high temperature, low salinity, prolonged darkness (as in a darkroom), and a number of other conditions. If conditions improve in a short time, the corals are able to take up new zooxanthellae from the surrounding waters, regain their colors, and live happily ever after—or at least till the next bad event. If stressful conditions are prolonged for several weeks, the corals begin to die, and in severe bleaching events, such as the one in 1998, there can be total mortality over wide areas.

A particularly strong el Niño event made 1998 the warmest year until then since weather records have been kept, so scientists were quickly in broad agreement that the mass bleaching that year was most probably induced by the extraordinarily high temperatures that prevailed. Subsequently, NOAA has been able to predict quite reliably where extensive bleaching would occur next by using a model that computes temperature anomalies and notes when and where nighttime sea surface temperatures exceed the long-term average (actually the 1985–93 average) by 1°C or more. When coral reef regions exceed this threshold for several weeks, extensive bleaching is the usual response. And events since 1998 have provided plenty of opportunities to test this model.

Mass bleaching first came to attention during the strong el Niño event of 1983, which resulted in heightened temperatures and mass bleaching of corals throughout the eastern equatorial Pacific.[10] Peter Glynn, then at the Smithsonian Tropical Research Institute in Panama, reported that mortality ranged from 50 to 98 percent at locations in Costa Rica, Panama, Colombia, and Ecuador. In preparing this chapter, I asked Peter Glynn whether he realized the significance of his observations at the time. He told me he had quickly made the connec-

---

10. *El Niño* is the term used to describe a weather anomaly that occurs periodically in the equatorial Pacific. During el Niño conditions, the surface waters of the eastern and central Pacific become warmer than usual, the equatorial current that normally carries water west slows or even reverses, and upwellings that sustain important Peruvian and Ecuadorian fisheries fail. El Niños are typically followed by anomalies in the opposite direction (stronger equatorial current, more upwellings, cooler surface waters termed *la Niña*) in an approximately cyclic climate modification also termed *el Niño southern oscillation*.

tion between mass bleaching and elevated temperatures due to a particularly strong el Niño event that year, and he did wonder what might unfold if global temperatures were to grow warmer. Still, his colleagues actively dissuaded him from this very pessimistic view at the time. Time appears to have proved his initial hunch correct.

Since 1983, there have been about nine mass bleaching events in which bleaching occurred in numerous sites and across two or more geographic regions. There is no evidence that such extensive, synchronized bleaching occurred prior to about 1980; indeed, the likelihood of extensive mass bleaching being missed any time between the 1950s and 1980s is very slim given the number of scientists and sport divers on reefs in those years and the conspicuousness of extensively bleached corals. That some massive seven-hundred-year-old corals on the Great Barrier Reef were killed during the 1998 bleaching also indicates that such bleaching must have been very unusual if it occurred at all over at least seven hundred years (or those corals would not have lived as long as they did). No, while bleaching has always been a response to stress, mass bleaching, such as what occurred in 1983 or 1998, is a brand-new phenomenon.

It's also one likely to become more common in coming years. The frequency of mass bleaching has picked up since 1983 as warmer-than-usual summers have become more prevalent. In addition, there is growing evidence that corals stressed in other ways are more likely to bleach when temperatures rise. Using the climate predictions developed by the International Panel on Climate Change, IPCC, Princeton University's Simon Donner and colleagues at Princeton and at the University of Queensland explored the likely frequency of high sea-surface temperatures for coral reefs worldwide for years up to 2059. They then computed the likelihood of the occurrence of temperature anomalies of 1°C or greater lasting at least a month for each coral reef location at years into the future according to the IPCC climate models. Their results, published in 2005, were alarming. It turns out that, even under the more optimistic of the IPCC scenarios, by 2030, temperatures this extreme are going to be reached in most coral reef locations every other year or so. By 2050 these high temperature episodes will be even more frequent. Subtropical regions fare somewhat better than equatorial regions, but by midcentury even these areas are that warm. In the dispassionate language of science, Donner and colleagues wrote: "Our global assessment indicates that the frequency of coral bleaching at reefs worldwide could become an annual or biannual event in 30–50 years because of climate change without an increase in the thermal tolerance of corals and their symbionts."

Will corals and their zooxanthellae become more thermally tolerant? Most animals show some capacity to acclimate to higher temperatures through physiological responses. This is the reason a cool summer day of 15°C (59°F) feels a lot colder to us than does a warm winter day of 10°C (50°F). A population can also adapt to warming temperatures through natural selection and evolution over several generations (in contrast to acclimation, this is a genetic response). Corals have rather long generation times and potentially very long individual lives. This may make the process of adaptation through natural selection rather slow for corals, but their zooxanthellae live much shorter lives and might be capable of adapting more rapidly. But is it enough for only the zooxanthellae to adapt? We simply do not know.

We do know that the critical temperatures that induce bleaching vary regionally, that most of the time when bleaching occurs not all individuals of a species bleach, and that some of those that bleach subsequently recover. In other words, there is local and geographic variation in the susceptibility of corals to warm conditions—a prima facie requirement if adaptation is to be possible. We also know, however, that the episodes of warm conditions that induce bleaching arise quickly and last only weeks, making acclimation difficult, and that the world's oceans are currently warming at an unprecedented rate, perhaps too fast for any adaptive capacity of the corals and their symbionts to keep up. More encouragingly, in the few places where repeated mass bleachings have been studied quantitatively, there seems to have been some improvement with time. That is, bleaching has been less intense for a given thermal shock the second time around. This may be a simple case of the most sensitive individuals being killed off the first time, so that the average tolerance to warm temperature increases without any individual having actually become better adapted. Or it may be a sign that some adaptation is occurring.

Whether corals can adapt to warmer temperatures and become less susceptible to bleaching, there are larger issues to consider when warm temperature events are expected to become annual or biennial in occurrence. Consider what has to happen after the bleaching event has occurred, and remember that coral reefs exist because of a balance between calcification and a number of erosional factors. Mass bleaching and resultant mortality is one of those factors that tend to erode coral reefs. Once bleached coral dies, it is rapidly broken down by bioeroders, by storms, and by slowly dissolving, and the loss has to be made up by new coral growth. Where does this growth come from, and how fast do reefs recover once seriously bleached?

New growth can arise locally through growth of surviving individuals and through recruitment of new larvae produced by these survivors, or it can arise through the recruitment of new larvae dispersing from other places. Obviously, in cases of extreme bleaching, such as in 1998, there will be very few local sources, and any larvae dispersing in will have traveled considerable distances. Corals that bleach but survive typically show reduced growth (less calcification) and reduced reproductive activity over several months. Put these together, and it's clear that when severe bleaching occurs, recovery is going to take several years. Peter Glynn, now at the University of Miami, and colleagues Andrew Baker and Bernhard Riegl have undertaken a detailed analysis of recovery of reefs following bleaching. The results are mixed. At forty-six of fifty-eight Indian Ocean locations from East Africa to Western Australia following the 1998 mass bleaching, coral cover increased in the four or so years between bleaching and subsequent remeasurement. In the Caribbean, however, sixteen of seventeen sites exhibited further decline in coral cover four to five years after bleaching. And in the eastern Pacific, the western Pacific, and the Arabian Gulf there were no clear trends: some reefs showed good recovery while others continued to decline.

Where deterioration in coral cover has continued, there are several causes at play. Sometimes the initial bleaching mortality has generated great fields of coral rubble that provide a continuously shifting terrain unsuitable for successful establishment of new colonies. This is a real risk wherever the original reef was dominated by branching colonies rather than by tablelike or massive forms. Sometimes the continued deterioration is due to outbreaks of diseases, outbreaks of the predatory starfish *Acanthaster planci,* which feeds on coral, or subsequent bleaching events. Where coral cover recovers following bleaching, it is sometimes rapid, restoring the coral that was lost in as little as two to four years. Usually it is a lot more modest. (At the forty-six Indian Ocean sites in the Baker, Glynn, and Riegl study that showed an increase in coral cover, that improvement averaged only 8 percent after 4.7 years.)

The pattern uncovered by Baker, Glynn, and Riegl is ultimately disappointing. Coral reefs are usually quite slow to recover following severe bleaching and sometimes continue to deteriorate. Galápagos coral communities, first bleached in 1982–83 and several times since, have not recovered after nearly twenty years. Coral reefs are now present only in one small region in the north of the archipelago. If temperature-induced bleaching events become frequent (happening every year or so), coral reefs are going to be degraded to the point that coral cover will typically be quite low—something on the order of 5 to 10 percent cover compared to the 50 to 70 percent cover that has characterized healthy coral reefs in the past.

All problems I have discussed previously are local. Even pollution of coral reefs is local if we consider distances of tens to hundreds of kilometers to be local. If Australia puts appropriate limits on agricultural practice in Queensland, it can control the impacts of onshore pollution on the Great Barrier Reef Marine Park. It can do this even if Indonesia does nothing about its onshore pollution. With climate change, things are different. No one country can mitigate the impacts of climate change on coral reefs, because coral reefs cannot be isolated from the effects of climate.

OCEAN ACIDIFICATION:
ANOTHER THREAT FROM CLIMATE CHANGE

Climate change has many aspects. Until recently, coral reef scientists have focused on the effects of heightened temperature, but acidification of the ocean is another aspect of climate change that seems to be having pronounced effects on reefs. (Rising sea levels and increased severity of storms are also features of climate change, but their effects on reefs may be less severe or even beneficial.)

As discussed in chapter 3, the surface layers of the oceans absorb some 40 percent of all the CO_2 that we put into the atmosphere, with the consequence that these waters are becoming very slightly acidified. This situation will endure for a thousand years, even if we stop adding CO_2 tomorrow, because ocean water mixes very slowly. Instead of being dispersed rapidly throughout the ocean, the CO_2 will remain predominantly in the surface layers—the very layers teaming with life, much of it dependent on building calcium carbonate skeletons. The climate scientists now have good models that show the geographic pattern in surface water pH and how it is likely to change over the next fifty years or so. And the coral scientists know a lot about rates of calcification by corals and how these are impacted by changes in pH. Putting these together gives us yet another bad news story.

Glenn De'ath is a coral reef scientist at the Australian Institute of Marine Science in Townsville, midway up the Queensland coast in approximately the center of the Great Barrier Reef. De'ath emphasizes the apostrophe when pronouncing his name, but even so, his name is unfortunate given what he reported in *Science* in January 2009. The rate of growth of colonies of the massive boulder coral, *Porites,* has dropped 13 percent since 1990 throughout the Great Barrier Reef.

Coral growth varies seasonally. Just as a section through the trunk of a tree reveals annual growth rings, a section through a coral's skeleton reveals annual growth bands—although the coral bands must be viewed with a gamma ray densitometer because they are bands of more dense (summer) skeleton and less dense (winter) skeleton. These annual bands can be counted to age a coral, and their widths reveal the coral's rate of growth each year. De'ath and his colleagues used sections taken from 328 coral colonies, from reefs up and down the length of the Great Barrier Reef. The colonies ranged from 10 to 436 years in age.

Using standard X-ray and gamma densitometry techniques, De'ath's team recorded average skeletal density and annual growth rate for each colony for each year of its life and from these data computed the rate of calcification. Their data show that the annual growth rate increased slightly during the period from 1900 to about 1980, presumably in response to warming temperatures, but then slowed and fell markedly between 1990 and 2005. Skeletal density declined throughout the period. The drop in calcification between 1990 and 2005 was 14.2 percent, and the drop in growth rate during the same period was 13.3 percent. The rate of change in both measurements was much greater than at any other time since 1900. A few months later, Barbara Brown and colleagues, working out of the Phuket Marine Biological Center in Thailand, reported comparable drops in calcification and growth rate in *Porites* corals at eight sites near Phuket.

This reduced growth is strong evidence that the reductions in ocean pH that have been occurring are affecting the ability of corals to calcify. While tropical ocean waters are supersaturated for aragonite (the specific form of $CaCO_3$ in coral skeletons), reduction in pH lowers the extent of this supersaturation, making calcification more difficult physiologically. In the past, most tropical waters were supersaturated for aragonite, while more temperate waters (where reefs do not grow) were less saturated. Now, most reefs lie in waters that are less saturated for aragonite and only marginally satisfactory for reef growth. Only a very few are in water with optimal saturation conditions. Once concentrations of CO_2 in the atmosphere reach 500 ppm, ocean chemistry models show there will be scarcely anywhere in the oceans where even marginal rates of reef growth will be possible. The calcification rates De'ath measured on the Great Barrier Reef are likely to continue to fall if we keep adding CO_2 to the atmosphere.

A GLIMPSE OF THE FUTURE IN THE CARIBBEAN

The future looks rather bleak for coral reefs, and the bleakness is not far off. Unless humanity shows rapid improvement in how we manage coastal environments and address problems of overfishing, pollution, habitat destruction, inappropriate development, and other forms of stress, coral reefs around the world are going to continue to decline. The Caribbean, which is in worse shape than many Indo-Pacific sites, may provide a glimpse of the future—a future we can still avoid, but only if we act quickly and aggressively to rein in our release of CO_2.

In the Caribbean, giant elkhorn coral, *Acropora palmata,* formerly one of the most important reef builders, now does not form the giant ramparts that bore the brunt of ocean waves when Caribbean reefs were being described in the first half of the past century. The ramparts that provided important coastal protection as well as an intricate habitat of cathedral-like, sheltered spaces for other reef species are now gone. Once so common at depths from 1 to 6 meters that this part of a Caribbean reef was formally known as the Palmata Zone, this species is now listed under the U.S. Endangered Species Act as "threatened" throughout its range. Disease, storms, and probably climate change have reduced it to an occasional species, and it may well be extinct by the end of this century.

Nor is the elkhorn coral the only species in decline on Caribbean reefs. Overall coral cover has continued to decline on Caribbean reefs since the first mass bleaching event of 1987–88. The first discovery of a coral disease (black band disease) was in the Caribbean, in 1973, followed shortly by the discovery of white band disease. Both have played major roles in the decline of elkhorn coral. Since then a broad array of coral diseases has become prevalent, particularly at times when corals have been stressed by warm waters. Many of these diseases appear to be new, and their prevalence has led experts to refer to the Caribbean as a coral disease hot spot. Aspergilliosis is one of these new diseases. It erodes sea fans (a close relative of corals), leaving gaping holes with angry purple edges in the delicate network of the fan. Serious outbreaks result in fans so weakened that they are broken apart by wave action and succumb. This disease is caused by the fungus *Aspergillus sydowii,* a widespread inhabitant of soils. The infective form of this species, isolated from infected sea fans, has been detected in air samples taken over the Caribbean during periods when easterly winds bring dust from Africa. Remember the desertification of West Africa mentioned in chapter 2? Desertification there has doubled the amount of dust being transported west since 1970. This dust has brought at least one new pathogen that has found a susceptible host in Caribbean sea fans.

New diseases, repeated mass bleaching events, and more intense hurricanes have all increased the mortality of corals in the Caribbean. Ocean acidification has likely combined with the stress of temperature-induced bleaching to reduce corals' capacity to recover. And overfishing has added another major problem—allowing algae to escape from herbivore control so that they can cover all dead, rocky surfaces with a lush algal turf. Actually, the algal problem is caused by overfishing, nutrification from coastal communities and agriculture, and an additional disease. Before 1983 one of the major herbivores on Caribbean reefs was the long-spined sea urchin, *Diadema antillarum*—an organism that, despite its tendency to hide away during the day, was exuberantly abundant and a constant nuisance to divers. Now, it's quite probable that *Diadema* was so common during last century because we had already killed off many of its large predators as we fished the reefs. Still, it was common and ecologically important nonetheless because it grazed algal turfs alongside the parrotfishes, surgeonfishes, and other herbivorous fish. In 1983 a disease appeared that was quickly lethal to *Diadema* and spread rapidly across the Caribbean, virtually eliminating this species over the span of a few months. Even now, there are only sparse populations of this urchin in most parts of the Caribbean, despite the abundant

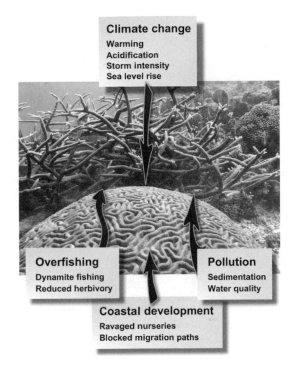

Climate change
Warming
Acidification
Storm intensity
Sea level rise

Overfishing
Dynamite fishing
Reduced herbivory

Pollution
Sedimentation
Water quality

Coastal development
Ravaged nurseries
Blocked migration paths

FIGURE 6. The deterioration of coral reef ecosystems seen throughout the world is due to a broad range of anthropogenic stresses. Here they are grouped as three sets of locally acting impacts (overfishing, pollution, and coastal development) and one set of globally acting impacts due to climate change. Image: Bonaire, Netherlands Antilles, 2005, © R. Steneck.

food and even fewer urchin predators than before. The loss of *Diadema,* which may or may not have been caused by us, and the removal of grazing fishes through our overfishing have permitted Caribbean coral reefs to undergo a phase shift—a relatively sudden switch from a coral-dominated to an alga-dominated state. Like most phase shifts, this one is very difficult to reverse because the lush algal turfs are an inhospitable habitat for the survival and growth of newly settled corals.

The Caribbean story is not unique to that region. Similar phase shifts have occurred in other parts of the world where reefs have been under strong pressure. Overfishing, coastal pollution, habitat destruction, bleaching, disease, and inappropriate coastal development have played variously large or small roles from one place to another. The eventual result, however, is monotonously consistent. First there is a loss of big fish, maybe some deterioration in water quality, a few more diseases. Then comes the progressive decline in coral cover and the growth of luxuriant algal turfs. Healthy coral reefs commonly had 50 percent to 70 percent coverage of living coral; it is now rare in most parts of the world to find such abundance. Instead, coverage of 30 percent, 20 percent, or less is becoming the norm. It is not pollution, or overfishing, or mass bleaching, or climate change, or any of the other factors I have mentioned that is killing our coral reefs (see Figure 6). It is all of these factors together. Or, to put it more plainly, the cause of the destruction of coral reefs is us.

ASSESSING THE PROBLEM, EVALUATING THE LOSS

Remember those 10-million-year gaps in the fossil record of coral reefs? Reefs have disappeared globally several times before, but each time, after a multimillion year pause, they have come back again. While many of the corals and other reef species have become extinct, a few have survived to provide a starting point for the evolution of reef communities every bit as diverse and wondrous as those that existed before. There is growing evidence that changes in ocean chemistry were the primary factor leading to previous instances of reef decline and disappearance. Indeed, the pattern seen in the fossil record—decline very early in each mass extinction event followed by a lengthy gap before reef building resumes—strongly implicates changed ocean chemistry as the cause, because recovery of chemical composition would take that long. Therefore the observation that the oceans are now becoming more acidic is reason for very real concern for the continued existence of coral reefs in our world, although this does not preclude them from eventually returning once more.

There are many possible reasons for changed water chemistry in past times. The evolution and proliferation of terrestrial plants is believed to have rapidly reduced atmospheric CO_2 concentrations during the late Devonian and contributed to that mass extinction event through much cooler climates. Pronounced volcanic activity puts CO_2, SO_2, H_2S, and other gases into the atmosphere in sufficient quantities to radically alter ocean chemistry. Movement of the earth's tectonic plates can rearrange continents into patterns that favor or prevent ocean currents that transport heat from equator to poles, thereby altering the rate at which the oceans mix. There remain gaps in knowledge, but it is clear that substantial alterations in the marine environment have happened before. They seem now to be happening again.

Local impacts such as overfishing, pollution, and inappropriate development can all be remedied using technically rather straightforward, relatively inexpensive approaches, and I will discuss some of these in chapter 9. We have the knowledge we need to address the various problems. On the other hand, the resources of people, information, and funding to support active intervention are seldom sufficient, and political will is frequently lacking. Therefore, while solutions exist that could make a great difference, we have not implemented these solutions nearly as consistently and aggressively as we need to for reef management to be improved. Because the matter is so urgent, we need to commence major efforts to mitigate the effects of local impacts so that reef ecosystems may better withstand the consequences of climate change.[11]

The climate problem can only be solved globally, and its impacts on coral reefs seem likely to be as severe as, if not worse than, those on any ecosystem on the planet. I am optimistic that we will ultimately address greenhouse gases sufficiently to mitigate many of the effects of climate change, but I seriously doubt the world will respond quickly or forcefully enough to prevent climate change from going beyond the point at which reefs cease to exist in any form resembling the reefs of the 1970s.

A desirable level of atmospheric CO_2 for coral reefs is 350 ppm—a lower concentration than now present, and one that we last experienced in the late 1980s. A critical level of atmospheric CO_2 for coral reefs is 450 ppm, about 60 ppm more than at present. At this concentration of CO_2, reefs will be in a world where enhanced frequency of bleaching-induced mortality combined with reduced capacity to build carbonate skeletons due to acidification will have shifted the balance everywhere in favor of reef erosion rather than reef building. This critical level is between 50 and 100 ppm *lower* than the targets that world leaders are

11. Well-managed reefs support higher abundances of coral, and one recent Australian study has shown that corals are better able to withstand high temperatures if water quality is high.

currently talking about—and talk is not action. I suspect we will know in another five years whether we have acted in time to save coral reefs.

Suppose reefs do disappear. Some reef species will survive, and reefs are very likely to come back in the distant future. The rocky structure that is the reef will persist for some considerable time (hundreds of years), occupied by various calcifying organisms, including some of the corals, but their calcification will not be sufficient to keep pace with the forces of destruction. The rocky structure will become a limestone bench, slowly eroding, the live corals and the ecosystem they support replaced by a rich algal flora. Fishery production will decline. The coastal protection value of former reefs will decline as they degrade, at the very time that climate change is likely to increase the severity and perhaps the number of tropical storms. Sea level rise and reef degradation will operate in consort to reduce protective value. Many species that depend on corals will go extinct, and the simplification of the physical structure will be paralleled by a simplification in ecology: fewer species, fewer complex associations, fewer wonderful ways of being alive. Much of this simplification will happen quite quickly, judging by the changes that have already occurred on reefs in the Caribbean, the Galápagos, and other particularly unfortunate places.

We now know that new reefs will not form in more temperate latitudes as the world warms, because the aragonite saturation state is already too low for reef growth outside the tropics. We know they cannot move deeper. They are trapped, and they will degrade and simplify drastically. They will lose the enormous productivity, the intricate recycling of nutrients, and the complex interactions among species that make reefs what they are. And substantial numbers of species will become extinct. But this has happened countless times in the geological past, and there is every reason to imagine a future when reefs blossom again. Ecologically, the loss of an ecosystem currently covering just 0.1 percent of the ocean surface, even a fantastically rich one, is not catastrophic. However, for humanity, the loss of coral reefs may be profound.

Hectare for hectare, coral reefs are economically the most valuable of all coastal marine ecosystems, whether one measures only the products we obtain from them or includes the environmental services they provide. With a growing world population that is increasingly coastal, these valuable ecosystems are only going to become more valuable if we can keep them with us. Their shoreline protection value alone will increase as sea levels rise and storm intensity increases. The economic cost of their loss will be felt.

However, I am not thinking about economic costs when I conclude the loss of reefs may be profound for us. Throughout our history—since the end of the Pleistocene if not earlier—we have excelled at hunting species to extinction. More recently we have proved capable of causing extinction in other ways as well. But if we finish off coral reefs, this will be a new first for mankind—the "extinction" of an entire ecosystem. That it happens to be one of the two richest ecosystems on the planet makes this first a particularly shameful one. I hope it does not come to that. I know we have the capacity to prevent this, but only if we act to address the impact of our ecological footprint.

CORAL REEFS AS AN EARLY WARNING SYSTEM

Coral reefs have been called canaries in the ecological coal mine. One of several risks of coal mining as an occupation, I am told, is being overcome by carbon monoxide or methane gases leeching from the rock face. Canaries are more sensitive to air quality than miners, and taking a caged canary into a mine became an early form of air quality monitoring—when the canary falls off its perch, it's time to get to the surface.[12] As detailed in this chapter, marine ecologists working on coral reefs in recent years have witnessed an extraordinary range of stresses that have impacted these amazing ecosystems in disturbing ways. They have such narrow ecological requirements (for light, depth, temperature, and water quality) that their highly intricate relationships and processes can be disturbed by many different factors and in many different ways. The notion that a coral reef is, like a canary, particularly sensitive to environmental quality and therefore a valuable indicator of damaging changes is not particularly novel and not based on much in the way of science. However, the possibility that coral reefs and certain other kinds of ecosystems (such as arctic regions) may be particularly susceptible to environmental change while other ecosystems may be more tolerant is worth pondering, because our impacts on this planet

---

12. Only in 1986 did the British government announce it would gradually phase out coal miners' canaries in favor of digital carbon monoxide detectors!

are not uniform across places and ecosystems, and the more sensitive ecosystems—the canaries—can warn us of impending danger.

Coral reefs are already telling us that pollution and overexploitation of biological resources can act synergistically to tip an ecosystem from one state to another, one of substantially lower economic value for us. They are also showing us how local stressors of various types can interact with climate change factors to result in less satisfactory outcomes for an ecosystem than if each operated separately. And their obvious decline in many locations over the past half-century is driving home to us just how serious our overuse of this planet may be.

PART TWO

UNDERSTANDING

*Why We Don't Comprehend
the Scale of Our Problem*

5

THE PROBLEM OF
SHIFTING BASELINES

I first met Daniel Pauly at an intensive workshop in Sydney, Australia, in January 1981. At that time he was based in the Philippines at ICLARM, the International Center for Living Aquatic Resource Management. He stayed at ICLARM (which became WorldFish and moved its headquarters to Malaysia) until 1994, when he joined the Fisheries Centre at the University of British Columbia. He remains one of the world's most prolific and widely cited fisheries scientists.

In 1981 Daniel was a young scientist and was somewhat impatient with the way his field moved forward. Fisheries science had grown up in the context of the North Sea and the North Atlantic—large, commercial fisheries targeted a few species in relatively simple northern food webs and were managed by relatively wealthy agencies using sophisticated science to understand the population and the catch. As a consequence, fisheries science was not readily transferable to the management of multispecies fisheries in developing countries. Most fisheries scientists were not terribly concerned about this, but Daniel was. I saw Daniel's frustration in the dynamic of our workshop—a week-long roundtable of just twenty people who engaged in discussion and debate from morning to night, all on the topic of management of tropical (multi-species) fish-

Facing page: The gorgonian soft coral *Pseudopteragorgia bipinnata*, Glovers Reef, Belize, 2003. Photo courtesy of R. S. Steneck.

eries. Most of the participants were senior fisheries scientists with substantial reputations, but there were a few younger participants, among whom Daniel was clearly the most engaged and outspoken. He made a considerable impression on me, and I can still remember one point during the week when he thumped his fist loudly on the table, practically jumped on top of it, and burst out that he was tired of people talking about fisheries science methods that were useless in developing countries where the need for improved fisheries management was greatest and the capacity to deliver sophisticated science was the weakest. (He expressed this idea with somewhat less temperance than I have suggested.)

Throughout his career, Daniel Pauly has said what others in his field were perhaps too timid to say and has developed ideas and approaches that have proven to be much more useful than the efforts of many of the more conventional fisheries biologists. Among his early accomplishments was the development of simple, rule-of-thumb, analytical methods that could be applied to a catch of fish, using minimal data and a pocket calculator, to give approximate but useful answers to basic questions such as "Are too many fish being taken?" or "Can this fish population sustain more fishing effort?" (The answers are only slightly less accurate than those gained using the much more labor- and data-intensive "standard fisheries approaches" that are simply unavailable to a fisheries manager in an impoverished developing country.) He also invented FishBase, now an immeasurably valuable online tool for fisheries scientists or ecologists unable to drop in to the local world-class museum or library, and the simple ecosystem modeling tool Ecopath, beloved by many coral reef ecologists, among others. Above all, he asked the difficult questions, such as "What do those FAO statistics really tell us about our global fishing effort?" The world needs more Daniel Paulys.

In 1995 Daniel Pauly introduced the term *shifting baseline syndrome* as a way of explaining why fisheries biologists, carefully scrutinizing abundance trends over many years, seemed not to be noticing the widespread declines in fishery stocks until it was too late. He suggested that scientists failed to identify and use the appropriate reference point, or baseline, for evaluating current fish populations. Instead of using the population in its unfished state as the permanent baseline for comparison, each individual scientist tended to compare current data on stock abundances with his or her memories of what abundances had been when commencing his or her professional career. Effectively, the baseline was being shifted each generation. This resulted in a distorted perception of change. The situation never seemed that bad compared to what fisheries biologists and managers thought of as "normal" or "natural."

Jeremy Jackson, also an important communicator of difficult news, expanded this term, suggesting there was a general tendency among both professionals and the lay public to look back only a few years when evaluating environmental changes. He suggested that the problem is that a person tends to assume an ecological system's "natural" state is something resembling its condition when he or she first saw it, perhaps because we typically do not expect substantial changes in our world.

As we discussed in chapter 1, Jackson used evidence available from paleontological, archeological, and historical records to identify three types of change: a measurable reduction in the sizes of fish of a particular species that were being landed, a change in the mix of species being caught, and a change in the quantity of fish caught for a given fishing effort. He pointed out that there were abundant examples of very substantial change of all three types over relatively short periods of time. He invoked the idea of the shifting baseline to reconcile this evidence of profound change and our apparent absence of awareness of it. In short, the shifting baseline hypothesis says that in looking at temporal changes in environmental measures—such as the sizes of fish being caught—we tend to compare the present-day data with what we personally remember from only a few years ago rather than look back a lot further to see the overall extent of the change. We shift the baseline we use when examining today's data.

This idea has now been extended to a wide range of other kinds of environmental change. It appears to be a general rule of human perception.[1] We tend not to look too far back, and thus we see only modest incremental change. Shift the baselines back to earlier times, however, and those increments add up to major shifts in conditions.

IGNORING OLDER DATA

Scientists don't consciously shift baselines, intent on erasing the past. We ecologists are all honorable men and women, stumbling about, try-

---

1. Not all scientists are as susceptible to the problem of shifting baselines. Earth scientists, for example, deal explicitly with processes that operate over thousands to millions of years and are therefore less likely to shift baselines.

ing to do our best. What has happened is that ecologists have simply failed to recognize the benefit of going back to older, often less precise data when assessing trends in environmental conditions. Part of the justification for not using older data is that these were rarely collected systematically or with the precision available using modern instrumentation, and scientists pride themselves on being precise and up to date. But the more important reason is surely that, until relatively recently, ecologists have not expected to find long-term trends in ecological data. We have operated within a paradigm that holds that the usual situation is for natural ecosystems not to change through time. This widespread faith in the overall balance of nature gets discussed in chapter 6.

When you operate within a framework in which long-term trends are not expected, one in which any variation present will be small fluctuations around mean conditions, you tend not to see evidence of real change even when it is present in the data. As Marshall McLuhan is reputed to have said, "If I had not believed it, I never would have seen it."

Given that long-term trends are not expected, ecologists frequently describe environmental conditions using only a relatively short time span of observations. This acceptance of short runs of data also fits the natural span of research projects, which are often timed to the durations of M.S. or Ph.D. programs in universities and the funding cycles in research and management agencies. There are many graduate theses and papers published from theses that have evaluated annual cycles in such things as abundance or production of particular species using a span of data barely twelve months long—clearly not long enough to see whether the pattern repeats reliably from one year to the next. Research studies including three years of field data are relatively uncommon, and those spanning a decade are quite rare. The risks in such a short-term perspective were recognized in the 1960s, and Joe Connell and Wayne Sousa, both then at the University of California at Santa Barbara, explored this issue in a carefully written review in 1983. They concluded that, to determine if a particular ecological community was stable in structure, it would be necessary to track it at least until every individual present at the start of the study had died and been replaced. This need for data from one complete turnover of the biota seems a reasonable minimal rule, but their well-reasoned plea did not cause a radical rethinking of how to evaluate long-term trends. Our level of satisfaction in drawing conclusions from very short runs of data is apparently quite difficult to disturb!

Even now, with the term *shifting baseline* having become widely recognized and with a "shifting baseline" site available on the web (www.shiftingbaselines.org), resistance to (or at least a dogged failure to embrace) the idea that changes have been occurring in many ecological systems directly due to human activity remains surprisingly strong. As discussed in part 1, our impacts on the world are serious, frequently unsustainable, and becoming worse. We cannot afford to continue not seeing the truth, but somehow we resist seeing what is before our eyes. When resistance is this strong, I tend to look for more fundamental reasons for failing to see what could be obvious. We really do fail to see long-term changes because we generally do not expect them. This is not a problem unique to ecologists and fisheries scientists. There is something about the way people think and experience the world and remember what we have seen that causes us to focus on the immediate events and fail to see the long-term trends.

THE BIASES IN HUMAN PERCEPTION

Shifting baselines is an operational explanation of what we are doing. Why do we shift them? And even more to the point, why don't we *notice* we are doing this? Why do we consistently fail to see the big picture, even when it is demonstrated to us? We seem to have this behavioral trait—a willingness and ability to notice immediate changes but not see the bigger changes over longer time periods. I think there are three possible and intertwined reasons for this trait, all of which relate to how we experience the real world. One is rooted in physics, one in sensory physiology, and one in evolution.

Let's take the physical reason first. We detect our environment by receiving stimuli of various kinds via our sense organs. These stimuli—light, sound, odor—travel to us through space, and the intensity of any stimulus is reduced as it travels from its source to our sense organs. The inverse square law states that the intensity of a stimulus is reduced at a rate proportional to the inverse of the square of the distance over which it has traveled. That is, if a lamp is 2 km away, it will appear only ¼ as bright as if the same lamp is only 1 km away; if it is 3 km away, it will appear only ⅑ as bright as at 1 km.

Now think of the apparent brightness of the headlights on a car approaching us as we stand together on the highway. The brightness of the light (as it reaches your eye) will obey the inverse square law and will appear to change very little until the last minutes. If the car is driven toward us at a constant speed, the apparent intensity of its headlights increases at an exponential rate—that is, the rate of change in intensity is itself also constantly increasing. If the car accelerates as it races toward us, the intensity of the headlights increases at a rapidly accelerating rate. Only if the car is slowing down (at an exponential rate) does the rate of change in the apparent brightness of the headlights become linear.

While most people do not live very long if they stand in the road watching approaching headlights, we have all heard the apparent changes in the sound of a car's engine, tires, or horn as the vehicle approaches, passes, and recedes into the distance. There are two changes here—loudness and pitch. The change in frequency occurs because pitch depends on the rate of travel of the sound wave, and this rate is relatively faster as the vehicle approaches than it is as it departs because the vehicle's motion adds to that of the sound wave. This change, called the Doppler effect, is a bit of a red herring in the present context, but I mention it because it may mask the change in the intensity of the sound. This change in intensity, like the brightness of the light, obeys the inverse square rule and is exponential when the car approaches at constant speed.[2]

Ignore the Doppler effect for now and notice instead that the intensity of the stimulus increases at an exponential rate when the source is moving toward us at a constant rate. This is a real phenomenon, quite independent of whether we or any other organism are there to see or listen. Linear changes in the distance of the stimulus source (the headlight) from the observer result in exponential changes in the intensity of stimulus received. While the object is moving but still far away, changes in the stimuli it provides will be quite difficult to detect, but when it is near and moving, the rate of change in the stimuli becomes far greater.

Now we add the physiological reason, which interacts with the physical. The old metaphor of the eye as camera does a good job of explaining the physics of vision up until the light hits the retina, but it leaves the impression that the visual system is a faithful recorder of intensities of light. Seeing, hearing, or any other form of perception is a far more

2. Of course, if the car were to be traveling really fast, at a large fraction of the speed of light, we could see a similar Doppler effect in the visual stimulus, and the color of the light would change—but that herring is so red it glows in the dark.

complex process than that—more analogous to modern image analysis than to exposure of film in a camera. The core constituent of a complex sense organ such as the human eye or ear is a set of specialized cells, the sensory receptors. Although I am simplifying greatly, each of our sensory receptors is a transducer, sensitive to a particular type of stimulus that translates that type of stimulus into the common currency of the nervous system—the action potentials of neurons. Neurons are much-elongated and branching cells, usually with many fine branches called *dendrites* and a single, usually longer and stouter branch, the *axon*. The action potential is a cyclical pattern of depolarization and repolarization of the electrically charged cell membrane that propagates along the dendrites or axon and, via synapses, from one neuron to another. Neurons "talk" to one another in a language of action potentials. Sensory receptors translate specific kinds of stimuli into action potentials so that more intense stimuli result in a greater frequency of action potentials. In other words, intensity of the stimulus being received is encoded as the rate of production of action potentials. But not quite.

Our sensory receptors are not automated translators that faithfully convert the intensity of the stimulus being received into a set rate of action potentials. They are forgetful, and they get bored. They respond most strongly (that is, they initiate action potentials at the highest rate) to new stimuli but become progressively less responsive as the stimulation continues. Switch on a bright light and the light receptor springs into action, but leave the light on, and after a while the receptor ceases to respond to it. This process, termed *adaptation,* is shared by all sensory receptors. It explains why background noises can be ignored while we listen to a conversation in a crowded bar, and why we do not continuously feel our clothing once we put it on in the morning. It also explains why we are very bad at estimating the brightness of light, and why I made lots of poorly exposed photographs back when cameras used film and required some skill to operate.

In addition to adaptation, groups of similar sensory receptors (such as the light receptors of the retina, the sound receptors along the cochlear wall, or even the touch receptors on a patch of your skin) also exhibit a trait called *lateral inhibition.* They interact with their neighbors so that the neighbors of an active receptor tend to be less active than they otherwise would be. As a consequence, if light shines onto a part of the retina, receptors in the center of the patch of illumination are less active than those at the edge. Those at the edge have some neighbors in darkness and therefore fewer neighbors inhibiting them than do receptors in the center.

The consequence of adaptation and lateral inhibition is that our sensory systems do a good job of emphasizing edges in space and in time: they tell the central nervous system when stimulation starts, where the edge of a patch of stimulation falls, and when stimulation stops. They are great at detecting change—the more sudden the better—and lousy at reporting unchanged or slowly changing conditions. The approaching car provides a dramatically increasing intensity of a variety of kinds of stimulation, visual and auditory, and our sense organs are good at reporting these changes to our central nervous systems. But a car that approaches very slowly may not even get noticed. The same is true for a predator—or for a threatening environmental change.

Now let's add in the evolutionary reason. Natural selection is a simple process that acts on variation in traits among individuals. Those individuals with inheritable traits that make them most likely to survive and reproduce in the environment in which they find themselves (the fitter individuals) are favored by natural selection: they produce more offspring than other individuals, and their traits become progressively more common in the population. The most direct selection occurs when individuals possess traits that facilitate their survival when faced by danger, such as an approaching predator or car. The ability to respond rapidly and effectively to approaching danger has high selective value, and we can anticipate that the attributes of all organisms are shaped to maximize these abilities. Selection is less effective in shaping responses to events that are not linked to imminent danger. That is, the ability to evade the predator's jaws is more likely to be strongly selected for than is the ability to notice the movements of a predator some distance away that is not an immediate threat.

Because natural selection works in this way, we should anticipate that organisms will be more responsive to signals of imminent danger or opportunity and less responsive to signals of more distant danger or opportunity. Like other organisms, we should be selected for traits that cause us to pay most attention, perhaps all attention, to immediate threats and opportunities. If we are relatively unresponsive to signals of future or distant danger or opportunity, that should not surprise us—selection to be responsive to more remote events will not have been very strong.

Putting these three factors together, an interesting pattern emerges.

First, for purely physical reasons, at least some of the changes that occur in the world generate stimuli that change exponentially, even though the environmental change is linear. The approaching predator or car on the highway is such a change, and in such circumstances, we interpret the experience of exponential change in stimulation as a case of linear change in distance of the entity causing the stimulation. The rate of change in stimulation is most extreme when the predator or car is nearly upon us. Second, the physiology of our sense organs ensures that they pay attention to sudden changes in stimulation but cease to respond to stimuli that are constant or only changing slowly. The exponential increase in brightness of those headlights probably will not be noticed until the car is getting pretty close, and as a consequence, our transducers further bias the message delivered to the central nervous system in favor of immediate events. Finally, natural selection has honed both the sensory physiology and the interpretive activity of the central nervous system (the actual seeing or perceiving and the remembering and decision making that will follow) to ensure that we respond to immediate events that are dangerous, such as approaching cars, by getting out of the way. There is likely to be little selection for general responsiveness to stimuli that are changing slowly or not at all. As a result, we are quite good at dealing with immediate events but not at responding to distant or gradual threats. To summarize, we are not built to respond to the big picture, the long-term change. Near and immediate events are emphasized, made more prominent than they really are, and our responses to those events will have been more precisely shaped by our evolution.

Now, I have been writing as if we are trapped by the laws of physics, biology, and evolution, but we also have culture, language, rationality, and the collective memory that language has provided. While I know we cannot transcend the laws of physics, and I believe that our biology and evolution trap us more than we might like to admit, of course we can rise above these limitations and learn new ways of viewing environmental change. In one sense we have been learning not to shift baselines ever since Daniel Pauly coined the phrase, but we still have a ways to go.

There is one other factor that may be important in explaining our poor ability to evaluate data on environmental change (as opposed to evaluating change directly). When we compile environmental data, bringing together objective measurements made at different places or, more particularly, at different times, our compilation removes the time and space relationships among those data. Our sensory systems no longer experience the changing intensity of stimuli that could have been available if the changing conditions were watched directly. What I mean to say is that a graph showing the distance of a car from the subject (us) and how this changes with time does not provide the apparent exponential increase in intensity of stimuli that we experience as we are about to get run over. The data are accurate, they show the car approaching with its headlights on, but they do not have the urgency of the direct experience of standing in the middle of the road. Even a graph of headlight brightness as measured close to the subject (us), which will be an exponential curve, still won't have the "feel" of the real thing.

Finally, there is also the possibility—I am out on a very thin limb here—that the combination of the inverse square rule, adaptation, and lateral inhibition causes us to perceive real exponential changes in our environment as only linear. Since a predator or car approaching at constant speed provides perceptions that increase exponentially in intensity, it may be that we routinely but incorrectly "reconvert" other exponential patterns to linear ones. I believe something like this must be taking place to explain our appallingly poor ability to subjectively appreciate the consequences of exponential change, such as in the growth of our own population. Nearly everyone who watched *An Inconvenient Truth* remembers how Al Gore had to use a cherry picker to lift himself high above the stage[3] in order to reach the point on the graph representing our global population in a few years' time. Yet very few of those same people truly appreciate what this graph tells us about the growth of our population.

EXPONENTIAL CHANGE: BEYOND OUR GRASP

Environmental changes that occur at rates that are themselves increasing (or decreasing) give rise to many of the most serious environmental problems we face, yet we have great difficulty appreciating them. This inability to see the implications of exponential change—to appreciate

3. Al Gore's Academy Award–winning documentary film, *An Inconvenient Truth,* did much to awaken people to the issue of climate change. In it, as a way of dramatizing the extent of growth in the human population, Gore tracked a graph across the stage as it moved from prehistory to the present, but as it inexorably inflected and shot toward the ceiling, he climbed into a cherry picker to keep up with it. *An Inconvenient Truth,* directed by Davis Guggenheim and starring Al Gore, is a 2006 Paramount Classics and Participant Production.

what it really means—seems to be a fundamental characteristic of the way we are built. It can perhaps be best seen through the story about the young man traveling in strange lands who had the opportunity to rescue a beautiful princess from the jaws of a dragon.

To reward him for this act of valor, the king of that country offered the young man anything he desired that was in the king's power to give. Being an astute and mathematically gifted young man, he stated that he wanted just one simple thing. He wanted one grain of wheat on the first square of his chessboard, two grains on the second, four on the third, and so on until all squares were full. The king protested that this was far too modest a request. The young man insisted. As the king gathered the grain needed to pay the reward, everything seemed fine at first, but then he began to see that he had made a huge mistake. He emptied his granaries and then exhausted his treasury buying grain from his neighbors. The young man sold the wheat, married the princess, and lived happily ever after.

It is a delightful tale, and I've never been sure what message it was intended to convey.[4] But it does provide a wonderful entrée to exponential growth. Intellectually, it is possible to make the calculations and discover the size of 2^{63}—the number of grains of wheat on the last square. What proves exceptionally difficult is to appreciate, subjectively or emotionally, the enormous size of 2^{63} or the shape of the whole progression. Working out that it will take only 255 grains of wheat to fill the first row of the chessboard and reconciling this with the need for 2^{63} grains of wheat on the final square is a simple piece of computation (although writing out 2^{63} as a simple number would be difficult without a rather large piece of paper). Appreciating the full extent of the change over just sixty-four steps is much more difficult. So is appreciating that if the king reached the point when sixty-three squares were filled, he would still have put on the board one grain of wheat less than half the number of grains it should eventually contain. I suppose it would also be difficult to find a chessboard big enough to hold all that wheat.

I think the difficulty we have in appreciating the pattern in this story is the same one we face whenever confronted with evidence of any kind of increasing rate of change. The pattern of growth of the earth's

4. Possible messages: always carry a chessboard, pay attention in math class, and, for kings, if a request sounds too good to be true, it probably is.

human population, for example, has been presented to us many times in the last forty years,[5] but we still don't get it. We still do not appreciate the real magnitude of the change that has already occurred and that is expected by 2050.

The pattern of human population growth is broadly exponential, as can be seen in Figure 7. There are several points of inflection on the curve that can be tied to events in human history. It is thought that the development of culture in the distant past, around the time *Homo sapiens* differentiated from ancestral forms, brought the size of the human population up to about 5 million at the close of the Pleistocene. The agricultural revolution resulted in a better-documented jump up to about 250 million, a level reached about a thousand years ago. The Industrial Revolution caused another major upswing in population, and the rate of growth continued to increase until quite recently. The world population reached 1 billion in 1802 and exceeded 6.8 billion in 2010. It has tripled in size since 1942 and is currently growing at the rate of more than 80 million people per year. While the rate of growth now seems to be declining slightly, the trend will be steeply upward for some time to come unless one or more major disasters strike.

It should be impossible to look at this growth trajectory and be complacent, because it should be impossible to conceive of the world supporting an ever-increasing number of one species. By 2050 it is estimated that our population will be 50 percent larger than it was in 2000. If each of these people uses resources at the rates we used resources in 2000, we will need 50 percent more of all the resources we use—food, water, raw materials, energy. If they all use resources at the rates at which people in developed countries currently use them, the need for additional resources will have increased astronomically—far beyond what the earth could possibly support.

REALLY SEEING WHAT'S HAPPENING TO THE WORLD

So, how do we stop shifting baselines? Or, more generally, how do we overcome our perceptual and cognitive limitations and learn to visualize the changes that are happening around us? Baseline shifting is not the

---

5. The Stanford University ecologist Paul Ehrlich deserves special credit for working long and hard to make us understand back in the 1970s.

FIGURE 7. The human population has grown slowly since the Stone Age, but growth became approximately exponential with the invention of agriculture. Growth rate reached a peak in the early 1960s. The slight slowdown in rate of growth since then is not visible due to the condensed time frame but should cause population size to level off at 9.2 million by 2050 and then begin a slow decline. The projection into the future is hypothetical. Graph redrawn, with permission, from a Population Reference Bureau figure that used data from United Nations, World Population Projections to 2100, prepared in 1998.

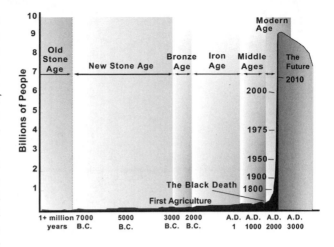

result of a conscious decision or of indifference in the face of exponential change. I think it is an inevitable consequence of the way we are built, how we evolved, and the physical nature of the universe. We will have to learn to appreciate the nature of change and to avoid readjusting our points of reference. One way to begin would be to put more effort into teaching all people, not just the environmental scientists, about how modest incremental change can have substantial effects given enough time, and how modest but exponential change can have very dramatic effects. These are the same lessons people need to learn if they are to understand the value of a disciplined savings or investment program, the benefit of even a modest lump payment on the ultimate cost of a mortgage, or the damage done by carrying credit card debt. Simply appreciating the difference between a thousand, a million, a billion, and a trillion might be a good start.

In addition, we need to teach people that the world is a place where we should expect changes, whether caused by us or not. Nature is not in perfect balance, and our universe can be a dangerous place. Given that many of our impacts on the environment are growing exponentially, we should anticipate a growing number of surprises unless we master the ability to look at the long-term view. Remember the king, when he had just managed to round up the wheat for the second-to-last square on the chessboard. If only he could have seen what was coming.

6

OUR UNREALISTIC BELIEF IN
THE BALANCE OF NATURE

My academic advisor in graduate school in Hawaii was the late W. A. (Bill) Gosline, a crusty old ichthyologist (fish biologist) who made many contributions to our understanding of the evolution of fishes. Being crusty, he did not like to mince his words—but he also had a gift for letting the naive student learn gently. I told him that for my Ph.D. research I wanted to pick a group of ecologically similar species and figure out what it was that permitted them to occur together on the reef. Without so much as a wink or a slight smile, Bill said, "I think you should work on moray eels."

He then elaborated: there were thirty-two species of moray eel in Hawaii, including fifteen in the single genus *Gymnothorax;* they were all cylindrical, 60 cm to a couple of meters long, with lots of sharp, pointed teeth; they all lived in holes in the reef not much bigger around than they were, where they hunted at night for the fish that were their prey. I realized quickly that he was not really suggesting I study eels; he was quietly telling me that my idea that species that occur together must differ was a quaint belief I had gathered in the much less biodiverse lakes of Ontario.

I duly registered Bill's skepticism in my mind, but I continued to wonder about what ecologists referred to as "the problem of coexis-

---

Facing page: Fishing boats, Philippines. Photo courtesy of Yvonne J. Sadovy de Mitcheson.

tence of similar species" (even though I ended up working on a rather different question for my Ph.D). For a long time, ecologists had been guided by the idea that species that occur together in nature must have unique ecological characteristics and that these essential differences between species are what permit them to coexist. In particular, members of the same guild—such as seed-eating birds, rainforest trees, or territorial damselfishes—must differ in how they exploit their habitats because otherwise competition among them would inevitably lead to competitive exclusion—the local elimination of one species by another until only the fittest species of that type survives in that region. You have probably heard this idea numerous times on the Discovery Channel, and you may even know the aphorism "No two species can occupy the same niche."

In those days, ecologists assumed that when one observed similar species coexisting in the same habitat, those species were somehow partitioning that habitat or its resources in ways that were not immediately apparent. Such situations were natural targets of research projects: you would observe the coexisting species with enough care and detail to determine the "hidden" mechanisms of niche partitioning. And so it was, several years later, that I came to be studying the real estate transactions of damselfishes on the reefs of Heron Island. The three species of damselfishes, you'll recall from chapter 4, had very similar requirements and yet occurred together, even defending territories from one another, in small rubble patches on the reef.

Luckily for me, four years of study and research at the University of Hawaii had taught me that much of what I had believed about natural ecological systems was simply not true in the tropics. So I was much more open-minded than I might otherwise have been, ready to look critically at this widely accepted idea that each species has unique characteristics and thus a unique "niche." What I discovered not only offered an entirely different explanation for how similar species could coexist, it began to poke some holes in an even bigger idea—the idea of the balance of nature.

STABILITY AND HOMEOSTASIS IN NATURE

Central to our understanding of the natural world is a deeply rooted belief in the essential homeostasis of nature. We liken nature to a living thing, investing it with the same inherent ability to maintain itself in a state of equilibrium, to heal itself when injured. This belief is frequently referenced as the "balance of nature." The belief that nature is homeostatic goes back in Western thought at least as far as the Greek philosophers and their concepts of the ideal. Plato's "forms" and Aristotle's "causes" helped build a rational, materialistic approach for understanding existence, fostering a belief that what might appear to be random or chance events were usually events with logical causes that we simply did not yet understand. With the amalgamation of Greco-Roman and Judeo-Christian thought came the idea that the universe was in many ways perfect, mechanistic, and logical in operation. The Renaissance and the rise of modern scientific approaches consolidated such ideas, along with the idea that humanity was appropriately an external observer of the natural world rather than a part of it.

By Darwin's time, the natural world was widely thought of as orderly, well designed, and capable of being understood rationally. Most people believed nature to be close to perfect in form and that this perfection was evidence of the magnificence of its perfect creator. It was logical to assume that the natural world was in its intended state and that it would be maintained by mechanisms or processes that existed for the purpose of maintaining that state.[1] This basic assumption has been retained in Western society up to the present day, forming the essence of our idea of the balance of nature—that the natural world is a homeostatic system able to maintain its current state through time and to return to that state if perturbed by some external agency. The Gaia hypothesis, which sees the biosphere as essentially a single living being, is a logical, if extreme, extension of this concept.

The problem is, natural systems on Earth offer no evidence that a balance of nature really exists. Ecological investigations over the last few decades have revealed that despite the comfort that a stable natural world would bring, it really doesn't work that way. Nature appears to have no inherent self-regulating, equilibrium-creating ability, although there are times and places in which conditions remain constant for peri-

---

1. This view of nature inadvertently created a problem for evolution, in that the tendency to believe that evolution must be progressing toward some superior goal, usually with *Homo sapiens* prominently present, continues to distort understanding. Evolution involves change, but it does not involve changes leading to predefined goals.

ods of several years or decades that might encourage us to continue searching for regulatory mechanisms. In short, the balance of nature is a myth. And more important, it is a myth we can no longer afford to have guide our thinking about the natural world.

"The great enemy of the truth," said John F. Kennedy, "is very often not the lie—deliberate, contrived and dishonest, but the myth, persistent, persuasive, and unrealistic. Belief in myths allows the comfort of opinion without the discomfort of thought." Our belief in a homeostatic nature has not been quite that bad, as myths go. It has encouraged rational approaches to understanding how nature functions and provided a helpful conceptual lifeline at a time when understanding of complex systems was limited. But it has led ecologists down some incorrect paths and given conservation a very fragile framework from which to build a science. Our tendency to extrapolate from very short time-series of data, assuming that nature is at equilibrium (or in a rhythmically repeating seasonal cycle), is a clear example of the problems it has caused. In forming the underlying paradigm of the conservation movement—just keep people away and it will remain as it currently is forever—it has complicated the life of more than one natural area manager. And I am certain that the strength of our belief in this myth has played a role in our tendency to shift those baselines without any thought to the consequences. It has certainly now outlived its usefulness, because nature is far less balanced than we believe, and its resilience is also necessarily far weaker.

To properly appreciate the extent to which we are damaging our world and what we will need to do if we decide to redress this damage, it is necessary to have a more accurate and up-to-date understanding of how the natural world functions. The following pages are a rushed journey through about 150 years of accumulated study that will show how ecology became seduced by the idea of the balance of nature and then how it broke free.[2] We will touch on what terms like *community* really mean in ecology, spend considerable time on the idea of the balance of nature itself, and trace the revolution in ecological ideas that

2. I am deliberately taking this historical approach because, over years of teaching, I have seen how compelling the idea of the balance of nature can be. Many ecology students never really let go of it, although they cleverly park it in the back of their minds while taking the final exam in my course! It is a comforting idea that gets continually reinforced in the media, entertainment, and carelessly written science.

took place in the waning years of the twentieth century. I will minimize ecological jargon and try to entertain, surprise, and delight you, but I will also do my best to ensure that you emerge thoroughly up-to-date ecologically, ready to contemplate the world of the twenty-first century.

THE CONCEPT OF THE ECOLOGICAL COMMUNITY

In ecology, one manifestation of the pervasive belief in nature's balance is our understanding of the concept of the community. The term *community* has a long history in ecology. The American ecologist Stephen Forbes used it in 1887 to describe the ecology of a lake. He referred to the lake as a microcosm, largely independent of what went on in the terrestrial world surrounding its shores, and spoke of a "community of interest" possessed by its inhabitant species. This community of interest was achieved by the individual organisms adjusting their interactions so that all prospered. Like many at the time, he reasoned that any predators that became so proficient that they took more prey than the prey species could produce would eat themselves out of house and home and go extinct. Since predators and prey continue to coexist, he argued there must be a community of interest, a degree of cooperation that had evolved to prevent such imbalances from occurring. (The tendency to award such altruism to species was largely ended by the work of geneticists, who showed convincingly that self-interest wins over altruism every time when natural selection is involved. In a Darwinian world such as ours, nice guys really do finish last.)

Since Forbes's time, the term *community* has been used to refer to the microcosm itself rather than to any mutual agreements among its members. *Webster's* definition of community—"an interacting population of various kinds of individuals (as species) in a common location"—well expresses the usual current ecological meaning. The community is the group of (presumably interacting) species that occurs at a set place and time.

Unfortunately, this is not what scientists call an "operational" definition. In practice, group, place, and time are all subject to interpretation and are often not specified, so that our theoretical concept of community does not closely match the things ecologists studying communities usually work on. *Group* often refers to species of a particular kind of organism—herbaceous plants, insects, birds, herbivores, or zoo-plankton—rather than to all species present. (This taxonomic restriction makes less valid the assumption that interactions are primarily among species within the group.) *Place* may be well bounded; it could, for example, be a lake, stream, or island surrounded by a very different environment largely inimical to the survival of the species from within it. Interactions across the border would be slight in such cases, and they are at least quantifiable as inputs and outputs. More often than not, however, *place* is far less clearly bounded, and interactions between community members and nonmembers are potentially frequent. The shallow subtidal, the meadow (bordered by forest or farmland), the small body of water within the Venus flytrap, and the decaying log on the forest floor have all been considered a community's place at one time or another. These are all poorly bordered, and some are also small or ephemeral (the log and the flytrap). *Time* is almost always measured simply by the duration of the ecologist's attention to the place and may range from a single visit one afternoon to a study of several years. Until recently, ecologists interested in community structure seldom specified what they meant by "the same time," although most, like Forbes, assumed their observations were sufficiently lengthy to encompass the range of temporal variation the community was likely to display over much longer periods of ecological time. I doubt whether this is usually true.

Where does this leave the concept of community? One problem is that a lot of the theoretical ideas about the structure and dynamics of communities have been based on the *theoretical* community—an all-encompassing group of species in a well-bounded place over an ecologically long time. Yet the *empirical* data used to support, test, or extend the theory are derived from studies of "communities" of restricted groups in poorly bounded places for short times. Is this a good foundation? No, but other fields of study have similar problems, and the important thing is to remember that the problems exist. In particular, when exploring ecological theory, principles, or rules, it's good to remember the assumptions that underlie them—assumptions that usually go unspoken. I could dissect concepts such as population and ecosystem in a similar way, but all that is necessary is to remember that populations are groups of individuals of one species, that groups of populations of different species comprise communities, and that communities blur into ecosystems as one thinks larger scale. Ecology really is a more complex subject than physics.[3]

CHANGING VIEWS OF THE COMMUNITY THROUGH HISTORY

A definition of *community* is one thing, but to understand the functioning of communities, I want to delve more deeply. A good place to start digging is provided by Charles Darwin. It is always surprising (and very humbling) to browse through his *Origin of Species,* published in 1858, because Darwin anticipated so much of the ecology that has developed since. (It's also fun because his language is so different from that of modern science.) *The Origin* is a very good place from which to begin a brief survey of the history of thought on communities and balance. Although Darwin emphasized that the strongest interactions an organism was likely to have were competitive interactions with closely related (and therefore ecologically similar) individuals, his "struggle for existence" included far more than intra-specific competition. In chapter 3 of *Origin of Species,* he stresses that the struggle for existence is a struggle *by the individual,* both to survive and to reproduce successfully. Darwin makes clear that it includes the struggles of intra- and inter-specific competition, the struggle against weather and other environmental challenges, and the struggle to avoid being eaten by a predator.

In the same chapter, he comes close to defining a community without using the word when he talks of "how complex and unexpected are the checks and relations between organic beings, which have to struggle together in the same country." He gives an example that is so complicated that Rube Goldberg would have loved it, if Rube had been an ecologist. Based on simple field experiments in his garden, Darwin knew that Heartsease (*Viola tricolor*) rarely ever set seed unless visited by humblebees (bumblebees). In addition, he had collected experimental data showing the importance of humblebees to pollination of a second species (Red clover, *Trifolium pratense*): "100 heads of red clover . . .

3. I do not believe ecologists are any less careful in their use of language than other life or environmental scientists, but most of us do not think as rigorously as mathematicians. However, the main point I want to make with this chapter requires that we see more clearly than we usually do.

produced 2700 seeds, but the same number of protected heads [from humblebees] produced not one." He then developed a chain that linked abundances of humblebees, field mice, and cats by referencing the reports of a Colonel Newman, "who has long attended to the habits of humblebees." Newman reported that field mice destroy humblebee nests and stated that nests of humblebees were more numerous near towns. Newman attributed this greater abundance of humblebee nests near towns to "the [greater] number of cats which destroy mice." Darwin nicely concludes that the differential abundance of cats near centers of human habitation may indirectly influence the abundance of Heartsease and Red clover through its direct effects on the abundance of field mice.

There is no doubt here that Darwin had a clear conception of the community as a group of interacting species, although there is nothing to suggest he anticipated a tightly balanced, equilibrial community or a system organized primarily by competitive processes. (All the processes in this example are predatory ones—even the fertilizing of flowers by bees is a consequence of foraging.) As for Newman, we hear no more of him, although it must have been nice to be a nineteenth-century gentleman of leisure with the time to "attend to the habits of humblebees."

While he did not explicitly propose a balanced, equilibrial community, Darwin lived in Victorian England—a time and place in which the natural world was viewed as a marvelous creation that reflected the glory of its maker. Herbert Spencer, Darwin's contemporary and the man who coined the phrase "survival of the fittest," was an engineer who saw the natural world as an equilibrium among opposing forces. The world was complete and, at the same time, an intricate and self-perpetuating mechanism, and Darwin and his contemporaries expected orderliness. Thus Darwin commented, later in chapter 3 of *Origin of Species,* on the "numerous recorded cases of the astonishingly rapid increase of various animals in a state of nature, when circumstances have been favourable to them during two or three following seasons," but he also noted that "in the long-run the forces are so nicely balanced that the face of nature remains uniform for long periods of time."[4]

4. In other words, the balanced condition of similar numbers each year is *normal,* and the outbreak in numbers is *unusual.* Nature usually keeps itself in balance—it's homeostatic.

Darwin's concept of adaptation through natural selection, though it challenged the prevailing religious view that the world and its creatures had been created in their present forms by a Supreme Being, still provided a mechanism accounting for the excellent design people thought they saw in the natural world. And he had a view of an overall orderliness that tolerated the occasional disorderly outbreak or massive decline of a species.

While the concept of the balance of nature has long been well entrenched in Western thought, it was F. E. Clements who codified the view of the community as an intricate mechanism in balance, although even he was careful to note that only what he called the "climax community" possessed a stable equilibrium structure. Other communities were engaged in progressive slow change toward this climax state.

Clements was an American plant ecologist at the turn of the twentieth century who became the most influential English-speaking ecologist of the time and, in 1905, wrote the first real ecology textbook, *Research Methods in Ecology*. Clements studied the structure of plant communities. He viewed communities as complex entities that, like individual organisms, could be considered to develop and mature, to possess a metabolism, and to display homeostatic abilities that shielded them from the vagaries of the environment. The process of community development was termed *succession* and was the central focus of much of his work.

Clements viewed succession as an inexorable set of changes in species composition that shifted the composition of a community away from its initial form until a final stage was reached in the climax community, the composition of which was determined by the local climate and geology. He recognized that the successional process could be interrupted or diverted by factors such as fire or overgrazing, but his emphasis was on the predictable march toward the climax. In Clements's conception, the climax community had many special properties, such as greater efficiency of transfer of energy from sunlight to consumer organisms, a greater ratio of biomass to production, and a greater preponderance of long-lived species—all because it was a more finely adapted entity than the various successional stages that preceded it.[5] All in all, Clements conceived of the

5. In fact, most of these properties are what might be expected of communities containing larger, longer-lived species, such as the mature forests Clements studied. His underlying belief in a balanced nature caused him to jump to a conclusion about causes.

community as a very intricate mechanism that changed only slowly and in predictable ways in response to orderly universal laws. These ideas, sometimes only nascent in Clements's writing, were embroidered more fully by his students and ultimately found their way into the concept of *ecosystem,* which refers to all the physical and biological components of an environment, or "the set of communities at a place."

Animal ecologists were strongly influenced by Clements. A considerable amount of time during the first half of the twentieth century was spent in enumerating which animal species belonged in each biome (ecosystem writ large) and in tracing patterns of animal replacement during succession. Despite this, animal ecology was an essentially separate discipline from plant ecology, and animal ecologists developed some important community concepts of their own because of their preoccupation with what animals did.[6]

Niche is one such concept. A *niche* is a species' place within the community, and it existed as a warm fuzzy idea for a long time (until Evelyn Hutchinson tried to make it explicit and operational in 1959). American ecologist Joseph Grinnell first used the word *niche* in 1917 to refer to an animal's ecological role, or profession, within the community—what it did. In his 1927 text, British ecologist Charles Elton used *niche* for the animal's habitat, or address, within the community—where it lived. Both usages were attempts to integrate the broad range of ecological requirements possessed by each species, but neither integrates them fully, because habitat needs and trophic (feeding) needs are two parts of a single set of requisites needed to sustain the individual. Both usages of the term *niche* help to indicate the structure of interrelationships that was presumed to exist between a species and other components of its environment: other species and factors such as temperature, rainfall, and so on, that impinge upon this structure within the community.[7]

Our rapid journey through time is masking some of the intricate shifts in meaning that occurred in this march forward from Darwin. Notice, for example, that in developing the concepts of *climax commu-*

---

6. Behavior is an important attribute of animals and virtually absent in plants. As an animal ecologist myself, I confess I have enjoyed watching animals do the things they do, and I find watching plants an excellent way to enter a deeply meditative state.

7. Incidentally, it was Grinnell who stated that two species could not occupy the same niche and thus began a very rich area of ecological inquiry into the mechanisms permitting coexistence of similar species.

nity and *niche,* ecologists shifted the focus toward the species and away from the individual. Why they did this is not clear, but with this subtle change, Darwin's "struggle for existence" waged by individuals, predominantly against similar individuals, was converted into a struggle among species.

Animal ecologists greatly strengthened the edifice that was the balance of nature when they developed strong arguments for the regulation of population numbers. Although Charles Elton stated forcefully in 1930 his belief that "the balance of nature does not exist, and perhaps, never has existed," because he had observed great variations in "the numbers of wild animals," he subsequently (in 1946) modified his views considerably and came to support the prevailing argument that population sizes were rather closely regulated by density-dependent biotic interactions such as competition.[8] This perspective, which sees the balance of nature as one in which the abundances of particular species are continuously being controlled, chiefly through their interactions with other species of the community, was given important impetus by the work of the Australian insect ecologist A.J. Nicholson, who became a leading advocate of this homeostatic view of the dynamics of populations and communities. In the mid-1930s, Nicholson went so far as to introduce the notion that populations were at, or very close to, an equilibrium state even when they were fluctuating markedly in size. Fluctuating populations were simply tracking a changing equilibrium set by changing conditions.[9]

In 1954 David Lack, a British bird ecologist, summarized the prevailing view in a very influential book, *The Natural Regulation of Animal Numbers.* Chapter 1 begins: "Most wild animals fluctuate irregularly in numbers between limits that are extremely restricted compared with what their rates of increase would allow"—an interesting contrast to Elton's statement just twenty-four years earlier.

Nicholson's view of continuous density-dependent control, when

8. *Density-dependent biotic interaction* is an interaction between organisms, the strength of which varies in some way with population density. *Density-dependent competition* is competition that becomes more severe as the number of competitors present increases. Therefore, animals competing for food or nesting sites will experience greater difficulty (greater competition) in obtaining these as the number of animals increases.

9. You may perhaps appreciate the difficulty of testing a hypothesis this flexible! Ecologists are not always noted for the precision with which they frame hypotheses. The late Robert Peters of McGill University, Montreal, has written extensively on this topic.

reinforced by Lack's supporting arguments, became the accepted dogma, despite a vigorous call in 1954 by two other Australian insect ecologists, H. G. Andrewartha and L. C. Birch, for an alternative, nonequilibrial view. The explosive interest in modern competition theory that began in the late 1950s and continued into the 1960s, with its mathematically convenient focus on only slight departures from equilibrium states, clinched the victory for a balance-of-nature view—and made it far more restrictive than had ever been intended by those who first used the phrase a hundred or more years earlier.

The concept of the ecological web developed by Andrewartha and Birch is in many ways an analog of the niche. However, unlike *niche,* which describes the species' role in a community, *ecological web* focuses strictly on the individual organism. Andrewartha and Birch viewed the organism as suspended at the center of a web of interactions with components of the environment, including other organisms as well as abiotic factors such as light and temperature, which acted to affect that individual organism's ability to survive and reproduce. Andrewartha and Birch directed their research so completely toward the individual that their ideas were largely put aside by ecologists of the day interested in community processes. They, in turn, disparaged a community approach as too complex to be likely to yield useful results for either understanding or managing dynamics of specific species. Yet their thinking about the network of directly and indirectly acting factors that together influence an individual's ability to survive and multiply was crystal clear, nondogmatic, and far more modern in its multifactorial approach and absence of assumptions about homeostasis than the thinking of the majority of ecologists at that time.

This brings me to two of the most influential American ecologists of their day—Evelyn Hutchinson and Robert MacArthur. Hutchinson was, in every sense, a Renaissance man interested in a broad range of subjects inside and outside ecology. His small textbook of 1978 is a delightful, sometimes whimsical book compared to other ecology texts of that time. He did what he could to make the concept of the niche operational,[10]

10. He was unsuccessful, because a niche is essentially a hypervolume with an indefinite number of dimensions. There is no way to fully measure a niche or to test whether two species have niches that overlap. Robert Peters explained this in 1976, but many ecologists did not notice.

and he asked delightful and provocative questions about community structure, whether of stable or of nonequilibrial communities. Above all, he seems to have encouraged in his students the idea of ecology as a hypothesis-testing science rather than a purely descriptive one. Robert MacArthur was, simply, Hutchinson's greatest student. MacArthur's contribution was to make field community ecology quantitative and closely tied to theory. To do this, however, he was obliged to concentrate on the more manageable theory of closed, equilibrial communities, and in most of his work he assumed that the communities of birds he studied were well bounded and at equilibrium.

In tracing the development of the concepts of community and the balance of nature, I have dealt mainly with what leading ecologists thought about communities rather than with the data that guided or supported the development of this body of thought. By the 1970s ecologists had a coherent body of theory, some scattered data, and a clear conception of what a community was and what community dynamics were like. Detractors such as Andrewartha and Birch were around but were not usually listened to. The prevailing paradigm was of a community of species that interacted in predictable ways, such that the interactions among them regulated the growth of each population, maintaining the community as a dynamic equilibrium. This simple view of the ecological community was perfectly in tune with a Victorian view of the natural world as a divine machine—a system with internal checks and balances that ensures that the composition of the community is maintained in its present form. It's a balance-of-nature view of ecological systems, one that appears to provide satisfactory explanations for a broad range of observations, such as the observation that similar kinds of places tend to contain similar kinds of organisms in similar abundances, that numbers of a species often do not appear to fluctuate markedly from year to year, or even that there appear to be regularities, patterns, in the distribution of species in nature—patterns that suggest underlying causal processes. This homeostatic community concept has certainly provided the framework for a considerable flowering of good science that has quantified the ways in which both species and individual organisms interact with one another and with the abiotic components of their environments.

Embedded within this community concept, however, are assumptions about the way the world works that are simply not true. It took a major revolution in ecological thinking, beginning in the 1970s, to illustrate how different ecological communities are from that community concept. Even now, the ramifications of the changed understanding have yet to permeate the ecological knowledge of the general population or make their way into the less-stellar university courses on the topic.

THE ECOLOGICAL REVOLUTION
OF THE LATE TWENTIETH CENTURY

The last few pages must be recognized for what they are—a very quick summary of prevailing thinking over a period of 120 years, from Darwin to the 1970s. Various skeptics in addition to Andrewartha and Birch worked outside of the mainstream during this period, but their research tended not to command lasting citations, and when it did, the studies would be cited as interesting exceptions to the rule. This is unfortunate, because some of these scientists reached conclusions and elaborated theories that anticipated the revolution in ecological thought that would come decades later.

A seminal article by British plant ecologist A.S. Watt, published in 1947, on the important roles played by small-scale disturbances and particular patterns of individual growth and senescence in shaping the dynamics of shrub communities was rediscovered in the late 1970s after being ignored for decades. It is a remarkably prescient view of what came to be called *patch dynamics,* a nonequilibrial view of community structure that recognizes that locations are a mosaic of patches with different histories of colonization, growth, and mortality of organisms. The overall pattern and dynamics in the location is the summation of the histories of all the component patches. Once rediscovered, the paper was hailed as ahead of its time. C.B. Huffaker's classic 1958 laboratory experiments, which pitted herbaceous insect pests of the California citrus industry against predatory mites in an artificial world of patches of fruit more or less difficult to move between, never got "lost," but the deeper meaning of what it explored—the significance of spatial arrangements and the distribution of resources for biotic interaction (in this case, predation)—was not recognized at the time and did not get properly integrated into our developing understanding of the nature of ecological communities until many years later. I personally am convinced that if chapter 14 of the classic 1954 text by Andrewartha and Birch had been read carefully by ecologists interested in community structure and dynamics, a more realistic understanding of communities could have been reached far sooner than it was. While this chapter retained the pair's strong focus on the individual or occasionally on its local population, it is a brilliant statement of a nonequilibrial perspective.

The core idea of chapter 14 is that any region may contain few or many suitable locations for small local populations of a species, so that on this broader scale, the species may possess a low or a high density of local populations. In addition, immediate past history may have resulted in very different abundances, relative to resources, among the local populations. In some suitable sites the species may be common, and individuals will be in competition for available resources, while in other sites it may be currently rare and able to grow exponentially (see Figure 8). In other words, at any given time, the demographic trends may vary substantially among the different populations of the species.

Andrewartha and Birch introduced the term *relative shortage of resources* to describe the situation in which a patchily distributed species is, on the broader scale, rare relative to its supply of food and other resources but, in many local sites, is common and suffering resource shortages. They noted that dispersive ability will play a crucial role in determining if a species is likely to suffer such relative shortage of resources (because more dispersive species can move easily among patches). If the species is locally common but inefficient at finding or colonizing new sites, many suitable sites may lie vacant or underutilized.

The most important feature of chapter 14, however, is not the specific ideas it contains (which were definitely novel in 1954) but that Andrewartha and Birch present these ideas as the norm for most populations. This is remarkable because the subdivided population is, in fact, the usual type of population in nature. Most ecologists did not reach this understanding until the 1980s, and the conventional wisdom still does not reflect it.

This is the view today: Natural systems are comprised of a mosaic of ephemeral patches, within which the component species exist as populations of individuals variously struggling to survive and reproduce against a broad variety of impediments—a shortage of resources, the presence of predators and competitors, a harsh climate or season, and

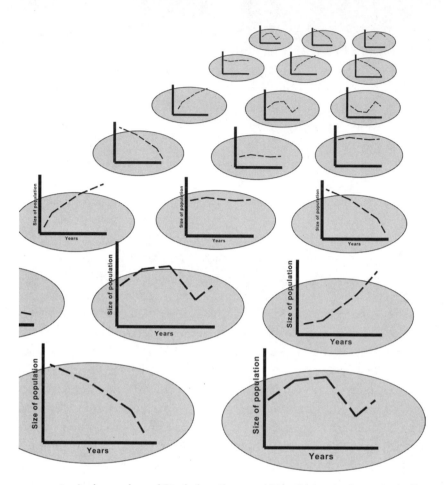

FIGURE 8. Andrewartha and Birch describe a world in which a single species is distributed over a landscape with a large number of patches (ovals) of suitable habitat. Because of varying conditions at each patch and varying histories of success in colonizing that patch, the population in each patch has a different size and pattern of growth or decline (as represented by the graphs of population size). Their model emphasizes that the overall success of the species is a function of the individual patterns of success in survival and reproduction by the individuals living within each patch of suitable habitat and stresses that conditions affecting population growth can be quite different from patch to patch as well as through time.

unanticipated disturbances that impact them suddenly and negatively (see Figure 8). Life is tough, but it is tough in varying ways from place to place and time to time.

Another feature of chapter 14 should be mentioned here. Andrewartha and Birch argue that far from being an unusual phenomenon, extinction of local populations (extirpation) is happening all the time, and extinction of whole species occurs only when all local populations of the species happen to disappear at the same time. This is a deceptively simple point, but one which radically revises our thinking. If we believe in the balance of nature and focus on whole species populations, we expect extinction—the total and final elimination of a species—to be a very rare event. For extinction to be rare, there must be mechanisms that prevent populations from declining to zero—hence the emphasis on density-dependent regulation of population growth. But if we think as Andrewartha and Birch did, each species exists as numerous local populations, and both the abundance relative to resources and the trend in numbers of individuals vary among local populations all the time. Under these circumstances, we realize that attempts to model the growth of the total population as if it was regulated in any particular way—and certainly as if it was prevented from reaching zero (or very large numbers)—are fallacious. This is because the total population is not a unitary entity. It is the algebraic sum of all the local populations, whose numbers are being determined in separate and independent ways and are variously growing or declining. At the level of these local populations, extinction and exponential population growth that outstrips resources are both relatively common events. This way of thinking is now far from novel, but each of the arguments that Andrewartha and Birch made in a widely read book in 1954 had to be rediscovered twenty to thirty years later!

Given that some ecologists were delving into nonequilibrium open systems as early as the 1940s and that Andrewartha and Birch provided a simple model of a distributed set of open local populations in the mid-1950s, why is it that the body of ecological thought through the mid- and late twentieth century focused so strongly on density-dependent, biotic regulation of closed homeostatic communities? The answer surely lies in the "power of the paradigm," the tendency for scientists to see what their body of theory (and its underlying, taken-for-granted assumptions) tells them to expect and, indeed, a tendency to report results that are likely to be approved of by their peers. The paradigm of closed, equilibrial systems made up of species whose populations are closely regulated by density-dependent factors was coherent, internally consistent, and amenable to exploration using simple mathematics and theory; it also conformed to long-standing, widely held Western beliefs in an orderly universe and a balanced natural world. As paradigms go, that's a pretty robust one. Science travels on bandwagons, which every now and then spin out of control. Only after they have crashed is it easy to look back and see all the evidence that a crash was imminent. Hindsight makes it easy to see where we failed to get it right.

So, what happened in the 1980s? I think the short answer is that the theoretical study of closed, equilibrial communities had gone about as far as it could go, while studies of natural systems kept revealing things that would not be expected if they operated around some static equilibrium state with numbers of each component species more or less constant through time. In this context, disturbance, patch dynamics, and other essentially nonequilibrial concepts became more interesting (and also more theoretically tractable because of computing advances). But most of all, the perspective changed because the equilibrial model could not explain biologists' observations of patchiness and high diversity.

The conventional theory of communities as homeostatic assemblages of species, internally structured by their biotic interactions, appeared to do quite well at explaining the apparently stable coexistence of three or four species but struggled when confronted by the high diversity characteristic of many tropical communities. Not being a spatially explicit theory, it could not comment on highly patchy spatial patterns in the presence or composition of communities, and because it focused on conditions at or near equilibrium, it had difficulty with natural communities in which there was sometimes dramatic evidence of change through time. Yet each of these conditions was regularly encountered by ecologists studying real communities.

Communities that included a high diversity of species had always been a bit of a problem because, inevitably, they contained many sets of very similar species. This fact brought back into question seemingly long-settled concepts such as the "survival of the fittest" or the exclusivity of the species' niche. If only the fittest survive, how is it possible that there can be so many similar species of fish on a reef or trees in a rainforest? The explanation offered by one ecologist with a sense of humor for the existence of huge numbers of rather similar beetles—the Creator must have an inordinate fondness for coleopterans—does not really provide a scientific answer. But neither does a tortured explanation that supposes there are many different ways to be a beetle, or a territorial damselfish, or a tree extracting nutrients from the soil and light and CO_2 from the air, and that the differences are just too subtle for us to see and measure.

For an example of just how big this high-diversity problem is, consider the following. Two plant ecologists working at the Smithsonian Tropical Research Institute, Stephen Hubbell[11] and Robin Foster, reported in 1986 that a single 50-hectare plot on Barro Colorado Island, Panama, contained three hundred different species of woody plants with stems of at least 1 cm dbh (diameter at breast height) and nearly two hundred species if one considered only those with stems greater than 20 cm dbh. And this island is not a particularly rich example of tropical wet forest. Furthermore, because they had mapped every tree within the plot, they were able to show that individuals were typically surrounded by many different species. For the greater than 20 cm dbh specimens of the ninety-eight most common species, the twenty nearest neighbors included, on average, fourteen different species, and the set of neighboring species varied greatly among individuals of any one species. Effectively, the ninety-eight species were almost randomly intermingled on the plot.

Given that trees gain all their nutrients through their roots and receive all the light and CO_2 they need through their leaves (and do not move about), it seems reasonable to assume that individual trees must compete most intensely with their nearer neighbors. For the ninety-eight species to coexist in some sort of equilibrium while competing for nutrients and light, each species must possess some distinctive trait that makes it competitively superior in some special way. But on this Barro Colorado Island plot, each individual is confronted by a different mix of many species of neighbors, making it very difficult to visualize a selective mechanism that could lead to evolution of specializations that

---

11. Steve Hubbell, now at UCLA, has taken his thinking about ecology a long way, notably in his engaging 2001 book, *The Unified Neutral Theory of Biodiversity and Biogeography* (Princeton University Press).

would make each species competitively superior in some way to all others.[12] Thus there is a paradox—numerous species with similar requirements living together successfully, and no plausible mechanism that can explain this in terms of a closed equilibrium.

Such "guilds" of ecologically similar species are a characteristic of many tropical faunas and floras and even of some in the temperate zone. The fish species flocks of the African Great Lakes have long been recognized as posing a similar paradox, and if the rich assemblages of fish and corals on coral reefs are not a big enough problem (and they are), there is the report by Fred Grassle, a biological oceanographer now at Rutgers University, of extracting more than 1441 individuals belonging to 103 different species of polychaete worms from a single dead and eroded coral head 4.7 kg in weight that he collected on the southern Great Barrier Reef. How many ways are there to be a polychaete that creeps about within dead and eroded coral heads? Yet if we take a less homeostatic view, particularly one that focuses on the individual organism's struggle for existence, the coexistence of large numbers of similar species is more easily accommodated. If the place can support (has sufficient resources for) lots of individuals and if large numbers of species are available, there is no reason why the set of successful individuals at any one time might not belong to a large number of species. They will not be living in an equilibrium set by their interactions, but they will still be living side by side. The trick is to discard the idea that nature is usually in balance.

The topics of patchiness and patch dynamics are also more compatible with a more variable system. The random spatial distribution of organisms is a rare phenomenon in nature, even among tropical forest trees. Instead, organisms of like kind tend to be clumped in distribution. When they are not clumped, they are more likely to be regularly spaced than to be dispersed at random. The clumping arises (1) because the resources they need are clumped (perhaps these are other organisms), (2) because they respond socially to one another in ways that bring them together into groups, (3) because they were hatched, born,

---

12. Each individual would face a different pattern of competition, and if one tree was successful and its offspring inherited its traits, there is every likelihood that they would each grow up under radically different competitive conditions than those of their parent because each would grow up surrounded by a different, rich set of neighbors. Their traits would not necessarily make them successful when faced by their particular neighbors.

or germinated together and have never moved apart, or (4) because factors causing mortality tend themselves to be clustered in their effects, removing all individuals in some places but sparing individuals some distance away. This tendency to be clumped occurs in many organisms and across spatial scales. Regular distributions, which are far rarer, arise when social interactions cause individuals to be spaced apart or when resources are regularly distributed. Nonrandom spatial distributions of species create patchiness in species composition and abundance.

The ubiquity of spatial patchiness is perhaps best exemplified by pointing to open ocean pelagic systems. While vertical structure may be anticipated because of the changing conditions of light, temperature, pressure, and other factors with depth, we find that in what appears at first to be a horizontally uniform environment, phytoplankton, zooplankton, and fish are all far from randomly distributed in the horizontal plane. Indeed, the strongly clumped patterns of distribution on scales of meters or even less help make the sampling of mid-water organisms particularly frustrating—replicate plankton tows, taken using nets towed side by side through the same body of water, are frequently very different in composition and abundance. True, there are physical and chemical attributes of water masses that we now understand are variable on these small scales, and these may be responsible for causing some of the nonrandom horizontal distributions of the fauna, but the fact remains that even in one of the apparently most featureless habitats, patchy distributions are the rule. Similar patchiness arises in apparently uniform mud flats and desert plains.

This tendency for individual species to be patchily distributed, even if no other factors came into play, will tend to ensure that assemblages of particular taxonomic composition will also be patchy in distribution. When the effects of patchily distributed disturbances to community structure are added (e.g., tree falls, mud slides, lightning strikes), it's not surprising that the natural world is characteristically a patchy place— a mosaic of assemblages, like those discussed by Watt. What is surprising is that this evident patchiness of nature was so little focused on— was literally not even seen—by community ecologists for so long. One of the most provocative points in Andrewartha and Birch's chapter 14 is that what we usually think of as a population really exists as a set of small local populations of differing abundances, in which the trends in population size (whether the population is growing or shrinking) may even be going in opposite directions. This is another way of saying that organisms are usually patchily distributed. At the time Andrewartha and Birch published their book, this was not a widely appreciated view.

Recognition of the importance of disturbances to the dynamics of communities came slowly. In intertidal ecology it perhaps began in 1971 with the observation by Paul Dayton, then a student at the University of Washington, that the dynamics of rocky intertidal communities depended, at least partly, on such unanticipated events as the smashing of drifting logs and other flotsam into the shore, ripping off and killing the rocks' sessile organisms such as mussels. These local-scale disturbances opened up small patches of bare rock for recolonization. In 1978 Joe Connell at the University of California at Santa Barbara developed the intermediate disturbance hypothesis to account for the way in which disturbances impacted coral communities. As the frequency and intensity of disturbances rose, he showed the diversity of the community also rose at first, then peaked and declined. His explanation was that under conditions with few disturbances, species prosper until they are limited by shortages of resources. In the ensuing competition among species, all but a few are eliminated. With a greater frequency of disturbances, the competitively superior species keep getting beaten back, and bare space is made available for colonization, sometimes by the competitively inferior species that would have been eliminated by competition. With very high frequencies of disturbance, however, conditions become too harsh or too frequently interrupted for all but a very few tolerant species to persist. In 1981 Bob Paine at the University of Washington teamed up with Simon Levin, a theoretical ecologist then at Cornell University, to produce an innovative study of the rocky intertidal in which they modeled the demography of patches of bare rock (hence the term *patch dynamics*). Instead of attending to the organisms that occupied the rock and created the community, they examined the "birth rate" of new patches of bare rock, their growth (usually negative as the patch shrunk due to colonization by sessile organisms around its edges), and their ultimate death as they became refilled with a carpet of sessile organisms. Most of their patches were born as the result of disturbances.

Among terrestrial ecologists, the discovery (really a rediscovery, since Watt had written about this phenomenon in 1947) of patch dynamics can be attributed to those who studied forests, particularly rainforests, and fire (usually in forests but sometimes in grasslands). Fire and falling trees were the two major forms of disturbance that created patches in forests, and the dynamics of such patches seemed to mirror those seen in the intertidal, except that forest patches were usually measured on scales of 10 meters to several kilometers, while intertidal patches were measured at scales of meters or less. Connell, identified above as a coral reef ecologist, is also a tropical forest ecologist, and his 1978 paper discussed the dynamics of communities of rainforest trees as well as communities of corals.

The study of patch dynamics in terrestrial and intertidal systems proceeded at about the same pace and during the same period of time, culminating in 1985 in an important book edited by two plant ecologists, S. T. A. Pickett and P. S. White (of Rutgers University and the University of Tennessee, respectively), called *The Ecology of Natural Disturbance and Patch Dynamics*. Since that time, the recognition of the importance of patchiness and the role of disturbance in maintaining patchiness has grown to include examples from many different kinds of communities and involving many different taxa.

With patchiness and disturbance come openness and dispersal. While it was possible to conceive of a homeostatic community as an essentially static thing organized by the biotic interactions taking place within its borders, the world of patch dynamics requires appreciation of change through time. This change can be sudden and massive, as when a disturbance occurs, and is certainly intermittent rather than gradual and continuous. But if disturbances cause mortality within a patch and the clearing of the patch is followed by recolonization, this recolonization must come from outside that patch. The patches are open, and the organisms surrounding them have important dispersive capabilities. The phenomenon of dispersal had been studied by ecologists for a long time, but now its role in the maintenance of community structure and dynamics was recognized.

It is but a tiny step from patch dynamics to metapopulation biology and the view of communities as metassemblages or metacommunities. (I prefer the former term because it mangles the English language slightly less.) The concept of the metapopulation, a population of nearby populations, was coined by Richard Levin, a theoretical ecologist at Princeton University, in two classic papers of 1969 and 1970. In Levin's simple formulation, the metapopulation consists of a set of populations, each of which has both the capacity to contribute new recruits to the others through dispersal and a tendency to go extinct. Levin's interest was in the extent to which dispersal among the populations could serve to reinitiate extinct populations, thereby maintaining the global population at some positive number of individuals. It turns out that quite modest amounts of interaction among the populations (very limited movement of individuals between them, what is now termed *connectivity*) can stabilize the system and reduce the chance of widespread extinction.

Levin's ideas were not picked up by ecologists studying real communities until the early 1990s, when it became recognized that many terrestrial species lived as sets of small and scattered populations, often because human activity had turned formerly continuous habitat into a much more patchy world. These small populations were communicating through dispersal, and metapopulation ecology was born as a way of understanding the resulting dynamics. It is even more recent that the metapopulation concept has spread into thinking about communities.

The individual most closely associated with metapopulation theory is Ilkka Hanski, a Finnish ecologist at the University of Helsinki who has done much to develop the theory and to apply it to the populations of butterflies with which he works. One of the human impacts on the terrestrial world has been to make patches of natural habitat even smaller and more isolated than they may once have been, with the result that the ecology of many species can best be studied by recognizing that they exist as numerous, small, and perhaps poorly connected populations. A metapopulation approach is ideal for doing this.

While the theory of metapopulations has advanced considerably since Levin's time, the metassemblage concept has only recently received attention. What makes metassemblages difficult to deal with is the fact that the individual species that together comprise the metassemblage are very likely to operate on differing spatial scales, recognize different patterns of habitat patchiness, and exhibit differing capacities to move between local patches. They also may operate on different temporal scales, with generation times varying greatly from one species to another. At this time, it is perhaps best to speak of the metassemblage as a useful concept rather than a theory. It is a way of helping ecologists remember and deal with the spatial variability that exists in habitat, species composition, and patterns of species interaction in the real world. It is proving very useful in developing the scientific basis for conservation management using networks of protected areas both on land and in the marine environment. It also helps us understand temporal change in the dynamics of species and communities, something that is now recognized as very important in the real world. The members of an individual local group of species may still interact in thoroughly deterministic and predictable ways and even show long-term equilibrium in numbers due to density-dependent feedback mechanisms of the type discussed by Nicholson in the 1930s. But these patterns of interaction are not universal, and they do not persist indefinitely, even within single local patches.

A RADICALLY DIFFERENT PERSPECTIVE

A modern view of community ecology must begin by acknowledging that the idea of the balance of nature, so beloved of twentieth-century theory, is more myth than reality. There do not exist sets of species that reliably occur together in particular places, with well-defined boundaries, across which few if any important interactions take place. Nor do sets of co-occurring species continuously interact in density-dependent ways to homeostatically regulate one another's abundances. Instead, the world is a constantly changing mosaic that, at any given moment, comprises a set of patches of different history, occupied by sets of species that have succeeded in colonizing them and in continuing to occupy them. To the extent that some neighboring patches are similar in their physical attributes, their histories, and the species that are present, we can recognize classes of similar patches. These classes of similar patches are the communities that ecologists study, but ecologists used to give them far more uniformity and permanence than they deserved. They overemphasized the degree to which patches of one class were similar, and their persistence through time. And they exaggerated the extent to which the component species recognized a common set of patch boundaries and limited their interactions to those other species that shared the same class of patch. In reality, these patches and the sets of species that occupy them are ephemeral, because each individual patch has its own history, and the individual organisms (rather than the individual species) are each doing their best to survive, reproduce, and get their offspring into suitable locations for life.

I suggest that this is a radically different view of ecological communities than the view developed during the first century or so of ecological investigations. It's a view that remains compatible with the basic observation that there is apparent pattern in the distribution of organisms in nature—the world does not contain a random hodge-podge of species jumbled together. To survive and reproduce, an organism must be able to tolerate both the conditions and the other species present at particular locations, and therefore particular types of places will tend to be occupied by predictable sets of organisms. At the local scale it is also compatible with ideas such as competitive exclusion, niche preemption, and density-dependent regulation of numbers—within a patch that is not currently undergoing a change in conditions, predictable biotic processes will occur with predictable results on species' populations. But this view also embraces ideas of change, disturbance, and spatial heterogeneity in the way the world's ecology is put together. And it readily accommodates ideas of dispersal, through both space and time.

Dispersal through space occurs via pelagic larvae, wind-distributed seeds, migratory juveniles, and so on. While most dispersing organisms must die (probably well over 99 percent of pelagic larvae die) and survival probably is best closest to home, some dispersers will succeed in establishing themselves in suitable patches a long way from home. The individual that disperses its offspring is hedging its bets on where good places to live will be next season.

While most organisms reproduce at predictable seasons in temperate habitats, producing their dispersive stages at the "right" time of year, many also gamble against the variability of the environment by distributing their offspring through time into several future seasons. This is done by having "resting eggs," a diapause, or, in plants, a seed bank. In less seasonal locations, this distribution of offspring through time is partly achieved by frequently reproducing instead of producing all the eggs for that year in one clutch. It's also done in both temperate and tropical regions by living longer than one reproductive year. The net result of all these tricks is to ensure that the offspring of one individual are distributed through time, just as the dispersal tricks ensure they are distributed through space. Each of these mechanisms gives the organism that practices it the ability to scatter its offspring through time or space, thus increasing its chances of success. Darwin saw the struggle for existence as a continuous struggle by the individual to survive and reproduce. So did Andrewartha and Birch. This view of ecological communities comes right back to that starting premise—the composition of species at a specific time and place (the community) is a consequence of the variable success of all the individual struggles for existence by the individual organisms of a broad range of species with differing capacities and tolerances. The structure of this community changes because a multitude of factors buffet each struggling individual and its progeny and because a changing world ensures that the buffeting is also changing in intensity and type.

That the world offers a heterogeneous and changing set of environmental conditions is fundamental to this dynamic view of community ecology. Heterogeneity means there is patchiness. The existence of patchiness and the ability of organisms to disperse among patches contribute to the openness of natural assemblages. As well as causing the immigration and emigration important to understanding the dynamics of an open metassemblage, such events give rise to "invasions" of novel species into assemblages. Changeability means that conditions at a particular site are not constant through time. The patches are not static in their conditions, and organisms display ubiquitous yet diverse life history attributes that allow them to accommodate to this fact. Distributing one's offspring in space by laying eggs in several places or by hatching dispersive offspring and distributing one's offspring in time by reproducing multiple times or by producing offspring with variably long periods of diapause are the two main classes of bet-hedging strategies adopted by organisms. Both kinds of dispersal are important for understanding the dynamics of metassemblages because the particular mix of species present at a particular place and time is a direct function of the history of that place, a history of arrivals and departures, successes and failures by individuals of different species.

This view of communities demands that we recognize a world that changes. That ecological conditions may vary through time is counter to our well-entrenched Western belief in the essential balance of nature, and many people find it difficult to accept, yet we all know of warmer-than-usual summers or wetter-than-usual winters—even these simple changes have effects on living organisms. By Darwin's time, scientists had largely come to terms with the profound environmental changes that had occurred in geological time and been preserved in the paleontological record.[13] Recognition that the world changes on geological time-scales has not transferred easily to ecological time-scales. For the most part, and perhaps only subconsciously, we have kept geological and ecological time separate and have considered major changes in conditions to be restricted primarily to the former. Yet ecological conditions do change on ecological time-scales, and those changes play a substantial role in driving the dynamics of ecological communities.

In recognizing a world that changes, we also need to put aside our expectation of gradualism—the idea that changes will always be slow and incremental. Those who model complex systems have long been aware that the state of such systems can change suddenly when thresholds in governing conditions are reached, and ecological modelers recognize that theirs are definitely complex systems. Sudden ecological changes are being seen more frequently now than they used to be: sudden weather events such as major storms that profoundly modify a forest or coastal community in ways that take decades or longer to ever disappear; sudden outbreaks of pest species, such as that of the mountain pine beetle (*Dendroctonus ponderosae*), which is devastating large regions of pine forests of British Colombia and the northwestern United States;[14] and phase shifts such as the relatively rapid switch from coral-dominated to algal-dominated coral reefs at many Caribbean sites. Changes that are sudden are also frequently unexpected and correspondingly far more difficult to deal with, and they happen in our world.

13. This coming to terms was reluctant, as can be seen by noting that it took forty years (from the 1920s to the 1960s) for the geological community to accept the possibility of horizontal continental movements on geological time-scales, even though by that time there was widespread acceptance of the notion that there had been pronounced vertical movements of land masses in the past. The reality of continental drift was only accepted once overwhelming evidence had accumulated and a potential mechanism for this movement had been proposed.

14. The western pine beetle is currently killing off much larger areas of pine forest than it ever has before. A combination of milder winters, which favor survival of individual beetles into the next year and provide access to higher-altitude and more-northern forests, and forestry practices that have left pine forests filled with older and therefore more susceptible trees has resulted in much larger and therefore more destructive populations of this pest.

WHEREFORE RESILIENCE, RECOVERY, AND ECOLOGICAL STABILITY?

If we are able to put aside our desire for a balance of nature and the reliable universe that it conjures up, we can embrace this modern and excitingly dynamic picture of ecology. In doing so, however, we must recognize that there are some additional beliefs we had better reexamine. The most important of these is the concept of ecological recovery and its relationship to resilience and stability. Resilience is conventionally defined as the ability of an ecological system to resist disturbance and maintain its current state. Recovery is the return of an ecological system to a previous state following disturbance. Ecological stability is the sum of resilience and recovery; as an imputed attribute of the ecological system, it is said to come from the suite of regulatory mechanisms that give the system its homeostatic character.

But real communities—which are patchy, open, dynamic, and dependent entirely on the successes of individual organisms in surviving and reproducing to determine their current state—cannot possess this kind of stability. There is no homeostatic mechanism that would drive the return of the community to prior conditions following disturbance and therefore nothing to produce equilibrium conditions. Without recovery, ecological stability is a meaningless term, although ecosystems can still be said to possess resilience. I think, however, that the word *inertia* more properly describes this attribute of an ecosystem—a tendency to resist change until external stressors become too strong and then to shift under their influence. *Inertia* better describes how ecosystems usually respond to our impacts than does *resilience,* with its usual analogy of a rubber band that returns to a former shape after being stretched.

I am not denying that what we see all around us appears to be stability and sometimes even recovery. Burnt forests do regrow. Forests that are not burnt tend to remain about the same from year to year. We are not imagining these processes and patterns. Nor are we imagining what we see when a coral reef damaged by a major storm regains its former glory and an undamaged reef nearby remains biotically rich and attractive year after year. I think we are misinterpreting these things. The observations are valid, but we have been too quick to assume that resilience is a lot more than inertia and to confuse change with recovery and lack of change with stability.

Inertia or resilience in an ecological system is the tendency for it not to depart from its current condition because no forces of sufficient strength are operating to cause such change. One way to understand sudden changes in ecosystems is to think of them as the result of resilience failing—something that will happen when stresses on a system are sufficiently strong. Systems will vary in the extent of inertia primarily because they vary in the demographies, particularly the longevities, of the individual organisms that comprise them. Forests and coral reefs contain substantial inertia because they have long-lived, slow-growing individuals among their most dominant species. Forests and reefs, in the absence of fires, storms, or outbreaks of disease, do not appear to us to change very much because they are changing on time-scales very different from our own. Other kinds of systems, dominated by short-lived, rapidly breeding species, may appear much more variable, and they are—but only because they change on shorter time-scales.

Recovery implies a directed pattern of change toward a prior state. When we think in balance-of-nature terms, recovery occurs because homeostatic mechanisms—such as density-dependent competition among species—function to bring the system back to its initial equilibrium state. Yet if the forest is burned but tree seeds survive and begin to grow into trees, the forest is "recovering" only in a much looser sense than this. All that is really happening is that some individuals of tree species have been successful in their individual struggles to survive and reproduce at that location. There is no mechanism working to force the forest back toward its previous state. There are only far simpler mechanisms in play that continue the survival of particular genomes. If the individual seed has the characteristics it needs to survive in the place it is when the fire passes through and the luck to receive the needed water and nutrients, it germinates. Its survival and growth is not a part of a mechanism that has been evolved *in order to regrow* the forest. Rather, the forest reappears only because individual tree seeds in sufficient number survive and grow. The trick to understanding this distinction is to remember that the struggle to survive is waged by individual organisms against the myriad factors that oppose them. It is not a struggle by the community to maintain its usual structure. Because we tend not to think in these terms, the forest as an ecological entity is almost a myth of our own creation.

Let me say that again in still different terms. The stable ecological community is a human construct. We can now see its artificiality when we apply a modern metassemblage perspective. The community is the set of patches of habitat that happen to be similar in structure and species composition at the time we examine them. (Imagine Figure 8 with several species present.) We classify the set of patches as a single entity *in our minds* because the same set of species happened to have individuals present *at those places* at that time. If those individuals are taken away, more like them may colonize and prosper, or they may not. If they do, we will think that the community *recovered*. But all that really happened is that new individuals colonized the vacated patches in ways that resulted in an assemblage resembling their previous species composition.

When you start looking for evidence of recovery in the balance-of-nature sense, it turns out to be pretty hard to find, even at the level of single species. In fishery after fishery, for example, we have overfished, drastically reducing the abundance of a favored and economically valuable species. We have then stopped fishing, often because everyone went broke, but sometimes because regulators stepped in and tried to correct a failing enterprise. Then what happens? The waited-for recovery often does not occur. Canada took somewhat tardy but ultimately bold action in the early 1990s and closed all eastern Canadian waters to cod fishing. We are still waiting for cod stocks to recover. But why should a species that has become rare in the environment suddenly become common? Each individual fish still has its own struggle to survive and reproduce, and there is little reason to suppose that by greatly reducing the number of individuals of that species we should have made each individual's chances a lot greater than they were before. If each individual has at best a slightly better chance of surviving and reproducing, why should we expect stocks to rebound and recover? How many years and under what kinds of conditions did it take to build those immense populations of cod that sustained our increasingly efficient fishery for five hundred years? Do we really expect them to recover in a couple of years after we stop fishing? And do we expect Australia's orange roughy to recover, or eastern North America's Atlantic salmon, or the California sardine, or the Chilean seabass? The answer, of course, is "yes." We do expect it, because we still think a balance of nature exists. Unfortunately, expecting things does not always make them happen.[15]

The irony and tragedy of our present situation is that, just at the time we are causing ever-increasing impacts on the natural ecosystems that sustain us, we appear to be trapped in a way of thinking about ecology that suggests there is far more internal capacity for regulation and repair in ecological communities than actually exists. We consequently think, first, that our actions will not cause any serious environmental effects because ecological systems are strongly resilient. Then we assume that even though some of our actions have caused measurable disturbance, the system will recover quickly and completely as long as we correct our behavior. Then we become surprised when an ecosystem changes radically, undergoing a phase shift when it passes a critical tipping point.[16]

Our expectation of strong homeostasis in natural systems is buried deep in our belief systems as Westerners and encoded in the conventional view of ecology that developed through the 1970s. It is so broadly accepted that it is rarely discussed and seldom examined in detail, despite the radically changed understanding of ecological communities that has been developed in the last twenty-five years. Many ecologists and most environmental managers, policymakers, and politicians still believe implicitly in the balance of nature. It underpins the conservation movement and the concept of national parks and other protected areas as places that will persist in perpetuity, ecologically unchanged, as long as we minimize human impacts. I fear it also underpins our remarkable complacency about our growing capacity to do serious harm to the ecological systems that sustain us. *Homo sapiens* needs to think a lot more carefully, because the ecological world that sustains us is not a stable system, and we are now more than powerful enough to disturb it substantially.

15. On the other hand, expected events sometimes do occur. Along the East Coast of North America, the striped bass, *Morone saxatilis,* responded very well to restoration efforts and a couple of seasons of very favorable reproduction after reaching very low numbers in the late 1980s. Commercial and recreational fishery landings now are greater than at any prior time.

16. Terms such as *phase shift* and *tipping point* are appearing ever more frequently in discourse about natural ecosystems. They are emotive descriptions of very serious events—the sudden and often catastrophic change in the nature of a place because its resilience has been overwhelmed by our pressures on it. They become more frequent as our impact on the natural world grows.

PART THREE

MOVING FORWARD

Why It Matters and What We Need to Do

7

WHAT LOSS OF ECOLOGICAL COMPLEXITY MEANS FOR THE WORLD

The dodo (*Raphus cucullatus*), known primarily for being dead, was a substantial, flightless bird that, at 23 kg, was about twice the size of the largest Thanksgiving turkeys. It was endemic to Mauritius, a set of islands east of Madagascar, and was first discovered by Europeans when Dutch sailors landed there in 1598. Typical of birds on isolated islands without mammalian predators, the dodo was "fearless" and sometimes used for food by European sailors. Habitat destruction and the introduction of egg predators including dogs, pigs, cats, rats, and crab-eating macaques (European explorers were not noted for their care in what got left behind) played the larger role, and the last living dodo was seen sometime between 1662 and 1700. One century to extinction! It then vanished, more or less, until resurrected by Lewis Carroll in 1865. Unfortunately, being resurrected as a character in a children's book does not bring an extinct species back to life.

The polar bear (*Ursus maritimus*), a top predator exquisitely adapted to its rigorous arctic environment, emerges from hibernation in the early spring at a time when the ringed seal population has pupped. Defenseless, fat-rich seal pups scattered in snow lairs across the sea ice

---

Facing page: Indo-Pacific lionfishes (genus *Pterois*) have been accidentally introduced to the Caribbean. It is too early to know the impact these beautiful but voracious predators will have on numerous prey species. Photo courtesy of A.J. Hooten.

make easy prey, and the bears consume large numbers of them before the sea ice begins to break up in midsummer and this easy source of food becomes inaccessible. This spring feast represents a substantial proportion of the annual caloric intake for the bears, and the fat laid down enables them to survive the winters and produce their own offspring. So it has always been, it would seem. Except that the arctic is changing, and the sea ice is breaking up earlier in the season. Progressively warmer weather has led to break-up occurring two to three weeks earlier than was the case fifty years ago, curtailing the seal-pup feasting. Warmer weather with more rain has possibly also led to increased mortality of bears during winter due to collapse of their snow dens. The condition of the bears has declined, and numbers have also fallen. On 15 May 2008 the U.S. Fish and Wildlife Service listed the polar bear as Threatened under the Endangered Species Act, despite the political difficulty this might cause if conservation activists attempt to force curbs to production of greenhouse gases to save polar bears. Polar bears are not extinct yet, but there is reason for concern. They may not be able to adapt to the ice-free Arctic Ocean that appears to be around the corner.

Dodos failed quickly, many other species have failed since, and polar bears are just the latest in a long list of species that appear to be having trouble surviving in the modern world. Dodos and polar bears, along with creatures such as pandas, humpback whales, chimpanzees, whooping cranes, tigers, albatrosses, and monarch butterflies, are among the threatened species that have attracted the most attention (and it is for this reason that they are called "iconic" or "charismatic"), but it is the smaller, far less well-known organisms threatened with extinction that should concern us more. There are somewhere between five and fifteen million species of eukaryotic organisms, including humans, polar bears, Atlantic salmon, honeybees, elkhorn corals, *Amanita* mushrooms, giant kelp, Bermuda grass, and white pine, alive on Earth at the present time. The numbers of prokaryotes—bacteria and blue-green algae—and of viruses are much less precisely known but still substantial. All of these organisms play roles in the ecosystems that sustain us. While extinctions of species have always occurred, the rate of extinctions has vastly accelerated. Although the rate averaged perhaps one species per million per year over the past sixty-five million years, it has increased to nearly one thousand species per million per year today. This means that about

0.1 percent of all extant species disappear every year, and the rate continues to increase. For the most part, we are the cause.

In reality, the extinctions are just the sharp tip of a much larger problem. Our activities are causing a substantial simplification of the earth's ecosystems—a loss of redundancy, diversity, and biomass. We touched on this problem in chapters 1 and 2 and again in chapter 6. Here we explore the changes that are happening and the possible consequences for ecosystem function and for us. I'll deal with extinction first and then turn to ecosystem function and the environmental services we depend on that may no longer get delivered as a result of biodiversity loss.

HOW WE CAUSE EXTINCTIONS

Species are going extinct for a variety of reasons. We carve up their habitats into smaller and smaller, more isolated patches, sometimes to the extent that the patches become too small to sustain populations of viable size. We pollute their habitats in a variety of ways, with chemicals or other wastes that may have much more deleterious effects on them than on us. We usurp their habitats to our own ends as farms, towns, and strip mines, often making them unsuitable for many of the native species to continue to survive there. Our tendency to subdivide, eliminate, or pollute habitats plays by far the largest role in eliminating other species; however, we also sometimes compete with them for resources other than habitat, and we often harvest them as resources ourselves. Finally, by transporting other organisms around the world we introduce exotic competitors, predators, or pathogens to their environments. Our activities are so extensive and create such big stresses for other species that we are now witnessing a rate of loss of species through extinction that is as rapid or more so than at any past time, and there are plenty of signs that the pace of loss is increasing. We are at the start of the Holocene mass extinction event, and we are the cause.

Our impact on extent and integrity of habitat can best be seen in time-series maps of forested land, whether in North America, Amazonia, or elsewhere in the world. Over time, large acreages of continuous forest cover become smaller and fragmented. The same process happens with other types of terrestrial habitat, and the barriers to movement among patches can be considerable. An aerial view of a complex highway network on the outskirts of a city is a map of small patches of grassland separated by cement barriers continually patrolled by cars and trucks. To the field mouse, cricket, or frog, these patches might as well be separate universes because crossing the road is nearly impossible. To survive in an isolated patch of habitat, a species needs to maintain a population of sufficient size, and to do this it needs to be able to obtain the resources of food, shelter, and other needs in sufficient quantity. Those resources need to be present inside the patch. The patches of grassland common inside cloverleaf loops are probably sufficiently large to support adequate populations of crickets. But for frogs, which need ponds, or field mice, which need more space than crickets, they may not be large enough. Animals that got trapped there when the highway was built may live out their lives and produce some offspring, but over time harsh winters, droughts, or attention from hawks all take their toll, and populations become smaller. If the members of those populations do not have adequate food and other resources, their ability to rebuild their numbers is reduced, the chance of recovery is reduced, and local extinction is waiting. Once the species is lost from such a patch, the likelihood of recolonization is quite low—those cars and trucks again—and over time, patch after patch loses its population of that species until the species has disappeared from the entire region. While cloverleaf loops are an unusually isolated type of patch, more natural patches of habitat—fencerows, woodlots, and unplowed patches of grassland—experience the same kind of decline and loss of species. Repeat this process of habitat fragmentation in place after place, and many species become globally rare or extinct.

The effects of habitat fragmentation on extinction have been elegantly demonstrated in a long-term experimental study of Amazon rainforest. In the late 1970s, Tom Lovejoy, then at the World Wildlife Fund and now at George Mason University, wondered how large patches of rainforest needed to be to still be able to retain a reasonable proportion of their species. This question is critical to any plan to conserve biodiversity through the creation of reserves or parks, because there is little point in protecting one or more small patches of habitat if they are too small to be able to sustain populations of many of their species. Put simply, how large do protected areas need to be to be effective in conserving their species? Discussion of this question among conservation biologists was so contentious over several years in the 1970s and 1980s that it gained the acronym SLOSS (single large or several small). Did it actually matter whether one fought to protect a single large patch of habitat or made do with protecting several small patches of equivalent total area? The "several small" approach would likely be politically and financially easier to achieve.

Such questions can be argued about for quite a while, or they can be tackled using well-designed manipulative experiments[1] and thereby answered more or less definitively. Lovejoy chose to do an experiment. It was a collaborative effort between the Smithsonian Institution and Brazil's National Institute for Amazonian Research that became known as the Biological Dynamics of Forest Fragments Project. It became the largest, longest-running ecological experiment in forest community dynamics ever. Indeed, it is still producing results. Working with the companies that were felling the forest near Manaus to harvest timber and to create grazing land, his team arranged for the clearing process to leave untouched a series of twelve square patches of forest, each 1, 10, or 100 hectares in area and separated from any nearby forest by 70 to 1,000 meters. Each plot was carefully censused for a variety of taxa before clearing took place around it and then was fenced to keep cattle out but otherwise left undisturbed. Then, over many years, the scientists carefully monitored changes in composition of species present and in the sizes of their populations. They showed conclusively that size does matter in this case, but also that the effect of patch size varies among species.

For example, to examine effects on tree community composition and dynamics, Smithsonian Tropical Research Institute scientist William F. Laurance and colleagues mapped all trees in a set of sixty-six square 1-hectare plots, thirty-nine occurring within the isolated forest frag-

---

1. Ecologists distinguish two types of field experiments. Manipulative experiments are much like typical lab experiments in which there are experimental and control units (separate plots or populations), and a treatment is applied to the experimental units. Natural experiments take advantage of an event (such as a fire, a tree fall, or a storm) that has occurred and compare plots or populations impacted by the event with ones that were not impacted, as if the event was an experimental treatment. Manipulative experiments are more powerful (they have randomization, replication, and appropriate controls in their favor), while natural experiments permit asking questions about types of events that the ecologist would not have the capacity to (or be permitted to) undertake. Lovejoy's experiment was manipulative—he arranged for specific portions of contiguous forest to be turned into isolated patches of specific size.

ments of various sizes and twenty-seven in nearby continuous forest. They then followed these sixty-six plots for eighteen years[2] to determine the effects of fragmentation. Their data, reported in *Ecology* in 1998, convincingly demonstrated that forest fragments experience a substantially higher rate of tree damage and mortality than do patches within continuous forest and that this greater damage is predominantly near the edge of the fragment. Edge forest, the outside band extending up to 60 meters inside the forest, is a different environment, with more wind damage to trees and a different microclimate that many forest species cannot tolerate well. As a consequence, tree mortality is almost four times higher in edges than in the fragment core (4.01 percent per year in edges, 1.27 percent in the core). This difference is a permanent one, not one that disappears a few years after fragment creation. Because of these strong edge effects, small fragments, which have a much higher proportion of edge to total area, show very different dynamics than do larger fragments or the continuous forest, and these dynamics lead to loss of many species and general reduction in average age of trees remaining. Laurance and colleagues found that fragments needed to be from 100 to 400 hectares in size[3] before they were large enough to resemble continuous forest in the dynamics their tree communities exhibited.

Similar results have been obtained in the many studies of different kinds of biota that have been analyzed. Small fragments of forest habitat do not behave like continuous forest, and a large number of small fragments, even if well protected, does not maintain biodiversity as effectively as the same area of continuous forest. While similar experiments have not been done in most other kinds of habitat, the general rule seems to be that our tendency to increase patchiness of habitat is going to have substantial effects on community dynamics and therefore on the survival of specialist species. In conservation, size really does matter, and we are naive if we believe that postage-stamp-size protected areas will suffice to preserve the biodiversity of our world.

2. I don't mean to make a big deal about this, but ecology is a science in which getting answers can take a long time because ecological systems move at their own pace. We need to understand this fact when we consider how rapidly we are changing the natural world—are we taking sufficient time to discover the consequences of our actions?

3. That's equivalent to between 187 and 747 American football fields in area, including the end zones.

To flush a toilet is to perform a task that human societies have performed repeatedly over the last four thousand years—using water to remove unwanted wastes from our immediate environment. The water, and whatever is in it, travels through pipes or channels, usually downhill, and ends up most frequently (usually after some sewage treatment) in some natural stream, river, lake, or ocean. This system works well in getting wastes away from us, and when human populations are small, it works well more generally too. The environment is sufficiently large that the wastes are diluted and pose little harm. Four thousand years ago, dilution really was the solution to pollution.

Because the system worked, there was little incentive to explore other ways of ridding our surroundings of waste products. A pity, because as we became more highly urbanized and developed more complex manufacturing processes and more chemically rich societies, we continued to send waste products of all types downhill to aquatic environments, often in considerable quantities and seldom with much thought to how well the receiving water body would be able to deal with the stuff we sent it. Aquatic ecologists have witnessed the consequences. There really is a limit to how much waste you can ship downhill to the local aquatic environment before that environment begins to choke.

This choking happens in two ways. Organic waste, the stuff the toilet was invented to dispose of, is organic matter rich in nutrients. Plants will frequently grow better when supplied with extra nutrients—whether fertilizer or manure—and there is nothing inherently wrong in placing this material into aquatic habitats. The problem is that the presence of too many nutrients leads to excess demand for oxygen by the phytoplankton and microorganisms busily breaking them down, and this excess demand depletes the supply of oxygen dissolved in the water faster than it can be replenished by diffusing through the water's surface from the atmosphere above. The result is a body of water lacking dissolved oxygen and a massive die-off of those aquatic organisms such as fish that depend on dissolved oxygen to live. How massive? At present, marine ecologists are becoming concerned at the number and size of "dead zones" appearing in the world's oceans. One of the largest and best known now forms each summer over an area about 15,000 square km from the mouth of the Mississippi westward as far as the Texas border and far offshore. Bottom waters in this zone are nearly devoid of oxygen, a condition that has major impacts on benthic fauna and important fish and shrimp resources.

The story is different for other kinds of waste, the chemicals that we wash down the drain in concentrations far greater than would normally occur in the environment and the novel chemicals that did not exist in the natural world before we invented and manufactured them. Mercury is a good example of the former; DDT, an example of the latter.

Some of our industries—notably mining and pulp and paper manufacturing—produce mercury, a highly reactive and toxic metal, as a by-product in its methylated form. Mercury poisoning is cumulative as concentrations of the metal build up in the tissues of animals and humans. Its effects are most pronounced on the nervous system, producing, in humans, Minamata disease. Symptoms of this disease include ataxia; numbness of hands and feet; general muscle weakness; damage to vision, hearing and speech; and, in extreme cases, insanity, paralysis, and death. Minamata disease was first documented in the late 1950s among residents of Minamata City, Japan, who ate fish and shellfish from Minamata Bay and the surrounding ocean. Methyl mercury released as waste from a local chemical company was incorporated into the tissues of fish and shellfish and passed to the tissues of those who ate the fish. Let's not suppose that methyl mercury affects only humans; it affects all organisms high enough up the food chain for bioaccumulation to result in significant concentrations in their tissues. (Bioaccumulation is the progressive increase in concentration of a substance within the tissues of animals progressively higher up a food web.)

DDT does not occur naturally. It's a manufactured chemical that was widely used because of its effectiveness as an insecticide. Being a strongly hydrophobic chemical, it tends to accumulate in fat deposits when ingested or absorbed through the skin. First synthesized in the late nineteenth century, it became an important insecticide during World War II and was very widely used during the 1940s and 1950s. Nonexistent in the environment before that time, it is now present in the tissues of every living vertebrate on Earth, including polar bears and humans. While DDT is relatively nontoxic to higher vertebrates, it has one important effect in birds. DDT in sufficient concentration causes birds to produce eggs with dangerously thin shells. Raptors such as hawks and eagles easily develop tissue concentrations that are sufficiently high because they feed upon mammals and other birds, and bioaccumulation means that concentrations become greater higher on the food chain. During the mid- and late twentieth century, many raptor populations crashed because eggs were too fragile to survive the period of incubation. The reduction in use of DDT since the 1970s, chiefly because its use has been banned in most developed countries, has led to the recovery of many raptor populations. DDT is also toxic to many aquatic organisms. Its widespread initial use, plus its continued legal and illegal use in many countries, particularly for mosquito control in malarial regions, has made it a widely distributed chemical in aquatic habitats, with deleterious consequences for the organisms that live there.

Mercury and DDT are just two of a growing list of chemicals we are introducing into the environment, either in concentrations rarely seen naturally or as totally new chemicals for the ecosystem to deal with. These include other heavy metals; pesticides and herbicides that can be toxic in various ways to various species; pharmaceutical breakdown products that can disrupt the endocrine systems of animals, altering sex determination and reproductive behavior and physiology; and fertilizers that overstimulate growth of plants and microorganisms. Novel chemicals are being invented every day, brought to market with limited testing for effects, and flushed into the environment with seldom much thought for the consequences. When the birth control pill was introduced, nobody imagined that estrogenic by-products from its use would find their way into aquatic environments in sufficient concentration to disrupt the reproductive physiology of fish populations.[4]

Pollution can make a habitat unsuitable for some or all of the species that usually live there, causing them to gradually disappear. By contrast, when habitat is consumed by human development, it becomes impossible for most native species to continue to live there. We consume most habitat by turning it first into plowed fields, then into towns and cities. Other habitat disappears as clear-cuts and strip mines. The extent

---

4. Over seven years, in a classic "whole lake" experiment, Karen Kidd and coworkers at Canada's Department of Fisheries and Oceans added the synthetic estrogen 17α-ethynylestradiol used in birth control pills to a lake in Canada's "experimental lake district" in northwestern Ontario, in concentrations that would be typical of places downstream from a small town (less than 1 to 5 nanograms per liter throughout the lake), and showed dramatic feminization of males of a common minnow—an important forage species for larger fishes in the lake.

of habitat usurpation can be gauged by a glance at the same aerial photographs that display habitat fragmentation. In Western Europe there is scarcely any natural habitat remaining. In North America there are now vast tracts of megalopolis, such as the Boston–New York–New Jersey–Washington corridor, the Los Angeles basin, or the Toronto–Hamilton crescent in Canada, that have replaced what was once near-continuous forest or open grassland. We really have taken control of vast quantities of the available real estate. By reducing the area of natural habitat, we reduce the sizes of populations of native species. Smaller populations are closer to zero, that ultimate low population size when local extinction occurs. Too many local extinctions, and another species is gone forever.[5]

While usurpation of habitat is primarily a terrestrial phenomenon (we are land dwellers), the intensity of some trawl fisheries has reached a level where the act of trawling is comparable in its impact on the benthic marine environment to plowing or clear cutting. As reported in chapter 1, in 1998 Les Watling and Elliott Norse estimated that an area of sea bottom equal to half the total area of the world's continental shelves was being trawled every year. Their estimate suggests that many parts of the world's continental shelves are being scraped clean by trawls at least every other year. The effect on the organisms that live there must be comparable to what would happen if giant combines were rolled across all native grasslands every other year to harvest a hay crop—actually worse, because the sponges and other creatures that provide structure in benthic habitats grow back much more slowly than grasses that have been cut.

We used to introduce species with scarcely a second thought. Sometimes we introduced deliberately; sometimes, accidentally. With our increasing capacity to travel quickly over long distances and ship freight all over the world, we have become progressively better at this, despite taking ever more steps to control the problem. The Polynesians purposely transported pigs, chickens, dogs, and coconut trees throughout

---

5. While our cities have replaced large areas of natural habitat, there is considerable benefit in encouraging urbanization rather than the suburbanization that prevails in North America. Compact urban centers house more people, use energy more efficiently, and enjoy other benefits of scale compared to the extensive suburbs and exurbs that blight many parts of this continent. European countries seem to do a better job of keeping the city from spreading into the countryside.

the Pacific; the European explorers added goats and cattle. Between the two groups, rats, fleas, mosquitoes, and cats were delivered unintentionally. Largely as a consequence, some of the highest rates of extinction of native plants, birds, mammals, and other terrestrial species have occurred on the islands of Polynesia during the last three hundred years, and Hawaii is now reported to hold more introduced than native bird species. Many island-dwelling species (remember the dodo?) are poorly adapted to terrestrial predators (rats, cats, dogs, and goats) or novel competitors. They succumb quite quickly.

We do not have to look to exotic locations in the South Pacific for examples of damage due to introduced species, however. Back in history a century or slightly more ago, the British had the quaint habit of trying to turn the rest of the world into an English country garden. Among many other examples, they brought foxes and rabbits to Australia, a whole host of "beautiful" songbirds (starlings, house sparrows) and garden plants (common dandelion, dame's rocket, purple loosestrife, rambler rose) to North America, and hedgehogs to New Zealand. Each of these "escaped" and became pest species in their new homes. Some have caused major disruptions, including loss of native species.

While we have learned to make deliberate introductions only very cautiously if at all, our accidental introductions continue. The accidental introduction of the zebra mussel, *Dreissena polymorpha*, to the waters of the Great Lakes and the Mississippi drainage has had major effects. This fingernail-sized filter feeder from the Caspian Sea came in from Europe as larvae traveling in ballast water that was then discharged in Great Lakes ports. First identified in Lake Saint Clair (the not-so-great lake between Lakes Huron and Erie) in 1988, it has become so abundant that it has eliminated numerous populations of native mussel and clam species, modified food webs by removing phytoplankton from the water column through its own voracious feeding, and caused direct economic damage through its proclivity for blocking cooling-water intake pipes in power plants and other places. Carried in the bilge water of pleasure boats or attached to neglected, mossy outboard motors on these boats, it has subsequently hopped from lake to lake across a large portion of east-central North America.

A major new introduction is currently unfolding across the reefs of the Caribbean, Bahamas, and Bermuda and along the U.S. East Coast from North Carolina south through Florida. Two species of the Indo-Pacific lionfish, *Pterois,* were first sighted off Florida in the early 1990s and are now becoming conspicuous members of the coral reef and rocky reef fish fauna from North Carolina down into the Caribbean, with populations in the Bahamas and Bermuda. Abundances are much higher in some locations than in their native habitat. These beautiful animals with long toxic fin spines are popular aquarium species and were introduced, probably more than once, when aquarium specimens escaped (in one case a hurricane led to the release of six fish) or were liberated. They are now clearly well established over a wide region. They are voracious predators of small fishes and crustaceans—their diet in the Bahamas consists predominantly of small reef fishes such as wrasses, damselfishes, gobies, and small specimens of many other families. It is too early to tell what impact they will have, but their accidental introduction is yet one more probably serious disturbance to Caribbean reefs.

We continue to harvest a number of wild species, and our harvests, as discussed in chapters 1 and 2, are frequently excessive. Our hunter-gatherer forefathers caused extinction mainly through overharvesting, but now direct harvest is far less important as a source of extinction than are all the indirect ways in which we impact other species. Still, egregious cases of overharvesting continue to exist. Currently, the sharks of the world are endangered by the quaint custom of finning, which is depleting global shark populations so that some wealthy people can have soup. Ships engaged in the shark fin trade routinely catch sharks, remove their fins, and toss the rest of the animal, often still alive, overboard. On September 25, 2009, President Johnson Toribiong of Palau announced at the United Nations that Palau had declared its entire EEZ as a shark sanctuary, where fishing of these magnificent fishes would not be permitted. As he said to a BBC reporter at the time, "The need to protect the sharks outweighs the need to enjoy a bowl of soup." Few others have been that eloquent or that clear in their understanding of this issue, and in Doha, Qatar, in March 2010, the world failed to agree that trade in several particularly endangered shark species should be halted. Palau cannot save the world's sharks by itself.

Populations of most of the world's sharks are falling because we harvest them for their fins. Rhinos are declining because we covet their horns. Bears get killed for their gall bladders, and tigers, for their whiskers and bacula.[6] Sea turtles are declining because we occupy and light the beaches they use for nesting and because we still, occasionally, harvest them for food—sometimes illegally, but usually in "traditional" hunting activities.[7] I discussed the problem of overfishing in chapter 1, and there is plenty of evidence that we tend also to overhunt, depleting populations of larger animals in an unsustainable way. We are currently overhunting African and Asian forest species for "bush meat" (see chapter 2). When it comes to certain types of fishing on coral reefs, our rates of harvest may be getting perilously close to causing numerous extinctions.

The Banggai Islands are a small archipelago of tiny islands located due south of the town of Luwuk in east-central Sulawesi, Indonesia. There is one cruise operator here who offers live-aboard dive tours. It's an out-of-the-way place. It's also home to the Banggai cardinalfish, *Pterapogon kauderni,* a small, boldly banded black-and-white coral reef fish. Its lack of a pelagic larval stage perhaps accounts for its very limited geographic distribution (only 34 square km of potential habitat around the islands). Where it occurs, it can be quite abundant, but it is susceptible to being collected for the international aquarium trade. The International Union for the Conservation of Nature (IUCN) placed the Banggai cardinalfish on its Red List as an Endangered species in 2007, when surveys had indicated that the population might have declined by 89 percent since harvest began in the mid-1990s. Its uniqueness, in combination with its diurnal habits, small size, and attractive appearance, is what makes this fish valuable to the aquarium trade. Local fishermen collect perhaps 900,000 fish per year, for which they receive US1 or 2¢ per fish. (You can buy one over the internet for $20 to $25—guess where the profit is in this fishery.) With a current total population of more than two million fish, the Benggai cardinalfish is not

6. The baculum, or os penis, occurs in some but not all mammals. Many wasteful harvests, including those for tiger bacula, bear gall bladders, and sun-dried seahorses, exist to provide humans with potions that may or may not improve libido, virility, sexual prowess, or all three.

7. For native peoples to be granted continuation of their traditional rights to hunt, fish, or harvest timber can be an appropriate way to ameliorate the effects of colonization. Problems arise when the native group uses its traditional right as a way to flaunt limits on harvest or ignore other management tools such as closed seasons. Political correctness can make it difficult to address the need for sustainability when a traditional harvest is involved.

extinct yet, but it is one of a growing number that are now being listed by IUCN because exploitation is pushing it close to extinction. The other eight species of coral reef fishes considered to be Endangered or Critically Endangered by IUCN are all larger than the Benggai cardinalfish. They include six groupers and one wrasse that are favored in the live reef fish restaurant trade, a subject explored in chapter 4.

CURRENT EXTINCTION RATES IN CONTEXT

We are responsible for most of the extinction occurring today, and the rate is somewhere around 0.1 percent of extant species per year. Species are now disappearing at a rate of about a thousand times faster than the average rate of extinction over the past five hundred million years, but there have been geologically brief periods of exceptionally high extinction rates several other times in geological history, and five of these stand out. Let's see how the present period compares to those.

We can estimate average rates of extinction during geological history by painstakingly examining the rates at which new taxa appear and old taxa disappear through the fossil record. Studies of this type indicate that the average species has a lifespan of about five to ten million years. This varies among taxa, however; the average mammal lasts for about a million years, and the average planktonic foraminiferan (a type of single-celled alga) survives some thirteen million years. A reasonable approximation, then, is that species endure from one to ten million years. The rate at which new species appear can also be estimated, in this case by examining the number of mutational changes between related species and assuming a more or less constant rate of occurrence of such changes. It takes, on average, about one million years to accumulate sufficient genetic differences for two related populations to be considered different enough to have become two species—further support for the idea of a one-million-year lifespan for species. (This is an average: species with short generation times will speciate more rapidly than those with longer generation times such as people or elephants.)

Figure 9 shows the pattern of extinction through time as revealed by the fossil record since the start of the Cambrian, five hundred forty-two million years ago. Presumably, earlier, less well-fossilized faunas experienced a similar pattern. There is an underlying low rate of extinction, punctuated with occasional geologically sudden increases in extinction

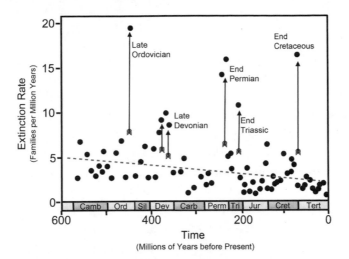

FIGURE 9. The pattern of extinction through geological time as represented by the rate of loss of families (number lost per million years) of marine vertebrates and invertebrates from the Cambrian period to the present. There are five periods, the mass extinctions, in which the rate has been noticeably higher than usual. Analysis based on records of 3,300 families of organisms. Figure redrawn from D. M. Raup and J. J. Sepkowski, "Mass Extinctions in the Marine Fossil Record," *Science* 215 (1982): 1501–3.

rate. In addition, there is a general downward trend in the average rate (number lost as percentage of existing taxa) because there has been a continuous slow increase in the total number of species present at one time as evolution has built an ever-expanding tree of branches—with more species present, the number being lost each year is a smaller percentage of the total.

The sudden peaks of extinction are termed *mass extinction events,* and we can argue about how many of these exist, depending on where we draw the line denoting "exceptionally high." Many people speak of five major events prior to the present: the Late Ordovician, Late Devonian, End Permian, End Triassic, and End Cretaceous events. (That three of the five occur at the end of geological periods is partly because so many geological boundaries have been defined based on the differences in faunal composition across the boundary.) The most extreme of the five is the End Permian event, in which some 96 percent of all marine species and 70 percent of all terrestrial vertebrates went extinct. (Other terrestrial taxa suffered as well.) The event lasted a couple of million years, with one particularly sharp peak about ten to sixty thousand years long around two hundred fifty-two million years ago. The End Ordovician event, the next most extreme, included two primary pulses of extinction a million years apart, about four hundred forty-four million years ago, and resulted in the loss of about 49 percent of marine genera. The Late Devonian extinction, most likely a series of smaller events over a period of about three to fifteen million years, occurred three hundred sixty-four million years ago and was of similar size. Fifty-seven percent of marine genera are estimated to have been lost. The End Triassic event, two hundred million years ago, was somewhat less severe: in the course of as little as ten thousand years, 20 percent of marine families and almost 30 percent of genera became extinct.[8] Finally, the End Cretaceous event, sixty-five million years ago, resulted in the loss of about 30 percent of genera and 50 percent of species over a period of a few thousand years.

How does the present rate of extinction stack up against what occurred during these past mass events? What people are now calling the Holocene mass extinction commenced during the final years of the Pleistocene with the losses of numerous large mammals. These losses of large organisms had been attributed to inability to survive a warming climate, but increasingly scientists argue that they are the result of over-exploitation by human hunters. The pace of extinction quickens into historical time with the migrations of human populations into Pacific islands, Australasia, and the Americas, followed by the exploration and colonization of these same locations by Europeans. Numerous mammals and even more birds disappeared as a result, the dodo being just one. The pace has continued to quicken into modern times, and E. O. Wilson of Harvard University predicted in 2002 that we are likely to cause the extinction of two-thirds of all living species within the next one hundred years.

While 67 percent of all species is not quite as great as the End Permian's 96 percent, Wilson was not predicting that the pace of extinction would

8. Stop and think for a moment. In this least severe of the mass extinction events, in a period as short as the time since the last Pleistocene retreat, 30 percent of all genera became extinct. At present, the world's mammals belong to about two hundred genera. This rate of loss, if applied to today's mammals, would result in the total loss of sixty of these two hundred kinds of animal. Would we notice? These mass extinction events all result in massive losses in diversity.

slow at the end of those one hundred years, and one hundred years is an incredibly short time in which to lose that many species. Furthermore, Wilson's prediction is based on the effects of habitat destruction alone— the loss of species due to increase in patchiness and overall reduction of area of habitat. The effects of overexploitation and climate change and the introduction of exotic competitors, predators, and diseases will only increase the rates of loss further. Many of these newly extinct species will have the dubious distinction of having gone extinct before they were ever collected and described by science—it's difficult to be missed when you are gone if nobody knew you when you were alive. Missed or not, these newly extinct species will be participating in a mass extinction event that clearly rivals the five major ones that have gone before and is occurring much more rapidly. And we will have caused it.

Because there have been five mass extinctions in the past and the world still turns on its axis, it is legitimate to wonder if the Holocene mass extinction really matters. After all, most of the species being lost are ones that are of little direct economic value to us. And, to alter the phrase slightly, if a species goes extinct and nobody is there to see, does it really disappear? Putting this perspective more positively, as long as we ensure that the species we depend on directly remain (chiefly our domesticated species), can we just engineer a world that will continue to provide for our needs in the absence of the extravagant biodiversity that presently exists? Many people, perhaps even a majority if pressed, would consider this a perfectly reasonable proposition. Yet I guarantee we will deeply miss these newly extinct species when our world becomes simplified and ecosystems cease to function as they once did. A sizeable number of biologists would agree and would consider the proposition that the predicted loss of species does not matter to be naively optimistic. I turn now to their arguments for why the Holocene mass extinction definitely does matter. However, before doing that, it is necessary to take a short side journey and discuss the concept of environmental, or ecosystem, services.

VALUING THE ENVIRONMENTAL SERVICES PROVIDED BY INTACT ECOSYSTEMS

Ecosystems provide both goods that we use and services that make our existence on the planet more tenable. The goods are easily valued economically. They include fishery and forestry products; if we include the agroecosystems that produce our food, then the goods provided by ecosystems include everything we eat.[9] The services provided by ecosystems are much more difficult to value economically because they do not usually enter our economy as services that are bought or sold. They include a broad range of communal benefits, including regulating gases in the air, regulating climate, dampening weather variability, regulating water flow, cycling nutrients, purifying waters, and so on. They also include protection of coastlines from storms—a particularly important service given our proclivity for living close to coasts—and the provision of habitat of particular types that support tourism or recreational activities or provide essential nursery habitat for valued species that live (and are harvested) in other habitats in later life.

In 1997 Robert Costanza, then at the University of Maryland and now the University of Vermont's Gund Professor of Ecological Economics, joined with a dozen colleagues to publish an article in *Nature* that attempts to value the environmental services of all natural ecosystems on Earth. They followed a logical line of reasoning to evaluate the current economic value of seventeen environmental services for the total area of sixteen natural biomes, including forests of various kinds, open ocean, deserts, tundra, and everything in between. They came up with the amazing value of $33 trillion per year (actually, the range was between $16 and $54 trillion) for these environmental services. This was a good deal larger than the total world GNP of $18 trillion at that time.

Although broadly accepted, the Costanza estimate received some sharp criticism due to the methods used, particularly the extrapolation from marginal to total value. So, in 2002 Costanza teamed up with an even larger group of ecologists and economists led by Andrew Balmford

9. Although agricultural systems differ from natural ecosystems because humans manipulate them to such a great extent, they are nevertheless built from natural components—all domesticated food species, plant and animal, originally came from wild species, and the world's agricultural soils were all created through natural geological and ecosystem processes. Further, no matter how artificial, agroecosystems ultimately depend on natural ecosystems for their continued functioning: natural systems provide them with soil, water for irrigation, raw genetic material for breeding new varieties, natural enemies of pests, pollination, beneficial soil microorganisms, microclimate modification, and so on. Loss of biodiversity in natural ecosystems will surely affect our ability to feed ourselves, particularly as the fossil fuels upon which today's agriculture is based are depleted.

of Cambridge University to use a different approach to estimate the value of conserving the world's natural systems. Their effort was described in chapter 2 as it related to forest ecosystems. They approached the problem by seeking out examples in which it was possible to compare the economic value of an area of relatively undisturbed natural habitat with that of a similar and reasonably adjacent area that had been modified and exploited. As mentioned in Chapter 2, only five studies of the three hundred they reviewed met their criterion of a comparison of relatively undisturbed and transformed habitats: tropical forests in Malaysia and Cameroon, mangrove habitat in Thailand, wetlands in Canada, and coral reefs in the Philippines. That only five existed shows how much more needs to be done to properly value natural ecosystems.

In every case examined, the difference in the value of nonmarketed environmental services between the relatively undisturbed system and the exploited one exceeded the marketed marginal benefits of conversion, often by a wide margin. Put another way, the economic gain achieved by exploiting a previously unexploited system was less than the economic loss due to the reduced capacity of the exploited system to provide environmental services.[10] Across the four ecosystems studied, conversion resulted in mean losses in total economic value (TEV) of roughly one-half of the TEV of relatively intact systems (mean of 55 percent, with a range from 14 percent to 75 percent). While there have undoubtedly been cases in which conversion of natural ecosystems to human use—clear-cut logging, farming, cities—has been economically beneficial in the broadest sense, these results suggest that at the present time, with so much of the world's surface already converted to human use, conversion of still more is not economically prudent.

Their next step was to use the estimate of the cost of conversion to human use (55 percent of TEV) to estimate the cost of documented losses in area covered by natural ecosystems worldwide—such as the seven-million-hectare, West Virginia–sized forest being lost each year. At the current rate of loss across all natural ecosystems, the economic

10. Costanza, Balmford, and colleagues measured total economic value (TEV), the sum of the value of goods (resources) exploited and entered into our market economy, and the value of environmental services, the unmarketed benefits that the ecosystem provides. In their comparisons they contrast the TEV of an unexploited piece of habitat (no goods captured and marketed) with that of a piece of habitat that had been exploited and degraded (value of goods harvested plus services remaining following exploitation).

cost of the conversion that occurs during a single year is approximately $250 billion per year, every year into the future, because that loss continues to be felt essentially forever. Read that last sentence carefully—the losses in one year cost $250 billion that year *and every future year;* the losses the next year represent *another* $250 billion that and every subsequent year, and so on. Such compounding means that there is a very substantial cost accumulating. Perhaps because this is literally mind-boggling (see chapter 5), we mostly pay no attention to it.

Constanza and Balmford go on to discuss such interesting political details as the value of governmental subsidies to private landowners to clear their forests (Cameroon) or drain their wetlands (Canada). These subsidies, which globally amount to something between $950 and $1,950 billion per year, distort the private value of conversion (making it more profitable to the developer) and are well in excess of the total of about $6.5 billion spent per year to manage natural areas being protected for conservation. A slight shift in policy on subsidies so that owners were rewarded for creating and managing protected areas would be a very useful move.[11]

Precisely because we do not usually purchase environmental services, taking such things as the purification of water in wetlands, the protection of coastlines from storm damage by reefs and coastal mangrove forests, or the regulation of run-off and erosion by forests as uncosted entitlements, these environmental services go unvalued and frequently unnoticed. Yet in many instances they are far more important than the goods or resources we harvest from the service-providing natural systems and sell into our markets. As I write this, we are undertaking an unplanned experiment to examine the value of environmental services provided by the coast of Louisiana and Mississippi (and perhaps Alabama and western Florida). By oiling this coast with product from the Deepwater Horizon well, plus copious amounts of chemical dispersants, BP is helping to show us the true economic value of nursery habitats for fish and shrimp and beaches for tourism.[12] I suspect we

11. I know it's a radical idea—that governments might spend funds to foster actions that preserve the public good instead of spending the same funds to foster private profit at the expense of the public good.

12. The Gulf of Mexico currently produces about a third of all capture fishery product in the North American market. I see no future in which our cost for seafood is not going to rise because of the Deepwater Horizon incident.

will "discover" that the value is substantial. Unfortunately, we will discover this only because we lose that value and the economic benefits that coast was routinely bringing to fishermen and tourism operators year after year, all for free. To return to our discussion of whether mass extinctions matter, we have to keep in mind the enormous value of environmental services. These are an additional benefit, beyond the value of any resources harvested, and they are normally provided free of charge. We also have to remember that the extinctions are just the end point of gross reductions in biomass that have potentially far-reaching impacts on ecosystem function.

ECONOMIC ARGUMENTS
FOR CONSERVING BIODIVERSITY

Arguments for conserving biodiversity fall into three groups: the ethical, the aesthetic, and the economic. The economic arguments are the ones easiest to evaluate because they are based on science and rational cost-benefit analyses. Ecosystems provide us with various goods and services. These have value. Loss of species or gross reductions in abundances will reduce their value, and we can measure the cost per species of such loss.

The most frightening of the economic arguments is that the loss of critical species will lead to total and perhaps sudden collapse of ecosystems—the loss of the ecosystems' ability to function in important ways, such as in the cycling of nutrients, the creation of biomass through photosynthesis, and the movement of the energy fixed by photosynthesis through the different trophic levels of food webs. Such a collapse, if widespread, would have profound economic consequences and even more fundamental consequences for our well-being. This argument hinges on the notion that ecological systems are highly evolved mechanisms that carry out their functions in efficient ways and that losing parts (the species) must lead to system failure. It's an important argument, and one I will discuss in some detail. First, however, let's examine the other economic arguments.

Other economic arguments concern either the loss of goods or services provided by particular species or the loss of adaptability or resilience of ecosystems when they become simpler because of species loss. The direct economic impact of the loss of particular species is easy to assess for many species that are already directly used. The loss of economic value often precedes actual extinction, as in the loss of value of the numerous fisheries that have crashed around the world, and for species that are harvested, we can be precise about the value they represent.

Direct economic impact is harder to assess for those species that provide services. What is the value of mangrove forests along a low-lying tropical shore, and what would happen if the handful of mangrove species that provide the structure for such forests were to go extinct? Their value lies partly in their effectiveness at ameliorating the effects of wave action on coastal communities and partly in their role as nursery habitat for a variety of coastal marine species, including valuable fish, shrimp, and crab species. Our appreciation of their protective value increased following the devastating Indonesian earthquake and tsunami that created damage and loss of life to communities across the Indian Ocean and into the South Pacific in 2002. In some instances, coasts fringed with mangrove forests were far less impacted than were those lacking such buffers; many coastal villages protected by mangroves were spared.[13]

What about the coast redwood of Northern California and Oregon? It has measurable value for the timber it provides, and it has equally valid but less easily quantified value for the tourism it promotes, the carbon it sequesters, and the local weather and cycling of water it creates. Finally, there are all those species that may be able to provide goods but have yet to be discovered and exploited, and those that provide services of which we simply are unaware. Chief among the providers of not-yet-discovered goods are species that may produce novel compounds in their tissues that will turn out to have pharmaceutical or other industrial value once we discover them. The pharmaceutical industry employs many biologists to comb oceans and tropical forests for species that may yield products with therapeutic properties or that can be manipulated chemically to create valuable compounds for medicine or manufacture. Nanotechnology will undoubtedly find biological products of use as building blocks, and research using proteins or DNA molecules to build novel nano-scale machines is already well under way. While we may not know the potential economic value of a particular species at risk of extinction, a precautionary approach would

13. This story is a little more complicated: it turns out that mangroves definitely protect from modest storms and wave action but not so much from extreme storms and waves.

suggest we should not be too sanguine about rampant biodiversity loss, because some of the species lost could have had substantial value to us if they had been saved.

The loss of resilience, and therefore of adaptability, of ecosystems due to the loss of species is even more difficult to evaluate. It's a given that ecosystems generally contain numerous examples of similar species that do similar things in similar ways. The many different trees in a forest are an example. In the beech–oak–maple forests of eastern North America, the various species of tree all contribute to the canopy, and all carry out photosynthesis to build organic matter that sustains the animals and other organisms that live in the forest. It is a reasonable assumption that, over ecological time-scales, each of these species of tree has its own particular "expertise." It does best under slightly warmer, drier, colder, or wetter conditions than do other species of tree in the forest. Under one set of prevailing climatic, geological, or soil conditions, or even under one set of prevailing abundances of herbivorous insects and tree pathogens, certain of these species will be functioning at their best while others will be performing suboptimally. Overall, the forest does what forests do: converting sunshine and nutrients into organic matter and sustaining the rich array of animals and other organisms that live there. If there is a change in conditions, certain other of the tree species will begin functioning at their best, while the prior best performers will begin to perform suboptimally. The diversity of tree species present allows the forest to continue to provide its goods and services even though conditions are changing. Of course, over longer geological time-scales, any of these tree species may undergo evolutionary changes that will change its "expertise." Therefore, if climates are becoming colder and wetter over decades or centuries, many of the trees may shift their capabilities so that they become better adapted to the new conditions.

Because the forest contains a number of different canopy tree species with their different specializations, the forest ecosystem is buffered from the effects of changes in its environment. By contrast, a forest containing a single species of canopy tree will be more directly impacted by cooling trends or by insect or disease outbreaks. In this sense, the more diverse forest has greater inertia, or resilience.

The Holocene mass extinction will rob forests and other ecosystems of their diversity and will reduce their capacity to function in a consistent way despite changing environmental conditions. Many people frame this argument in the context of genetic diversity. When mass extinction removes species, it removes unique genetic patterns. These genetic patterns may be valuable for ecosystem function right now, or they may be ones that will come into their own at some future time when environmental conditions particularly favor them or when further evolution changes them into particularly well-adapted forms.

Now, how realistic are these two arguments? On one level they are compelling. The ecological world does provide us with goods and services, and loss of species does remove the goods and services they formerly provided. Further, there are undoubtedly instances of novel products yet to be discovered, and if the species capable of supplying that product is lost before the product is discovered, there has been a loss of future value. From another perspective, however, these arguments can be overstated. The very redundancy of natural systems— the several canopy tree species, the far more numerous beetle species, and so on—ensures that in many cases one or more species can be lost without any measurable loss of economic value for us. Northern forests with ten or fewer species of canopy tree function quite well, and I am far from convinced that losing a few species of tree or beetle or anything else will result in a measurable degradation of the goods and services forests provide. Only where a species provides economic benefits that cannot be provided by other species does its extinction result in demonstrable economic loss.

I am aware that my career working with diverse tropical systems may have biased me against the idea that the loss of a single species could have significant effects on an ecosystem's capacity to provide its services. When the forest has ten tree species, each species plays a more important role than if the forest has one hundred species. Still, let's agree that species losses will become cumulatively significant sooner in the less-diverse ecosystems than in the richer ones. In fact, my possible bias may be moot, given that we should be focusing not on the loss of one or two species but on the near-term loss of substantial numbers of species. When we talk of losing two-thirds of all species, we are entering a very different arena. We will not be able to lose two-thirds of all species without losing all members of particular functional groups. It is the sheer scale of the mass extinction now taking place that should be causing us to worry. The genetic diversity lost when a single species goes extinct is rarely worth worrying about. Nor in most cases are the goods and services that that single species provided. But the removal of over half the species presently on Earth is loss at a vastly different scale. It will have substantial consequences, some due to the loss of goods and services, others to the loss of genetic resiliency that their extinction will result in. The problem is not in the details of how the loss of each species will affect us economically, but in the fact that such a large proportion of species is being lost. Death by a thousand cuts is still death, even when the individual cuts are small.

The concept of ecosystem collapse as a consequence of extinction is somewhat different from the other economic arguments. This argument does not hinge upon the intrinsic value of the particular species that are going extinct but on the idea that there are ecosystem-level properties that are important for providing goods and services and that these properties will be so irrevocably changed by species loss that the goods and services will not be provided. I wrote in chapter 6 that ecosystems are less finely coevolved than the prevailing wisdom suggests and that community structure is not nearly as strongly regulated as many might claim. This perspective might support the argument that biodiversity does not matter—if community structure is relatively loose, the loss of a single species will not be expected to ripple across the community. And it could follow that the loss of two-thirds of species could still result in a biosphere that functioned much as the current one does and provided for our needs. I do not believe this chain of reasoning is correct, however. I have not changed my mind concerning community organization, but when we talk about eliminating the majority of all species, we have to recognize that ecological systems are going to be profoundly changed, sometimes in unexpected ways. We have growing evidence that ecological change can be abrupt rather than gradual, that thresholds and tipping points really do exist. It is possible the that loss of certain species will increase the likelihood of loss of certain other species strongly dependent upon them, so that the rate of loss spirals up to much higher rates than at present. It is also possible that the growing stresses on the environment caused by our activities will accelerate species loss. In both these cases, thresholds and tipping points are likely to loom up unexpectedly. So, while we know that species are going extinct at a fast rate, what we do not know at present is how far down this path of lost species we can go before the situation becomes critical and we find ourselves at the threshold of a nightmare. I would prefer not to find out.

At the present time honeybees (*Apis mellifera*) are in decline. They are suffering a broad range of problems, each of which lowers their capacity to survive and reproduce. These include the effects of pesticide use in agriculture, the introduction of disease agents due to the increased international transport of bees to supply the needs of the agricultural sector, and the reduction of habitat as farms become ever-neater checkerboards of adjacent fields. Honeybees themselves are not in danger of extinction yet because there is a substantial industry that cultivates them and distributes them to provide pollinator services to farmers. However, wild populations of this bee have declined significantly—by about 90 percent in the last fifty years in most parts of the United States—and the factors that are responsible also impact other species of bee and other insects.[14]

Insecticide use remains heavy in many agricultural crops, and the chemicals used rarely target only specific pests. In the developed world, insecticide use is also rampant in suburbia, where we have been taught to value green monocultures of grasses in preference to the whimsical diversity of meadows with their wildflowers, clover, and dandelions. And in many places there continue to be spraying programs for mosquito control. The consequences are that many insect pollinators are in decline. Loss of habitat also makes life difficult for insect pollinators and for other species such as bats and birds that play important roles as pollinators as well.

A quick survey of pollination tells us that a large fraction of plant species are dependent on animal pollinators to fertilize their seeds. Of one hundred fifteen crop species in a recent worldwide study, eighty-seven relied partly or entirely on animals for pollination, and it's estimated that about one-third of human nutrition depends on insect pollination. Further, all pollinators are not the same. Some can service some plants and not others. Different lengths of tongue, different body shapes, and

---

14. A somewhat analogous situation exists for the Atlantic salmon, *Salmo salar,* which is native to the rivers and streams of northeastern North America. This animal has been extirpated in many of its native rivers, due primarily to habitat alteration, but it is among the most abundant aquaculture species on the planet and is cultivated along the coasts of all continents. Probably more numerous than at any time in the past, it is not going to disappear any time soon, but *ecologically* it is approaching extinction.

different behavior when visiting a flower all play a role in determining whether a particular insect is able to extract the nectar it seeks from a particular flower (and thus whether it will bother to visit the flower) and whether it is effective in carrying pollen when it does visit a flower.

While many pollinators, such as the honeybee, are generalists, some are specialists, closely adapted morphologically and behaviorally to the structure of the flowers they service. Indeed, the close matching of pollinators and flowers in such groups as the orchids was one of the first examples of coevolution—the closely complementary evolution of a pair of species to make them particularly well adapted to each other—that attracted scientific attention. So, turning aside from the particular problems of the honeybee or even of the farmer with a field crop that absolutely needs its pollinators, what happens when various species of pollinator start to disappear? A certain amount of pollination just won't get done, and plants will fail to produce seed in the quantities they might otherwise be capable of producing. Rachel Carson's silent spring becomes a silent and unproductive spring. In time, plant species begin to disappear as well.

What about other forms of tight coevolution that would result in cascades of loss? This is where things get difficult because there simply has not been sufficient study of the extent to which species are truly dependent on one another for their continued existence in a community. The concept of the guild, or the functional group, is useful here, because in most species-rich communities it is a relatively simple task to recognize that there are particular types of species that play particular roles and that several species of each type may be present. The forest is made up of canopy and understory species of tree as well as a host of different kinds of other plants. Its animals can similarly be grouped into sets of species that do similar things, or play particular roles in the community. Loss of one or two members of a functional group can therefore be managed by other species stepping forward to carry the extra load. As with pollination, where most plants can be pollinated by more than one insect and most insects will visit more than one plant species, other coevolved relationships tend to include groups of species.

In the coral reefs of the vast Indo-Pacific, stretching west from Hawaii and Easter Island all the way to the Indian Ocean and the Red Sea, there are some behaviorally fascinating examples of commensalism, a particular form of coevolution. One of the best known is of the anemone and its anemonefish—"Nemo," to that cohort who had their childhood in the late 1990s. All but one of the twenty-eight anemonefishes belong to the single genus *Amphiprion*. They all use anemones as an obligate habitat and occur as small, permanent groups, usually with a single dominant female, resident in a single anemone. They use a variety of anemone species as hosts, preferring ones of relatively large size, providing lots of cozy space among the tentacles in which to revel. And here is the catch. All twenty-eight species never occur together, because they have different geographic distributions across that vast expanse of ocean, but many places include five, six, or more of the twenty-eight among their native species. Careful field studies have shown that the several anemonefishes present at any particular location will each exhibit definite preferences for particular species of anemone. However, every species of anemonefish can be found using more than one species of anemone, and every anemone offers space to more than one species of fish.

This commensalism is obviously coevolved. The tentacles of these anemones are toxic to most small fish, and the anemonefish either does not trigger the release of or is immune to the toxins. Both partners benefit, because the fish, gaining shelter and protection from the anemone, sometimes happens to lure other species within the anemone's reach or, more frequently, drops small food items that then become food for the host. Yet the commensalism has not developed as a strict one-to-one partnership but as a partnership between the members of two functional groups. In such cases, if one or two species of anemonefish or one or two species of anemone were to become extinct, the world would go on, and there would still be fascinating partnerships between fish and anemones.

Exactly the same story can be told of the somewhat less well-known partnership between certain burrowing gobies and shrimp that also live on reefs in the Indo-Pacific. Gobies of the genus *Cryptocentrus* grow 10 to 15 cm in length, a bit larger than Nemo, and live in burrows dug in the sandy floors of reef lagoons. Unlike many other gobies, they are unable to dig their own burrows. Instead, they team up with shrimps of several genera within the family Alpheidae. These shrimps are able excavators that build complex burrows big enough for two, or three if one is a fish. This is a true commensalism, in which both partners benefit: the fish obtains use of the burrow in return for sitting at the entrance and signaling approach of danger to the shrimp. (They usually signal by touch, and it's common to see the fish at the burrow mouth with one antenna of the shrimp draped across its tail.) While there are definite preferences for partner species, in most reef regions several species of fish occur with several species of shrimp. Once again, if one species of shrimp became extinct, the gobies would make do with whomever was left, and vice-versa.

If one searches carefully for other examples of commensal relationships, both the ones in which the partners are relatively independent, free-living organisms and the ones in which one partner is extensively modified to live within the other and does not spend time in the great outdoors, it seems that functional groups of commensals are more common than single pairs of species living closely with each other. At least this is the case in the tropics, where diversity is high (so again, my possible bias may be misleading me). In such cases, loss of one species will not lead irrevocably to loss of the partner.[15]

To summarize, studies of commensalism, in which we would expect to find very tightly coevolved species, usually reveal patterns in which several species of one type occur together with one or other of several species of the other type. The redundancy characteristic of most ecological systems, in which species commonly exist as members of identifiable functional groups, extends even to commensal pairs. This redundancy makes it relatively unlikely that the loss of one particular species will be followed by ecosystem collapse.

Therefore all three economic arguments—ecosystem collapse, loss of direct economic value, loss of environmental services—suffer the same problem. The impact of the *loss of a few* species tends to be overstated to argue in favor of working to prevent the *loss of large numbers* of species. Overstatement weakens the arguments, yet they are valid when we consider the loss of two-thirds of all species. It is quite unlikely that such heavy losses will be balanced across functional groups so that representatives of each group will remain behind. Loss of all the canopy tree species really does eliminate the forest. I would not call this eco-

---

15. In his 2006 book *Nonequilibrium Ecology*, Klaus Rohde provides numerous examples from the world of parasites that demonstrate the species-rich guilds of parasites adapted to life in specific regions of an organism's body and sometimes several species' bodies. Even here, the one-to-one partnership is apparently far from universal.

system collapse, but I would call it a distressingly simplified world, and one that will be economically challenging for us. Striving to prevent or at least slow the progress of the Holocene mass extinction seems, from the perspective of economic self-interest, to be a valuable goal, even if the precise arguments supporting this goal may be a good deal weaker than many believe.

ETHICAL AND AESTHETIC REASONS
FOR CONSERVING BIODIVERSITY

Ethical arguments for biodiversity conservation are often reduced to "we do not have the right to cause extinctions," and aesthetic arguments to "every species is a unique product of evolution and therefore of intrinsic value that we should honor." I think these simple assertions trivialize these arguments, and while I am uncomfortable venturing outside my rational and materialistic comfort-zone, we need to explore them.

I personally believe there are strong ethical arguments for developing a more responsible stewardship of the earth. However, I was influenced, a couple of years ago, by a colleague I greatly respect who claimed that ethical arguments were not particularly helpful, because for some people they weakened the general case. He offered a counterargument: No other organism behaves ethically toward other species, and it is a gross distortion of our animal nature to argue that we have a responsibility that no other organism has—a responsibility to act in ways that permit the continued existence of all other species. By making ethical arguments for more responsible management of the earth's ecosystems, one runs the risk of having the argument "thrown out of court" because the starting premise (that ethics are appropriate) is judged to be false. Far better, he argued, to restrict the arguments to ones based on economics than to introduce a possible distraction in the form of ethics.

I think there is much merit in this perspective, because ethical arguments will not fare very well against arguments from big business concerning loss of jobs, loss of GDP, and losses in the stock market. Far too often, the environmental movement has failed to win the critical battles because economic forces have opposed what the environmental movement sought to achieve, and the environmental arguments have been a mixture of "the sky is falling" and "it's the right thing to do." In fact, as I have tried to demonstrate throughout this book, there are good, economically sound arguments for responsible environmental management. Sustainable management, in the long run, produces greater quality of life for humans than does a less-responsible approach.

Still, it would be wrong not to admit that there are valid ethical arguments that can bolster the arguments based on economics. In my view, a valid ethical argument can be based on the observation that humans appear likely to be the only living organism on the planet with the capacity to identify and understand complex causal relationships and to anticipate the future consequences of present-day actions. Given that we have these special capacities, we are obligated to behave responsibly and to avoid behaviors that are likely to result in deleterious consequences for the biosphere of which we are but one part. Deleterious consequences are such things as a substantial alteration in the rates at which species become extinct compared to rates in previous times. To behave ethically, we should, as individuals and as a species, attempt to tread lightly on this planet. In the present context, that means we should attempt to avoid actions that lead to the extinction of any species. (I think it's notable here to remember that the extinctions we have caused have rarely been deliberate; they have been the accidental but inevitable consequence of our carelessness or greed.)[16]

In essence, I am arguing that all extant species have a right to life and that we do not have the right to knowingly cause extinctions. As my colleague would say, this is a pretty wishy-washy argument, and not one based on sound scientific principles. Still, it's an argument that some people will embrace, and it has its own validity: as creatures possessed of free will and the ability to anticipate the effects of our actions, we have a special obligation, perhaps only to ourselves, to avoid behaving in a way that knowingly causes the extinction of other species. We are more civilized if we live up to this obligation.

This ethical argument requires that we accept that there exist absolutely just states and transitions in this universe against which our actions can be measured. (The argument may also benefit from a Gaia worldview, but as one who long ago rejected Gaia, I do not think it

16. The smallpox virus is a rare exception that we deliberately sought to eliminate. It would now be extinct were it not for the archived samples retained in certain government labs.

essential.) The argument does not require that we not kill other animals (although many may try to stretch it in that direction), but it does require that we avoid unnecessary or excessive killing either directly or indirectly via pollution, habitat destruction, and so on. It does not require a belief in any higher power or an expectation of punishment for behaving unethically (although it does have a place in many religiously grounded worldviews). It does require acceptance of the idea that, unlike other organisms, we somehow have had bestowed upon us (or have taken to ourselves) greater responsibility for caring for the biosphere than they have. In this regard it clearly lies outside science, and while some will embrace it enthusiastically, others will reject it out of hand because of that fact, arguing that it is neither right nor wrong to undertake actions that lead to massive extinction, cause total collapse of ecosystems, or even endanger our own future survival and prosperity. Ethics is simply not a part of the natural world, and we should be no more concerned that our actions are responsible for the Holocene mass extinction than that great asteroid was when it was about to plunge into the Yucatán Peninsula sixty-five million years ago and cause the End Cretaceous mass extinction. Some may embrace this counterargument, but I like to think I am a more sensitive (that is, sentient) individual than some large lump of rock hurtling through space.[17]

The aesthetic argument is somewhat different. It is based on the notion that every species is a unique product of evolution that will never exist again if it goes extinct. Uniqueness has intrinsic value. We should no more countenance the extinction of a species than we should the destruction of the Mona Lisa or the paintings in the caves at Lascaux. As a unique creation of the evolutionary process—the fundamental engine of existence—each species has a precious beauty that deserves to continue to exist in the world, regardless of whether it provides us with goods and services or whether we have an ethical responsibility to preserve it. As with the ethical argument, to accept this argument requires acceptance of the existence of fundamental truths, such as that uniqueness is of value. Again, this is not a scientific argu-

17. Although there is excellent evidence for the asteroid that landed on the Yucatán and reasonable deduction concerning the nuclear winter that followed, it is doubtful that this event alone caused the End Cretaceous mass extinction, which killed off species throughout the world and in the depths of the oceans. It was the cymbal clash that marked the end of a complex series of events that coalesced to create this mass extinction.

ment, and it is easy to squelch. The Taliban, who destroyed the giant statues of Buddha at Bamyan, Afghanistan, would presumably squelch it with ease.

THE UNFOLDING OF THE
HOLOCENE MASS EXTINCTION

We are well into what may become one of the largest mass extinction events the world has seen. This Holocene mass extinction is occurring because of human abundances and human activities. It commenced for terrestrial species by the end of the Pleistocene and now includes marine organisms. In excess of two-thirds of all extant species could be lost by 2100, and there is no reason for the process to stop at that point. What will the world of 2100 be like?

Most larger species (coyote size and up), other than those directly cultivated by humans, are likely to be extinct or to exist only as threatened populations, with perhaps a few representatives in zoos. Truly wild landscapes (other than deserts) are likely to be nonexistent, except in parts of North and South America. Ecosystems, other than agricultural or urban ones, will be depauperate and remarkably uniform from place to place, but they will probably still function to cycle nutrients and capture energy. Environmental goods and services will be much reduced simply because of the loss of diversity of organisms. With the increased homogeneity and overall reduced diversity, there will be a much greater risk of pandemics that severely impact particular species and create massive change in ecosystem composition as a result. The risk of a species extinction that has major ramifications through the ecosystem will become ever greater as diversity falls, and our own population will be precariously dependent on just a few species to sustain its vast size.

This is not a world that I want to see, or one I want to help create. Yet I suspect it could be a sustainable world for a time, as long as we engaged in a fair amount of environmental engineering to help it along until it neared the point of final collapse. Ultimately, if our numbers and our demand for environmental goods and services remain high, it will have to collapse. I suspect the collapse will be sudden and unpleasant. At the same time, because it will be sustainable for a while yet, there is the real risk that only a few more people will be particularly concerned than are concerned at present. Increasingly urbanized populations, with increasingly virtual entertainment experiences, will watch the dying of the final wild species with no more concern than our ancestors gave to the loss of the passenger pigeon or (nearly) the bison. The dodo looks grand on a stamp or in a children's book, and there are lots of things that begin with the letter Z other than *zebra*.

To summarize, the problem with mass extinction is that there is little evidence for severe environmental consequences of increased extinction—the kind of consequences that would cause us direct harm—until the process has proceeded fairly far down the path. Ecosystems will continue to function, even as they become simplified, until suddenly they do not. The precautionary arguments for working to stem this massive loss of species are fairly weak, and when pitted against the need to make money and buy bigger cars and houses, they are unlikely to prevail. The ethical and aesthetic arguments are also weak in cultures that are strongly materialistic and selfish. As a consequence, it is going to be difficult to achieve the dramatic shift in attitudes that will be needed to reverse the trend. Yet, if we are going to solve our environmental dilemma, we have got to begin to change how we interact with the natural world. Finding the right enticements to encourage us to start down a more appropriate path is the challenge we must tackle in the remainder of this book.

While lapsing into abject pessimism is easy, there are two faint glimmers of hope. First, human attitudes can switch suddenly when the right symbol appears, and the conservation NGOs know this. Maybe we will lose the polar bear but, in that process, wake up to what we are doing to our world. Secondly, the Holocene mass extinction is not a phenomenon happening in isolation. Our activities are having many different impacts on this world. Loss of biodiversity is just one aspect of what we are doing. It is possible that some of the other consequences— such as loss of much of the Greenland ice sheet or permanent drought in many of our most important food-producing areas—will be more dramatic and will lead us to review our actions carefully. Mitigation of the effects of the large, growing, overconsuming human population will have benefits for biodiversity conservation even if the desirability of retaining diversity was not the reason for mitigation.

If we do nothing, and the loss of species continues, there remains one other important idea to keep in mind. The world has survived massive loss of species before. On each occasion, diversity has recovered, and the world's biota has become even richer in species after some time has passed. It's possible to be optimistic concerning the eventual resolution of the Holocene mass extinction. But we must also be aware that during every previous mass extinction, the species that were most dominant before the collapse were among the species that were lost. It takes considerable hubris to expect that millennia after the Holocene mass extinction has run its course, humans will still be present to enjoy the recovery of diversity. Hominids have never been a richly diverse group, and we are one thin thread out of Africa. Should we really expect to be here indefinitely? Do we deserve to survive if we take no steps to preserve the ecosystems upon which we still depend?

8

REDUCING OUR USE
OF FOSSIL FUELS

At 11 P.M. on April 20, 2010, something went wrong on board the Deep-water Horizon, a semisubmersible oil drilling platform located about 80 km southeast of the Mississippi Delta and almost one mile above a new well on the ocean floor. The well had been drilled a further three miles down into the estimated 3.5 billion barrels of crude oil lying below—about a six-month supply for the U.S. economy. There was an explosion and fire, and the rig burned furiously until April 22, when it finally sank beneath the waves, leaving broken pipes spilling crude oil at the bottom of the ocean. At the time of the explosion, there were one hundred twenty people on board; eleven lost their lives.

Drilling rigs are not supposed to explode. Oil wells have blowout preventers that close off the well at the first sign of trouble. Any oil spilled can be skimmed off the water's surface, burned off, or dispersed using chemicals made for this task. But that is not what occurred this time. The rig exploded and sank. The blowout preventer failed and could not be manually activated using robots. Over 7.2 million liters of the dispersant Corexit 9500A were sprayed over the ocean's surface or injected into the deep water below, a far greater quantity of this

Facing page: The Deepwater Horizon explosion resulted in the second-largest accidental oil spill in history. Image 100421-G-XXXXL-003-Deepwater Horizon Fire.jpg, courtesy U.S. Coast Guard Visual Information Gallery http://cgvi.uscg.mil/media/.

chemical than ever used before. The weather conspired to make skimming, burning off, and corralling the oil away from shore through the use of booms less effective than they might have been. And estimates of the amount of oil released continued to grow. Initial reports were of 5,000 barrels per day, but by mid-June, reliable estimates pegged the flow from the wellhead at 53,000 to 62,000 barrels per day.[1] At this rate, Deepwater Horizon was spilling the equivalent of an *Exxon Valdez* disaster every four to seven days. As I write this, the spill has covered more than 10,000 square km of the Gulf of Mexico, includes deepwater plumes as well as oil at the surface, and has been entrained to a limited extent into the Loop Current, which has the potential to whisk oil into the Atlantic, past the coral reefs of the Florida Keys and Cuba. It will take years to assess the damage caused to the gulf coast environment, the fisheries of the gulf, and the economies of Louisiana, Mississippi, and Alabama, all heavily dependent on oil exploration, fishing, and coastal tourism. And the chances of similar catastrophic spills in the future are only increasing, because much of our remaining oil reserves are in difficult-to-reach locations like the deep waters of the gulf.

As previous chapters have made clear, we have an enormous and multifaceted environmental problem facing us, one that gets worse every day and is not just about oil pollution. This problem is like a huge and growing elephant, standing deliberately unnoticed in the middle of our human soirée. Until now, we have been mostly able to ignore it, except when it tramples something we value, but that approach is proving less tenable. The problem has a multiplicity of parts—including pollution, overfishing, and greenhouse gas emissions. Most of these parts interact with one another, so that solving one part in isolation is not really feasible. Some parts are global in scale, particularly the changes that are happening to our climate, and can only be solved globally. This growing elephant is a problem of a complexity and scale that we have never faced before, but it is going to have to be faced in its totality if we

---

1. Oil is measured in barrels, equivalent to 159 liters each. Thus 62,000 barrels becomes 9.86 million liters per day. For perspective, the *Exxon Valdez* accident spewed a total of 270,000 barrels (or 43 million liters) of oil over Alaskan waters. Deepwater Horizon, by the time it was shut off, had spilled about 4.9 million barrels (779 million liters) of oil—eighteen times as much, and the largest accidental spill worldwide except for the 1910 Lakeview Gusher that released 9 million barrels of oil over Kern County, California, over eighteen months.

are to have any quality of life in the future. None of its parts offers up easy solutions, but some components are definitely worse than others.

One of those parts is energy use and its various consequences. As discussed in chapter 3, using energy freely is not a sin, because there really is more than enough energy for our foreseeable needs arriving from the sun every day. However, because most of the energy we use comes from fossil sources, our energy use has created enormous environmental problems, perhaps the biggest problems of all the ones confronting us. Our ways of gaining and using energy are largely responsible for the profound changes in climate now well under way, as well as for some of our most serious and ecosystem-changing examples of environmental pollution. If we are going to solve our environmental dilemma, changing our patterns of energy use will have to be a major part of the solution.

EFFECTS OF MINING OIL, GAS, AND COAL

While we have long used the energy stored in wood, falling water, and wind, we derive the bulk of our energy from fossil sources—coal, oil, and gas. To obtain these materials, we have to dig or drill. Long gone are the seams of coal open at the surface or the oil pooling on the land. Extraction of these fossil fuels is very often environmentally damaging, due both to the difficulty and the quantity needed.

Mining of oil and gas is now, relatively speaking, an environmentally clean process, but this has not always been the case, and "relatively speaking" can hide many problems—such as the disaster with which this chapter began.[2] The ecological footprint of an oil or gas well can be quite small, and properly capped wells can produce their corrosive or explosive products safely and securely for many years. Indeed, some oil companies would like us to believe that they build offshore rigs as habitats for marine life and that their onshore explorations proceed from noninvasive imaging processes for source location to surgically precise insertions of the pipes that bring the product to the surface. Relatively speaking, I suppose they are correct.

2. For perspective, close to nine hundred thousand oil and gas wells have been drilled within the United States and its territorial waters to date. The overwhelming majority have been drilled, brought into production, and eventually decommissioned without serious incident.

The truth is not quite so benign environmentally. The imaging procedures (seismic profiling) can cause serious physiological damage to marine creatures when used offshore. The surgical drilling always generates substantial amounts of solid and liquid wastes that may carry toxic chemicals and have to be disposed of appropriately. The drill is continuously lubricated with "mud" composed of oils, water, clay, and various chemicals that improve lubricating qualities. This mud also has to be disposed of. Drilling through numerous rock strata opens up the possibility of providing channels for the migration of water, oil, or gas, potentially contaminating groundwater in the process. Finally, the "product" does not arrive at the surface as something you can put into your vehicle or furnace. Instead, there is a mixture of variable proportions of crude oil, natural gas, and water, contaminated with sulfur, heavy metals, salts, and other minerals, while the crude oil and natural gas are themselves complex and variable mixtures of substances, many of which are unpleasant. Oil and gas exploration and extraction is a potentially very messy business, and accidents can happen. In the worst cases, a blowout can result in a prolonged flooding of a region by the untreated, highly complex, often toxic raw crude released from the geological structure where it had been trapped. It's to the credit of the oil and gas industry that they extract their "product" as cleanly as they do, but risks always remain.

The sheer scale of the oil and gas industry makes the potential environmental impacts enormous. Take the matter of drilling waste, the rock cuttings and drilling mud that must be disposed of as the well is drilled. Then realize that the average North American well is about 2 km deep and generates about a barrel of waste (159 liters, 67 percent liquid) for every 30 cm drilled. Now imagine a conical mountain of barrels of waste 1 km high and about 2 km in diameter at its base; this 1-km-high mountain of waste would easily bury any building in the world, including the Burj Khalifa[3] at 808 meters, the Taipei 101 Tower at 509 meters, or Toronto's CN Tower, 553 meters to the tip of its antenna. That pile of mine wastes has been generated by the drilling of the 877,000 oil and gas wells in the United States. Similar piles

3. Formerly known as the Burj Dubai, the building was renamed after Sheik Khalifa of Abu Dhabi just days before being opened and days after Khalifa provided enormous sums of money to bail out profligate Dubai during the world economic collapse—"Here's some money, cousin, but you will now name that building after me!"

can be imagined for other countries. Given that these wastes are loaded with toxic substances from the drilling mud, this is not a trivial disposal problem. In addition, there are the wastes, mostly contaminated water, that are brought to the surface with the oil or gas when the well goes into production. Many oil wells, particularly late in their production cycle, are yielding 90 percent water and 10 percent oil. I repeat: it's to the credit of the oil and gas companies that they have managed the exploration and extraction processes as effectively as they have.

So far, I have been talking about conventional oil exploitation—the extraction of crude oil via wells.[4] As the price of oil has increased, it also has become economically viable to attempt to extract useful product from vast, long-ignored, low-grade deposits, called *oil shales* and *tar sands*. In some quarters, the mining of these deposits is now seen as a responsible effort to enable us to continue to meet the global demand for oil. Yet the extraction of oil from these sources is far more damaging environmentally, and the scale of oil shale and tar sand operations is truly immense.

When the media discuss U.S. dependence on foreign oil, the usual impression is that the United States gets most of its oil from the Middle East. Actually, the chief supplier of oil to the U.S. market is Canada, which has supplies of conventional oil and gas far in excess of its own needs and has now ramped up exploitation of its truly vast stores of oil sands located in the Athabasca region of northern Alberta in response to the U.S. thirst for oil. Here, economically recoverable tar sands lie less than 100 meters deep under some 3,500 square km of boreal forest, wetlands, and rivers. The oil exists as bitumen (a viscous mixture of different hydrocarbons) bound with sand, silt, and water. It's like toxic peanut butter. But at 100 meters depth or less and in deposits 40 to 60 meters thick covered by an overburden of about the same thickness, it can be strip-mined. These tar sand deposits make Canada second only to Saudi Arabia in the quantity of its recoverable oil resources, but recovering this oil is far different from conventional oil extraction.

Typical medium-grade tar sands in the Athabasca deposits are 83 per-

---

4. While the term *conventional* suggests "routine," conventional production is shifting toward more difficult deepwater sites and into more environmentally sensitive regions because the "easier" sites have already been mined. This type of conventional production greatly increases the risk of environmental damage.

cent sand, 3 percent clay, 4 percent water, and 10 percent bitumen. Nearly 1 metric ton of ore must be mined to yield a barrel of oil (and the overburden that must first be stripped away is also about 1 metric ton per barrel of oil uncovered). That's 2 metric tons of waste for every barrel of oil.

The ore processing generates additional waste. The most common processing method is to crush the ore and mix it with water heated to 80°C, sometimes including caustic chemicals such as sodium hydroxide. The resulting slurry can then be piped to large settlement tanks, where much of the sand settles out. The bitumen tends to float to the surface, and between the bitumen and the sand is a layer of water with various contaminants. While the extraction process recycles much of the water, the sand and some of the water layer are waste by-products, or *tailings,* that have to be disposed of. These tailings include silt, unrecovered hydrocarbons, and various toxic chemicals that either existed naturally in the deposit or were added during extraction. They are fed into large tailings ponds in which the process of settling out continues. Sounds pretty straightforward, but the problem is in the sheer volume of tailings generated, their toxicity, and the length of time they have to be impounded in tailings ponds.

Tar sands mining has been under way in the Athabasca region since 1967. About 2.6 billion barrels of bitumen have now been extracted, and over 2 million Olympic-size swimming pools of liquid toxic waste remain behind in tailings ponds. On average, 1.5 barrels of these liquid tailings are produced for every barrel of bitumen extracted, and the growing U.S. demand[5] for the product is such that the rate of extraction of bitumen is predicted to grow from 1 million barrels per day now to 3 million barrels per day in 2015. That results in 4.5 million barrels, or 715.5 million liters, or another 286 Olympic-size pools of toxic waste added every day. Most of that contaminated water has been added during processing of the product. Where does all that water come from, and can we afford to store it away indefinitely, 286 swimming pools at a time?

Settling sand and silt and detoxifying contaminated water via a variety of "natural" pathways are very slow processes. They can be aided

---

5. While it is U.S. demand that creates the market, Canadian governments and the industry itself are not exactly being dragged kicking and screaming toward the waiting tar sands—we are all complicit.

by the addition of various flocculating agents to the liquid tailings, but the material that is settled out (termed *consolidated tailings*) remains highly toxic. All operating tar sand projects in Alberta are required to abide by a "zero-release" policy with respect to toxic by-products, meaning that none can escape to the environment. Plans at present call for burial of the toxic solids underneath reconstituted uplands that will then be encouraged to return to boreal forest; liquid tailings are to be retained indefinitely, first in tailings ponds and ultimately in "end pit lakes," enormous tailings ponds 65 to 100 meters deep established within excavated sites once all ore has been extracted. These end pit lakes will become permanent features of the environment. The expectation (hope) is that they will become biologically healthy aquatic ecosystems in which contaminated liquid tailings sit permanently in the deepest basins and do not mix with cleaner water above because of the greater density of the saline tailings. Upland restoration is proceeding successfully, and boreal forest is likely to result as long as the consolidated tailings are buried sufficiently deeply so that contaminants do not migrate toward the surface. Wetland restoration is proving more difficult. No end pit lake has yet been constructed (the first is expected in 2012), and it is not certain that they will behave as planned. It all sounds a bit like venturing out on thin ice and hoping for the best rather than using a carefully thought-out environmental policy.

Even apart from the environmental damage done, open pit tar sands mining uses immense amounts of energy for every barrel of oil produced. The digging, transporting, processing, and particularly the heating of the product and the long-term processing and managing of the waste consume almost as much energy as contained in the oil produced. Current estimates are that it takes the energy of two barrels of oil (or the equivalent) to extract three barrels of oil from the Athabasca tar sands. For comparison, conventional oil comes in at the rate of one barrel expended for every thirty or so barrels produced. At the present time, there is considerable discussion within Canada over whether the tar sands oil industry is worth encouraging, but so far governments and industry have not been listening. Meanwhile, tailings and contaminated water accumulate.

Extraction of our other primary fossil fuel—coal—has a sorrier environmental history than does the extraction of oil or gas, although it's better than the history that tar sands extraction seems now to be writing. Coal is rock and has to be dug out of the ground. Lots of other rock comes out with it. Sometimes the ground caves in; sometimes whole mountains are cut up and taken away. As in the case of tar sands extraction, it is the scale of coal mining that makes the environmental problems severe.

Unlike oil, coal is widely distributed around the globe and very abundant. Proven coal reserves at present are estimated to be 847 billion metric tons, enough to last 133 years at the current rate of use, and coal-fired power plants today provide about 40 percent of all electricity worldwide. But patterns of use are changing rapidly, largely because of the rapid industrialization of China. China holds 13.5 percent of the world's proven coal reserves but only 1 percent of global oil or gas reserves. Consequently, China uses coal for more than two-thirds of its energy needs—and those needs are growing rapidly. China's fossil-fuel energy use jumped from 990 million metric tons of coal equivalent (tce) in 1990 to over 2.6 billion tce in 2007 and is expected to more than double again by 2020. The extraordinary growth in demand for energy has meant that China is now building one new coal-fired power plant almost every week.

Coal is mined on an increasingly large scale in China. In the country's northwestern Shaanxi Province, the Dongsheng coalfield is the seventh largest in the world at 31,000 square km in area and contains an estimated 224 billion metric tons of coal, 25 percent of the coal in China. Shenhua Group is the world's largest producer of coal and manages a combination of underground and open-cut mines at Dongsheng. In 2006 their combined production exceeded 114 million metric tons and was continuing to grow.

In parts of the Appalachian coal district (from southwest Pennsylvania through Ohio, West Virginia, Kentucky, and Tennessee to northern Georgia), open-cut mining has evolved into mountaintop removal mining, in which the tops of mountains are blasted away to get at the seams of coal beneath and the waste overburden is dumped into adjacent valleys. As of 2008 at least 474 mountains had been cut down in this region and more than 405,000 hectares leveled by mountaintop removal and other forms of open-cut mining. Over 7 percent of Appalachia's forests have been destroyed and nearly 2,000 km of streams buried in the valley-filling process. The filled valleys look like dams from below; they leach contaminants into streams and sometimes fail catastrophically. Remediation following mining is minimal at best, given lax regulatory systems and an "out of sight, out of mind" mentality. (It's Appalachia, after all, one of the economically most depressed regions of the United States, and the scarring can only really be seen from the air or via Google Earth.)

Open-cut mines now account for 40 percent of all coal produced (67 percent of U.S. production) and leave more-obvious scars on the environment, but deep mines cause environmental problems too. When coal is uncovered or excavated, methane trapped in the coal bed can be released. David Kirchgessner and colleagues at the U.S. EPA measured releases at a number of mines and published a careful estimate of total methane releases from all U.S. coal mines for 1995. The 4.67 million metric tons of methane came primarily from active underground mines (74 percent), while coal handling (21.0 percent), abandoned underground mines (3.3 percent), and surface mines (2.1 percent) released 26 percent of coal mine methane that year. Methane from coal mines represents approximately 15 percent of all methane released into the atmosphere by human activities. (Oil and gas extraction are responsible for much of the remainder.) As discussed in chapter 3, methane is a particularly potent greenhouse gas.

In addition to releasing methane, coal mines release acidified water, often laden with toxic chemicals such as copper, lead, and mercury, either via drainage through underground mines or via seepage through the overburden waste resulting from open-cut mining. This acid mine drainage pollutes groundwater and surface streams, sometimes to the extent that fish cannot live in the water. It is a pervasive problem that has, for example, polluted about 4,800 km of waterways in Pennsylvania.

Two other major forms of environmental damage due to coal mining are subsidence and damage to groundwater sources. Once the coal is removed from an underground mine, it leaves vast underground cavities. These can collapse, with resulting sudden settling of the land above. The mining activities also open up new pathways for water that result in water tables falling at the same time that the groundwater is being contaminated with acid mine drainage.

Finally, coal mining usually involves washing the product before shipment from the mine site. The fine particulates (soot) that are removed allow the coal to burn more cleanly, but they still must be disposed of. At most mines they are stored as a slurry for long periods of time in impoundments that can leak or rupture. About 340 million liters (136 Olympic swimming pools) of slurry are generated each year in the United States alone. Mining is a messy business.

EFFECTS OF USING FOSSIL FUELS

Coal, oil, and gas cannot be extracted from the earth without causing environmental damage. But the damage they cause does not end once they are processed, packaged, and delivered to the sites where they will be used. Their use also carries environmental impacts because of the gases and other pollutants released when they are burned.

As discussed in chapter 3, it's now recognized that the burning of coal, without the use of suitable scrubber technology, results in acid rain over an area extending many thousands of kilometers downwind. Coal also contributes fine particulates (soot) to the lower levels of the atmosphere as well as a number of compounds such as SO_2 and nitrous oxides that react in the air to create ozone and cause smog. Oil and gas burning also can result in ozone if not carefully managed, and so can the burning of wood. Ground-level ozone and other components of smog have major human health effects, particularly respiratory problems, and many world cities are less healthy places than they would otherwise be because of this. Still, bad as smog can be, as an environmental impact, it pales in significance to acid rain or climate change.

When coal is burned, it also leaves behind mountains of waste, the fly ash and other noncombustibles laced with chemicals such as arsenic, lead, chromium, barium, and mercury. This has to be disposed of, initially in containment ponds similar to those at mine sites and then in landfills, although a portion gets diverted to roadbed construction and cement manufacture. Sometimes disposal fails. When it was built in 1955, the Kingston Fossil Plant, located west of Knoxville, Tennessee, was the largest coal-fired power plant in the world. Its nine generators consume about 12,700 metric tons of coal per day to produce 27 million kWh of electricity, enough to supply about seven hundred thousand homes. Fly ash generated at the plant is stored as a slurry in three large containment ponds behind earthen dikes. Early on the morning of 22 December 2008, one of these dikes failed, and the largest coal slurry spill in U.S. history resulted. The 4 billion liters of slurry—enough to fill sixteen thousand Olympic-sized swimming pools—damaged several houses, washed out a road, covered 160 hectares of land up to 2 meters deep, and partially blocked the Emory River. Chemical analyses of water downstream from the spill revealed significantly elevated levels of arsenic, lead, and chromium, and some fish mortality was reported. Like the 2010 oil blowout in the Gulf of Mexico, this is a mess that is going to take time to clean up. It should cause us to wonder about the advisability of building all those far larger tailings ponds full of comparably nasty wastes in the Athabasca tar sands region.

Carbon dioxide, CO_2, is a natural by-product of the burning of any organic material, and all fossil fuels produce CO_2 when they are burned. As discussed in chapter 3, our use of fossil fuels is now putting so much CO_2 into the atmosphere that our climate is warming substantially. We have a critical need to stop warming the planet, and the most straightforward way of doing this is to turn away from the burning of fossil fuels. Indeed, it is difficult to see how we are going to address our environmental problems without reducing our production of CO_2 and other greenhouse gases. Wind, water, tidal, solar, and nuclear power are all available to us, and their use does not generate greenhouse gases. Given all the other environmental problems in the extraction and use of fossil fuels, it is not surprising that the shift away from fossil fuels has begun. However, this is a difficult transition to make, and the current pace indicates that we are likely to fall well short of what is really needed.

SHIFTING AWAY FROM FOSSIL FUELS

We turned toward fossil fuels in the first place because of two particular attributes they all share. They are high-value fuels, meaning that they contain relatively large amounts of energy per kilogram or liter, and they occur in concentrated pockets in the ground from which relatively large quantities can be extracted. This makes it possible to establish the industrial-scale mining operations we have built to obtain the fuel and ship it economically to where it is needed. The large-scale mining and shipping operations naturally favor construction and operation of large-scale energy-transforming power plants that use the fossil fuel to produce electricity that is then transported further to provide the small amounts of energy we need in individual houses and factories. Thus, the nature of fossil fuels has led us to provide energy to populations by way of highly centralized, industrial-scale enterprises, frequently state-owned and often monopolistic, that deliver energy where it is needed in the form of electricity or as highly refined liquid fuels to power cars, planes, and trains.

This coordinated, one-way delivery of energy from centralized power plants and fuel refineries to individual homes, farms, and factories is not well suited to the use of some of the alternative sources of energy. With the exception of water power, which can be tapped at large waterfalls or dams, wind, water, tidal, and solar power are all distributed, low-value sources of energy that cannot be converted into useful, transportable fuels. For a centralized power supplier to use a non-fossil source and distribute energy to a city, it would be necessary to gather supplies of energy from a large number of relatively power-poor sources. This is typically more expensive than opening another coal mine or drilling a new oil well. Further, since the energy generated by water, wind, or sunshine will likely be stored as electricity, the technology requires not a centralized power plant but a large number of much smaller installations and a network to distribute the power to individual users. These infrastructural differences make a transition from the use of fossil fuel logistically and administratively difficult for any extant power authority.

Nuclear energy is an exception of course. The production of electricity using nuclear power begins with a "fuel," uranium yellowcake, that can be mined, refined, and transported to sites where the energy contained in it is converted into electricity. Therefore, nuclear power is not only conducive to centralized generating stations analogous to those powered by fossil fuels, it requires them. A switch from the use of fossil fuels to nuclear energy is structurally and administratively a relatively easy transition, and it is in part due to the ease of this path that we are now seeing renewed enthusiasm for the use of nuclear power. But as we all know, nuclear energy has significant problems of its own, not the least of which is waste disposal.

Analogous infrastructural commitments make it difficult for North America to transition away from reliance on private cars and semitrailers toward more energy-efficient forms of transportation such as high-speed rail for moving people and railroad freight for moving goods. In contrast to some other parts of the world, North American communities have been built in such a way that a private car is almost a necessity, and the railroad systems that originally opened the West have declined and deteriorated to the point that even bulk freight is moved as often by truck as by train. Shifting back toward rail would be a wise move, but it is expensive and difficult to achieve because the existing infrastructure of roads is not easily reconfigured into the needed rail.

Shifting away from using fossil fuel is also difficult because most other sources of energy are available only intermittently and are less easily stored than are coal, oil, or gas. Sunlight is only available on clear, sunny days; winds occur only on windy days; and the tides, though very reliable in their timing, are cyclical, with four peak flows per day and flows that wax and wane every fifteen days. By contrast, we use energy more continuously, on cycles reflecting our lives rather than the pattern of energy delivery to us. Of course, solar, wind, or tidal energy can be collected and stored until needed as electricity in batteries, heat in the ground, hydrogen in a pressure tank, or any of a number of other ways. But all of these approaches require substantial innovation, something that existing power companies will be slow to undertake without economic or legislative inducements.

The irony, of course, is that there are so many good reasons to change that we need to figure out how to smooth the transition rather than delay action because the transition itself will be costly. Delay for this reason would be like continuing to use a horse to pull the plough because the barn has horse stalls and a feed bin but no fuel pump for a tractor. As a way of beginning to consider how the transition might be accomplished, it is worthwhile to look at the environmental issues associated with the use of alternative energy sources, because understanding these will avoid unexpected problems as the transition takes off.

PROS AND CONS OF ALTERNATIVE ENERGY SOURCES

Nuclear energy has always been attractive because of the extraordinarily high yield of energy per kilogram of fuel; in this sense uranium is more energy-rich than oil or gas. Nuclear energy is now doubly attractive because it releases no greenhouse gases or other environmental pollutants except some heat, but it is not problem-free, and two problems are quite significant: spent fuel rods and the risk of meltdown. The former is a certain problem; the latter, only a problem in the event of an accident.

At present, 439 nuclear power plants operate around the world generating 15 percent of the world's electricity. There are 39 more under construction and a further 376 in the early planning stages. The 104 plants in the United States supply 19.4 percent of its electricity, while 18 Canadian plants produce 14.7 percent of electricity there. Nuclear power is more important in Europe, where it supplies more than 25 percent of the energy in many countries and 77 percent of all electricity in France. The use of nuclear energy is going to grow because the technology exists, it is readily compatible with existing transmission grids and our other major forms of power generation, and it produces no greenhouse gases. Indeed, there is probably no way for us to transition away from dependence on fossil fuels without substantial increases in the use of nuclear power. The generation of nuclear waste is going to continue; in the United States it is growing at about 2,000 metric tons per year.

The waste from U.S. nuclear power plants is a nasty mix of about 96 percent uranium, 1 percent plutonium, and 3 percent other nuclides and actinides. It comes out of the plant extremely radioactive and thermally very hot. It is stored underwater both to cool it and to serve as a barrier for the radiation. Eventually it is supposed to go to a central secure containment facility, where it will remain dangerously radioactive for several hundred thousand years.[6] In one sense, government policy has made a serious problem worse because much of this spent fuel could be reprocessed and used again. During the Carter administration, the U.S. government made a decision not to develop facilities for reprocessing spent fuel because it was seen as a way for plutonium to get into the wrong hands. By not reprocessing, the plutonium stays with the stored spent fuel, but as a result, there is far more waste than there might otherwise be.

Other countries have not followed the U.S. lead, and because they reprocess spent fuel they produce less (and less long-lasting) waste per kWh of power produced. The United States is now reexamining its position and exploring a number of reprocessing methods, some of which are already in use in many European countries, Russia, and Japan. Reprocessing means that far more of the available fuel is used, the quantity of waste that must be stored is reduced, and (when reprocessing removes all longer half-life elements from the waste) storage can be for far shorter times (about a thousand years). The issue of nuclear waste is not a trivial one. There is always the risk that an accident will

---

6. Yucca Mountain was going to be that facility, but increasingly it looks as if the "not-in-my-backyard" and anti-nuke forces have combined to prevent that or any other solution to this important problem.

release radiation into the environment, and the material remains dangerous for a period longer than our civilization has been around. But there are signs that with the renewed interest in nuclear power, there is also interest in using the fuel more efficiently, which will materially reduce the waste problem.

The other environmental issue for nuclear power is the risk of an accident or terrorist attack leading to a serious release of radiation or, at worst, a meltdown of a reactor's core. The accident in reactor unit 4 at the Chernobyl Nuclear Power Plant in eastern Ukraine on 26 April 1986 stands as the only major accident in a nuclear power plant worldwide, and it was substantial. The catastrophic loss of cooling water led to some melting of the reactor core and a fire that lasted ten days; this resulted in the escape of very large quantities of radioactive particles into the atmosphere, particularly downwind. More than five million people lived in the 200,000 square km of European countryside, chiefly in Ukraine, Belarus, and Russia, that was classified as "contaminated," meaning that it received more than 37 kBq per square meter of cesium (^{137}Cs) in the fallout,[7] and more than four hundred thousand of these people lived in areas classified as requiring "strict radiation control" (a fallout dose yielding over 555 kBq per square meter of ^{137}Cs).

This level of radiation contamination has had marked health and environmental impacts, although the true extent of damage remains difficult to discern because of the initial effort by the then–Soviet government to cover up what had happened. Fewer than thirty people are known to have died directly due to acute radiation illness, but there have been demonstrable increases in the prevalence of some cancers, most notably childhood onset thyroid cancer (more than five thousand cases reported) due to drinking contaminated milk in the first weeks following the accident. Environmental effects were mostly short-term because of the rapid decay of most of the radionuclides released; however, some plutonium and americium will be around at low levels for a very long time in the countryside within 100 km of the reactor (these heavy elements settled out early), and strontium (^{90}Sr) and cesium (^{137}Cs) will be around for decades over the wider contaminated zone.

7. The becquerel (Bq) is the international unit of radioactivity equal to one radioactive decay per second. Thus 37 kBq per square meter is equivalent to 37,000 decay events per second per square meter of land.

Evidence of negative impacts of the radiation on plants and animals has been limited, except in particular instances. The rapid uptake of ^{137}Cs by lichen has created significant difficulties for the Sami people of Finland, Norway, Russia, and Sweden, because reindeer eat the lichen and the Sami eat the reindeer. The efficient "recycling" of ^{137}Cs in forest ecosystems has meant that many forest products remain unsafe for human consumption twenty years after the accident, while most other agricultural products can now be produced safely over most of the region. Ironically, the major ecological impact of the accident may be that numerous native species have improved opportunities for life due to the forced out-migration of humans and reduced agricultural and other economic activities.

The Chernobyl accident occurred because of a flawed reactor design, including lack of any containment structure surrounding the reactor, and because plant operators made a series of monumentally bad decisions that progressively shut off all backup water supplies when the initial problem was first detected. The nuclear industry continues to point to these design flaws and inadequate training as the reasons for the disaster while implying that only the Soviets are that incompetent.[8] Although the industry might wish that this were so, the expectation that accidents will never happen because everybody is now competent seems naive. While nuclear accidents remain a small but finite risk, terrorism may actually be a less serious problem because containment structures are built to resist massive destruction, and nuclear power plants are, by their nature, high-security facilities. Despite the risks, it may be that we do not have an alternative to nuclear power for a significant part of our electricity generation in the next decades.

Hydroelectric power generation already contributes 17 percent of the world's electricity, which is achieved either by diverting water past a natural waterfall and through turbines or by building dams to create a significant vertical drop and sending the water through turbines on its way down. While the flow of water generates energy without producing damaging wastes or greenhouse gases, there are still some environmental impacts. This is particularly so when dams are built.

---

8. The Three Mile Island incident in 1979 was far less serious, but it proved that Western countries could have major accidents too. This book was in final proof before the Fukushima Daiichi accident occurred in 2011.

The loss of salmon populations in western North America is widespread and has complex causes. Overfishing and water pollution have played a big role, but the damming of rivers, even when fish ladders provide for fish migration, has also played a significant role. When a river that formerly flooded and ebbed becomes a tranquil series of pools behind dams, the change can be profound—lack of new supplies of silt and nutrients to formerly fertile downstream deltas being the most obvious. The increased evaporation from the large lake surfaces behind those dams also helps move a river toward failure (when it stops flowing altogether), although the ease of diversion of that impounded water to irrigate farms plays a larger role.

The other big problem with hydropower, if we seek to increase its contribution, is that there are few places left where it is possible to capture the energy of falling water. In North America the only remaining undammed large river is the Yukon, and there is pressure from environmentalists to keep it that way. Undeterred, hydroelectric futurists plan mega-schemes such as Quebec's James Bay Project in the rugged country east of James Bay. Phase one of this giant project commenced in 1972, using nine dams and two hundred six dikes to divert four major rivers into the La Grande River, creating massive spillways and power stations and achieving 16,000 megawatts of capacity. This is four times larger than the generating capacity of Niagara Falls (Canadian and U.S. stations combined) and eight times larger than the capacity of the giant Hoover Dam. Worldwide, it is exceeded only by the Three Gorges Project in China, which has a capacity of 18,300 megawatts. The production capacity of the James Bay Project was gained at considerable environmental cost, including submerging 11,300 square km of boreal forests and radically altering hydrological regimes over a wide area. All this was done without consulting the people who lived there. Phase two was to have been about as large but was canceled in 1994 under strong pressure from aboriginal groups and environmentalists. Such large-scale terraforming projects can generate more hydroelectric power but at major costs to the environment and to the typically poor, rural, and often aboriginal communities that get displaced. These are also extremely costly projects, and one of the arguments against phase two was that for far less expenditure, improvements in efficiency and energy conservation would generate as much or more benefit.

Biofuels now provide just under 2 percent of the fuel used in transportation worldwide. These are organic fuels manufactured from agricultural products; agricultural, industrial, or municipal organic waste; manure; and other organic sources. Like wood, these fuels release CO_2 when burned, but because the carbon in this CO_2 was only recently removed from the atmosphere via photosynthesis, these releases do not comprise new additions of CO_2 to the atmosphere. While these fuels can be useful products when derived from waste materials that would otherwise add to pollution, the growing of crops to provide sources of biofuel competes directly with the use of agricultural land to grow food crops. In addition, the energetic and other costs of the conversion of biomass into useable fuel often make these fuels less environmentally attractive than they might appear to be. Overall, these features make biofuels likely to remain a minor player in our mix of energy sources.

Wind, geothermal, and solar power currently contribute slightly more than biofuels to the world's energy needs—about 2.1 percent combined—but their use is growing. All are essentially emission-free, and other environmental impacts are few. Earlier wind turbine designs killed a lot of migrating birds, but newer designs are far less lethal, and the requirement for open space in which to set out solar arrays will be reduced as solar panels become incorporated directly into roofing or other surfacing materials. Photovoltaic roofing tiles and wall panels are already available in Europe and are starting to appear in North America, and research to put photovoltaic collectors into paved surfaces such as parking lots, roads and walkways has passed the proof-of-concept phase. The idea of the green neighborhood, in which the roofs and sidewalks generate all the energy needed for operating the homes, is no longer science fiction, although it is yet to become routine in the construction industry, and there will need to be a major regulatory or tax-benefit push to have it broadly adopted.

As wind farms and solar arrays become more common, environmental issues beyond the ever-present not-in-my-backyard effect are appearing. Offshore wind farms as well as tidal or wave power generators will need to be sited and installed in ways that preserve connectivity in the underwater ecosystem. Large wind farms may even modify local climate by dissipating wind more quickly. Still, at present, the environmental impacts of these forms of renewable energy production seem far more modest per kilowatt than do the impacts of fossil fuels.

USING ENERGY MORE EFFICIENTLY

A second major step that allows us to maintain the high-energy lifestyles we favor while reducing use of fossil fuels is well under way but seems to have stalled. This is to improve the efficiency of energy delivery and use and to conserve energy by using less of it. Until recently, the world was one in which power-generating industries were paid for delivering power, and there was little incentive for them to encourage conservation or efficient use. That world has been changing slowly, and pressure to conserve and to use more efficiently is now coming from the industry, from enlightened governments, and from the conservation community.

In 2008 the International Energy Agency (IEA) of the OECD— Organization for Economic Co-operation and Development—published a detailed report on worldwide trends in energy use and energy efficiency. According to this report, if the improvements in energy efficiency that occurred between 1973 and 2005 had not occurred, we would now be using 58 percent more energy worldwide than we are. This makes energy savings through increased efficiency the most important "fuel" during this period, in that the amount of energy use avoided was actually greater than the total amount of energy generated from any single source during that period. However, the IEA also reported that current rates of improvement in efficiency, even though substantial, are not sufficient to counteract the trend of increasing energy use. This growth in energy use is simply unsustainable in terms of demand for fuels and impacts on environment, especially the production of greenhouse gases.

The IEA study also showed that improvements in efficiency between 1973 and 1990 (about 2 percent per year) were substantially higher than those between 1990 and 2005 (only 0.8 percent per year), suggesting either that effort to improve efficiency has waned or that we have reached a limit and can improve efficiency no further. In fact, there are plenty of ways to increase efficiency further, and there is an urgent need to discover why we have slowed our efforts to do so.

In North America, energy use has increased about 20 percent over the past fifteen years and is approximately evenly divided among three primary needs: transportation, operation of buildings, and industrial, commercial, and service activities other than maintaining the buildings where the work is done. In 2004 the percentages for these three categories of use were 29 percent, 30 percent, and 38 percent, respectively, in Canada, and 27 percent, 40 percent, and 33 percent, respectively, in the United States. (The difference is due to the proportionately greater importance of pulp and paper and mining industries in Canada, which have a high demand for energy.) In each of these categories of use, there exist ample opportunities for additional improvements in energy efficiency using only currently available technology.

Housing is a good example. About 50 percent of all energy use in North American homes is for heating and cooling, and the trend toward larger homes in recent years has offset the modest improvements in climate control that have been introduced. Yet the technology to radically improve efficiency is readily available. In Canada, 57 percent of energy use in the home is for heating, and a further 24 percent is used to heat water. Homes built to the R-2000 standard for insulation require two-thirds less energy for heating than do conventionally built homes of the 1970s. Water heating in North America wastes energy because of our insistence on keeping a forty-gallon tank of water piping hot whether hot water is needed or not. Application of European technology that heats water only when needed, usually at the tap where it is needed, could cut energy use for providing hot water by at least two-thirds. With the exception of stoves, major appliances being manufactured today are significantly more energy-efficient than those of just a decade ago. Appliances use 13 percent of the energy in a North American home, and upgrading to newer models can cut this use in half. Even the routine replacement of incandescent with fluorescent or halogen bulbs and adopting the habit of switching smart appliances off at the wall, making them dumb and truly off when switched off can result in significant savings in electricity.[9] Overall, adopting current technology will cut the energy cost of running the average home in North America by at least 50 percent. And this is all achieved without any reduction in quality of life—the house is just as big and just as warm in winter and as cool in summer, and the appliances and electronic toys are all still there. Even the showers are as long and hot as they were before. Think what could be done if we went still further than what is possible with "current technology" or learned to be happy with smaller houses, shorter showers, and warmer indoor temperatures in summer.

Design the house to suit its location, and build it using elements of pas-

9. Their little psyches are not troubled by this, although they will need time to come back to life when switched on.

sive solar design such as south-facing windows and appropriately sized roof overhangs to provide shade in the summer. Plant evergreen trees north of the house to block cold winds. Plant deciduous trees in the south to shade the house in summer but allow it to be warmed in winter. Put solar panels on the roof to heat water and to generate some electricity. None of these steps is costly or difficult, but together they can make the house energy neutral. Widespread adoption of these design, construction, and operation changes could wipe out 20 percent of the energy used in North America today. Yet our building industry continues to produce development after development of cookie-cutter homes with inefficient climate control systems, positioned on their lots with no regard to whether they face north or south, east or west. Smart buyers purchase the home that is sited with its largest windows facing south or east.[10]

A similar argument can be made for increasing efficiency in the transportation sector. Estimates are that with better use of existing technology, we could easily cut the energy used in transportation by more than 50 percent. The case is particularly extreme in North America, where railroads have been allowed to wither and die. Transportation uses over a quarter of all energy consumed worldwide, and because the sector relies heavily on petroleum, it uses over 70 percent of all oil produced.

In the United States, transport is overwhelmingly by road. Of the energy used for transportation, air transport accounts for 8 percent; water transport, 4 percent; and rail transport, a whopping 2 percent. Apart from the 4 percent of energy used to transport liquids such as water or oil through pipelines, all the rest (81 percent) goes to vehicles on roads. Light vehicles (cars and light trucks) account for 62 percent, larger trucks for 19 percent, and buses for a mere 0.19 percent of transportation energy used. The media talk proudly about the "NAFTA superhighway," that moderately organized stream of semitrailers that flows back and forth between northern Mexico and southern Canada, supporting all the trade that the North American Free Trade Agreement has generated. At its occasional bottlenecks, such as at the Ambassador Bridge between Detroit, Michigan, and Windsor, Ontario, trucks are lined up bumper to bumper, barely above idle speed, making air qual-

---

10. Readers in the Southern Hemisphere are used to this flagrant hemispherical chauvinism by northerners and are chauvinistically secure in their knowledge that their hemisphere has the best climate and beaches.

ity in the vicinity abysmal. These goods should be shipped by a smart, coordinated, truck-to-train conveyor belt that puts trailers on flat cars for most of the journey, but it has been easier to continue down the same bad path we were already on and add more trucks and more miles.

North Americans spend major parts of their lives as commuters, sitting in their idling cars in traffic jams every morning and evening in every large city, one person per car, because it is easier to drive one's own car than to take public transport. Architects and planners are now talking about redesigning communities so that walking or biking to work, shops, or school will be simple and far more pleasant than driving. Once we begin to redesign our cities this way, we will reduce our consumption of energy enormously while building a new job-creating industry.

WHAT DOES THE FUTURE HOLD?

If current trends continue, our overall use of energy is going to keep on growing, and we will continue to depend primarily on fossil fuels. The use of coal will grow significantly because it is abundant and widespread. The use of gas and oil will grow as long as new supplies can be found, and the fuel will be ever more expensive because the easy-to-get-at supplies have been used up. Nuclear energy will also grow in importance. Solar, wind, geothermal, biofuel, and water power will remain fringe players, relatively speaking. Energy will become proportionately more expensive, and the environmental impacts will be greater than ever.

But current trends are not likely to continue. As discussed in chapter 3, there is growing awareness of the environmental costs of using fossil fuels, and while we may well not act quickly enough to effectively mitigate climate change, we will likely act to curb our use of these fuels, much as we have been doing over the past fifteen years, taking little steps to be more energy-efficient and to make non-fossil sources a more important part of the mix. We probably need a crisis or two to jolt us out of our complacency and help us achieve the magnitude of change in behavior and in government regulations that is necessary to really shift away from fossil fuels. Indeed, there is some hope that the Deepwater Horizon accident will help shift public opinion in the United States away from reliance on fossil fuels.

It is certainly true that the advances that have been made in energy efficiency and energy conservation should be implemented promptly as developing countries ratchet up their need for energy. This would enable them to avoid the mistakes made by Western countries in the past and minimize their use of energy right from the start. The rapid economic growth and rising standards of living now being seen in China are certainly going to be unsustainable if China continues to focus on use of fossil fuels, particularly coal. I say this not because China risks running out of coal—it has plenty of it—but because the deterioration in the environment that is likely to result would be a human health disaster for that country. There is already ample evidence that China has paid a high environmental price for its economic growth: it now has the worst air pollution and some of the worst water pollution of any country, and these problems are directly impacting the health of its citizens. Much of this pollution, particularly the SO_2 and fine particulates in the air, comes from the use of coal to power its economy and heat its homes. The Chinese health services sector is strained by the deteriorating health of its citizens, and some of the statistics are daunting: government sources report that over 300,000 people die each year because of air pollution–induced diseases, chiefly heart disease and lung cancer; about 26 percent of all deaths are due to respiratory diseases; and SO_2 emissions—the highest in the world—have risen more than 27 percent since 2000 as energy demand has grown. In many ways, China is an experiment in rapid progress: the pressure to grow its economy is intense because that is the only way to lift its population out of poverty, but much of the energy required to fuel that growth comes from the dirtiest fossil fuel of all, and the Chinese environment suffers as a consequence. Time will tell how these contradictions will affect China's trajectory.

Throughout the developed world, particularly in North America, our past choices have been poor ones, and they have given us attitudes difficult to change and habits difficult to break. These habits, and their mimicry by developing countries such as China, are the reason that the climate is warming on a trend that is above the most pessimistic predictions by the International Panel on Climate Change (see chapter 3). The paradox is that we are nowhere near any real limit on availability of energy, and we have technologies that can provide that energy safely. The problem with using fossil fuels has real solutions that we can implement once we decide to do so.

9

SLOWING GROWTH OF
THE HUMAN POPULATION

Since 1950 demographers at the United Nations Population Division have been reliably tracking our growing population and predicting growth into the future. Their predictions have proven quite robust in the short term (for periods up to fifty years into the future). They advise us that, barring a catastrophe comparable in scale to the Black Death of the fourteenth century or a dramatic shift in human behavior, the global population will reach 9.2 billion by 2050. At present, the earth supports almost 6.9 billion people, so we are talking about an increase of about 2.3 billion people over the next forty years. That's a 33 percent increase, the equivalent of adding almost two new Chinas to the world. Each of these people will add to the already-too-heavy burden the human species places on the world.

In the previous chapter, I likened our multifaceted environmental problem to a giant elephant that we seem intent on ignoring, despite the fact that it's in the middle of our living room. I noted that when we do recognize the problem, we do so in a piecemeal fashion, focusing on overfishing, or pollution, or climate change, or deforestation alone, as

Facing page: Ever since 29 December 1968, when Apollo 8 emerged from behind the moon and the astronauts saw our beautiful but lonely planet in the sky of an alien world, we have known that we share a finite world. Photo GPN-2001-000009, *Earthrise,* courtesy of the U.S. National Aeronautics and Space Administration.

if paying attention to the elephant's trunk alone could keep the animal from trampling us. Of the many parts of our environmental problem, human population growth is perhaps the part most clearly interconnected with the other parts: it has direct and important linkages with every other aspect of our environmental problem. It is also the issue that we have the most difficulty acknowledging or discussing.

The issue of human population growth has received little discussion over the past thirty years because it has been considered "politically incorrect" to mention it since the 1970s. Why is this so? Because any discussion of it intrudes on matters considered by many to be outside the bounds of public discourse in three different ways. First, such discussion cannot avoid invading the traditionally private topic of reproduction and the intensely personal decisions of whether and when to have children. Second, it invades a sphere considered by at least some religions to be sacred; the procreative process is not only outside the realm of public inquiry but properly beyond societal intervention. Third, because the rate of population growth is not uniform across the world and because the fastest growing populations are mostly in less-developed countries, the discussion becomes susceptible to charges of racism, as individuals from wealthy, slowly growing populations demand that less wealthy, more rapidly growing societies do something about their fertility rates. Paul Ehrlich, of Stanford University, led a valiant attempt to break down these barriers to discussion in the 1970s, but it ultimately failed; ever since discussion has been avoided or diverted.

Most usually, discourse concerning population growth has been diverted into discussion of ways to raise living standards and economic status in the developing world. This is because of the well-documented observation that when a society raises its living standards and its people experience a rise in economic status, it shifts toward smaller family size and later commencement of family building. Lowered rates of population growth result. This so-called demographic transition is a quite reliable societal change coincident with rising living standards, particularly if these improvements also include greater equality and greater educational opportunities for women. But unfortunately the demographic transition does not come quickly enough to make a significant difference. Living standards have risen in many developing countries over the past forty years, but during the same period, although the rate of growth has slowly declined, we have seen the human population grow from 3.7 billion to 6.9 billion, with average family sizes remaining distressingly high across much of the world. I think it is time that we put political correctness aside and confront the issue of population growth directly.

Figure 7, in chapter 5, presents the well-known dramatic rise in the human population since the Stone Age. It's the graph that Al Gore reached to the top of by using a cherry picker. While the rate of growth of the human population has slowed from the peak rate achieved in the early 1960s, the human population is still growing very rapidly, and the addition of 2.3 billion more people by 2050 is all but inevitable unless we act collectively to change the rate of increase. This growth will not be evenly distributed around the world. Just as now, there will be places that experience relatively modest growth and ones that experience profound growth. Unfortunately, those experiencing the more rapid rates of growth are likely, as now, to be among the ones least able to afford the considerable stresses that a growing population brings, such as the need for more food, water, housing, infrastructure, and jobs.

At the present time, rates of growth vary greatly among countries, and the age structure of populations varies commensurately, with some countries occupied predominantly by young people and others with a higher proportion of older people. Growth rates in the so-called first world now tend to be low, and in a number of European countries birth rates are lower than mortality rates. This is the case in countries such as Germany and Croatia as well as in all of Eastern Europe (Belarus, Bulgaria, Czech Republic, Hungary, Moldova, Poland, Romania, Slovakia, and Ukraine), where rates of growth average −0.4 percent and run as low as −0.7 percent (Ukraine). Several other European countries have growth rates of 0 percent at present. In the rest of the world, only Lesotho and Botswana, in southern Africa, have population growth rates that are negative (due in both cases to the prevalence of HIV/AIDS). In Europe, immigration is usually being permitted at levels that result in a net growth rate that remains slightly positive. Net immigration is an important component of overall population growth in other developed countries as well. Thus, during the decade 1994–2004, Canada's 1.0 percent annual growth rate was made up of a 0.39 percent growth rate in the existing population and a 0.61 percent rate of growth due to immigration from other countries. Similarly, the 1.1 percent growth rate in the United States was the result of a 0.58 percent internal growth rate combined with a 0.52 percent net immigration rate.

In most but not all developing countries, fertility rates[1] and growth rates are higher than those in Western countries. Fertility rates have generally been falling in these countries, and most population scientists anticipate that fertility rates in developing countries will continue to fall until they come to match the low rates of Western countries. However, they differ in how quickly this will occur and how large the world's human population will therefore become before the rates converge. They anticipate this decline in rates of growth because of the demographic transition I mentioned earlier. In general, a demographic transition tends to occur when a human population gains a certain level of economic prosperity and individuals choose to have fewer children for a variety of reasons: they have more options for spending their time in a culturally richer society and do not wish to be perpetually burdened by child care; they no longer feel obliged to produce numerous offspring simply to ensure they will be looked after in their old age; they no longer require more household members to grow food or contribute to household income. The result is that the age distribution shifts from one dominated by children and young adults to one in which older individuals are more prevalent.

In cases such as India and China, the demographic transition is being helped along by governmental policies that actively promote (India) or require (China) limits to the number of children produced. China's mandatory one-child policy, while more authoritarian than India's promotion of birth control, is proving more effective at limiting the growth rate, and in time may be seen as a wise step for the country to

1. Fertility rates, measured as the number of children born during the child-bearing years of the average woman, currently range from 0.91 (Macau) to 7.19 (Niger). Countries such as mainland China (1.73) and Brazil (1.90) already have fertility rates between those of the United States (2.05) and Canada (1.53), although India's (2.81) is a good bit higher, and 130 countries have rates in excess of 2.0. A fertility rate of 2.1 will produce a stable population size in developed countries, assuming no net immigration from other countries; however, because of higher childhood mortality, developing countries require rates higher than this for stable population size. For the world, assuming the mortality schedules of 2010, a stable population could be achieved with a fertility rate of 2.33. It's currently about 2.56.

have taken. As it is, China's population is currently 1.338 billion (2010) and growing at a rate of 0.6 percent per year, while India's is currently 1.182 billion and growing at 1.6 percent per year.

I do not believe that our world will be able to support the 9.2 billion predicted for 2050. That 9.2 billion estimate includes assumptions about the pace and timing of the demographic transition across developing countries, assuming current trends in economic prosperity continue. I would like to believe that the demographic transition can be hastened by changes within societies brought about by wider awareness of the challenges posed by population growth and by new attitudes—and perhaps new policies—on the part of governments. I want to see these changes because lowering birth rates seems far preferable to letting famine, pestilence, and war raise death rates, and one of these must happen if the current explosive growth is to be curtailed more quickly. I worry that if we continue to avoid the issue of population growth, we may build ourselves a future over the next few decades in which epidemic disease, starvation, and strife prevail.

The problem, of course, is that if we simply wait for economic development to stimulate a demographic transition worldwide, all those developing countries have to gain a sufficient level of economic prosperity. Will it be possible for standards of living to be raised sufficiently for the decline in fertility rates to take place before the supply of resources needed to sustain those high standards of living runs out? Or, to put it another way, in 2050, how well off and how large will our population really be?[2]

Some people dismiss the problem of population growth by inferring that it is only a problem in developing countries and that it will be solved in due course by a combination of the demographic transition and by immigration that evens out rates of growth across regions. According to this view, societies that currently have growth rates close to or even less than zero (meaning that their populations are stable or growing smaller) can easily absorb much of the world population growth by accepting immigrants from other parts of the world. Unfor-

2. There is a clear tradeoff here. If active measures can be taken to lower population growth rates, it will also become easier to raise standards of living, and we will achieve a smaller population living better in 2050. This appears to me to be a better approach than to simply continue the struggle to raise living standards, in the hope that the improvements will result in lowered birth rates later.

tunately, there are not enough of these low-growth societies, and current rates of immigration are much too low to solve the problem of excessive rates of growth in the more rapidly growing countries. The issue of illegal immigration, which waxes and wanes but is usually present in most advanced countries, is a sure sign that there are serious social inequities in the world and that there are more individuals wishing to relocate to find a better life than there are places available legally. Furthermore, the world population of humans is simply the sum of all the individual country populations, just as a species' population is the sum of all the small local populations (see Figure 8), and while immigration away from the most rapidly growing countries will reduce the variation among individual rates of growth, it cannot make the overall growth disappear.

Some other people dismiss the problem of population growth with a calm assumption that somehow we will be able to supply the needed resources to provide all these people with a reasonable quality of life. Frequently, if the issue of population growth is raised, these people counter with the argument that it is the disproportionately high consumption of resources by individuals in developed countries that is the real environmental problem and that people in developing countries live well within the capacity of the world to support them. While this makes it possible to continue to avoid the taboo subject of human population growth, both aspects of this argument have very serious flaws. First, as demonstrated a number of times through this book, there is mounting evidence that our needs are pushing up against finite limits to what the world can provide. Second, it is trivially easy to show that if North Americans, Australians, and Europeans reduced their per capita use of the world's resources to levels comparable to those of the least-developed nations, their selflessness would not compensate for the basic needs of the large numbers of humans that current projections say we will add over the next forty years. Let's briefly elaborate on each of these points.

In chapter 1 I showed that there is solid evidence that we are now gaining less fish protein from the oceans, even though we have increased our fishing efforts. Wild fishery yield has been slowly declining since the mid-1980s, and while substantial increases in aquaculture have enabled us to sustain total fishery yield, we have been unable, so far, to increase total yield to keep up with our growing population.[3] As a consequence, the proportion of protein food delivered to the human population by wild fisheries and aquaculture combined has been falling.[4] It is expected to continue to fall as our population grows and, indeed, may begin to fall more rapidly as our overfishing of wild stocks leads progressively to collapse. Now, people do not have to eat fish, but they do have to eat, so the reduction in per capita fishery yield has got to be replaced by something else. Chapter 2 reported similar problems in our unsustainable use of forests, and chapter 8 has shown how our use of fossil fuels cannot be sustained unless we are prepared to accept a future in a world with a rapidly changing climate. I will expand on this subject in chapter 10, but suffice it to say that the idea that we can somehow add two new Chinas' worth of people to the world's population and be able to provide for their needs by increasing our use of the world's resources is neither realistic nor logical.

The claim that it is the high consumption of environmental goods and services by people in Western nations that is the real problem has some validity—we should certainly be questioning and reducing the wasteful rates of consumption so common in these communities. But there simply are not sufficient numbers of people in Western countries for a reduction in their profligate rates of consumption of resources to compensate sufficiently for the increase in resource use that goes along with adding 2.3 billion people. As I will detail in chapter 10, the difference between the rate of consumption of environmental goods and services by the average African and the average North American is less than an order of magnitude, and North Americans become a smaller proportion of the human family every day. (Currently they make up about 5 percent of humanity.) Adding 2.3 billion people, each with a Chinese per capita footprint, does much more to overtax the capacity of the earth to continue to provide the goods and services we

3. Dirk Zeller and Daniel Pauly reevaluated the rate of decline, including data on bycatch as well as on fishery landings. The substantial reductions in bycatch (a good thing) add to the overall decline in total marine catch (bycatch plus marketed fish) so that the actual reduction in metric tons of fish caught is about six times greater than the rate reported originally by Watson and Pauly. Not good news for sustainability.

4. It declined from 16 percent to 15.3 percent of our total animal protein food supply between 1996 and 2005.

crave than could ever be compensated for by encouraging, or forcing, Americans to live a Chinese or African lifestyle. The blunt fact that we have refused to look at is that if we are going to continue to work to lower mortality, making it possible to expect every child born to have an excellent chance of reaching old age, we also are going to have to deal with our propensity to produce excess offspring. Given all our other problems, adding almost two Chinas or seven-and-a-half United States in the next forty years while also maintaining or improving current average quality of life is simply impossible, even if it is politically incorrect to say so.

As the foregoing makes clear, growth in the human population and per capita consumption must be considered in tandem. They affect each other in several important ways, and together they determine humanity's impact on the earth. So, as we begin to discuss the seriousness of the population problem and what to do about it, we must do so in a broad context that takes consumption into account. This means recognizing, first of all, that rates of consumption of goods and services in developing countries are going to rise as economies strengthen. This is already happening in China, India, and Brazil, and it will tend to happen elsewhere also. Every third world villager has known about the American Dream for generations, thanks to Hollywood. Now the Internet lets every villager think about needing all those material possessions. And as wealth rises in developing nations, the rate of shopping goes up, and what were formerly wants become needs. It is common for small developing nations to leapfrog over "normal" stages of material development, bypassing them completely on the way to greater consumption. Give the village electricity, and television sets blossom. If there are no accessible broadcast signals, DVD players also blossom, and villagers learn to sit around watching reruns of American sitcoms. Keeping per capita consumption in check while also encouraging the needed growth of a retail economy to generate employment and lift standards of living is going to be quite difficult, even with charismatic leaders and well-crafted messages, but it is also very important. We will be well served to encourage conservation, energy efficiency, and recycling as each country enters more completely into the market economy, because otherwise our demand for resources will outstrip supply even more rapidly.

At the same time, North Americans and Europeans must continue to be encouraged to adopt more sustainable lifestyles, because we really can have quality lives while consuming a lot less. Are North Americans ready to leave the malls in droves and build status by doing or creating rather than by consuming? Can our economy change so that we buy what we need instead of what we have been taught to want? This shift is also possible, but difficult. It can best be achieved by focusing on efficient use and smart recycling rather than by preaching a Spartan existence. We owe it to the rest of the world to demonstrate measurable reductions in our per capita use of resources while encouraging them *not* to follow our path through the temple of consumerism.

Still, controlling per capita consumption in developed and developing countries is not sufficient by itself. Realistically, we need to find a way of undercutting that projection of 9.2 billion people by 2050, because our opportunities to solve our environmental dilemma are expanded the more we undercut it. What can be done to talk up the benefits of the demographic transition? Just as dynamic leaders and Madison Avenue can teach us to value a less exploitative lifestyle, these same forces can teach us to value small families and make childless unclehood a desirable choice. The growing acceptance of gay lifestyles in many societies may prove to be an important step toward solving our environmental problem. It affirms that our human need for love and companionship does not have to be based on the traditional family. But we will probably need additional incentives to forego the joys of multiple births, and we may also need penalties for having too many children, such as the ones in China's one-child policy.

There are already a few economic incentives to keep families small. As soon as communities begin to gain some wealth, the value of extended education is recognized, and education costs money, even if it is only the wages foregone while the child remains in school. In the small community on Apo Island, the Philippines, where a sustainable, locally managed, reef fishery and tourism economy has been built (see Chapter 10), families are becoming smaller, and the village includes a dispensary that provides family planning literature and contraceptives. Residents see the value in giving their children opportunities for further education, and they are choosing to have fewer children to do this. An American parent with two teenage children getting ready to go to college knows that the financial cost of raising children who are likely to remain in full-time education until their early twenties is not trivial. This cost influences many decisions about family size.

Unfortunately, misguided population policies also abound, partly because politicians who provide tax exemptions or child allowances to voters are more likely to be reelected than those who take steps to add to the financial burden of building a large family. In countries where growth rates have started to trend down, misguided policies also exist because of the stresses that an aging population places on the social systems of a country.[5] Fear of a lack of workers to support the costs of the elderly is bolstered by economists who seem unable to see the big picture and argue for incentives to ensure that the population continues to grow. Economists should travel more—there are plenty of young people looking for better lives in new parts of the globe, and the solution to a shortage of labor in a country should be obvious. Any government in a developed country that provides incentives to increase birthrates or provides allowances or tax benefits to help defray child-rearing costs beyond the first child needs to seriously reexamine its policies. So should any government that responds to pressure from religious or other right-to-life groups to prevent free access to birth control, abortion, or family-planning information or materials. It is possible to respect the right of individuals, religiously affiliated or not, to express views concerning the sanctity of life, the rights of the not-yet-born, or the virtue of letting pregnancy happen naturally. But this does not require that we condone any interference with the right of other citizens to disagree, or even with the right of the society to pass laws that penalize the production of extra children.[6] This moral and ethical discussion should never be tangled up in the provision of contraceptive services to a population that routinely accepts the vaccinations,

5. When population growth rate slows, the age distribution of a population shifts toward older ages. This puts added burdens on medical and retirement pension programs, and the transition can be particularly painful. If we want long lives in a population that is not growing, we will have to invest more carefully to provide for needs during the post-employment years. It's not impossible, but it will require a disciplined savings and investment plan by individuals and by governments.

6. The right to express beliefs must not be automatically turned into a right to act. Just as most societies find polygamy, incest, or the selective abortion or infanticide of children of one gender abhorrent even though some members may believe in these practices, it should be accepted that a society can decide to introduce measures to encourage a limit on births, even if some members do not agree with this restriction on their rights.

pharmaceutical services, and medical interventions that prolong and improve the quality of our lives once born.

Unchecked population growth presents substantial (I am tempted to say *insurmountable*) impediments to our need to achieve sustainable use of the earth's goods and services. If those of us who understand this do not speak up concerning our population problem, who else will? I fear we have been complacent for far too long.

IO

OUR ALTERNATIVE FUTURES

Paradoxically, our global thirst for oil, which featured in chapter 8, is the reason the world has the Great Barrier Reef Marine Park. Established by the Australian government in 1975, it was until very recently the largest marine management area in the world, encompassing 344,400 square km of ocean and reef, perforated occasionally by island pieces of the state of Queensland.[1]

In the late 1960s, Australia was actively promoting a search for oil to achieve energy independence, and multinational oil companies were lining up for leases. Since the continental shelf off Queensland was thought to have good oil potential, the Great Barrier Reef became Australia's early version of the U.S. Arctic National Wildlife Refuge, except that the reef was not protected in any way and was certainly not a wildlife refuge. The tiny Queensland Littoral Society led a vigorous conservation movement under the simple slogan "Save the Barrier Reef." In March 1970, the collision of the fully laden oil tanker *Oceanic*

Facing page: We owe it to our children and grandchildren to choose our future carefully. Photo courtesy of Yvonne J. Sadovy de Mitcheson.

1. A very effective collaborative environmental management of national marine park reefs and ocean and the Queensland islands makes the Swiss cheese nature of the Marine Park invisible to all except lawyers, who spend idle hours wondering whether the boundary between state and national jurisdictions is based on shorelines at high tide, low tide, or somewhere in between!

Grandeur with an unmapped coral pinnacle off the tip of Cape York resulted in a spill of 1,100 metric tons of oil and a 10-km-long slick, galvanizing public opinion. "Save the Barrier Reef" became the rallying cry. The government acted to establish a royal commission to make recommendations on the exploitation of the reef for oil. The commission met over the next four years and, in its monumental report, pointed to the paucity of scientific knowledge concerning the Great Barrier Reef, the potential risk if oil exploration was to proceed, and the urgent need to establish a special statutory authority responsible for ecological protection and for control of research and development within the Great Barrier Reef region. In June 1975 the Great Barrier Reef Marine Park Act became law, and the process of creating the world's largest marine park began. It remains the world's best example of sustainable management of coral reefs, despite an enormous growth in human pressures, and is free, in perpetuity, of any risk of oil exploration.

The protection of the Great Barrier Reef was hugely important for the organisms living there, but for our purposes it is most important for what it tells us about people. When the Queensland Littoral Society began its campaign, Australia was a country in which the prevailing outlook on conservation was well described by the saying, "If it moves shoot it; if it doesn't move, chop it down." Rural property was advertised for sale as "already cleared," meaning that *all* the trees had been removed. For many, *conservation* was a dirty word uttered by drug-crazed, stringy-haired hippies. Citizens knew about the Great Barrier Reef, but most did not know much. Few outside Queensland had ever seen it, and it was assumed it was way too big for anyone to have to worry about. Why shouldn't oil companies drill on part of it? But something happened after the *Oceanic Grandeur* incident, and it may have been as simple as the fact that the Queensland Littoral Society rolled out a national campaign with its simple slogan—Save the Barrier Reef—on a bumper sticker. They did not ask people to save the reef from any particular threat or to save specific parts of it; they just asked people to save it. Bumper stickers appeared on cars all over the country, and the Australian people changed their minds almost overnight: The Great Barrier Reef is important. We cannot risk letting it be damaged by oil exploration. We Australians have a responsibility to look after it.

Whenever a new idea catches on in a whole community, it is almost as if a fresh breeze has swept through and cleared the fogginess out of peoples' minds. The change is rapid, it is infectious, and the enthusiasm that is generated is very powerful and can achieve much. Communities can reach consensus on needed actions very rapidly once the inertia is broken. This kind of transformation is what is now needed on a global scale, and it will come.

Previous chapters have discussed the ways in which we are impacting this world that sustains us. Overfishing, deforestation, excessive production of greenhouse gases, and other human activities have ushered in the world's sixth mass extinction. Biodiversity is falling, and our food resources may be at risk. The renewable resources that clothe and house us are already less able to provide for all our wants, if not our basic needs. More urgently, the enormous industries based on renewable resources, which provide jobs, income, international trade, and quality of life, are at risk.

Meanwhile, our growing use of energy and our enthusiasm for fossil fuels add substantially to other forms of pollution of land, water, and the atmosphere. We are changing the climate more rapidly and extensively than it has changed in the last 10,000 years, while natural systems are becoming degraded and less able to cope with the new stresses an altered climate brings. Natural systems are also becoming less able to supply the environmental services that we take for granted and on which we depend.

All the time, our population continues to grow toward an anticipated 9.2 billion people in 2050. Most of this growth is in developing countries, which are ill prepared to absorb additional people. As a result, the inevitable droughts and crop failures will lead ever more often to large populations living in near-starvation conditions, bereft of hope for anything better. Our future does not look promising.

This future of doom and gloom is not inevitable. We have the opportunity to choose the future that will unfold and the capacity to make it happen; and we humans have a history of moving quickly once we make the collective decision to move at all. In this chapter, I will explore the various paths forward, the challenges of each, and the opportunities that exist.

In a sense, we have come to a point on our collective journey at which we face not a fork in the road or even a crossroad. We are at a place from which several alternative paths move off in quite different directions. The choices we make in the next few years will determine what our future will be, because on this journey, we can't reverse our steps, go back in time, and correct an error. We need to use all the information available to us to rationally choose the best path to take. This decision must be based far more on long-term communal benefits and risks than has been our usual practice through history and prehistory. Now is not the time to focus on short-term gains and losses; it is the time to plan carefully for humanity's future. I am confident that there is at least one possible future ahead of us that offers us high quality of life in a world of sustainable natural ecosystems. Perhaps we can find it quickly enough to save a large portion of the earth's present biodiversity.

UNDERSTANDING OUR DILEMMA

A number of possible solutions to our current predicament exist, but before we can evaluate them we must understand clearly what the problem really is. I've described it as an elephant that we try not to see, a huge and growing elephant with many different parts. Previous chapters have concerned particular parts of this metaphorical elephant—overfishing, deforestation, climate change, and so on. To solve our problem we are going to have to deal with the whole elephant, because the seemingly separate parts are interconnected and affect one another.

Unfortunately, most discussion of our environmental problems presents them as separate. Indeed, most government agencies and universities are structured in ways that partition these problems—separate groups of experts deal independently with fisheries management, forestry, watershed issues, climate change, energy use, air pollution, ocean acidification, and so on, and the average citizen is left hoping that all these experts know what they are doing. By thinking of our environmental problems this way, we have come to think that they also have separate solutions, but they do not. Worse still, there has been a tendency to think of them as unique to specific locations or nations or even to play them off against one another. Reducing the loss of biodiversity is less or more important than combating climate change. Drought and desertification are problems of Africa. Loss of coral reefs will impact coastal communities in certain developing countries.

This tendency to partition the problem into smaller bits and then place these bits at a distance can help make the problem appear more tractable—tackling one bit at a time makes it less daunting. However, the parts of the problem are too interconnected to permit us the luxury of solving some of them in some places. We live on one planet, and we have one problem: we are using the resources of our only planet at rates and in ways that are not sustainable in the long term, and we are now beginning to see the effects of that overuse and misuse in a general deterioration of the capacity of the world to support us.

The plight of coral reefs demonstrates very clearly the interconnections among the parts of our problem. As discussed in chapter 4, reefs are not being destroyed solely by overfishing, pollution, or inappropriate development of coastal areas, but by all of these and by climate change as well. The climate change effects themselves are diverse, including warming, acidification, increased severity of storms, and potentially even sea level rise. If we focus effort on overfishing but ignore the other parts of the problem, reefs remain damaged. If we focus on climate and ignore everything else, again, reefs remain damaged. We have got to think holistically and treat the whole patient rather than the particular symptoms, one at a time.

One way of thinking holistically is to use an idea called the *ecological footprint*. This concept provides a common currency for most of our different types of impact on environment, and while it does not ease the task of deciding how to proceed, it does portray the scope and scale of our dilemma with clarity.

The footprint concept was invented in the early 1990s by William Rees and his Ph.D. student, Mathias Wackernagel, at the University of British Columbia. It starts by recognizing that every thing and every service we use is provided by this planet and the energy it receives from the sun. It is a methodology for relating all the *renewable* resources we use to the amount of space on Earth that would be required for natural processes to produce them. This makes it possible to combine everything that goes into supporting us—food, water, manufactured products, and most energy—by converting each to a measure of how much of the earth's surface would be required to produce it or produce the resources we use in constructing or transporting it. The footprint can quantify those environmental services that are dependent on biological productivity in ecosystems, but not those services that are tied to other aspects of ecosystems, and it does not give a very good measure of sustainability or ecosystem resilience.[2] The footprint is a standardized measure of consumption, not a measure of all uses we make of the environment. Still, it can be used to examine per capita requirements, national use of resources, global demand for resources, and so on. Turned around, the same methodology can be used to compute the production of resources by the earth, by particular nations, or by particular ecological systems on the earth's surface.

Footprint measurements are expressed in global hectares (gha)—one gha equals the average overall production of renewable resources per hectare of land surface across the world given current levels of technology. Over the past fifteen years, the methodology has been refined to account for oceanic and freshwater resource production and use, although there remain gaps and problems. Fishery yield per hectare of fishing ground appears to be overestimated at present, for example, while much of the damage done by pollution, other than nutrification or release of greenhouse gases, is not captured because pollution by plastics, other novel chemicals, or heavy metals is not ameliorated on ecological time-scales. Use of energy is not measured directly but rather by the amount of land required to take up, via photosynthesis, the carbon released to the atmosphere through burning of fuel. Since most of our energy comes from fossil fuels at present, this approach captures most energy use. An increase in use of nuclear, wind, or solar energy would go uncounted. Ecological footprint methodology and calculations are continuously updated by Global Footprint Network, an international NGO dedicated to this task.

The ecological footprint can provide a quantitative index that captures most human demands on the earth's ecosystems. This index can be compared across various sectors (nations, regions, industries) and through time. The related concept of *biocapacity* provides an equivalent measure of the capacity of the earth's ecosystems to restore and replen-

---

2. Note that the ecological footprint does not account for everything. Our use of minerals, such as copper or iron, for example, is not part of the footprint. These items are not renewed by ecological processes. Our use of fossil fuels, however, is included in the ecological footprint by referencing the amount of forested land that would be needed to take up the CO_2 released from mining, processing, and burning that fuel, to prevent it from being added to the atmosphere. The ecological footprint is also dependent on technology in the sense that the capacity to produce resources depends on the particular mode of environmental management or agriculture—well-managed wetlands are more productive than polluted and otherwise degraded ones, and well-managed croplands can be much more productive than lands subject to poor agricultural practices.

ish the environmental goods and services humanity uses. Biocapacity can also be compared across sectors and through time. Together, the analysis of footprints and biocapacity has provided an effective way to demonstrate the overuse of environmental goods and services that characterizes the human condition today.

Calculations of the global ecological footprint for 1961 (the earliest year for which adequate data are available) yielded a value of 7 billion gha, about half the global biocapacity for that year (13 billion gha). But our consumption of resources and energy has been continually shifting upward, and by 1980 the data revealed a global footprint that was larger than the earth's biocapacity. This trend has continued. Our global ecological footprint for 2006[3] is reported as about 1.44 times the global biocapacity (17.1 billion gha versus 11.9 billion gha). What this means is that we are using about 40 percent more environmental goods and services than the earth's ecological systems can supply each year. The overage is covered by using goods and services produced in the past and stockpiled as forests, coal deposits, and so on. We can overshoot for a number of years, but ultimately we will run out, a fact now becoming apparent in the progressive deterioration of the planet's capacity to produce those goods and services.[4]

Because of its ability to permit quantitative comparisons among nations or regions, ecological footprint analysis has revealed some instructive contrasts. As expected, citizens in countries such as Canada and the United States have large ecological footprints (5.8 and 9.0 gha per capita, respectively), while eleven African countries have ecological footprints of 1.0 gha per capita or smaller. The United States is currently ranked third for the size of its per capita footprint—the United Arab Emirates (10.3 gha) and Qatar (9.7 gha) have the dubious distinction of demanding more per person from the earth than any other nation—but with its much larger population, the total footprint for the United States is the largest of any nation (2.7 billion gha in 2006). Despite a

3. Information on the Global Footprint Network website in 2009 is based on data compiled for 2006.

4. Global biocapacity barely changed between 1961 and 2006, despite the introduction of more efficient agricultural technologies that greatly improved the productivity of croplands during the 1980s and 1990s. Degradation of natural environments over those years approximately balanced those improvements. Now overall biocapacity is starting to fall, despite continuing improvements in agricultural yields.

much lower per capita footprint, China is second, with a total footprint of 2.4 billion gha. But China's use of ecological goods and services is growing so rapidly that it will soon surpass the United States. Canada, with its much smaller population, has a total footprint (189 thousand gha) that is much lower than either of these.

One patently obvious conclusion is that it will be very difficult indeed for all people on Earth to raise their standards of living to U.S. levels if we continue to measure standard of living by the amount of things we consume. The current 44 percent overage in use of ecological goods and services is occurring with an average global per capita footprint of 2.6 gha; if all people on the planet had an American-sized footprint, the overage would be more like 400 percent (global footprint of 59 billion gha versus 11.9 billion gha global biocapacity). While it may be politically incorrect to say that we can't all live like Americans, it is ecological common sense. We cannot continue indefinitely to take more than our world produces, even if it would be nice to believe that we could. I'm not sure where we would find the four extra Earths.

Footprint analysis also helps us clearly see the second aspect of our problem: the situation we are in gets a little bit worse every day. Per capita use of environmental goods and services worldwide is increasing as countries such as China and India become wealthier and living standards rise. The rate of increase has slowed in developed countries, but here too the trend is usually upward. And the global human population is continually growing as well. We expect to add over 2 billion consumers by 2050, bringing us to 9.2 billion overall. If those two new Chinas' worth of people each have the same footprint as the average person in China did in 2006, we will add 4.7 billion gha to the world's global footprint, bringing it to 21.8 billion gha. If instead they each have the 2006 global average per capita footprint of 2.6 gha, the world's global footprint jumps to 23.9 billion gha. If all these additional people live like Americans, the global footprint will more than double to 40.6 billion gha, and if they plus everyone else on Earth manage to achieve a U.S. lifestyle, the global footprint balloons to 82.8 gha—about seven Earths' worth of goods and services.

To sum things up as clearly as possible, our problem is that we are already overusing, by a significant margin, the resources and services the earth provides, and, because of continued population growth and increases in standards of living, the total human footprint is increasing very rapidly. Most of the ecological deterioration we see—loss of species, collapse of food webs, growing dead zones in the ocean, changing climate—is due to our growing overuse of the planet. Our ecological bank account is in overdraft, we are spending more each month than we get in new deposits, and we are spiraling ever deeper into debt. We are using the ecological capital built up in the world over millennia. How much longer can this go on?

POSSIBLE SOLUTIONS

Continuing the financial analogy for a moment, there is one solution that is frequently used in economic markets but is not available to us: we cannot declare bankruptcy and start over. Bankruptcy is a process whereby an individual seriously in debt is permitted to wipe away that debt. Effectively, the debt is spread among the creditors, who each absorb some of the loss, and life goes on. Unfortunately our growing ecological overage is not a debt that can be pushed off onto creditors, allowing us to start over. There is only us and our home planet of accumulated ecological wealth. So let's stop acting as if some ultimate bailout is possible and consider the real solutions.

An individual in serious financial difficulties is usually advised to do two things: (1) assess the various expenses being incurred and cut out those expenses that can be eliminated, and (2) use the money freed up to pay off those debts that have the highest interest charges first. To face our ecological problem responsibly, we need to pursue two analogous strategies: (1) increase the efficiency with which we use resources and energy so that we consume less and pollute less, and (2) shift environmental management toward sustainability, tackling those environmental problems that are most serious first. The complexity of our problem means that there are many different ways of doing these two things— some of these provide much better outcomes than others, but all are characterized as active efforts to find a solution.

There is one other path that many individuals in financial difficulty follow: do nothing different and hope for the best. Let's consider the hope-for-the-best option before dealing in more detail with strategies for taking action to solve our problem.

There are many reasons to hope for the best. Maybe the scientists will prove to have been wrong, despite the mounting evidence of real ecological dangers. Maybe new technology will be developed that will make all our problems (or at least the worst of them) disappear. Maybe market forces will find the best solution without us having to plan for it.[5] Perhaps God will give us a new start without nasty ecological constraints to our activities. Maybe if all the children who believe clap their hands, Tinker Bell will come back to life with a magical solution. While I have serious problems with several of these possibilities, intelligent people believe in each of them, so they cannot be dismissed outright. (Well, maybe Tinker Bell can.) What can be stated, however, is that there is as yet no evidence suggesting that any of these scenarios are realistic possibilities. Given that we only have one Earth and one chance to get things right, I prefer to adopt the precautionary principle: let's take active steps to reduce our demands on ecological systems while also addressing the most serious cases of ecological degradation as quickly as possible. If one of these alternative possibilities turns out to be true, we will still get to a better situation more quickly by taking some prudent action. And if Tinker Bell still has no magical solution, we will have begun the process of solving our problem ourselves.

Here is why I am not prepared to just hope for the best. We are already overusing the goods and services provided by this planet. The trend is toward greater overconsumption, because populations continue to grow and consumption rates continue to increase. Many of these growth rates are approximately exponential, meaning that the situation gets worse at an increasingly rapid rate. The consequences of our overuse are becoming ever more apparent. There is absolutely no doubt that continuing down this path will, short of a miracle, result in substantially bad outcomes for people, including me, our children, and our grandchildren. The hope-for-the-best strategy leads us to a future of greatly reduced quality of life for 9.2 billion people in just forty years' time. It's very likely to be a dismal downward ride.

FOUR CHOICES FOR THE FUTURE

I am confident that humanity is taking the first step toward adopting an active strategy to solve its problem right now. That first step is a

---

5. The financial collapse of 2008 should cast renewed skepticism on the argument that markets do a good job of regulating themselves.

small and difficult but vitally important one. It is to acknowledge that this problem is real, shared, and must be addressed. It is a difficult step because we have always avoided accounting for the environmental costs of our activities. By treating resources as free for the taking, by assuming that the environment can handle our wastes and continue to provide other essential services, we have built economies that are artificially more profitable than they have been in reality. The true costs are off the ledger, and they are shared. Usually the poorest of us carry the largest share of these costs. This is the case in rich countries and poor, in democracies and dictatorships, in countries with a thriving middle class and those without. It has always been the case, because we have not seen ourselves as part of the ecosystem but as individuals who are free to use the goods and services that ecosystems provide. Indeed, Western thought has been quite explicit that the riches of the world are there for our use and enjoyment. Recognizing now that our strange accounting practices have resulted in a serious situation that threatens all of us to some extent and many to a considerable extent is a difficult step to take. We have been struggling with it for perhaps thirty years, but I think we are finally getting to the point of acceptance.

The second step is also a small but difficult one: to recognize that this problem cannot be solved without taking explicit action. We are tackling this step right now, and none too soon. The biggest stumbling block at present seems to be how best to share the responsibility for our problem and the cost of its solution, but this is a big advance over not admitting a problem existed or that we needed to act to solve it.

The third step is to choose a specific path forward, to make fundamental choices about how to proceed. At present I can see four possible paths (or perhaps four groups of similar paths) leading to quite different futures. All four futures are better than the one we will arrive at if we simply hope for the best, but some of them are preferable to others. Only one is sustainable over the long term, but all of them provide reasonable quality of life for many of us over the next several decades. I call them Belvedere, Woodstock, Technopolis, and New Atlantis.

Belvedere is the future we will move toward if we each continue to think "me first" and use whatever power we have selfishly. Unlike hoping for the best, it involves acting, but the actions taken are for individual or in-group benefit. Those of us who have wealth and power will ensure our own quality of life, using our wealth to purchase the goods and services we need or want, while the great majority of humanity will live in increasingly straitened circumstances in a world of deteriorating ecosystems. At first there will be wealthy nations and poor ones; then there will be wealthy fiefdoms within once-wealthy nations. Members of privileged classes, relatively few in number, will enjoy an American lifestyle or perhaps something even more extravagant, but they will live in gated communities in a world that will be increasingly violent as the underprivileged struggle among themselves and against the upper class to obtain the absolute necessities of life. The wealthy will provide assistance as charity, but only to the extent that it is in their own self-interest to mollify the masses.

The Belvedere world is colonialism taken to a new level. High standards of living for the very few will be gained at the expense of the many, who will experience growing squalor; severe shortages of food, water, and other basic necessities; pandemic diseases; wars; and mass migration of ecological refugees. The privileged classes will be scattered in small, defended communities across North America, Europe, and Asia that will function as separate feudal states. They would do well to remember that gates do not keep pandemics at bay. In the long term, this future will become increasingly unattractive to everyone, but the Belvedere world is probably sustainable for a couple of generations, and during that period life will be quite pleasant for the few. The developed countries of 2010 are already quite good at harvesting and sequestering environmental goods and services for their own benefit; their techniques can be readily extended to the more extreme requirements that are coming. Indeed, the road to Belvedere may be the easiest active path to choose, the four-lane superhighway stretching out ahead of us, and the danger is that we may take it without first weighing carefully the other options available.

The Woodstock future is at the end of a road along which we substantially cut back our use of environmental goods and services. We solve the problem of climate change by substantially reducing our use of energy and returning to simpler lifestyles. We solve the overuse of resources by reducing consumption. On the road to Woodstock, the American footprint will decline from 9.0 gha per capita to something closer to the global mean of 2.6 gha. With a general turn away from technology and use of energy, we will depend more on our own physical labor, but there will be greater equitability across the globe, and that may translate into less conflict and greater understanding. Getting to Woodstock will not be easy, because it requires a significant reduction of economic activity and a substantial renunciation of present-day signs of high social status. This is unlikely to happen on a sufficiently wide scale unless inspirational leaders appear on the scene, with the power and social connections to harness the media to promote the virtues of a simpler life. Still, with the right leadership, the necessary shift in thinking could happen quickly—if people can be convinced to want huge houses, multiple cars, and lifestyles of conspicuous consumption, they can also be convinced to want modest lifestyles and to live smaller. One central tenet of the Woodstock world would be that the earth's environmental systems are a precious inheritance that we must manage sensitively for future generations. Under sensitive, sustainable management, global biocapacity would increase, and the global environmental footprint would be brought back toward balance with it. The Woodstock future may be sustainable long-term if standards of living can be lowered substantially; however, there is a real risk that continued population growth will ultimately swamp any reduction in per capita consumption.

The Technopolis future is the one we will move toward if a belief in our capacity to develop new, innovative technologies to solve our environmental problems becomes dominant. Through aggressive technological innovation, we will be able to alter the way in which we obtain and use energy, allowing us to solve our climate problems without reducing our use of energy to provide for our needs and wants. Technological innovation will move our agriculture increasingly from the farm into the factory, greatly expanding our efficiency in food production and creating a new green revolution. Our foodstuffs, however, will move very far from the types of organisms we have consumed through history. It's conceivable that we will be able to duplicate photosynthesis, building our own foodstuffs in closed hydroponic systems to which we add sunlight and nutrients. By freeing food production from the need for naturally productive land, it will be possible to locate food production factories closer to centers of human population and to expand our cities across the land. Sustainable management of what natural environments remain will be practiced, but only to the extent that they are useful to provide resources or recycle wastes from our communities, and these needs will be progressively reduced as we develop technologies to do those tasks efficiently and independently of natural ecological processes. With abundant, nonpolluting energy and an increasingly information- and service-based economy with reduced demand for natural resources, we will develop a civilization in which recreation and entertainment are entirely divorced from the natural world. Indeed, it is not a big stretch to imagine the implanting of a data transfer port just behind the left ear as a normal perinatal procedure that equips the individual for operating in an increasingly connected and virtual world. Going to the Holodeck[6] for several days may well become the vacation of choice for billions of people.

The Technopolis future will be attractive to many because it follows our tradition of inventing ourselves out of difficulties. Indeed, there is already considerable interest, by serious scientists, in what is called geoengineering—the use of engineering approaches to mitigate climate change by shielding the earth from the sun's rays or by extracting CO_2 from the atmosphere and sequestering it somewhere safe. I worry about the lack of ecological redundancy that will occur in the Technopolis future—loss of species, loss of genetic variation, loss of important but poorly understood ecological processes—and the risk that some small link in our totally engineered world will not work.[7] Biosphere 2 failed dismally[8] because its designers did not understand enough about the cycling of carbon and oxygen to build a system that could be totally closed to the outside and still function ecologically—they had to continually monitor and adjust the atmosphere to keep the place habitable. In Technopolis there will be no engineers on the outside able to monitor and repair when things go wrong. I also worry about the progressive iso-

6. I assume *Star Trek* has invaded the global consciousness sufficiently that all will be familiar with this space in which a holographic simulation of a place of one's choosing provides a stage on which to have virtual adventures.

7. The precautionary principle does not only apply to fisheries management. While ecologists and other environmental scientists understand a lot about how the complex systems of our world work, we do not understand them completely, and as we tinker with natural systems (or try to replace them entirely), there will be surprises.

8. Built near Oracle, Arizona, in the late 1980s, Biosphere 2 is a fully enclosed ecosystem covering 1.28 ha, or more than two football fields. Planned to be a self-sustaining biotic system and including representative rain forest, cloud forest, savannah, desert, coral reef, and ocean systems, it turned out to be incapable of maintaining an atmosphere that would sustain animal life without inputs of additional oxygen and could not produce sufficient food for the four people who attempted to live inside it.

lation of humanity from the natural world that will occur. I am not sure that we can be truly human if we do not have the opportunity to interact with the world around us. I fear the Technopolis world will become culturally sterile as increasing numbers of people live increasingly constrained lives. I love tofu, but I do not want to eat a factory-made equivalent morning, noon, and night. Nor do I want the Holodeck to be my only option for recreation. Still, Technopolis is an option with a long-term, more-or-less positive outcome. Continued population growth will probably ultimately degrade it, and I suspect that as it degrades, civilization will become stark, monotonously homogeneous, and constricting. I do not see Technopolis generating much art or literature.

The path to New Atlantis may be the most difficult one to follow. This is the path we take if we recognize that there are finite limits in the world and that we must use our technological expertise and ethical principles to build a civilization that lives in harmony with the natural world while still aspiring to foster all the creative exuberance of which humanity is capable. This is the path of quality, not quantity, and it differs from the other three in one important way. Moving toward New Atlantis requires that we value every human life while actively constraining our natural capacity to grow more abundant. Taking this path means that we embrace the idea that a world population of fewer than the current 6.9 billion is the only way in which we can have sustainably high standards of living across the world.

To move down this path, we aggressively innovate to develop carbon-free sources of energy and make our use of energy highly efficient, confident that the sun is not yet anywhere near close to limiting the amount of energy we want to use. We apply our best environmental science and enlightened social policy to ensure that all natural environments are brought under sustainable management; we alter our economic methods so that the value of healthy natural systems is appropriately measured and applied when business decisions are being made. We maximize the efficiency of our agriculture, and we price agricultural products according to the true cost of producing them—beef will become a lot more expensive, but agricultural efficiency will improve. And we build a civilization based on efficient borrowing of natural resources rather than on wasteful plundering of natural systems. In short, we take the best ideas from Technopolis and Woodstock, couple these to a rational awareness that the human population cannot keep growing unless we find some additional Earths to inhabit, and build a truly sustainable, globally equitable society.

Economists will dismiss New Atlantis as unworkable until they recognize that their conventional economics is fundamentally flawed by its assumption that growth is essential for economic prosperity. Talk of perpetual growth within a finite universe has always been unrealistic, but economists got away with it for many years because we were not butting up against limits. We have reached those limits now. Yes, it will be difficult to transition to a non-growth economy, just as it will be socially and culturally difficult to transition to a non-growing population. But it will become even more difficult the longer we delay starting on this journey. There is a world out there that we can get to in which a stable population lives in harmony with its environment, using goods and services sustainably, all while maintaining a culturally rich civilization. New Atlantis may well have Holodecks and people who prefer virtual reality to hiking in an alpine valley. But the Holodecks will be green, and the meadows will be available for those who still enjoy hiking. And there will be art and literature.

Doing nothing and hoping for the best is not a realistic option, so we are going to move along some active path in the next few years. No path will be easy, and the destinations are very different from one another. Is there any evidence that we will be able to choose the most appropriate path? Can we get to New Atlantis?

SOME REASONS FOR OPTIMISM

Throughout this book, I have emphasized the ways in which we have been overusing the natural world. Overfishing, deforestation, biodiversity loss, climate change—each was an example of our excesses. The myriad ways in which we have been degrading coral reefs made for a particularly distressing tale. Is there any reason to believe that we can change our ways and move toward a more sustainable future?

In fact, we already have most of the needed tools and techniques, and if we act intelligently and make our decisions rationally, we can make that move. There are no excuses for not acting.

As discussed in chapter 3, there is enough energy arriving on the earth's surface each day to supply our energy needs several times over without releasing more greenhouse gases. Our technologies for tapping into carbon-free sources of energy are developing rapidly and are already able to provide energy at only a modest premium compared to fossil fuels.[9] As was made clear in chapter 1 (in relation to fisheries) and in chapter 2 (in relation to forests), we already have the tools we need for sustainable environmental management. Our current understanding of ecosystem processes, set out in chapter 6, is already sufficient to radically improve our management of natural ecosystems of all types. Our current failures to manage sustainably arise from our inappropriate (insufficient) valuation of the goods and services supplied by natural ecosystems and our willingness to permit the costs of resource use, in the form of pollution and ecosystem degradation, to be hidden and shared widely while the benefits provide profits for the few. Changing our ways of accessing the earth's wealth is certainly going to be difficult, because economic and national interests strongly favor the status quo, but there are no technological or scientific barriers to shifting to a sustainable economy.

Of course, as discussed in chapter 8, knowing that we already have the technology to supply most of our energy needs with solar power does not help an electricity provider make the shift away from fossil fuels. A major investment in still-functional power plants designed to use coal or oil cannot be paid off by abandoning the plants and replacing them with new, expensive solar collection and distribution networks. Society must provide strong economic incentives to change, enabling the electricity provider to invest the extra funds needed to begin the transition. Similarly, the farmer operating a large, highly mechanized operation dependent on use of fossil-fuel-based fertilizers and pesticides will be unable to quickly shift to sustainable methods based on nutrient cycling, ecological relationships, and biodiversity, as these methods will likely not be as bountiful, particularly on the worn-out, chemically overdosed soils on his farm. He will need economic incentives to do so, and unless he begins to change his practices, his farm will continue to pollute natural environments, use external inputs that boost atmospheric CO_2, and undermine the natural fertility of the soil.

9. The possibility of developing fusion power should not be dismissed, and, if achieved, this would provide effectively unlimited nonpolluting energy.

The fisherman who understands that taking too many fish drives down populations and ultimately leads to fishery collapse might stop fishing, but his income collapses, and other fishermen take the fish he would have taken. If he is an artisanal fisherman who fishes primarily to feed his family in the only way he knows how, he cannot stop fishing without starving. And the manager charged with preventing fishery collapse has limited options when any reduction of fishing effort impacts earnings and employment throughout the fishing economy. Fishermen and managers alike need clear economic incentives to move toward sustainable fishing. The same is true for those who harvest forest products and for those who merely undertake construction projects in environmentally inappropriate locations or use environmentally inappropriate methods and materials. Making changes to the incentive systems operating in all communities needs to begin as soon as possible. This will require an informed and committed public and political leaders with vision, but it is what governments should do.

EXAMPLES OF SUSTAINABLE MANAGEMENT

Making the shift toward sustainability will be difficult. Yet I am encouraged that there are many instances where more sustainable approaches are already in place. People have managed to make this shift, and these precious examples can teach us how to build the incentives we need. Let's look first at sustainable management of resources.

While the FAO reports that 78 percent of fishery stocks are either "fully exploited," "overexploited," or "depleted," and while tales of fishery collapse are numerous and distressingly similar, there are some well-managed fisheries around the world. At one extreme, the Alaska pollock fishery—the largest fishery by volume in U.S. waters and the largest white fish fishery in the world—has been sustainably managed for more than thirty years. One of the secrets to its success is what's called a *limited access privilege program* (LAPP).

Under a LAPP, fishery-independent stock assessments help define the total allowable catch (TAC) each year, and a rigorously enforced set of "catch shares"[10] guarantee each shareholding fisherman access to a spe-

10. LAPPs share out the total allowable catch (TAC) by allocating access to a specified percentage of fish. Individual transferable quotas (ITQ) share out the catch by allocating

cific fraction of the TAC, regardless of when those fish are taken during the season. The allowable catch (and the actual catch) have fluctuated over the years and have been trending downward over the past decade. Catch share programs, first introduced in the Western Australian rock lobster fishery, have become increasingly common tools to manage limited access commercial fisheries, and most sustainable fisheries now build ownership in such ways.

The Alaska pollock fishery is also certified by the Marine Stewardship Council (MSC), an international, nonprofit, charitable organization that evaluates and certifies fisheries deemed to be sustainably managed. Product from these fisheries bears the distinctive blue MSC logo and can be advertised as certified sustainably managed. Now ten years old, the MSC currently certifies fifty-nine fisheries distributed across all oceans, although the preponderance are in northern Europe. The MSC logo is used by retailers and restaurants to inform consumers when they are making their choices about seafood. It is a market-based mechanism for building the economic value of sustainable management. Similar certification programs now exist for forest products, agricultural products, and tourist destinations.

Artisanal fisheries have been among the most difficult to manage sustainably, but considerable success is being achieved in Chile. There, the Fisheries and Aquaculture Law includes provisions for management and exploitation areas for benthic resources (MEABR). Areas considered MEABRs, lying between the shoreline and five nautical miles out to sea, are formally allocated for exclusive fishing use by artisanal cooperatives that participate in co-management of the fishery for particular mollusks, crustaceans, echinoderms, and algae. Individual fishermen are registered as co-op members, and cooperatives pay for baseline assessments from which TACs and management plans are established. Cooperatives police themselves, and this includes excluding nonmembers from fishing within the MEABR. MEABRs were first introduced in 1989, and at present there are more than five hundred of them in

---

a specified proportion of the catch to each shareholder. LAPP and ITQ are legally slightly different instruments, but they achieve the same ecological goal. Each fisherman shareholder is guaranteed a specified portion of the total catch permitted that season, assuming he can catch it. This avoids the overfishing and the tendency to glut the market early in the season that result when all fishermen are trying to maximize their individual catches before the TAC has been landed (and the season closes).

Chile, totaling over 1,000 square km of the Chilean coast. Their presence has increased the value of the catch while reducing its size to sustainable levels. They have also encouraged more effective cooperation among the fishery co-op members, including some partnering of neighboring co-ops in marketing efforts. Chilean MEABRs represent a strategy different from the use of catch shares, and they operate in a much smaller and very different fishery, but they have the same effect—building ownership (in this case, communal) in the fishery stocks at specified exclusive locations. With ownership comes the possibility of sustainable management.

Chilean MEABRs have also been shown to foster conservation of nontarget species within their borders. While the exclusive areas are set up to manage a fishery for specific benthic invertebrates, demersal fish and nontarget benthic invertebrates are now more abundant and diverse within protected areas than outside them. In this regard the Chilean experience mirrors that in the central Philippines, where a long-term program led by Angel Alcala of Suliman University and his colleague, Garry Russ of James Cook University, Australia, has resulted in the creation of a number of small, locally managed marine protected areas (MPAs). This program started in 1974 when Alcala established a small 12.5 hectares reserve at uninhabited Sumilon Island, near Cebu Island in the Bohol Strait. The reef surrounding this island was traditionally fished by people from nearby towns on Cebu. Initially, the fishermen supported the concept of a reserve, and stocks of fish within it began to build up. This gave Alcala the opportunity to bring fishermen from nearby Apo Island to see the effect of protecting the fish.[11] Seeing the effectiveness of the reserve, the fishermen joined Alcala in creating a reserve (about 10 hectares in size) on the Apo Island reef in 1982. (This timing was fortunate because a change of local governments on Cebu in 1980 brought in people opposed to the concept of a reserve on their traditional fishing grounds at Sumilon. Fishing resumed, and the impressive gains were wiped out. Since then the Sumilon Reserve has been sometimes protected, often fished, and has not been effective.)

Apo Island was inhabited by about seven hundred people who fished

11. Fishermen are more impressed by the improved fishing outside reserve borders (due to animals living there that have moved out of the reserve) than they are by the quantity of big, inaccessible animals inside the reserve.

its reef. The reserve was established with their support and involvement, and they have continued to manage it—now under a license from the federal management agency. Repeated ecological monitoring by Russ, Alcala, and their colleagues has documented a great increase in numbers, biomass, and diversity of fish species inside the Apo reserve and also a spillover of this production to augment the fishery in the surrounding fished area of reef. The attractive, protected reef has enabled a small but profitable tourist industry based on diving. Villagers on Apo are now wealthier and work shorter hours to catch the fish they need to support their lifestyles and send their children to school. Continuously managed now for nearly thirty years, Apo Island's tiny MPA is cited worldwide as an outstanding example of an effective strategy, based on protection from fishing, for managing a coastal fishery. Alcala has encouraged a number of other small reserves in the general region based on the initial success at Sumilon and the continued success at Apo. Some are functioning very well, some less so, but the overall result is definitely positive.

The use of MPAs of various types has been a favored strategy for sustainable management of coastal waters for several decades. The concept is simple: by excluding human activities, principally fishing, from a specific region of coastal environment, the target species, their habitats, and the ecological processes that sustain them are all protected from damage due to extraction. Fish live longer, grow larger, and are correspondingly more fecund; their habitats escape the damage caused by nets, trawls, or dynamite fishing; and other species are undisturbed also. These positive changes inside the reserve spill over to surrounding areas, improving fishing outside the reserve.

In reality, of course, most MPAs are protected only on paper and have no effect on sustainability, but a minority are well managed and produce the expected results. Among these are the Great Barrier Reef Marine Park at one size extreme, the Land and Sea Park in the Bahamas, the Apo Island MPA in the Philippines, and a number of others. These successful MPAs share three essential features: they are actively managed; there is a high degree of compliance with the regulations that exist; and the community values these places and takes personal pride in the success of the conservation effort. Unsuccessful MPAs characteristically lack at least one and usually all three of these features.

EXAMPLES OF CHANGES IN ENERGY USE

In chapter 8 I commented on the benefits that could be achieved by increasing the efficiency of our energy use and by shifting toward use of non-fossil fuels. Perhaps spurred more by higher prices for oil than by pleas to go green, innovative industries are now peppering the market with new products that can make our homes energy efficient and perhaps even energy neutral. Wind farms are becoming an almost routine part of the scenery and contribute usefully to satisfy energy demands. Solar collectors are now being embedded in building products, particularly roofing shingles and tiles and wall panels. Window technology is being dramatically improved. Ground-source heating is becoming fashionable if not routine in some regions, and houses that pump excess energy into the power grid are being built occasionally in all Western countries. The "green building" initiative has benefited from the establishment of the U.S. Green Building Council, a Washington-based NGO that supports the LEED[12] green building certification program used internationally. Now we are beginning to see the production of entire housing developments, office towers, and high-rise apartment buildings that are certified green. In some cases these are not only energy neutral but also supply excess energy to the grid. LEED-certified buildings are energy efficient, using alternative energy sources, passive solar design, and sustainably produced construction materials.

Our transportation sector is also a hotbed of innovation as hybrid, fuel-cell, and plug-in electric cars are rushed into production. Light rail lines are being implemented for inner city transportation, and there is starting to be talk in North America concerning high-speed rail links between major population centers. Maybe we will catch up to Europe one day.

In a particularly interesting development, several manufacturers are planning to bring "micro-nuclear" power plants to market by 2012. These will be factory-assembled and preloaded with fuel to last twenty years. Sandia National Laboratories is developing one about the size of a modest two-to-three-story office building; it will generate 100 to 300 megawatts and is designed to have its fuel cartridge switched out and replaced with a new one. The expectation is that construction costs will be far better controlled compared to those for much larger site-built

12. LEED: Leadership in Energy and Environmental Design.

projects. There is even talk of using micro-nuclear generators at tar sands mine sites to replace the current use of fossil fuels in the extraction process—I am not sure this is a "good idea" but at least oil companies are aware that the outrageous amounts of energy (and release of CO_2) used currently for extracting oil from the tar sands is not going to be tolerated much longer.

Greensburg, Kansas, was flattened by a tornado on May 4, 2007, destroying about 95 percent of homes in this tiny town of fourteen hundred people. Rather than disperse to other towns in the region, the inhabitants decided to rebuild, and to rebuild green. What inspired them to do this is unclear, but rural populations sometimes display an intuitive understanding of the need to be good stewards of the earth, and this may have made them already aware of the need for, and the potential benefits of, green technologies. The tornado merely provided the opportunity to put theory into practice. Now the streets are lit with LED technology; the new arts center, city hall, hospital, and school are being built to LEED platinum standards, the highest possible; and the new homes being constructed are deliberate experiments in exploring the use of specific materials and design elements. A wind farm south of town is destined to provide for the town's energy needs, and the new school will have geothermal heating and air conditioning.

These examples and many others prove that it is possible for human communities to develop management programs that provide for environmental sustainability and to undertake other projects to reduce their demands for fossil fuels. Knowing that it can be done, and has been and seeing the consequences in more valuable goods and services provides a powerful incentive to people elsewhere to strive to make this transition. The most critical requirement for getting a group started appears to be building ownership in the process and commitment to the goals. Greensburg turned the tragedy of its tornado into an opportunity—a marked contrast to the response in much-larger New Orleans, which has rebuilt using conventional methods on the floodplains that Katrina wiped clean. Do they understand that sea level is rising? Or did they just lack the needed leadership or not realize that it was possible to organize around the cause of rebuilding on more secure land? Now is a time for community organizing while central governments or the United Nations develop the incentives. Let's see how quickly we can change.

CAN WE SAVE THE CANARIES?

Ecosystems and species vary in the degree to which they are being damaged by human activities. Some of each are proving to be particularly susceptible and have been termed canaries in the ecological mine. The sad reality is that the damage we have already done is unlikely to be undone before some of these particularly susceptible species or ecosystems disappear. Coral reefs and polar bears are clearly such canaries. Under any imaginable scenario, many species are going to become extinct, more fisheries are going to collapse, and more forestland is going to disappear before we get our impacts on the world under control. How well we do is going to depend, intrinsically, on what path forward we decide to take. Hoping for the best and doing nothing will lead to the worst outcome, but most active paths forward are also going to fail to save species already on the brink or ecosystems as fragile as coral reefs.

As I noted earlier, selfish Belvederians, luxuriating in their protected enclaves of plenty, will ultimately succumb when they are swamped by the huddled masses. Before that happens, demand from the wealthy and those masses of poor will have overexploited and polluted all environments other than a few tokens protected inside luxury enclaves as natural parks. I doubt any coral reefs will make it, but rainforests and coastal wetlands are also unlikely to be saved. In Woodstock, the idealism that leads initially to sustainable management and smaller footprints risks ultimately being swamped by the growing population. Idealists may be willing to reduce their footprints somewhat from U.S. levels, but they will not reduce them to levels now seen in Africa, and that is all the Earth of 2050 will support if 9.2 billion people are present.[13] The result will be failure to prevent overexploitation simply because there will be too many of us around.

The Technopolis world, which moves us even further away from sustaining the ecosystem than we are at present, is also not a world in which we might look for sustainably managed ecosystems. The pressure to provide a quality life for growing numbers of people will force

13. Assuming today's biocapacity of 11.8 billion gha and a population of 9.2 billion, the average sustainable per capita footprint would be 1.3 gha, less than the current average for Africa of 1.4 gha.

adoption of technologies that solve climate problems by building domes over cities or by vacuuming CO_2 from the air rather than by mitigating releases of greenhouse gases. And the focus on technology as the answer tilts us toward replacing natural ecosystem processes with lab-based mechanisms of our own devising. It's possible that in Technopolis there will be a new opportunity for human population growth, even beyond the 9.2 billion now forecast for 2050. If we can devise novel food production methods, effective desalination and purification processes for drinking water, and distribution systems that get food and water to populations needing them, we can avoid the deaths caused by drought and famine. If we can harness ample energy, we can move to a totally urban, passive entertainment culture of which Second Life may be an early example. It may even be possible to retain a reasonable semblance of civilization, with the arts well catered for. Under such circumstances, the limit to the number of humans may get adjusted upward once more. But this Technopolis world will certainly not be a place in which currently threatened ecosystems are sustainably managed. We will have moved beyond the need for them. They will only need to be preserved holographically for history lessons or for the atavistic few who want to walk on a beach, climb a mountain, or cast a fly for trout along a river running free. This all assumes that the Technopolians do not make any mistakes—they will only have one chance.

Only New Atlantis provides a future where coral reefs and other fragile ecosystems might survive, because only New Atlantis confronts the twin problems of our growing population and our growing per capita environmental footprint. It is the only future that attempts to do something about the two new Chinas' worth of people who are expected to be produced over the next forty years unless we change our behavior. Remember our difficulty in appreciating exponential change. Remember what is happening to the human population. If reducing our use of fossil fuels and adopting more sustainable use of environmental goods and services seems difficult now, just think how much more difficult it will be when the earth adds another 2.3 billion people with all their needs and aspirations. The path to New Atlantis accepts the need to address this problem as part of the solution to our overall problem of not living sustainably. So, how do we move down this path?

UNDERSTANDING OUR LINKS TO
THE NATURAL WORLD

In 1974 the marine ecologist Bob Johannes traveled from the University of Georgia to spend a sabbatical year in the west Pacific. He did not spend his sabbatical in a library of an East Asian university, as would be typical, but in the village of Ngeremlengui in Palau, Micronesia, where he learned from traditional fishermen. For sixteen months, Johannes interviewed fishermen, went fishing with them, met their families, and generally learned whatever he could of their customs, beliefs, and practices with respect to fishing. Palau has been home to people for over three thousand years, and during this time they learned to fish its reefs and offshore waters while tending vegetable gardens and maintaining a few chickens and pigs. Perhaps because he was a fish biologist, Johannes knew the right questions to ask and could interpret the answers provided. I talked about the wondrous breadth of fish hook technology in ancient Palau in chapter 1, but Johannes reported many other aspects of the fishing crafts as practiced there.

One feature that was clear in Johannes's book *Words of the Lagoon* was the very effective way in which Palauan societies had managed their fisheries through a clear appreciation of how the reef ecosystem produced fish and of the need to fish sustainably. Their deep understanding of the natural history of the species they fished enabled them to recognize critical times and places when fishing should not occur because of potential disruption to spawning or juvenile survival and recruitment. Their fishing was organized to conform to the natural cycles of the reef, and this organization was maintained through a complex series of rules or laws, mostly with spiritual overtones. Above all, the Palauans saw themselves and the fish as sharing their world and exhibited a sense of responsibility for sustainable management to ensure that this state would continue.

These attitudes were not unique to Palau but widely represented across Micronesia and Polynesia. They also were dying fast when Johannes visited. Japanese colonization in the 1920s opened Palau to the world and to new markets for fishery products. The ravages of World War II and the associated overfishing of the reefs to feed large numbers of occupying troops damaged the fish stocks, their environment, and the social structures that had kept fishing sustainable. By the 1970s many of the old practices had been abandoned, and fishing was a far less lucrative activity than it had been. In addition, young Palauans, back from business school in the United States and becoming influential in government, were tilting Palau ever forward toward the overexploitation that would inevitably degrade its fragile environment. Johannes finished his book not knowing what the future would bring.

But Palau has been a fortunate country. By the end of the 1970s, a new generation of young Palauans, just back from their own American educations, brought a different perspective, one that enabled them to form alliances with people in their grandparents' generation who remembered the old days of sustainable fishing and had pride in their culture. Palau was able to recover, to develop diving-based tourism as a better driver of the economy than the export of fish and other natural resources, and to restore an appreciation for the old ways, even if the majority of people did not go back to living in small fishing villages. Conservation was boosted by international NGOs that recognized an opportunity to help. In September 2009 President Johnson Toribiong of Palau announced the declaration of the nation's entire 600,000 square km exclusive economic zone as a shark sanctuary. This was to be Palau's answer to the widespread finning of sharks for the Asian soup industry—the need to protect sharks is indeed more important than the need to enjoy a bowl of soup.

The story of Palau reveals how decisions about fishing or sustainable management are inevitably bound up with belief systems, economic structures, governmental decisions, and a certain amount of serendipity. It could have gone either way, but Palau has looked deeply and chosen a sustainable future.

We can learn from Palau. We must rebuild formal education so that citizens understand how we are linked to the natural world that sustains us. Ancient civilizations understood this viscerally, but we have increasingly forgotten it as we have become wealthier and as our lives have become less directly connected with nature. In addition, we must recognize the true economic value of sustainably managed ecosystems and reflect this in the structure of our economies. Above all, local populations need to be empowered to take ownership as stewards of their environments, because we only care for the things we value. If in the course of building understanding of the economic value of the natural environments around us we should also happen to reconnect with the aesthetic and even spiritual values of these places, so much the better.[14]

There are many ways to value some thing or some place, and economics is not everything. Above all, we must stop tolerating the inappropriate, destructive use of natural systems and be prepared to speak truth to power when it is governments that are acting irresponsibly. Each of these small steps can be taken locally. There is no need, initially, for global agreements on attitudes to natural ecosystems. What is needed is for local communities to come together in looking after the places where they live.

NO TIME TO WASTE

Like all of us, Palau now needs to deal with climate change, and its risks as a SIDS (small island developing state) are particularly severe. A number of island nations are destined to disappear completely beneath the sea in the next few decades due to sea level rise. Like the coral reefs and the polar bears, these SIDS may well be sacrificed while the rest of us struggle to find that path that we can follow to New Atlantis.

For those of us not on small islands, there is some good news: shifting to a carbon-free economy is going to offer economic opportunities to those who are first and best in developing the new technology. Let's not naively think these benefits will fall to the United States, let alone to non-entrepreneurial Canada. Europe is well ahead of us. China is the world leader in manufacturing solar panels. Putting chauvinism aside, the fact that there are fortunes to be made also means that there are jobs in creating the new economy. Shifting to a carbon-free economy is not a step that only has costs.

Despite these pluses, the longer we wait, the costlier the process of shifting over to non-fossil fuels is going to be. Thus, there should be a far greater sense of urgency than I see when heads of state, government administrators, economists, or others discuss this subject. By applying

14. On 18 March 1968, speaking at the University of Kansas, Robert Kennedy said, with reference to the GDP, that it "does not allow for the health of our children, the quality of their education or the joy of their play. . . . It measures neither our wit nor our courage, neither our wisdom nor our learning, neither our compassion nor our devotion to our country, it measures everything, in short, except that which makes life worthwhile."

new efficiency standards and using existing technologies to increase our energy efficiency, we can reduce the need for energy while still doing the things we want to do. This provides a bridge to the new path, lowering our CO_2 emissions while we put plans in place to transition to non-fossil sources. Many aspects of this bridge, such as the use of passive solar design elements in our buildings, should have been routine decades ago.

But real changes in the use of energy are only going to come when we unite and commit to real change in each country. There is movement at the international level, but at present it is glacial, and many countries (including Canada and the United States) are dragging their heels. It is worth remembering that the reports from the International Panel on Climate Change have consistently underestimated the extent of impacts and the rapidity with which our emissions of greenhouse gases have risen. There are going to be more nasty surprises, because the climate system is complex and multifaceted. We are still learning to understand it. Soon to come is the realization by the public of what the scientists mean when they talk of committed climate change—that we have already done the damage that is going to cause about 1°C of global warming. Also coming soon will be a growing awareness that sea level has already risen enough to be causing problems in the deltas of Bangladesh, on the Maldives, or in Venice; that storms really are bigger now; and that droughts and famines are worse than before. Given this continual rain of bad news, we need to get to work with actions to mitigate and adapt, simply to provide glimmers of good news that will counteract an otherwise inevitable sense of despair. There is no time to waste, and politicians have got to be persuaded to stop thinking in terms of short time frames and local economic advantage.

ROOM TO HOPE

Take a quick breath, hold your mask and regulator in place, and step off the stern of the boat. Readjust your buoyancy compensator. Look around. There it is below you, blue in the distance, dappled light and dark, some hints of topography. Drift slowly down, reveling in the weightlessness. As you come closer, the topography becomes more apparent, much as it does when the plane commences its descent, gliding down toward a city from 30,000 ft. The colors become richer and brighter. Coral in its many varied forms creating pinnacles, spurs with deep groves between them, caves and overhangs, fields of branched *Acropora* shrubbery with finger-thick branches standing up to 2 meters high, terraced layers of flat plates a meter wide marching up hillsides, giant boulders and smaller ones, on and on and on. Everywhere there is life, moving, from larger fishes of numerous shapes and color patterns to myriads of tiny shrimps, crabs, and starfish. Look closer and see tubeworms waving their fluffy orange tentacles, crinoids perched high on top of corals waving their strangely mechanical arms slowly and moving plankton to their mouths, or minute gobies living out their lives among the tiny canyons created by the pattern on a boulder coral's surface. If this is an average reef in 2010, it is still something well worth seeing. It retains much of the wondrousness that makes coral reefs what they are. It is certainly different from any other environment on which you could have a dive.

But there remain some reefs, even today, that preserve more of the qualities that reefs used to have, back when Darwin marveled at them or Cook cursed them. Reefs in which the profusion of life dazzles the mind with its abundance and diversity. Reefs over which the fishes stream past so thickly that you doubt you can swim between them. Reefs where fish grow large, really large, and where the coral covers nearly 90 percent of all available surfaces. I haves seen reefs like this off the south coast of Cuba along the Archipiélago de los Canarreos, seaward of Golfo de Batabanó. Enric Sala of the Scripps Institution of Oceanography recently reported on the wonderful environment at Kingman Reef, a tiny atoll lying almost in the center of the Pacific (6°N, 162°W). At Kingman, there are not only lots of fish, but the larger groupers and sharks dominate the fish community they way they used to hundreds of years ago on other reefs.

Such near-pristine reefs share several features. They are well removed from sources of pollution, have usually been fished only lightly if at all, are well placed with respect to clear ocean water, and are in places that humans visit only occasionally. Off Cuba the reefs have benefited from a political situation that has prevented people from getting out to them to go fishing. At Kingman the protection comes from the area's utter remoteness. That such reefs exist tells us that there is still room to hope.

Back in the 1970s and 1980s, I used to spend several weeks each year at the One Tree Island Field Station, a tiny, primitive research outpost on One Tree Reef, just east of Heron Reef at the southern end of the Great Barrier Reef. One Tree Reef is only about 5 km by 3 km in size, and the single island is only a few hectares, with a maximum elevation of 2 meters above high tide. One of my favorite things to do at One Tree Reef, when I was not doing science, was to wander out across the reef flat at low tide and get to the outer edge a kilometer or more from the island. Alone, on the edge of the reef, watching the seabirds fishing and arguing over the catch or the parrot fishes, tails thrashing in the air, eager to regain access to the productive shallows as the tide came in, and listening to the ceaseless roar of the Pacific swell as it broke just outside the reef edge, I would get an almost mystical sense of the time-lessness of the natural world and my own relative insignificance. I was standing on a solid limestone rampart built up over thousands of years by the growth of corals and other calcifying organisms, facing waves that might have traveled across the Pacific before smashing into this wall of limestone. The wall, submerged at high tide, was only about thirty meters tall because the southern Great Barrier Reef is a post-Pleistocene phenomenon that grew on a hilly limestone plain formed much earlier, when southern Queensland was outside the tropics. It was impressive nonetheless: a solid limestone wall, 30 meters high, 100 km off the Queensland coast, with a pavement on the top that would eas-ily support a Hummer or a 747, if anyone wanted to put one there, built over nine thousand years by the calcifying activities of minute coral polyps and coralline algae. I still think back to those hours alone on the edge of the reef; reefs are amazing in so many different ways.

One Tree Reef comes close to being as idyllic as remote Kingman Reef. A hundred kilometers off the Queensland coast, washed by waves that might have crossed the Pacific and protected from fishing for thirty years because of its status as a scientific reserve within the Great Barrier Reef Marine Park, One Tree Reef has been a low-impact location for long enough that its fish populations are abundant and full of large individuals and its corals are generally healthy. Lying on the Tropic of Capricorn, it is less diverse than more northern parts of the Great Barrier Reef, but it remains impressively rich. It does not have the shark populations of Kingman (few places do anymore), but it still provides many magical dives.

We can keep atmospheric concentration of CO_2 below 450 ppm and even move it back toward 350 ppm, if we get busy now and make the changes we have to make quickly.[15] We can revitalize management of coastal waters so that more reefs begin to look like those off Cuba or at One Tree and perhaps even like Kingman. We can treat reefs as the precious jewels they are, while using them as living ecological canaries, telling us daily how well we are doing in caring for the planet. And we can develop similarly responsible management of other natural environments. We need to start now on our long-overdue journey. My hope is that we will make that journey, that we will get to the best destination, and that my granddaughter will one day snorkel over a marvelously rich coral reef and relish the joy of being one part of a wonderful world.

15. The consensus among coral reef scientists at present is that a move back to 350 ppm (a 1980s level) would permit reefs to flourish once more.

BIBLIOGRAPHY

INTRODUCTION

My trip to the Swains Reefs commenced a research project that resulted in a number of technical publications, strung out over many years. None relates to the subject of this book. The last to be published was P. F. Sale et al., "The Relation of Microhabitat to Variation in Recruitment of Young-of-Year Coral Reef Fishes," *Bulletin of Marine Science* 76 (2005): 123–142.

E. O. Wilson's autobiography, *Naturalist* (Washington, D.C.: Island Press, 1994) is a delightful account by a leading environmental scientist. A twenty-first-century view of ecology is presented in the better modern college texts on ecology, such as Charles J. Krebs, *Ecology: The Experimental Analysis of Distribution and Abundance,* 6th ed. (San Francisco: Benjamin Cummings, 2008), or Michael Begon, Colin A. Townsend, and John L. Harper, *Ecology: From Individuals to Ecosystems,* 4th ed. (Oxford, U.K.: Wiley-Blackwell Publishing, 2006). Information on the size of the human population is readily available from the Population Division of the Department of Economic and Social Affairs of the United Nations (www.un.org/esa/population/unpop.htm) or from the International Database maintained by the U.S. Census Bureau (www.census.gov/ipc/www/idb/index.html).

A recent account of stromatolites' role in the creation of the oxygen atmosphere can be found in an article by A. Bekker et al., "Dating the Rise of Atmospheric Oxygen," *Nature* 427 (2004): 117–120.

CHAPTER 1. OVERFISHING

The U.N. Food and Agriculture Organization, FAO, regularly publishes extensive data on the state of the world's fisheries. Its primary reporting tool is "State of World Fisheries and Aquaculture," published every two years and available at www.fao.org. I have used the 2004, 2006, and 2008 versions (published in 2005, 2007, and 2009, respectively), as well as articles by Botsford, Jackson, Myers, and Pauly to describe global trends: L. W. Botsford et al., "The Management of Fisheries and Marine Ecosystems," *Science* 277 (1997): 509–515; J.B.C. Jackson et al., "Historical Overfishing and the Recent Collapse of Coastal Ecosystems," *Science* 293 (2001): 629–638; R. A. Myers and B. Worm, "Rapid Worldwide Depletion of Predatory Fish Communities," *Nature* 423 (2003): 280–283; D. Pauly et al., "Fishing Down Marine Food Webs," *Science* 279 (1998): 860–863; D. Pauly et al., "Toward Sustainability in World Fisheries," *Nature* 418 (2002): 689–695; and R. Watson and D. Pauly, "Systematic Distortion in World Fisheries Catch Trends," *Nature* 414 (2001): 534–536.

The decline and collapse of the Northwest Atlantic cod fishery is well documented. A delightful little book by Mark Kurlansky, *Cod: A Biography of the Fish That Changed the World* (Toronto: Alfred A. Knopf, 1997), tells the story of our five-hundred-year association with this fish. I also relied heavily on an article by W. H. Lear of Canada's Department of Fisheries and Oceans, "History of Fisheries in the Northwest Atlantic: The 500-Year Perspective," *Journal of Northwest Atlantic Fishery Science* 23 (1993): 41–73.

The theory of logistic population growth is covered in all basic ecology texts, and the relationships among effort, cost, and yield leading to the idea of MSY are in any introduction to fishery science. The precise shape of the line in Figure 2 and the symmetrical yield curve are based on the assumption that the fish population obeys the logistic growth curve. The general rule that cost increases linearly with effort, while yield rises to a maximum and then falls, does not depend on this assumption. Inevitably there will be an intersection between cost and yield. Increasing effort beyond this intersection point will result in lower yield and greater financial losses, while reducing effort below this point should result in better yields (if all fishermen cooperated).

In 1981 the marine ecologist R. E. Johannes published an account of a year he spent in Palau: *Words of the Lagoon: Fishing and Marine Lore in* the *Palau District of Micronesia* (Berkeley: University of California Press, 1981). In chapter 9 and in an appendix of this book, Johannes tells us what the exquisite fishhooks of Micronesia were for and how they worked. In general, his book reveals the immense depth of knowledge of the natural world held by traditional fishermen.

In addition to the article by Watling and Norse that informed my discussion of trawling in the text (L. Watling and E. A. Norse, "Disturbance of the Seabed by Mobile Fishing Gear: A Comparison to Forest Clearcutting," *Conservation Biology* 12 [1998]: 1180–1197), I recommend two articles documenting the seriousness of clear cutting through trawling, one by Rijnsdorp and colleagues (A. Rijnsdorp et al., "The Micro Distribution of Beam Trawl Effort in the Southern North Sea," committee meeting, International Council for the Exploration of the Sea, Copenhagen, 1991) and another by C. R. Pitcher and colleagues (C. R. Pitcher et al., "Implications of the Effects of Trawling on Sessile Megazoobenthos on a Tropical Shelf in Northeastern Australia," *ICES Journal of Marine Science* 57 [2000]: 1359–1368). The "four hundred times per year" estimate in the text (for trawling in certain areas) comes from Rijnsdorp's 1991 calculation of beam trawling intensity for sites in the North Sea; if you want a still higher extreme, Pitcher and colleagues reported that there are parts of Hong Kong harbor that have trawls pass over them three times per day ("Implications of the Effects of Trawling").

Garrett Hardin's 1968 article on the problems of open access, "The Tragedy of the Commons," *Science* 162 (1968): 1243–1248, is more than forty years old but still relevant.

CHAPTER 2. REMOVING FORESTS

The U.N. Food and Agriculture Organization, FAO, reports regularly on the global forestry industry; I have used three FAO publications in preparing this chapter. The estimates of economic value and of forested area in 2005 come from FAO, *Global Forest Resources Assessment 2005* (published in 2006), which also provided data on the value of timber and nonwood forest products globally and in specific regions. The 2005 and 2007 editors of the biennial FAO reports, *State of the World's Forests,* provided additional information. *Key Findings: Global Forest Resources Assessment 2010* is also now online, providing some preliminary information from the report due out in late 2010. All are online at www.fao.org.

Margaret E. Lowman's website, www.canopymeg.com, provides an interesting portal to forest canopy research and much more.

Data on extraction of bushmeat from forested land came primarily from J.E. Fa et al., "Bushmeat Exploitation in Tropical Forests: An Intercontinental Comparison," *Conservation Biology* 16 (2002): 232–237. The article by D.S. Wilkie and J.F. Carpenter, "Bushmeat Hunting in the Congo Basin: An Assessment of Impacts and Options for Mitigation," *Biodiversity and Conservation* 8 (1999): 927–955, was also helpful. This appears to be a serious problem in some tropical forests for which there are few data.

Valuation of ecosystems to include non-harvest services is an emerging activity. I used three articles that dealt with forest valuation approaches: A. Balmford et al., "Economic Reasons for Conserving Wild Nature," *Science* 297 (2002): 950–953; B. Kaiser and J. Roumasset, "Valuing Indirect Ecosystem Services: The Case of Tropical Watersheds," *Environment and Development Economics* 7 (2002): 701–714; and T.H. Ricketts et al., "Economic Value of Tropical Forests to Coffee Production," *Proceedings of the National Academy of Sciences (USA)* 101 (2004): 12579–12582.

My source for the information on the collapse of the Easter Island civilization and the more general idea that societies tend to overuse their resources and then collapse came from Jared M. Diamond, *Collapse: How Societies Choose to Fail or Succeed* (New York: Viking Press, 2005).

Information on desertification came chiefly from the FAO's *State of the World's Forests 2007* and from a report from United Nations University: Z. Adeel et al., *Overcoming One of the Greatest Environmental Challenges of Our Times: Re-thinking Policies to Cope with Desertification* (Tokyo: United Nations University, 2007), available at www.inweh .unu.edu. The claim that dust from Africa has brought novel pathogens to Caribbean coral reefs is covered well in a 2003 article by V.H. Garrison et al., "African and Asian Dust: From Desert Soils to Coral Reefs," *Bioscience* 53:469–479.

Charles C. Mann's book *1491: New Revelations of the Americas before Columbus* (New York: Knopf, 2005) introduced me to pre-Columbian agriculture in the Amazon Basin. In reading further, I waded into the anthropological literature and ultimately drew information from two articles dealing with *terra preta*: N.J.H. Smith, "Anthrosols and Human Carrying Capacity in Amazonia," *Annals of the Association of American*

Geographers 70 (1980): 553–566; and W. M. Denevan, "A Bluff Model of Riverine Settlement in Prehistoric Amazonia," *Annals of the Association of American Geographers* 86 (1996): 654–681.

CHAPTER 3. DISRUPTING THE OCEAN-ATMOSPHERE ENGINE

A paper presented by Ken Wilkening at the 48th annual convention of the International Studies Association, Chicago, 28 February–3 March 2007, and titled "The Discovery and Scientific and Political Recognition of International Environmental Problems: Case Studies of Arctic Haze, Acid Deposition and Persistent Organic Pollutants" provided a good history of the scientific understanding of acid rain. It is online at www.allacademic.com/meta/p181116_index.html. The acid rain story, particularly as it related to the Sudbury smelters and the Aurora trout, was fleshed out using several websites and three articles: R. J. Beamish and H. H. Harvey, "Acidification of La Cloche Mountain Lakes, Ontario, and Resulting Fish Mortalities," *Journal of the Fisheries Research Board of Canada* 29 (1972): 1131–1143; Aurora Trout Recovery Team, *Recovery Strategy for the Aurora Trout (Salvelinus fontinalis timagamiensis) in Canada,* Species at Risk Act Recovery Strategy Series (Ottawa: Fisheries and Oceans Canada, 2006), also available at the Canadian Species at Risk site, www.sararegistry.gc.ca/species/speciesDetails_e.cfm?sid=65; Pollution Probe, *Sulfur Dioxide and Toxic Metal Pollution from Smelters in Ontario* (Pollution Probe, 2003), available at www.pollutionprobe.org/Publications/Smelter Report.pdf.

I used two documents from the U.S. Department of Energy for data on current and predicted patterns of energy use. These are *International Energy Outlook 2008,* report DOE/EIA 0484(2008) (Washington, D.C.: Energy Information Administration, U.S. Department of Energy), available at www.eia.doe.gov/oiaf/ieo; and *Annual Energy Outlook 2008, with Projections to 2030,* report DOE/EIA 0383(2008) (Washington, D.C.: Energy Information Administration, U.S. Department of Energy), available at www.eia.doe.gov/oiaf/aeo.

My information on the efficiency of photosynthesis came from FAO's agricultural services bulletin number 128 by Kazuhisa Miyamoto, published in 1997 and available at www.fao.org/docrep/w7241e/w7241e00 .HTM.

Information concerning the Norse expansion to North America came from several websites, including that for the L'Anse aux Meadows National Historic Site, www.pc.gc.ca/eng/lhn-nhs/nl/meadows/index .aspx. The description of the Bolca fossil site came from D.R. Bellwood, "The Eocene Fishes of Monte Bolca: The Earliest Coral Reef Fish Assemblage," *Coral Reefs* 15 (1996): 11–19, bolstered by web research, while more general information on geological history of coral reefs came from J.E.N. Veron, *Corals of Australia and the Indo-Pacific* (Sydney: Angus & Robertson, 1986).

My primary source for information on the science of climate change was the various reports from the Intergovernmental Panel on Climate Change, available from its website at www.ipcc.ch. These are written in a way that makes the science readily accessible by nonspecialists. The fourth assessment report (2007) is in four volumes; a formally approved synthesis volume and three more detailed reports from the three working groups. I relied primarily on the synthesis report and the report of working group 1. I also used two more recent updates on the science and the trends in climate: Catherine P. McMullen and Jason Jabbour, *Climate Change Science Compendium* (Nairobi: United Nations Environment Programme, 2009), available online at www.unep.org/ compendium2009/; and N.L. Allison et al., *The Copenhagen Diagnosis, 2009: Updating the World on the Latest Climate Science* (Sydney: University of New South Wales Climate Change Research Centre, 2009), available online at www.copenhagendiagnosis.org/.

Other references used in this chapter included Wallace S. Broecker, "Climatic Change: Are We on the Brink of a Pronounced Global Warming?" *Science* 189 (1975): 460–463; J. Hansen et al., "Climate Impact of Increasing Atmospheric Carbon Dioxide," *Science* 213 (1981): 957–966; James E. Hansen, "A Slippery Slope: How Much Global Warming Constitutes 'Dangerous Anthropogenic Interference'?" *Climate Change* 68 (2005): 269–279; Katja M. Meyer and Lee R. Kump, "Oceanic Euxinia in Earth History: Causes and Consequences," *Annual Review of Earth and Planetary Sciences* 36 (2008): 251–288; Ulf Riebesell et al., "Comment on 'Phytoplankton Calcification in a High-CO_2 World,'" *Science* 322 (2008): 1466b; and Glenn De'ath et al., "Declining Coral Calcification on the Great Barrier Reef," *Science* 323 (2009): 116–119.

CHAPTER 4. THE PERILOUS FUTURE
FOR CORAL REEFS

A more technical treatment of my studies of real estate transactions among damselfishes is in P. F. Sale, "Coexistence of Coral Reef Fishes— A Lottery for Living Space," *Environmental Biology of Fishes* 3 (1978): 85–102. Charles Darwin's comment on coral reefs came from his book *The Structure and Distribution of Coral Reefs. Being the First Part of the Geology of the Voyage of the Beagle, under the Command of Capt. Fitzroy, R.N., during the Years 1832 to 1836* (London: Smith Elder and Co., 1842).

There are numerous books about coral reef biology and some excellent websites. I have primarily used the technical literature, but NOAA's Coral Health and Monitoring Program website at www.coral.noaa.gov is an excellent gateway to much of the science. Two other excellent sites are the Great Barrier Reef Marine Park Authority site at www.gbrmpa .gov.au and the ARC Center of Excellence for Coral Reef Studies at www.coralcoe.org.au. The research studies I specifically highlighted are documented in P. L. Harrison et al., "Mass Spawning in Tropical Reef Corals," *Science* 223 (1984): 1186–1189; C. L. Hunter and C. W. Evans, "Coral Reefs in Kaneohe Bay, Hawaii: Two Centuries of Western Influence and Two Decades of Data," *Bulletin of Marine Science* 57 (1995): 501–515; D. R. Robertson, "Fish Feces as Fish Food on a Pacific Coral Reef," *Marine Ecology Progress Series* 7 (1982): 253–265; J. Stimson and E. Conklin, "Potential Reversal of a Phase Shift: The Rapid Decrease in the Cover of the Invasive Green Macroalga *Dictyosphaeria cavernosa* Forsskål on Coral Reefs in Kane'ohe Bay, Oahu, Hawai'i," *Coral Reefs* 27 (2008): 717–726; and R. R. Warner, "Traditionality of Mating-Site Preferences in a Coral Reef Fish," *Nature* 335 (1988): 719–721.

Many of the articles referenced in chapter 1 were used in dealing with overfishing of reefs, but the chapter by Yvonne Sadovy and Amanda Vincent was a valuable treatise on the live reef fish restaurant trade: "Ecological Issues and the Trades in Live Reef Fishes," chapter 18 of *Coral Reef Fishes: Dynamics and Diversity in a Complex Ecosystem,* ed. P. F. Sale (San Diego: Academic Press, 2002), 391–420.

A recent document from United Nations University provides a broad range of information on coastal mismanagement, much of it directly relevant to reef management: P. F. Sale et al., *Stemming Decline of the Coastal Ocean: Rethinking Environmental Management* (Hamilton,

Canada: UNU-INWEH, 2008), available online at www.inweh.unu
.edu/publications.htm.

Information on coastal pollution and the Great Barrier Reef Marine
Park was obtained from D. Haynes, ed., *Great Barrier Reef Water Quality:
Current Issues* (Townsville, Australia: Great Barrier Reef Marine Park
Authority, 2001), available online at www.gbrmpa.gov.au/corp_site/
info_services/publications#Water_Quality.

Information on geological history of coral reefs came from P. Copper,
"Ancient Reef Ecosystem Expansion and Collapse," *Coral Reefs* 13
(1994): 3–11; D. M. Raup and J. J. Sepkoski, "Periodic Extinction of
Families and Genera," *Science* 231 (1986): 833–836; J. E. N. Veron, *Corals
of Australia and the Indo-Pacific* (Sydney: Angus & Robertson, 1986); and
J. E. N. Veron, "Mass Extinctions and Ocean Acidification: Biological
Constraints on Geological Dilemmas," *Coral Reefs* 27 (2008): 459–472.

For information on the economic value of reefs and aspects of reef
management, I used a 2008 report from Access Economics: *Economic
Contribution of the GBRMP, 2006–07,* which was prepared for the Great
Barrier Reef Marine Park Authority, available online at www.gbrmpa
.gov.au/__data/assets/pdf_file/0004/29272/AE_GBRMP_19MAR08
.pdf; and R. W. Buddemeier et al., *Coral Reefs and Global Climate Change:
Potential Contributions of Climate Change to Stresses on Coral Reefs* (Pew
Center on Global Climate Change, 2004), available online at www
.pewclimate.org/global-warming-in depth/all_reports/coral_reefs.

The topic of climate change impacts on coral reefs is developing
rapidly, and I used a number of recent technical articles. The major
ones are listed here. The Coral Reef Watch website was also a useful
source of current information: http://coralreefwatch.noaa.gov/satellite/
current/products_ssta.html.

A. C. Baker, P. W. Glynn, and B. Riegl, "Climate Change and Coral
Reef Bleaching: An Ecological Assessment of Long-Term Impacts,
Recovery Trends and Future Outlook," *Estuarine, Coastal and Shelf Science*
80 (2008): 435–471; G. De'ath et al., "Declining Coral Calcification
on the Great Barrier Reef," *Science* 323 (2009): 116–119; S. D. Donner
et al., "Global Assessment of Coral Bleaching and Required Rates of
Adaptation under Climate Change," *Global Change Biology* 11 (2005):
2251–2265; V. H. Garrison et al., "African and Asian Dust: From Desert
Soils to Coral Reefs," *Bioscience* 53 (2003): 469–480; D. M. Geiser et al.,
"Causes of Sea Fan Death in the West Indies," *Nature* 394 (1998): 137–

138; P. W. Glynn, "Extensive 'Bleaching' and Death of Reef Corals on the Pacific Coast of Panamá," *Environmental Conservation* 10 (1983): 149–154; P. W. Glynn, "Widespread Coral Mortality and the 1982/83 el Niño Warming Event," *Environmental Conservation* 11 (1984): 133–146; P. W. Glynn, "Coral Reef Bleaching: Facts, Hypotheses and Implications," *Global Change Biology* 2 (1996): 495–509; J. M. Guinotte and V. J. Fabry, "Ocean Acidification and Its Potential Effects on Marine Ecosystems," *Annals of the New York Academy of Sciences* 1134 (2008): 320–342; O. Hoegh-Guldberg, "Coral Bleaching, Climate Change and the Future of the World's Coral Reefs," *Marine and Freshwater Research* 50 (1999): 839–866; O. Hoegh-Guldberg et al., "Coral Reefs under Rapid Climate Change and Ocean Acidification," *Science* 318 (2007): 1737–1742; J. A. Kleypas et al., "Environmental Limits to Coral Reef Development: Where Do We Draw the Line?" *American Zoologist* 39 (1999): 146–159; J. A. Kleypas et al., "Geochemical Consequences of Increased Atmospheric Carbon Dioxide on Coral Reefs," *Science* 284 (1999): 118–120; J. T. I. Tanzil et al., "Decline in Skeletal Growth of the Coral *Porites lutea* from the Andaman Sea, South Thailand, between 1984 and 2005," *Coral Reefs* 28 (2009): 519–528.

CHAPTER 5. THE PROBLEM OF SHIFTING BASELINES

The shifting baseline concept was introduced by Daniel Pauly and developed further by Jeremy Jackson. My discussion was based on D. Pauly, "Anecdotes and the Shifting Baseline Syndrome of Fisheries," *Trends in Ecology and Evolution* 10 (1995): 430; J. B. C. Jackson, "Reefs since Columbus," *Coral Reefs* 16 (1997): S23–S32; J. B. C. Jackson et al., "Historical Overfishing and the Recent Collapse of Coastal Ecosystems," *Science* 293 (2001): 629–638; and J. B. C. Jackson, "What Was Natural in the Coastal Oceans?" *Proceedings of the National Academy of Sciences (USA)* 98 (2001): 5411–5418. The concept now possesses its own website, www.shiftingbaselines.org, which is full of wacky stuff, some only marginally related to the concept.

Joseph Connell and Wayne Sousa, then both at the University of California, Santa Barbara, discussed the relative scarcity of long-term ecological studies and proposed a simple rule that few studies obey: to monitor a system for sufficient time for all individuals initially present to have died and been replaced. J. H. Connell and W. P. Sousa,

"On the Evidence Needed to Judge Ecological Stability or Persistence," *American Naturalist* 121 (1983): 789–824.

My explorations of the inverse square law, sensory physiology, and natural selection were based on material that should be present in any introductory college text in physics, physiology, or biology, respectively. That we appear to have so much difficulty in appreciating the consequences of exponential changes suggests our education systems should be trying to improve the job they do in this respect.

CHAPTER 6. OUR UNREALISTIC BELIEF IN
THE BALANCE OF NATURE

This chapter is a crash course on modern ecology. The ideas discussed are all covered in the better modern college texts on ecology, such as *Ecology: The Experimental Analysis of Distribution and Abundance,* 6th ed., by Charles J. Krebs (San Francisco: Benjamin Cummings, 2008) or *Ecology: From Individuals to Ecosystems,* 4th ed., by Michael Begon, Colin A. Townsend, and John L. Harper (Oxford, U.K.: Blackwell Publishing, 2006). *Foundations of Ecology: Classic Papers with Commentaries,* ed. Leslie A. Real and James H. Brown (Chicago: University of Chicago Press, 1991), reproduces many of the critical older papers that I refer to. Here are the key references for those who want to delve more deeply.

E. O. Wilson's autobiography, *Naturalist* (Washington, D.C.: Island Press, 1994), is a delightful account by a leading environmental scientist.

The concepts of the community and the balance of nature—the idea that the structure of a community of species is closely regulated and remains constant through time—have developed over time. My quick survey catches the high points. The core articles referred to (in order of appearance) are C. Darwin, *On the Origin of Species by Means of Natural Selection, or The Preservation of Favored Races in the Struggle for Life* (London: John Murray, 1859); F. E. Clements, *Research Methods in Ecology* (Lincoln, NE: University Publishing House, 1905); F. E. Clements, "Nature and Structure of the Climax," *Journal of Ecology* 24 (1936): 252–284; J. Grinnell, "The Niche-Relationships of the California Thrasher," *Auk* 34 (1917): 427–433; C. S. Elton, *Animal Ecology* (New York: MacMillan, 1927); C. S. Elton, *Animal Ecology and Evolution* (Oxford: Clarendon Press, 1930; the quote is from p. 17); C. S. Elton,

"Competition and the Structure of Ecological Communities," *Journal of Animal Ecology* 15 (1946): 54–68; A. J. Nicholson, "The Balance of Animal Populations," *Journal of Animal Ecology* 2 (1933): 132–178; D. Lack, *The Natural Regulation of Animal Numbers* (Oxford, U.K.: Clarendon Press, 1954); H. G. Andrewartha and L. C. Birch, *The Distribution and Abundance of Animals* (Chicago: University of Chicago Press, 1954); and G. E. Hutchinson, *An Introduction to Population Ecology* (New Haven: Yale University Press, 1978).

The final quarter of the twentieth century was an exciting time to be an ecologist interested in community structure and dynamics. The revolution I refer to did not involve guns, but the arguments among various protagonists did generate considerable heat, even verbal fireworks, as ideas and egos clashed—scientists can be passionate about their ideas. Again, I list the main references in the order of their appearance: A. S. Watt, "Pattern and Process in the Plant Community," *Journal of Ecology* 35 (1947): 1–22; C. B. Huffaker, "Experimental Studies on Predation: Dispersion Factors and Predator-Prey Oscillations," *Hilgardia* 27 (1958): 343–383; S. P. Hubbell and R. B. Foster, "Biology, Chance, and History and the Structure of Tropical Rain Forest Tree Communities," in *Community Ecology,* ed. J. Diamond and T. J. Case (New York: Harper and Row, 1986), 314–329; J. F. Grassle, "Variety in Coral Reef Communities," in *Biology and Geology of Coral Reefs,* vol. 2, *Biology 1,* ed. O. A. Jones and R. Endean (New York: Academic Press, 1973), 247–270; Paul K. Dayton, "Competition, Disturbance and Community Organization: The Provision and Subsequent Utilization of Space in a Rocky Intertidal Environment," *Ecological Monographs* 41 (1971): 351–389; J. H. Connell, "Diversity in Tropical Rain Forests and Coral Reefs," *Science* 199 (1978): 1302–1310; R. T. Paine and S. A. Levin, "Intertidal Landscapes: Disturbance and the Dynamics of Pattern," *Ecological Monographs* 51 (1981): 145–178; S. T. A. Pickett and P. S. White, *The Ecology of Natural Disturbance and Patch Dynamics* (Orlando: Academic Press, 1985); R. Levins, "Some Demographic and Genetic Consequences of Environmental Heterogeneity for Biological Control," *Bulletin of the Entomological Society of America* 15 (1969): 237–240; R. Levins, "Extinction," in *Some Mathematical Problems in Biology,* ed. M. Desternhaber (Providence, RI: American Mathematical Society, 1970), 77–107.

A good entry to metapopulation biology is the small text by Ilkka

Hanski, *Metapopulation Ecology* (Oxford, U.K.: Oxford University Press, 1999), and metapopulation ecology of marine systems is covered in *Marine Metapopulations,* ed. J. P. Kritzer and P. F. Sale (San Diego: Academic Press, 2006).

In 1976 the late Robert H. Peters clearly pointed out the lack of testability inherent in the concept of the homeostatic community as developed during the mid-twentieth century in his article "Tautology in Evolution and Ecology," *American Naturalist* 110:1–12, and subsequently in more detail in a very useful book, *A Critique for Ecology* (Cambridge: Cambridge University Press, 1991).

Many insect pests have populations that fluctuate widely and can only be understood using nonlinear modeling and concepts such as thresholds or tipping points. The mountain pine beetle is a typical example, and its current outbreak has been well researched. An entry to this literature is in W. A. Kurz et al., "Mountain Pine Beetle and Forest Carbon Feedback to Climate Change," *Nature* 452 (2008): 987–990.

I drew on John F. Kennedy's commencement address to Yale University, 11 June 1962, for his comments on lies and myths.

CHAPTER 7. WHAT LOSS OF ECOLOGICAL COMPLEXITY MEANS FOR THE WORLD

Information on the current plight of polar bears is available from a number of sources. I used the World Wide Fund publication that first drew public attention to this problem in 2002: S. Norris et al., *Polar Bears at Risk* (Gland, Switzerland: World Wide Fund for Nature), available for download at www.panda.org/about_wwf/ where_we_work/ europe/what_we_do/arctic/polar_bear/publications/index.cfm.

Study of the richness of the earth's biodiversity and the rates of extinction now and in the past has been active since at least the mid-1990s, when Stuart Pimm and others produced their seminal article on the topic: S. L. Pimm et al., "The Future of Biodiversity," *Science* 269 (1995): 347–350. I also drew from several other articles: N. Myers et al., "Biodiversity Hotspots for Conservation Priorities," *Nature* 403 (2000): 853–858; S. L. Pimm et al., "Can We Defy Nature's End?" *Science* 293 (2002): 2207–2208; and D. M. Raup and J. J. Sepkowski, "Periodic Extinctions of Families and Genera," *Science* 231 (1986): 833–836. Peter H. Raven put this subject into context as part of the human dilemma in his presidential address to the American Association for the Advancement of Science in 2002: "Science, Sustainability and the Human Prospect," *Science* 297:954–958.

The Amazonian forest fragment project has been going since 1979 and is still yielding new findings. One recent article I made use of is W. F. Laurance et al., "Rain Forest Fragmentation and the Dynamics of Amazonian Tree Communities," *Ecology* 79 (1998): 2032–2040. The project has its own webpage: www.stri.org/english/research/programs/ecology/index.php.

A good introduction to the current state of pollution of aquatic environments is in the United Nations Environmental Programme's *The State of the Marine Environment: Trends and Processes* (The Hague: UNEP GPA Coordination Office, 2006), available at www.gpa.unep.org/documents/soe_-_trends_and_english.pdf.

I referred to one classic study on effects of estrogen disruptors in aquatic systems: K. A. Kidd et al., "Collapse of a Fish Population after Exposure to a Synthetic Estrogen," *Proceedings of the National Academy of Sciences (USA)* 104 (2007): 8897–8901. Honeybee loss and its consequences are abundantly reported on the web, with plenty of misinformation. One recent reliable article is C. A. Mullin et al., "High Levels of Miticides and Agrochemicals in North American Apiaries: Implications for Honey Bee Health," *PLoS ONE* 5, no. 3 (2010): e9754, doi:10.1371/journal.pone.0009754.

Effects of trawling were discussed in chapter 1. Other examples of usurpation of habitat are easy to see all around us as our cities sprawl over farmland. The introduction of exotic species is well documented in any conservation text. My account of the lionfish invasion drew on two primary articles: P. E. Whitfield et al., "Abundance Estimates of the Indo-Pacific Lionfish *Pterois volitans/miles* Complex in the Western North Atlantic," *Biological Invasions* 9 (2007): 53–64; and J. A. Morris Jr. and J. L. Akins, "Feeding Ecology of Invasive Lionfish (*Pterois volitans*) in the Bahamian Archipelago," *Environmental Biology of Fishes* 86 (2009): 389–398.

In addition to several articles cited in chapter 2, I used the classic article by Costanza and colleagues on valuation of ecosystem services: R. Costanza et al., "The Value of the World's Ecosystem Services and Natural Capital," *Nature* 387 (1997): 253–260.

Klaus Rohde, whose expertise lies in the ecology of parasites, par–

ticularly those that occupy the exterior and interior surfaces of fishes, has provided an unusual perspective on parasite-host systems within a refreshing view of community ecology in his 2006 book *Nonequilibrium Ecology* (Cambridge, U.K.: Cambridge University Press).

In presenting the various arguments for why we should strive to mitigate species loss, I have tried to be clear and concise, and I hope that the presentation does not seem simply superficial. Chapter 2 of *Ecosystems and Human Well-Being: Our Human Planet. Summary for Decision-Makers,* from the Millennium Ecosystem Assessment (Washington, D.C.: Island Press, 2005), 15–39, provides a detailed review of the issue and the arguments for mitigating species loss.

CHAPTER 8. REDUCING OUR USE OF FOSSIL FUELS

The Deepwater Horizon accident happened while this chapter was being finalized, and I relied on ample press reporting. In addition, the NOAA sites available at its National Ocean Service Office of Response and Restoration, http://response.restoration.noaa.gov, and the site set up by the Joint Information Center for the response to this disaster, www .deepwaterhorizonresponse.com/go/site/2931/, were quite informative.

Information on environmental issues with oil and gas extraction came primarily from the National Center for Manufacturing Sciences' report on oil and gas extraction, available at http://ecm.ncms.org/ERI/ new/IRRoilgas.htm, and from the U.S. Environmental Protection Agency's *Sector Notebook Project: Profile of the Oil and Gas Extraction Industry (EPA/310-R-99–006),* published in 2000 and online at www.epa .gov/compliance/resources/publications/assistance/sectors/notebooks/ oil.html.

The Athabasca tar sands story was told using several sources, particularly C. Hatch and M. Price, *Canada's Toxic Tar Sands: The Most Destructive Project on Earth* (Toronto: Environmental Defense, 2008); D. Thompson, *Facts on Oil Sands and the Environment* (Fort McMurray, Canada: Oil Sands Developers Group, 2008); and J. Grant et al., *Fact or Fiction: Oil Sands Reclamation* (Drayton Valley, Canada: Pembina Institute, 2008).

Data on world coal reserves came from the World Energy Council's Survey of Energy Resources 2007, as reported in the *BP Statistical*

Review of World Energy 2008, online at www.bp.com. General information on the coal industry was gained primarily from World Coal Institute, *The Coal Resource: A Comprehensive Overview of Coal* (London: World Coal Institute, 2005).

I used the lobbying piece prepared by the Alliance for Appalachia in 2008, available at www.ilovemountains.org/resources, for information on the extent of mountaintop mining in Appalachia. I also used media reports from several sources that detailed the Kingston Fossil Plant fly ash slurry spill that occurred as I was writing this chapter.

Information on the Chinese coal sector came primarily from an article by P. Fairley in the January 2007 edition of *Technology Review,* "China's Coal Future," online at www.technologyreview.com/energy/17963/page1. Other websites from the World Resources Institute (http://earthtrends.wri.org/updates/node/274), the World Bank (www.worldbank.org/eapenergy), and the Shenhua Group (www.shenhuagroup.com.cn/english/index.htm) filled in additional data. Information on Chinese air and water pollution and their effects on health came from the World Resources Institute (www.wri.org) and from a short article on the risks to the medical system: Christina S. Ho and Lawrence O. Gostin, "The Social Face of Economic Growth: China's Health System in Transition," *JAMA: The Journal of the American Medical Association* 301 (2009): 1809–1810.

For information on methane emissions from mines, I used D. A. Kirchgessner et al., "An Improved Inventory of Methane Emissions from Coal Mining in the United States," *Journal of the Air and Waste Management Association* 50 (2000): 1904–1919.

I obtained information on the nuclear power industry from several web sources, including the U.S. Department of Energy (www.ne.doe.gov) and two predominantly private sector organizations, the Nuclear Energy Institute (www.nei.org) and the World Nuclear Association (www.world-nuclear.org). I also used an International Security Advisory Board report prepared in 2008 for the U.S. Department of State: *Proliferation Implications of the Global Expansion of Civil Nuclear Power,* available at www.ne.doe.gov/pdfFiles/rpt_ISAB_GlobalExpansionof CivilNuclearPower_Apr2008.pdf. Finally, a congressional research service report updated in 2008 for the U.S. Congress, *Managing the Nuclear Fuel Cycle: Policy Implications of Expanding Global Access to Nuclear Power,* was also helpful. A report from the Chernobyl Forum, *Chernobyl's Legacy: Health, Environmental and Socio-economic Impacts and Recommendations to the Governments of Belarus, the Russian Federation and Ukraine* (Vienna: IAEA Division of Public Information, 2006), provided balanced information on the accident.

Information on alternative energy sources and on energy efficiency came from a number of sources, particularly the following articles: D. Arent et al., *Energy Sector Market Analysis,* technical report NREL/ TP-620–40541 (Golden, CO: U.S. Department of Energy, National Renewable Energy Laboratory, 2006), available from www.osti.gov/ bridge; International Energy Agency, *Worldwide Trends in Energy Use and Efficiency: Key Insights from IEA Indicator Analysis* (Paris: Organization for Economic Cooperation and Development, 2008), available from www.iea.org/books; and Office of Energy Efficiency, *Improving Energy Performance in Canada,* report to parliament under the Energy Efficiency Act for the fiscal year 2005–2006, M141–10/2006E–PDF (Ottawa: Office of Energy Efficiency, Natural Resources Canada, 2006). Their website is oee.nrcan.gc.ca.

CHAPTER 9. SLOWING GROWTH OF THE HUMAN POPULATION

Information on the size, age structure, and rate of growth of the human population is readily available from the Population Division within the Department of Economic and Social Affairs of the United Nations, www .un.org/esa/population/unpop.htm, or from the International Database maintained by the U.S. Census Bureau, www.census.gov/ipc/www/idb/ index.html.

My comments on fisheries yield came from the FAO's *The State of World Fisheries and Aquaculture, 2008* (referenced also for chapter 1). I also used D. Zeller and D. Pauly, "Good News, Bad News: Global Fisheries Discards Are Declining, but so Are Total Catches," *Fish and Fisheries* 6 (2005): 156–159.

CHAPTER 10. OUR ALTERNATIVE FUTURES

The history of the establishment of the Great Barrier Reef Marine Park and a great deal more is detailed in *The Great Barrier Reef: History,*

Science, Heritage, by James Bowen and Margarita Bowen (Cambridge, U.K.: Cambridge University Press, 2002). The Queensland Littoral Society has changed its name to the Australian Marine Conservation Society but is alive and well at www.amcs.org.au.

I have previously discussed our environmental dilemma with specific reference to coral reefs in the 2008 essay "Management of Coral Reefs: Where Have We Gone Wrong and What Can We Do about It?" *Marine Pollution Bulletin* 56:805–809. Information on our ecological footprint is available at www.footprintnetwork.org. I used the 2009 *Ecological Footprint Atlas,* downloadable from there, and the *Living Planet Report* (Gland, Switzerland: World Wide Fund for Nature, 2008), available at www.panda.org. Information concerning sustainable fisheries was primarily taken from a "newsfocus" editorial in *Science,* a document from the Marine Stewardship Council, and two technical publications: V. Morell, "Can Science Keep Alaska's Bering Sea Pollock Fishery Healthy?" *Science* 326 (2009): 1340–1341; Marine Stewardship Council, *Net Benefits: The First Ten Years of MSC Certified Sustainable Fisheries* (published in 2009 and available at www.msc.org/healthy-oceans/our -solution/net-benefits); J. C. Castilla et al., "Successes, Lessons, and Projections from Experience in Marine Benthic Invertebrate Artisanal Fisheries in Chile," in *Fisheries Management: Progress toward Sustainability,* ed. T. McClanahan and J. C. Castilla (Oxford, U.K.: Blackwell Publishing, 2007), 25–39; S. F. Walmsley and A. T. White, "Influence of Social, Management and Enforcement Factors on the Long-Term Ecological Effects of Marine Sanctuaries," *Environmental Conservation* 30 (2003): 388–407.

I used various media reports on the web for information on topics such as the LEED (Leadership in Energy and Environmental Design) green building program and the move toward micro-nuclear electricity generation. The story of the greening of Greensburg, Kansas, came from an article by F. Heeren, "Rebuilding Greensburg Green," in the *Smithsonian* magazine, posted online on 27 February 2009 at www .smithsonianmag.com.

I referenced Bob Johannes's book *Words of the Lagoon* in chapter 1. Information concerning Kingman Reef came from "An Uneasy Eden" by K. Warne, an article in the July 2008 *National Geographic* of and a technical article: S. A. Sandin et al., "Baselines and Degradation of Coral Reefs in the Northern Line Islands," *PLoS ONE* 3 (2008): e1548.

The Heron Island Research Station, now operated by the University of Queensland, is the oldest research facility on the Great Barrier Reef and was the only one when I arrived in Australia in 1968. The tiny field station at adjacent One Tree Reef, www.bio.usyd.edu.au/OTI/, originally an Australian Museum field camp and now operated by University of Sydney, is perhaps the smallest marine research station ever. Yet for about forty years it has provided valuable access to a more remote, less visited reef where long-term field experiments can be run. Its story is told in a 1981 book by island ecologist Harold Heatwole: *A Coral Island: The Story of One Tree Island and Its Reef* (Sydney: Collins).

INDEX

aquaculture, 19, 33, 34, 48–51, 55, 226, 266; coastal pollution and, 50; dependent on continued fishing, 49; fish and oil in, 50; focus on top carnivores, 49; growth of, 50; limited promise of, 48

Arabian Gulf, 140

aragonite, 142, 148

Archipiélago de los Canarreos, 302

Arctic National Wildlife Refuge: oil and, 273

Arctic Ocean, 86, 88, 103, 202

Aristotle, 169

Asia, 284

Aspergillus sydowii, 144

asteroid, and End Cretaceous mass extinction, 232

Athabasca, 241, 242, 243, 247, 318

Atlantic cod, 20, 24. *See also* cod fishery

Atlantic redfish, 39

Atlantic salmon, *Salmo salar*, 202, 226

Atlantic swordfish, 36

atmosphere, 103, 141, 143, 245, 251; acid rain pollution of, 77–80; chlorofluorocarbons and ozone layer hole, 83; in earlier epochs, 88–89, 102, 146; ground-level ozone, 246; release of greenhouse gases to, 82, 83–84, 90, 92, 97, 100, 104, 245, 247, 254; transfer of heat toward poles, 84; variable transparency of, 81, 83, 85–86

atoll, 113, 116

Aurora trout, 77, 313; threatened species, 78

Australia, 57, 73, 115, 131, 141, 197, 211, 273–74; Brisbane, 113; Cape York, 274; Gladstone coal and alumina exports, 131; Queensland, 131, 141; Sydney, 153; Townsville, 115, 142; value of Great Barrier Reef, 122; Western Australia, 117, 140. *See also* Great Barrier Reef

Australian Institute of Marine Science, 142

Australian Marine Conservation Society. *See* Queensland Littoral Society

B1 scenario of IPCC, 96, 97

Babcock, Russell, 115

baby boom generation, 28

bacalao, 20. *See also* Atlantic cod; cod fishery

baculum, 213

Bahamas, 117, 211; Exuma Cays, 10; Land and Sea Park, 293

Bahrain, 67

Baker, Andrew, 140, 141

balance of nature, 156, 179, 183, 193, 314; and complacency re human impacts, 195–98; evidence against, 180–81; faith in, 12; history of concept, 173–78; and metapopulation ecology, 189–91; myth, 168–71; patch dynamics and, 186–89; revolution in thinking, 183–91; unrealistic view of ecology, 178–80; view of Andrewartha and Birch, 181–83

Balmford, Andrew, 69, 218–20

Bamiyan statues of Buddha, Afghanistan, 233

Banggai cardinalfish, *Pterapogon kauderi*, 213, 214

Banggai Islands, Indonesia, 213

Bangladesh, 87; sea level rise and, 301

Banner, Albert, 128

Barro Colorado Island: diffuse competition, 186; random distribution of trees, 185; tree diversity, 185

Beamish, Richard, 79

bear, 212

Belarus, 251, 263

Belvedere, 283–84, 296; easiest solution, 284

Bermuda, 211

Bermuda grass, 202

bet hedging, 192, 193

bioaccumulation, 208, 209

biocapacity, 278, 279, 280, 285, 296

biodiversity: global, 202; in 2100, 233; intrinsic value of other species, 232; redundancy among parasites, 229; redundancy in ecosystem, 224, 227; resilience of forests and, 223

biodiversity conservation: aesthetic arguments for, 181–83, 221, 230, 232, 234; economic arguments for, 221–30; ethical arguments for, 221, 230–32, 234; reasons for hope, 234

biodiversity loss, 4, 216, 276; commensalism and, 227–29; direct harvest and, 212–14; habitat usurpation and, 209–10; introduced and invading species and, 210–12; pollination and, 226–27; pollution and, 206–9; redundancy protects ecosystems from impacts, 224–29

bioeroder, 116, 140

biofuel, 253, 258; competition with food crops, 254

biogenic environment, 58

biome, 176

Biosphere 2, 286

Birch, L. Charles, 178

bison, 234

bitumen, 241, 242

Black Death, 261

Black Sea: dead zone, 103

blast fishing, 46

blowout-preventer, 237

bluehead wrasse, spawning sites, 124

Bohnsack, Jim, 2

Bolca, Italy, 87, 310

boreal forest, 241, 243, 253

Botsford, Louis, 34

BP oil blowout. *See* Deepwater Horizon

Brazil, 268

breeding success, of fishes, 19, 28

bristlecone pine, 89

Britain, 73

Broecker, Wallace, 90

bryozoa, 120

Bulgaria, 263

Bull, Gordon, 115

bumblebee, 173, 174

Burj Khalifa, 240

Burma, 87

bushmeat, 62, 67, 68, 213, 308; harvest in Amazon basin, 64, 73; rate of harvest, 64

bycatch: impacts on non-target species, 43; magnitude of, 42, 44

Cabot, John, 20

calcium carbonate, 113, 114, 141, 143

Cambrian Period, 10, 214

Cambridge University, 69, 219

Canada, 78, 98, 220, 300, 301; action re cod fishery, 197; Alberta, 241, 243; CN Tower, 240; commitment at Copenhagen conference, 105; ecological footprint, 279, 280; energy use pattern, 256, 257; evidence of glaciation, 87; Halifax, 36; James Bay Project, 253; Kirkland Lake, 77; La Grande River, 253; Lake Erie, 211; Lake Huron, 79, 87, 211; Lake Ontario, 87; Lake St. Clair, 211; mountain pine beetle in British Columbia, 194; NAFTA Superhighway bottleneck at Windsor, 257; Newfoundland, 20, 21, 22, 86; Niagara Falls, 253; oil reserves, 241; Ontario, 60, 78, 87, 167, 209; population growth in, 263; St. Lawrence River, 86; Sudbury, 77, 79, 313; Yukon River, 253. *See also* cod fishery; tar sands

Cape Cod, Massachusetts, 21

carbon dioxide, 80, 81, 83, 88, 89, 90, 102, 104, 143, 146, 185, 247, 254, 297; desirable atmospheric concentration, 147, 303–4; effect on ocean pH, 100, 141; increasing atmospheric concentration, 82, 92, 95, 147. *See also* ocean acidification

carbon-intensive economy, 4

commensalism, 227, 228, 229

community, 170, 175, 179, 195, 196, 197, 314; climax, 175, 176–77; cooperating species in, 171; Darwin's view, 174; modern view, 191–94; openness of, 189, 193; problems with definition, 171–73; recolonization and dispersal in, 188, 189, 204; theory vs empirical data, 172

community dynamics, 174; dispersal and, 192, 193; disturbances and, 180, 183, 187, 188, 189; equilibrial, 174, 177, 179, 195; long-term data and, 155–57; modern non-equilibrial view, 178, 179, 180, 183, 184, 186, 191–94, 195; and recovery following human impacts, 198; of rocky shores, 188; role of history, 193

competition, 168, 173, 177, 178, 181, 186, 188, 196

competitive exclusion, 168, 192

conch, 49

connectivity, 190

Connell, Joseph H, 156, 188, 189

conservation science, 170

continental drift, slow acceptance of concept, 194

Cook, James, 302

COP15 (Copenhagen climate change conference), 73, 105; Canada's position, 105; positions of leading countries, 105

Copenhagen Diagnosis, The, 95

coral: acclimatization or adaptation to warmer temperatures, 139; African dust and, 72, 144; asexual reproduction, 114; aspergilliosis disease of sea fans, 144; black band disease, 144; evolutionary history, 87; growth rate declines, 142, 313; mass spawning, 115; planktivory, 120; sexual reproduction, 114–15; white band disease, 144

coral bleaching, 136, 144, 145, 147, 312–13; mass bleaching of 1998, 136–41; stress response, 137

coral reef: absences in past epochs, 117–18, 146; atoll, 113, 116; barrier, 116; beach replenishment impacts, 134; bioerosion, 116; biogenic, 114; calcification, 113, 143; as canary in ecological mine, 5, 109, 149, 296; carbon dioxide and, 141–43, 147, 303, 304; coastal development, 145, 147; consequences of decline, 148, 149; damaged by divers, 133, 134; decline in coral cover, 146; degradation of, 288, 296, 300; diverse human impacts, 277; diversity of, 118, 119, 302; drowned, 117; fossil, 87; fringing, 113, 116; growth and erosion, 113–14, 115–17, 195; herbivore depletion, 127; limited evidence of adaptation, 139; limited recovery, 140; loss of economic value, 148; managing local impacts, 147; mangrove removal impacts, 135; mass extinctions and, 117, 146; moral cost of loss, 149–50; as neighborhood, 110; nutrient cycling in, 119–22; nutrient-poor environment, 119, 121, 122; ocean chemistry and, 146–48; overfishing on, 123–28; phase shift to algal dominance, 128, 143–46, 148, 312; pollution impacts on, 128–32; primary productivity in, 121; sensitive ecosystem, 5; similarity to forests, 58; still time to save them, 301–4; sustainable fisheries on, 122; tipping point and, 150; tourism impacts, 132–36; upwellings and, 119; value of, 122–23; wall of mouths, 120

Coral Sea, 131

Corexit, 237

COSEWIC, 78

Costanza, Robert, 69, 218

Costa Rica, 70, 137

Cretaceous, 87, 118. *See also* mass extinction
Croatia, 263
Crown-of-Thorns starfish, *Acanthaster planci*, 140
crude oil, 237, 240, 241
Crustacea, 113, 118
Cuba, 238, 304; Archipiélago de los Canarreos, 302
cyanide fishing, 46, 126
cyanobacteria, 10, 117, 121, 305
cyclone, 131
Czech Republic, 263

Dalhousie University, 36
Dame's rocket, 211
damselfish, 111, 120, 123; grazing over turtle, 111; resource sharing in, 107–8, 109–10, 168; territoriality in, 107, 110, 311; three-spot damsel, 111
dandelion, 211
Darwin, Charles, 113, 116, 169, 173–76, 180, 193, 302
Dayton, Paul, 188
DDT, 208–9
dead zone, in Gulf of Mexico, 5, 103, 207–8
De'ath, Glenn, 142
Deepwater Horizon, 220, 237–38, 247, 258, 318; amount of oil spilled, 238
deforestation, 3, 59–60, 65–67, 70, 73, 74, 75, 90, 261, 275, 276, 288; consequences for global water cycle, 4; trend in, 71–72
demographic transition, 262, 264–65, 269
Denevan, William, 73
density dependence, 24, 26, 31, 177, 183, 191, 192, 196
Department of Fisheries and Oceans, Canada, 209
desertification, 5, 71–72, 97, 276, 308; in West Africa, 5, 144
Devonian. *See* mass extinction

Diadema, 42, 144; disease in Caribbean, 144
Diamond, Jared, 71
diapause, 192, 193
Dictyosphaeria alga in Kaneohe Bay, 128, 129, 311
dinoflagellate, 114
diversity, 188, 223, 233, 234, 235; high diversity systems, 184–85, 186, 229
dodo, *Raphus cucullatus*, 201, 211, 216, 234
Doha, Qatar, 212
Dongsheng coalfield, 244
Donner, Simon, 138
Doppler effect, 158
drilling muds and wastes, 240
drylands, 71
Dubai, 240
Durrell Wildlife Conservation Trust, 64
dynamite fishing, 46

early atmosphere, oxygen content of, 10
earthquake, 222
East Australia Current, 131
Easter Island deforestation, 71, 227
Eastern Pacific, 140
Echinodermata, 113
echo boom generation, 28
ecological footprint, 277–81, 284, 296, 297, 321; comparison among countries, 279; global overshoot, 255–58, 279, 280; growing globally, 280, 281; renewable resources and, 278
ecological guild, 109, 168, 227
ecological inertia, 195, 196
ecological recovery, 195, 196
ecological research, systems with and without human impacts, 3
ecological services. *See* environmental services
ecological stability, 195
ecological time, 172, 194, 223, 278
ecological web, 178

ecology: hypothesis-testing in, 179; as nature study, 5; out-of-date conventional wisdom, 6; poorly taught, 5; recent revolution in thinking, 6, 110, 170, 180–91

Ecology (journal), 206

Ecology of Natural Disturbance and Patch Dynamics, 189

economic extinction, 32

economic theory, finite world and, 288

Ecopath, 154

ecosystem: complex interrelationships in, 110–12; as complex system, 194; following biodiversity loss, 233; as homeostatic system, 168–71, 174, 175–76, 177, 179, 183, 184, 195, 196, 198, 315; loss of function in, 203; resilience of, 6, 9, 10, 170, 195, 196, 198, 221, 223, 278; tipping points in, 112

ecosystem collapse, 221, 229; biodiversity loss and, 225

ecosystem dynamics. *See* community dynamics

ecosystem resilience, 195–98

Ecuador, 137

Ehrlich, Paul, 118, 164, 262

elkhorn coral, *Acropora palmata*, 143, 202

el Niño, 137

Elton, Charles, 38, 176, 177

Emory River, Tennessee, 247

Endangered Species Act (U.S.), 143, 202

energy: alternative, 249, 254, 294, 320; conservation, 253, 259; global supply sufficient, 80–81, 288; micro-nuclear plants, 294, 295; non-fossil sources intermittent, 249; nuclear power, 247, 248, 249–52, 278, 319; solar power, 248, 254, 258, 278, 289; water power, 7, 248, 252, 258; wind power, 7, 81, 97. *See also* coal, use of; fossil fuel; natural gas; oil

energy allocation among sectors: Canada, 255; North America, 256, 313; in

transportation, 248, 257–58; United States, 255

energy efficiency, 255; crisis needed, 258; opportunity and trends in, 255–58; passive solar design and, 257; urban planning and, 258

energy use: China's growing environmental problems, 259; efficiency of, 294; future trends in, 258–59; global rate, 82; historical increase in, 7, 81; transition from fossil fuels, 247–48, 258, 289, 294–95, 300

environment: as a complex system, 11, 170, 194, 286; human impacts on, 3–9; human responsibility for, 12; natural changes in, 9–10; spatial patchiness, 8

environmental changes: growing seriousness of, 3; interlinked, 3, 4; invading species, 9, 210–12; multifaceted problem, 276; past "natural" changes, 9–10, 194; rate, nature and extent of, 4, 11, 190; tipping point, 10, 11, 112, 198, 225. *See also* biodiversity conservation; deforestation; overfishing; pollution

environmental crisis: acknowledge it, 11–12, 283; active solution needed, 281–82; Belvedere future, 283–84; complexity of, 122–23, 238–39, 276; four alternative futures, 283–88; good solutions exist, 288–90; holistic response needed, 275–77; hoping for the best, 281, 282; human population growth and, 13, 261–71; learning from Palau, 298–300; market forces, 282; New Atlantis future, 287–88; sharing the cost, 283; still time to act, 301–4; sustainable management examples, 186–89; Technopolis future, 285–87; timing of action to solve, 13, 296–97, 300–301; Woodstock future, 284–85

environmental engineering, 233

environmental goods and services: deteriorating capacity to provide, 7, 8; footprint and, 279. *See also* resources

environmental services, 7, 58, 59, 60, 62, 69, 71, 203, 229, 275; of mangrove forest, 222; unpaid use by tourism, 133; valuation of, 67–68, 72–74, 217–21, 317; and value of biodiversity, 217–21

environmental sustainability, 281, 290

Eocene, 87, 88; climate of, 88

Erikson, Leif, 86

erosion, 58, 61, 62, 68, 117, 147, 220

erratic boulders, 87

ethical arguments for conservation, 230, 231

Eucalyptus, 57, 65

eukaryote, 202

Europe, 250, 284, 300

evolution, 167, 169, 185, 215, 224, 227, 232; of plants, and climate effects, 146

experiment, types of ecological, 205

experimental lake district, 209

exponential change: chessboard parable, 163, 165; inability to appreciate, 162–64; learning to comprehend it, 164–65

extinction, 183; average global background rate, 202–3, 214; causes of, 203; and economic cost, 224; habitat fragmentation and, 203, 204, 206, 210, 317; increasing rate of, 225; of local populations, 183; patch size and, 204; temporal pattern of, 214

Exxon Valdez, 238

Fa, John, 64

FAO, 19, 34, 35, 38, 42, 50, 55, 59, 65, 67, 68, 71, 75, 154, 290

fecundity of fishes: size and, 18

fertility rate, in human populations, 262, 264, 265

finning of sharks, 44, 212

fire, use in forest management, 62

firewood, 59, 60, 62, 65

FishBase, 154

fisheries: artisanal, 19, 44, 53, 60, 62, 65, 123, 290, 291; bycatch in, 39, 42–45, 50, 267; catch share, 52, 290, 292; certification program, 291; Chilean benthic fisheries, 291; cost, catch and effort in, 25, 31; disrupted social structures and, 37; as economic activity, 30; economic value of, 19; ecosystem effects, 32, 40–47; effects on habitat, 45; global industry, 17; global trends in, 33–40; illegal, unreported and unregulated, 19; ITQ program, 290; LAPP program, 290; limited entry, 52; MEABR program, 291; open access, 51, 54, 307; overexploited, 32, 34; overreporting of Chinese catch, 34, 36; population effects of, 24–33; as predation, 24; protein food and, 19, 50, 55; recovery of, 47–48; recreational, 19, 35; regulation of, 31; societal influences on, 33; straddling stocks, 52; strong year class, 28, 29; sustainable, 19, 31, 122, 290, 299; total allowable catch, 290; traditional management of, 298; trophic level of catch, 38–40, 41, 44; tuna, 17; ways to avoid collapse, 51–55. *See also* cod fishery; overfishing

fisherman: as efficient predator, 30, 33

Florida, 212, 220; Florida Keys, 2, 238; Key Largo, 2, 134

fly ash, 246

foraminiferan, 101

Forbes, Stephen, 171, 172

foreign oil, sources of, 241

forest canopy, 57, 58, 63, 223, 224, 227, 229; ecology of, 57–58; research techniques, 58

forestry: agroforestry of Amazon rain forests, 73–74; firewood extraction,

64; resource harvest, 59–65; unsustainable, 60. *See also* logging

forests: annual cost of, 70; carbon markets and, 72–73; climate change and, 72; CO_2 sequestration by, 72, 73; coffee plantations, 70; edge, 206; interior, 206; loss of, 59, 65–67, 68, 70, 71, 74–75; nonwood products of, 60; old-growth, 65; pollination value, 70; primary, 62, 63, 65, 67, 68, 75; reforestation of, 59, 67, 73; regeneration of, 59; secondary, 59, 62, 65, 67, 68; second growth, 61; similarity to coral reef, 58; tree fall gaps, 63, 187; tree plantation, 67, 68, 70; value of, 67–71, 72, 219; water conservation value, 69

fossil fuel, 80, 81, 90, 95, 96, 218, 239, 250, 254, 255, 267, 275, 278, 288, 289, 295; CO_2 emissions, 82, 247; energy use patterns dictated by, 247; difficulties in transitioning from, 247–49; environmental costs of, 246–47, 258; health impacts in China, 259; high energy content, 247; origin of, 81. *See also* coal; natural gas; oil

Foster, Robin, 185

fox, 211

fragmentation, forest biodiversity and, 206

France, 73, 250

functional group, 224, 227

Gaia hypothesis, 169, 231

Galapagos Archipelago, 136, 141, 148

gall bladder, 213

gay marriage, 269

genetic diversity, 224

geoengineering, 286

geological time, 194, 223

George Mason University, 204

Georges Bank, 22

geothermal power, 254, 258

Germany, 263

Gettysburg College, 69

giant clam, 49, 120, 122

giant kelp, 202

glacier melting, mode of, 99

Global Footprint Network, 278–79

global hectare, 278, 279

global ocean conveyor, 103

global temperature. *See* climate change; temperature, global

Glynn, Peter, 137, 140, 141

goby, *Cryptocentrus* sp., 228

Goddard Institute for Space Studies, 90

Golfo de Batabanó, Cuba, 302

Google Earth, 245

Gore, Al, 162, 263

Gosline, W.A., 167

Grand Banks, 21, 22

Grassle, Fred, 186

Great Barrier Reef, 1, 119, 130, 131, 136, 138, 142, 143, 186, 274; coastal pollution, 132, 141; economic value of, 122; Heron Island, 1, 107, 108, 111, 116, 168, 303; Magnetic Island, 115; nutrification, 132; Oceanic Grandeur spill, 274; oil exploration and, 273; One Tree Reef, 303–4; Royal Commission into oil drilling, 274; save the reef campaign, 274; Swains Reefs, 1, 2

Great Barrier Reef Marine Park, 130–32, 134, 293, 303; establishment of, 273–74, 320–21

Great Barrier Reef Marine Park Act, 274

Great Lakes, Laurentian, 211

Greco-Roman philosophy, 169

Green Building Council, 294

greenhouse effect, 4, 83–84, 90

greenhouse gas, 82, 83–85, 95, 96, 97, 98, 102, 103, 104, 105, 147, 202, 238, 245, 247, 249, 250, 252, 255, 275, 278, 289, 297, 301; methane clathrates and, 88

Greenland: current rate of melting, 98; failing climate, 86; Norse settlement, 86, 88, 310

Greensburg, Kansas, 295, 321

green turtle, 111

Grinnell, Joseph, 176

groundwater, 240, 245

groupers, Serranidae, 37

guild, 224, 227

Gulf of Maine, 21, 41

Gulf of Mexico, 238, 247; dead zone, 5, 103, 207–8; fishery yield, 220

gulf stream, 103, 119

habitat loss to urbanization, 209, 210

Haddock, 39

Hake, 39

Hansen, James, 90, 99

Hanski, Ilkka, 190

Hardin, Garrett, 51

Harrison, Peter, 115

Harvard University, 216

Harvey, Harold, 79

Hawaii, 227; introduced species in, 211; Kaneohe Bay pollution, 128, 129, 311; Ko'olau Mountains, 69, 70; Oahu, 69, 128; Pearl Harbor aquifer, 69

Heartsease, *Viola tricolor*, 173

heavy metal pollution, 132

hedgehog, 211

herbivore, 38, 49, 57, 107, 144

Heron Island Research Station, 1, 107, 322

highways: as ecological barriers, 204

Himalaya Mountains, 87

Hjort, Johan, 28

Hollywood, 268

Holocene mass extinction, 9, 203, 223, 230, 232, 233–35; causes and rates of loss, 202–14; compared to earlier episodes, 214–17; extinction rate, 216; likely course over this century, 233–34

Holodeck, 286, 287

honeybee, *Apis melifera*, 202, 226, 227; colony collapse, 226, 317

Hong Kong, 126, 127

Hoover Dam, 253

house sparrow, 211

Hubbell, Stephen P., 185

Huffaker, C.B., 180

human footprint, 6, 280. *See also* ecological footprint

humanity, *Homo sapiens*, 51, 164, 169, 198; as dominant organism today, 11; as external to natural world, 169; extinction of, 235; special responsibilities of, 231–32

human population growth, 7, 63, 262, 270, 271, 280, 285, 287, 320; current trends, 263–68; economic and other incentives to reduce, 269–71; HIV/AIDS and, 263; immigration and, 263, 266; pattern broadly exponential, 164, 266, 297; and resource consumption, 268–69; taboo subject, 13, 262–63; by 2050, 261, 265, 269, 275, 280, 282, 296; in USA, 264; variation in resource use, 266

human society, capacity to change attitudes and behavior, 234, 274–75

humpback whale, 202

Hungary, 263

hurricane, 131, 144

Hutchinson, G. Evelyn, 176, 178

hydrogen sulfide, 102, 146

immigration, 265

Inconvenient Truth, An, 162

India, 264, 268, 280

Indian Ocean, 136, 140, 222, 227

individual transferrable quota (ITQ), 290

Indonesia, 47, 99, 136, 141, 213

Indo-west Pacific Ocean, 227

industrial pollution, 79

industrial revolution, 81, 100, 164

infrared light, 83

mass extinction *(continued)*
ecosystem services and, 221; End
Cretaceous, 87, 99, 215, 232; End
Ordovician, 215; End Permian, 87,
215–16; End Triassic, 117, 216; Late
Devonian, 215. *See also* Holocene
mass extinction
Mauna Loa, 90
Mauritius, 201
maximum sustainable yield, 26–27, 43,
54, 306; environmental variability
and, 27; non-stable equilibrium, 27
McGill University, 177
McLuhan, Marshall, 156
Medieval Warm Period, 86, 88, 97
Mediterranean Sea, 87
Melanesian, 30
Mesoamerican Barrier Reef, 130
metacommunity. *See* metassemblage
metapopulation, 189–91, 316
metapopulation dynamics, 189; butter-
flies, 190
metassemblage, 189–90, 193, 197
methane, 83, 98, 149; from mining
industry, 245
methane clathrate, 88
Mexico: Cancun, 129, 130, 133;
Tulum, 129
Micronesia, 298, 309
midden, evidence of aboriginal over-
fishing, 18
Middle East, 87, 241
Minamata City, Japan, 208
Miocene, 87
Mississippi, 220, 238
Mississippi River, 211; delta, 237. *See
also* dead zone, Gulf of Mexico
Moldova, 263
Mollusca, 113, 116, 118, 121
Mona Lisa, 232
monarch butterfly, 202
monkfish, 45, 53
mountain pine beetle, *Dendroctonus
ponderosae*, 194, 316

mountaintop removal mining, 244, 319
Mount Pinatubo eruption, 85
Mount St. Helens eruption, 99
Museo Civico di Storia Naturale, 87
mushroom coral, Fungiidae, 114
Myers, Ransom, 36
Myrberg, Arthur A., 111
myth, 170, 191, 196

NAFTA Superhighway bottlenecks, 257
National Institute for Amazonian
Research, 205
natural gas, 81, 82, 239–41, 245, 246,
249, 258. *See also* fossil fuel
*Natural Regulation of Animal Numbers,
The*, 177
nature, as perfect creation, 169
Nature (journal), 33, 34, 218
neuron, 159
New Atlantis, 283, 287–88, 297, 300;
controlling human fertility, 287
Ngeremlengui, Palau, 298
niche, 176–77, 178, 184; Hutchinsonian
model, 178; partitioning, 168, 192
Nicholson, A.J., 177, 191
nitrogen fixation: in coral reefs, 121
nitrous oxide, 83, 246
NOAA, 2, 94, 136, 137
Norse, Elliott, 46, 210
North America, 57, 60, 65, 79, 86, 94,
119, 126, 203, 210, 211, 223, 226,
248, 253, 254, 259, 284; energy use
among sectors, 255–58; fisheries of,
197, 198, 253
North American Free Trade Agree-
ment, 257
North Atlantic, 153
North Carolina Museum of Natural
Sciences, 57
North Sea, 28, 153
Northwest Atlantic, 20, 22, 39. *See also*
cod fishery
Norway, 73, 86, 252
Nova Scotia, 21

nuclear power, 248, 249–52. *See also*
    Chernobyl nuclear accident
nuclear waste, 250
nursery habitat, 220

ocean, transfer of heat toward poles, 84
ocean acidification, 144, 276, 310; cal-
    cification and, 100; and coral reefs,
    313; ecological impacts, 100; effects
    on coral growth, 101; effects on coral
    reefs, 141–43; effects on plankton, 101
ocean–atmosphere climate engine, 84–
    85, 103–4
ocean chemistry, ancient changes in,
    146
Odén, Svante, 79
oil, 81, 82, 241–46, 248–49, 257, 258,
    273, 274, 289; Royal Commission
    into drilling on Great Barrier Reef,
    274. *See also* oil exploration
oil exploration: blowout, 237–38, 247;
    conventional, 241, 243; environ-
    mental effects of, 240–41; seismic
    profiling, 240
oil rigs, habitat for marine life, 239
oil sands, 241. *See also* tar sands
oil-spill dispersant, 237
Oliver, Jamie, 115
One Tree Island Field Station, 302, 322
One Tree Reef, 302–3
Ontario Ministry of Natural Resources,
    78
open cut mining, 244–45
Orange Roughy, 53, 197
orchid: and pollinators, 227
Ordovician, 117. *See also* mass extinction
Origin of Species, The, 173
Orinoco watershed, 74
otter trawl, 21. *See also* trawl; trawling
overburden, 241, 242, 244, 245
overfishing, 3, 4, 17–18, 36–38, 48, 144,
    147, 212–13, 261, 267, 275, 288, 290,
    298; aquarium trade, 213; changed
    trophic structures and, 41, 155, 193;

collapse of stocks, 197; consequences
    for our food supply, 4; on coral reefs,
    123, 127–28, 277; declining fish size,
    155; declining yield, 19; economic
    drivers of, 53; ecosystem effects of,
    40–47; human population growth
    and, 55; live reef fish restaurant trade,
    123, 126, 214, 311; open-ocean fish-
    eries and, 54; reasons for, 51–54; of
    sharks, 212; societal reasons for, 48,
    53; synergistic effects of, 42; tourism
    and, 135; use of inappropriate fishing
    methods, 125. *See also* cod fishery;
    trawling
overstory tree, 61
Oxford University, 38
oxygen minimum layer, 103
oyster, 120
ozone: chlorofluorocarbons and, 83;
    ground-level, 246

Paine, Robert, 188
Palau, 212, 298–99, 300, 307; shark
    sanctuary, 299
Palmata Zone, 143
Panama, 41, 111, 137, 185; Isthmus of, 87
panda, 202
paradigm, 170, 179, 183
parrotfish, 49, 116, 127, 144
passenger pigeon, 234
passive solar design, 257, 294, 301
past climates: evidence, 87–89
patch dynamics, 180, 181, 184, 188–89,
    191
patchiness, 181, 184, 186–87, 189, 193,
    206, 217; effects on forest diversity,
    205–6; human impacts on, 190
Pauly, Daniel, 33–36, 38, 153–54, 161,
    267
permafrost, greenhouse methane and,
    98
Permian, 102, 215. *See also* mass
    extinction
Peruvian anchoveta, 35

pesticide, 132, 209

Peters, Robert, 177, 178

phase shift, 143–46, 194. *See also* coral reef

Philippines, 213, 219, 269, 292. *See also* Apo Island, Philippines

photosynthesis, 81, 82, 88, 114, 120, 221, 223, 254, 278, 285; creation of oxygen atmosphere and, 10, 146

Phuket Marine Biological Center, 142

Pickett, S. T. A., 189

piscivore, 39, 111

Plato, 169

Plectroglyphidodon lacrymatus, 109. *See also* damselfish

Pleistocene, 7, 51, 88, 117, 149, 164, 216, 233

plutonium, 250, 251

Poland, 263

polar bear, *Ursus maritimus*, 201, 208, 234, 316; extinction of, 296, 300; impacts of warming climate on, 201–2

political will, 52, 53, 132, 147

pollination, 173, 218, 226–27; economic value of, 70

pollinator, 226, 227

pollution, 4, 42, 50, 79, 103, 117, 141, 143, 150, 207, 232, 239, 254, 259, 261, 275, 278; air, 259, 276; of aquatic systems, 207; by chemicals, 208–9; on coral reefs, 128–132, 145–46, 147, 277; DDT, 208; eggshell thinning, 208–9; endocrine disruptors, 209; growing quantities of waste, 8; heavy metals, 209, 278; methyl mercury, 208–9; Minamata disease, 208; by nutrients, 207; oil, 238; pesticides and herbicides, 209; pharmaceuticals, 209, 222; scale and complexity of, 4; water, 253, 259

Polychaeta, 113, 186

Polynesia, 298

Polynesian: fishhook styles, 30, 307; species introduced by, 210

Pompeii, 99

population: cohort, 19, 27, 28; density-dependent growth, 177; exponential growth, 181, 183; logistic growth, 25, 306; per capita rate of increase, 25; recruitment, 27–30, 36, 47, 140, 305; subdivided, 181, 183

Precambrian, 117

precautionary principle, 54, 105, 222, 234, 282, 286

predation, size-selective, 24

Princeton University, 138, 189

prokaryote, 202

purple loosestrife, 211

Qatar: ecological footprint, 279

quality of life, 60, 97, 231, 239, 256, 266, 268, 275, 276, 282, 283

Queensland Littoral Society, 273–74

R-2000, 256

rabbit, 211

rambler rose, 211

reactor core, 251

recruitment, variable success of, 19, 28. *See also* population

red clover, *Trifolium pratense*, 173

Red Sea, 227

red snapper, fecundity of, 37

reef fish, 118; moray eel diversity, 167; recruitment of, 2

Rees, William, 277

reindeer, 252

Renaissance, 169

reproduction: of fishes, 19

Research Methods in Ecology, 175

resilience, 62, 170, 195–98, 221, 223–25, 278; biodiversity and, 223

resources: growing per capita use of, 8, 280; management of, 276; national differences in demand for, 8, 279–80; per capita consumption of, 7, 279–80; relative shortage of, 181; unsustainable use of, 8, 276–81; usurping use by other species, 8. *See also* eco-

logical footprint; energy use; fisheries; forestry
resting eggs, 192
retina, 158, 159
rhinoceros, 212
Ricketts, Taylor, 70
Riegl, Bernhard, 140–41
rights, of other species, 231
Robertson, D. Ross, 111, 121
rock lobster fishery, Western Australian, 291
Rohde, Klaus, 229
Romania, 263
Roumasset, James, 69
rugose corals, 87, 118
Russ, Garry, 292–93
Russia, 250, 251
Rutgers University, 186, 189

Sala, Enric, 302
Sami people, 252
sand cay, or key, 113
Sandia National Labs, 294
Saudi Arabia: oil reserves, 241
Scandinavia, 78–79
Science (journal), 28, 33, 34, 38, 41, 69, 90, 142
Scleractinia, 87
Scripps Institution of Oceanography, 41, 302
sea cucumber, 121, 122
seahorse, 213
sea level: change in, 10, 98–99, 301; melting of glaciers, 99
sea otter, 41
sea snakes, 2
sea urchin, 41, 42, 49, 109, 116, 144–45. *See also* phase shift
Second Law of Thermodynamics, 40
Second Life, 297
seed bank, 192
sensory receptor, as transducer, 159–60
sequential hermaphrodite, 37
Shaanxi Province, China, 244

shark, 212, 299
Shark Bay: Hamelin Pool stromatolites, 10
Sheik Khalifa, 240
Shenhua Group, 244, 319
shifting baseline, 12, 164, 313; confusion of linear and exponential change, 161–62; data vs. reality, 162; origin of concept, 154–55; reasons for doing this, 157–61; selection for responses to immediate change, 160; sensory perception and, 157, 159
Siberia, 98
SIDS, sea level rise impacts, 300
Sierra Nevada, 89
similar species: coexistence of, 167–68, 184–86; partitioning resources, 168
SLOSS, 205
Slovakia, 263
smart appliances and energy use, 256
Smithsonian Institution, 205
Smithsonian Tropical Research Institute, 185, 205
snapper (Lutjanidae), 37
sodium hydroxide, 242
solar collectors, integrated into building materials, 254
solar constant, 80
solar energy, rate of arrival on Earth, 80
solar power, 248, 254, 258, 278, 289
Sousa, Wayne, 156
South America, 64, 65
Southeast Asia, 30, 87, 126
South Pacific, 30, 211, 222
spatial distribution of species, 186–87
spawning aggregation, 123–25; tradition and, 124
species, threatened, potential value of, 222
species flock, 186; fish in African Great Lakes, 186
species introduction, 210–12
Spencer, Herbert, 174
sponge, 120

Text:	10.75/14 Bembo
Display:	Bembo
Compositor:	BookMatters, Berkeley
Printer and binder:	Thomson-Shore, Inc.